On Understanding Poverty

© 1968, 1969 by the American Academy of Arts and Sciences
Library of Congress Catalog Card Number: 71–78451
Manufactured in the United States of America

I

On Understanding Poverty

PERSPECTIVES FROM THE SOCIAL SCIENCES

Edited by

DANIEL P. MOYNIHAN

with the assistance of Corinne Saposs Schelling

Basic Books, Inc., Publishers

NEW YORK / LONDON

Volumes in the American Academy
of Arts and Sciences Library

The members of the
American Academy of Arts and Sciences
Seminar on Race and Poverty
respectfully dedicate this work
and its companion volume to
Martin Luther King, Jr.
1929–1968
and
Robert Francis Kennedy
1925–1968

Few ideas are correct ones, and what are correct no one can ascertain; but with words we govern men.

BENJAMIN DISRAELI, *Contarini Fleming*

⊂⊃ The Authors

ZAHAVA D. BLUM is Research Associate at the Department of Social Relations and at the Center for the Study of the Social Organization of Schools, The Johns Hopkins University, where she is also co-director of a research program entitled: "Education and Social Change: The Development of a System of Social Accounts."

OTIS DUDLEY DUNCAN, Professor of Sociology and Associate Director, Population Studies Center, University of Michigan, is co-author (with Peter M. Blau) of *The American Occupational Structure* and co-author (with Beverly Duncan) of *The Negro Population of Chicago*.

MARC FRIED is Research Professor, Institute of Human Sciences, Boston College, and was Director of the Institute. He has had extensive experience as a psychologist. Chapters by him are regularly included in books on the urban condition and renewal.

HERBERT J. GANS is Visiting Professor of Sociology, Columbia University. His major publications are *The Urban Villagers, The Levittowners,* and *People and Plans: Essays on Urban Problems and Solutions*. He has been Senior Staff Sociologist for the Center for Urban Education.

OSCAR LEWIS, Professor of Anthropology at the University of Illinois, is author of numerous articles and books including *Five Families, The Children of Sanchez, Pedro Martinez,* and *La Vida*.

S. M. MILLER is Professor of Education and Sociology at New York University and Program Adviser in Social Development at the Ford Foundation. He is the co-editor (with Frank Riessman) of *Social Class and Social Policy*. He is author of *Comparative Social Mobility* and other books.

WALTER MILLER, Research Associate, Joint Center for Urban Studies, is author of *City Gangs* (forthcoming) and many articles. He was Director of the Roxbury Delinquency Research Project.

DANIEL P. MOYNIHAN is on leave as Professor of Education and Urban Politics at Harvard University and was formerly Director of the Joint Center for Urban Studies. He was Assistant Secretary of Labor for Policy Planning and Research, 1963 to 1965 and is currently serving as Assistant for Urban Affairs to President Nixon. He is author of *Maximum Feasible Misunderstanding.*

LEE RAINWATER is Professor of Sociology at Washington University and a Research Associate in the Social Science Institute there. He is Senior Editor of *Trans-Action.* He has written *The Moynihan Report and the Politics of Controversy, And the Poor Get Children,* and *Workingman's Wife.*

PAMELA ROBY is a doctoral candidate and Research Assistant in the Department of Sociology at New York University. She is currently working on a study of perception of the distribution of resources and is co-author of several articles with S. M. Miller.

GERALD ROSENTHAL, Associate Professor of Economics at Brandeis University, is Senior Associate of the Organization for Social and Technical Innovation (OSTI). Much of his work has been in medical economics. He is author of "The Operating Structure of the Medical Care System—an Overview" for the Joint Economic Committee in *A Compendium on Human Resources.*

PETER H. ROSSI is Professor and Chairman of the Department of Social Relations, The Johns Hopkins University. He was Director of the National Opinion Research Center, University of Chicago. He is author of *Why Families Move* and *The Politics of Urban Renewal* among other books.

STEPHAN THERNSTROM is Associate Professor of History, Brandeis University, and a member of the Joint Center for Urban Studies. His books include *Poverty, Planning, and Politics in the New Boston* and *Poverty and Progress: Social Mobility in a 19th Century City.*

HAROLD WATTS, Director of the Institute for Research on Poverty, and Professor of Economics, University of Wisconsin, served as economist, Division of Research and Plans, Office of Economic Opportunity, 1965 to 1966.

ᴄᴃ *Preface* TALCOTT PARSONS

It is a pleasure, on behalf of the Council, officers, and staff of the American Academy of Arts and Sciences, to write a brief preface to this volume of studies on poverty in the United States. Its publication is the result of the first continuing seminar of the Academy dealing with American domestic problems.

The genesis of this study of poverty may be of interest to the reader. In the years 1963 and 1964, at the height of the newly revived civil rights movement, *Daedalus,* the journal of the Academy, initiated a project for a comprehensive survey of knowledge and opinion about the status of the Negro American. This project followed the common *Daedalus* pattern of calling together a group of knowledgeable and representative people for a planning conference, commissioning papers to be written, and holding a second larger conference for discussion of the draft papers. In this case it proved, however, to be a larger than usual undertaking and the immediate result consisted in two large issues of *Daedalus* (Fall 1965 and Winter 1966). In the second of the two the unusual course was followed of publishing most of the actual transcript of the discussion of the second conference. Most of this material, with a few additions, was subsequently republished in 1966 in the Daedalus Library in the volume entitled *The Negro American.*[1]

During the course of this study it became evident that the focus of the problem of the Negro was rapidly shifting to the urban North and that this shift was rapidly accentuating the intricate interlacing of the problems of race with those of poverty. Daniel P. Moynihan had been an active participant in the Negro-American study and was prevailed upon to assume, as chairman, the responsibility for organizing a continuing "seminar" on Problems of Race and Poverty. This group met for a day and a half once a month during the academic year 1966–1967.

The present volume, and its companion, edited by James Sundquist of The Brookings Institution, include the main fruits of these meetings, papers presented to the seminar and revised after discussion within the group. The first volume deals with theoretical aspects of the nature of poverty; the second with the development of federal anti-poverty policy. The editors and contributors to the two volumes would be the last to claim that they have presented a solution to the problem of poverty. In fact, the reader will observe considerable differences of opinion among the various authors. They have, however, certainly contributed to the description and clarification, on an interdisciplinary basis, of some of the issues which are currently being and will continue to be faced in working toward not one, but the necessary variety of solutions. This represents a considerable step in the mobilization of the resources of social science to provide a solid basis in empirical knowledge and theoretical analysis so urgently required in this area of public policy.

Perhaps then the Academy's initiative in this area can serve at the least a gadfly function. As an organization it has certain special advantages. It is not saddled with specific policy formulation or with operating responsibilities with all the attendant constrictions involved. Also, it does not "represent," in an activist political sense any of the groups with primary interests in the problem. It does, however, have contact with such expertise, in the academic as well as nonacademic world, as our society commands, not only in current knowledge about the problems, but also in potential for developing better methodology and more useful knowledge than is now available. If a substantial contribution in this direction has been made, the Academy will, I feel sure, consider its sponsorship of this enterprise to have been well worthwhile.

This volume and its companion inaugurate a new American Academy Library. A second phase of the seminar on poverty is now in progress: a series of conferences on four subjects relating to poverty which appeared to require further careful study. These are urban transportation, the question of income, evaluation of social-action programs, and social stratification. These conferences may lead to further books in the new Academy Library.

Note

1. Talcott Parsons and Kenneth B. Clark, eds., *The Negro American* (Boston: Houghton-Mifflin, 1966).

☞ *Acknowledgments*

The editors of the two volumes "Perspectives on Poverty" wish to express their appreciation to the authors included in this volume, to other participants in the seminar, and to the Academy staff. In addition, they thank the Research Funds Committee of the American Academy for providing support to initiate the seminar on poverty and the Stern Family Fund for its grant to the American Academy which has helped make this publication possible.

☙ Contents

On Understanding Poverty

Chapter 1

⊂⊇ *The Professors and the Poor*

DANIEL P. MOYNIHAN

At about the time the chapters of this volume were making their final round among the members of the American Academy seminar, at which their contents were presented, an almost chance encounter with a Negro poverty worker from the Roxbury section of Boston somehow compressed the themes of the preceding twenty months of analysis into a quarter hour's conversation. The lady in question came to see me at the Joint Center for Urban Studies, directed to me by a liberal business executive who had thought I might be of help in her effort to raise a quite large sum of money to establish a cultural center for the disadvantaged. I was not especially sanguine and said as much: The federal poverty program was then being cut back rather than enlarged, redirected toward employment as against community programs. My visitor's reaction, however, was not one of resignation, but of exasperation. Once again, or so it appeared to her, the demands of the black community were being rejected by the white power structure, in this case represented by me. In the manner of professors, I resorted to reason: Was it not the case, I asked, that a very considerable number of poverty programs had been begun in Roxbury in recent years? (The Boston *Globe* was shortly to publish a special supplement describing 262 such programs spread about the city as a whole.) "Exactly," came the retort, "but do you notice they only fund programs that don't succeed?"

This chapter was prepared for a seminar of the American Academy of Arts and Sciences, and all rights to it are reserved by the Academy. It has been published in the August 1968 issue of *Commentary*.

There in a few sentences were summarized the events of the preceding five years: the transformation of the war on poverty from a program concerned generally with the poor, to one understood to be primarily for Negroes (or blacks, as some members of the group increasingly insist they be designated) ; the proliferation of projects; the constant association of such projects with academic activists and academic conceptions such as "disadvantage" and "culture"; the precipitous rise of dissatisfaction with the program in the Congress, followed by restrictions in funding; the attendant rise of Negro militancy and hostility, accompanied by increasing sophistication (note the Bureau of the Budget verb "to fund") and fiercely asserted independence, but also a not less strongly held conviction that power continues to reside in a concealed, but ruthless and disciplined, freemasonry of the white elite. In the course of the conversation, the suggestion that the junior United States Senator from Massachusetts —a Negro—might be of help was dismissed, whereas it was readily agreed that his white colleague, howsoever out of favor with the incumbent President, would be a man of great potential influence on behalf of the undertaking. (Some might argue that my visitor's being a woman would suggest the further theme of the matriarchal nature of lower-class communities, but the female hegemony in cultural affairs in Boston has persisted so long that it has doubtless become a subculture all its own that allows for no endogenous inferences. Nor will the reader be surprised to learn that, nothing if not indomitable, she eventually got her center, although without public funds.)

My visitor had also elicited the essential themes of this volume, most especially the painful truth that a great national effort, so bravely begun not four years earlier, was by then widely deemed to have failed; and that American professors and intellectuals, having been so much involved with launching the initiative, were somehow implicated in that failure.

The question of failure must be put aside. It refers at best to a mood of the moment—and within the seminar, hardly a unanimous one—and not at all to anything that might be thought of as "facts." The success or failure of the Great Society's war on poverty is a question for historians, and the final verdict may be very different from the perception of the moment, not only as to what happened but as to what was relevant. Is it not, for example, possible that a twenty-second century Namier tracing the lives of those who influenced history in the decades either side of the year 2000 will conclude that early personal experiences in the poverty program of the Johnson administration had profoundly affected the process of personal formation that led to *their* later influence? But, for the present moment, the confidence of many persons in the nation's ability to master the congeries of social, economic, regional, and racial problems that were subsumed under the heading poverty in the winter and spring of 1964 has been badly shaken.[1]

This is not a judgment directed solely to the Office of Economic Opportunity (OEO). On the contrary, as Richard Rovere has noted, "The new federal agencies set up to deal with the distress of the cities—the Office of Economic Opportunity, the Department of Housing and Urban Development, the Department of Transportation—have turned in generally disappointing performances." But OEO, having got so much more than its share of the publicity, has attracted an equivalent proportion of the second thoughts. But worse than to be blamed in Washington is to be ignored, and as 1968 wore on, there were unmistakable signs that OEO itself was going through that institutional change of life that had come so prematurely and cruelly to so many of the bold enterprises of the 1960s. The pattern was by then almost a fixed one: the bright new idea, the new agency, the White House swearing in of the first agency head followed by a shaky beginning, the departure twenty-four months later of the first agency head to be replaced by his deputy, the gradual slipping from sight, a Budget Bureau reorganization, name change, a new head, this time from the civil service, and slowly obscurity covers all. In the spring of 1968, the irrepressible Sargent Shriver left as director of OEO, to be replaced by his deputy, a competent, even a distinguished political executive, but essentially an anonymous one, with strong connections to the Bureau of the Budget. As the 1968 political campaign became heated, new proposals for dealing with poverty began to flow forth from the candidates, almost all of whom began with the assumption that existing programs did not add up to much. When, in May of 1968, the Southern Christian Leadership Council's "Poor People's March" made its way to Washington and encamped on the Mall, it was as if they were lobbying for the establishment of an OEO: That one existed seemed almost unknown, or at best unacknowledged. Something, somewhere, had gone wrong. Rather, many things had gone wrong. This volume, and the one to accompany it, edited by James L. Sundquist, is an effort to suggest some of the sources of difficulty, both conceptual and operational, while at the same time looking to more promising options open to the nation, still committed, in Daniel Bell's phrase, to a policy of deliberate social change.

For the War on Poverty—rather like the war in Vietnam—was pre-eminently the conception of the liberal, policy oriented intellectuals, especially those who gathered in Washington, and in a significant sense came to power, in the early 1960s under the Presidency of John F. Kennedy. Kennedy's Presidential campaign had propounded a fairly radical critique of American society. The Eisenhower era had not been barren of government initiatives, but even when these were of massive dimensions, as in the case of the Interstate Defense and Highway Program, they had tended to be directed toward the needs and interests of the middle classes of Americans, with the concomitant inference that other, more pressing needs did not in fact exist. In considerable measure, the intellectual community accepted this assertion and directed its energies largely to deploring the uses of mass embourgeoisement. Affluence, indeed, became the master term for the period, such, for example, that when John Kenneth Galbraith devoted a book to that subject, his trenchant discussion therein of the persistence of poverty was all but ignored.

Kennedy changed that: in part, because he was a Democrat and by definition involved with the sources of Democratic strength and the tradition of Democratic concern; in part, also, because he was a Roman Catholic. This had forced him to make the crucial test of the campaign for the Presidential nomination the primary contest in Protestant West Virginia, where a decent, but impotent, people of impeccable pioneer origin were slowly, and without protest, sinking into the slag heaps they had too willingly piled up to make money for other men. Commitments were made in West Virginia and, just as important, impressions were gained that remained with the Kennedy administration throughout. But beyond these essentially political influences, there arose at this time an element of intellectual influence, deriving from the world of little magazines and large universities of the kind that abound on the eastern seaboard. (Much in the manner that those who least approve and those who most approve suppose to be the case!) In particular, two clusters of intellectual concerns came to bear on the problems of poverty. The first derived from the world of political economy. At the time John F. Kennedy took office, more men were out of work in the United States than at any time since the Great Depression. Kennedy's concern "to get America moving again" was perhaps primarily a concern to regain a satisfactory level of economic growth and to reduce the quite intolerable levels of unemployment that persisted, and even rose, in the period following the Korean War. A second cluster of concerns derived from the world of sociology, criminology, and social psychology and were concerned, essentially, with the problem of deviant behavior. It will be recalled—or will it?—that the issue on which Senator Kennedy and his next youngest brother came to national attention in the 1950s was that of trade-union corruption and organized crime—conservative-type issues, if anything. Certainly they were issues that directed attention to the seamy and disreputable side of working-class and lower-class behavior, hardly tending to convey any exalted notion of a redemptive proletariat purified by suffering. Both sets of concern were much in evidence in the legislative program of the Kennedy years, most notably in the emergence of the "new economics" and its concern for employment and economic growth, in legislation such as the Manpower Development and Training Act of 1962, and in the establishment of the President's Committee on Juvenile Delinquency and Youth Crime, which became almost a personal project of the President's brother, Attorney General Robert F. Kennedy. If the minimum wage legislation of 1961, with its emphasis on the low-paid Democratic voter (Negro washerwomen were a group specifically at issue), and the Area Redevelopment Act of the same year, with its emphasis on Appalachia, responded to the political themes of the administration and perhaps received greater public notice, these intellectual themes were not less in evidence and in ways were closer to the hearts of the purposeful and proud men then guiding the nation in their brief authority.

The political economy—the "new economics"—of the Kennedy era worked, or that at least must be our assumption, and in working provided perhaps the most impressive demonstration of the capacity of organized intelligence to forecast and direct events that has yet occurred in American government of the present era. If the fiscal and monetary policies that began at that time can be judged a social experiment, the conclusion is hard to escape that it would seem to be one of the few—certainly the only one of its size—that really can be said to have worked out as predicted. To be sure, events broke "with" the administration. The month Kennedy took office, the economy turned upward, beginning the unprecedented expansion that is now, as I write, in its eighth year. Kennedy's task here was essentially to sustain and then accelerate a movement that had begun on its own. This was not the case with the issue of deviant behavior. In at least a general sense, that problem probably worsened during this period—events were not on their own moving with the administration—but, paradoxically, concern for them appeared to recede. Juvenile delinquency and youth crime, for example, had been strong issues in the 1950s. Of a sudden, seemingly, they were no longer. Fashions change. Even so, the problem persisted; further, when unemployment, especially among Negroes, failed to recede in measure as the economy expanded, it, too, began to acquire certain overtones of deviancy. The "hard-core" unemployed either acted differently, were treated differently, or both. Something beyond macro-economic measures was required. Yet, somehow it was not forthcoming. This was a failure, in the proper sense of the term, of rhetoric. Kennedy was unable to impress upon the nation either the validity or the urgency of his administration's concern in this area. Thus, a bill that brought many of these strands together, the Youth Employment Act, was given the highest priority in the administration's legislative program; a bill any legislator might be presumed to favor, it somehow could not pass the House of Representatives. In effect, the Kennedy administration was making the first, tentative, groping efforts of the federal government to involve itself with the question of the "life style" of lower-class persons. With the long-dominant problems of cyclical economics gradually coming under control, the energies of government were turning to those persons who, for myriad reasons, lived lives of seeming permanent depression.

Some work in this area had already begun. Walter W. Heller, Chairman of the Council of Economic Advisers, had raised the subject with President Kennedy in December 1962, and in the spring of 1963 sent him a memorandum prepared by the redoubtable Robert Lampman. It was in this context that the President's advisers, in the fall of 1963, began to shape the issue of poverty as a central theme for the campaign of 1964, an effort that would begin with the sequence of Presidential messages and proposals in the early months of the year. On October 30, 1963, Walter W. Heller wrote to the relevant members of the Cabinet informing them that Theodore Sorenson had asked the council "to pull together for the President's consideration a set of measures which might be woven into a basic attack on the problems of poverty and waste of human resources, as part of the 1964 legislative program."

On October 29, a council staff memorandum that spelled out the anticipated strategy had been prepared. It read in part:

The Poverty Cycle

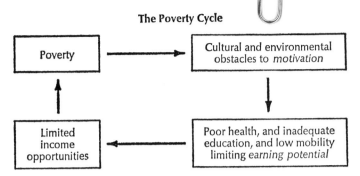

The sources of poverty are not listed in chronological sequence. The vicious cycle, in which poverty breeds poverty, occurs through time, and transmits its effects from one generation to another. There is no beginning to the cycle, no end. There is, therefore, no one "right" place to break into it: increasing opportunities may help little if health, educational attainments and motivation are unsuitable; making more education available may bear little fruit unless additional employment opportunities exist; altering adverse environmental factors may not be feasible or effective unless access to education and ultimately job opportunities is enhanced.

Programs to attack each of the three principal stages in the poverty cycle may be directed at one or more of three levels: (1) *prevent* the problem from developing, (2) *rehabilitate* the person who has been hurt, and (3) *ameliorate* the difficulties of persons for whom prevention or rehabilitation are not feasible. Each type of "treatment" is associated generally with a separate stage in the life cycle. Prevention of poverty calls for attention principally to youngsters (and to their parents, insofar as parents' attitudes and values affect the children). Rehabilitation of those missed by preventive efforts, or for whom these efforts were ineffective, seems best designed for adults in their productive work years. Amelioration of poverty seems called for in the case of the aged, the physically and mentally disabled, and those for whom prevention and rehabilitation are ineffective.

This was government staff work at its best: systematic, comprehensive, candid, practical, and optimistic. The administration was setting about its business in the manner of men who purpose to control events. Within weeks, of course, the nation spun wildly out of control as madness for the moment seized the levers of power and the President was assassinated. All the more, in the aftermath, was the desire to reassert the powers of rationality, and this had the effect, if anything, of intensifying the pace of the developing poverty program. The theme was attractive to the New Deal, populistic style of President Johnson, who, in the immediate aftermath of the assassination, directed that planning the poverty program proceed as a matter of administrative priority. Just as importantly, the effort provided a focus for the energies and emotions of the stricken men Kennedy had left behind. Much as it is said that German businessmen, in the ruins of postwar Europe, found in knuckle-whitening work an anodyne for memories they had to leave behind, so in a not different way the survivors of Kennedy's thousand days threw themselves into this effort, which became for them an assertion that they had indeed got the country moving again and that it would keep moving.

In the State of the Union Message of 1964, Richard Goodwin, who was to have been appointed special assistant for the arts on Kennedy's return from Dallas, turned his powerful pen to a sterner subject, and the new President spoke the words, even as he had prescribed their intent: "This administration today, here and now, declares unconditional war on poverty in America."

But already troubles were appearing. It was one thing to propose to do away with poverty; it was another to determine how to do so and yet another to find the resources and persuade the Congress to authorize the effort. Here the legacy of Kennedy's difficulties with Congress and the advent of the Johnson manner, with its justified pride and preoccupation with legislative maneuver, moved matters much too precipitously from phrase-making to vote-trading, with ominously little attention paid in between to the question of what exactly was the problem to be solved.

On taking office, President Johnson had found the Council of Economic Advisers and the White House staff in a state of some confusion and even deadlock brought about by the conflicting desires of the various Cabinet departments concerned to see their existing legislative programs given priority in the new package. It was one thing to outline a general strategy of intervention as the Council of Economic Advisers memorandum had done. It was another to state precisely the form and manner of the intervention, to assign responsibility for it, and to decide what level of resources would be required. Thus, for example, the Department of Labor, which was the "sponsor" of the Youth Employment Act, viewed employment programs as the master weapon to be used against poverty, discrimination, technological change, juvenile delinquency, or whatever the most fashionable formulation of the moment happened to be. Just three days before the State of the Union Message, the department had presented to the President the report of the Task Force on Manpower Utilization, entitled "One-Third of a Nation," which Kennedy had established the preceding August to analyze the extraordinarily high Selective Service rejection rates, with the hope of producing

evidence in support of his youth-employment proposals. The report
had succeeded in that, if nothing else, and was one of the few data
sources on which the emerging poverty program could draw. (The
study revealed, for example, the extraordinarily high rates of Negro
failure on the mental test, the great importance of family size for all
races, and the sharp differences in rejection rates not only between
races but between different regions of the nation.) But other departments had their own formulations. Most importantly, the Council of
Economic Advisers and the Bureau of the Budget had become strong
proponents of a proposal that had emerged from the President's
Committee on Juvenile Delinquency and Youth Crime to organize
the new effort around the essentially new concept of "community-
action programs." Through the President's Committee, headed by
the Attorney General, federal funds were already supporting a number of these programs on a "demonstration" basis. The idea of community action was in one sense the purest product of academia and
the Ford Foundation. Its underlying propositions concerning opportunity structure and anomie constituted a systematic theory as to the
origins and cures, if not of poverty, at least of juvenile delinquency.
Moreover, in making its way through the maze of the Executive
Office Building it had acquired a managerial gloss that—while never
fully, or even partially, intended by its original sponsors—nonetheless proved decisive in its adoption by the mandarins of the Budget
Bureau. Community action was originally seen as a means of shaping
unorganized and even disorganized city dwellers into a coherent and
self-conscious group, if necessary by techniques of protest and opposition to established authority. Somehow, however, the higher civil
service came to see it as a means for coordinating at the community
level the array of conflicting and overlapping departmental programs
that proceeded from Washington in seemingly ever-increasing numbers, legislative stalemates to the contrary notwithstanding.[2] In this
situation, President Johnson appointed Sargent Shriver, Director of
the Peace Corps, to head a White House task force to make peace and
assemble a program.

Thus the poverty task force inherited a series of intellectual
views—and conflicts. First was the generalized judgment of the Kennedy era that America was not performing at anything like the level
of which it was capable, whether measured in the material terms of
gross national product or the abstractions of world leadership. To
this was added an overlay of Johnsonian populism, with its concern
for the plight of those "peckerwood" boys in the hill country. Along

with this came the now well-established concern with problems of unemployment, with its increasing corpus of statistical and analytic material. To this there was now added the assertion that the problems of lower-class individuals required changes in the social structure and their perception of it, and the further, bolder assertion that these changes could be deliberately induced by means of group action. It would be inaccurate to state that the Shriver task force was unaware of these divergent views or that it was insensitive to them. But it had not the least interest in producing anything like an intellectual synthesis. This was in measure a reflection of Shriver himself, a man of "infectious energy" to quote *The New York Times*—truly one of the rare temperaments of the era—but with no taste and little patience for abstractions such as lay behind the community-action concept. Time, moreover, was short—the group did its work in about eight weeks. But, most importantly, the primary attention of all concerned was on the problem and—as the nation's reaction to the assassination became more clear—the real prospect of getting a program through the Congress. For the grief and shock of the assassination was followed—rather like the euphoria, even merriment, that will break out at a reception following the return of a funeral cortege—by an atmosphere in Washington of opening possibilities and widening expectations. Far from assembling a massive, in a sense defiant, program designed to affront and indict the Congress with its own unwillingness to act, the task force increasingly submitted to the discipline of political realism as it became evident that this was a bill that was going to be passed.

The concept of consensus took over. Shriver busied himself touching every conceivable power base—especially in the business community—while his associates in effect put together a poverty bill that included some part at least of just about everything that any department or agency had seriously put forth. (Especially attractive were measures for which budgetary provision had already been made, so that they were, in effect, already paid for.) Pride of place was given to the Labor Department's Youth Employment Act, which, with minor changes, became Title I of the proposed bill. The Community Action Program, which the Council of Economic Advisers and the Bureau of the Budget had originally envisaged as the *entire* poverty package, became Title II. Other departments followed, pretty much in order of precedence.

The resulting program, sent to the Congress March 16, 1964, thus represented not a choice among policies so much as a collection of them. Nothing of consequence had been added to the congeries of proposals that had been handed over to the Shriver group. This result was, if anything, emphasized by the fact that Shriver had tried to add one major new element to the program and had failed. The one element that might have been expected to be a central feature of any large scale anti-poverty effort but was nonetheless absent from any of the departmental proposals was that of an adult-employment program. Public works—jobs—has for a century or more been a primary governmental response to problems of this kind. Within the Shriver task force, the case for an "employment strategy" was made with some vigor and little opposition. As a result, the final package, which Shriver presented to a meeting of the Cabinet early in March, provided for a special five-cent tax on cigarettes to be earmarked for an employment program for the poor.[3] The tax originally proposed by Senator Gaylord Nelson of Wisconsin was calculated to produce something like 1.25 billion dollars per year. The Council of Economic Advisers had been anything but enthusiastic about the proposal. It was a regressive tax, the council argued, that would destroy almost as many jobs as it would create, and with no guarantee that the newly created jobs would be "on" the poverty target. (The council staff was at this time especially impressed by analyses of the Accelerated Public Works Program of the Kennedy administration that showed the various projects to have had only a minor effect on hardcore unemployment.) Even the most optimistic Labor Department analysis suggested a net increase of only 50,000 to 90,000 jobs. Shriver, however, believed that through various multiplier effects and other devices, a much higher number could be achieved, as much indeed as 500,000 jobs "on target." But the President would have none of it. The Chairman of the House Ways and Means Committee, he explained, was against earmarking. Besides, 1964 was the year for cutting taxes—the great Revenue Act of 1964 proposed by Kennedy in the spring of 1963 was then on its way to enactment; to propose simultaneously to increase taxes was no way to handle the Congress.

The matter ended there, without protest and with *no* public knowledge. Yet, it was in ways a decisive decision. Short of its provision for the employment of adult men, the War on Poverty unavoidably turned its attention to the provision of services to women and children, of marginal employment and some intensive training of late adolescents, and—to its eventual grief—to community organization. This was to have consequences great or small throughout the society, but most fundamentally for Negro Americans.

BLACK FOREBODINGS

In retrospect, it is possible to view the War on Poverty as a device that enabled the federal government to launch a fairly wide range of programs designed primarily to aid Negro Americans without having to specify their purpose. In some measure, this was understood to be the case at the time. The theme of poverty was a unifying one, a cause that the most diverse persons could share. (Thus, the legislation was sponsored in Congress by Senator McNamara of Michigan and Congressman Landrum of Georgia, men at opposite poles of the Democratic party with respect to domestic issues.) Yet, it would be a mistake to conclude that Negro matters were uppermost in the minds of administration strategists either before or immediately after the assassination. It was well enough understood that by any reasonable standard most Negroes probably lived in poverty; but they were nonetheless seen to be a minority of all those living in poverty, and much was made of this point. The emergence of Negro poverty as *the* poverty problem was yet to come: a development that accompanied, rather than preceded, the establishment of the poverty program.

This is largely a matter of historical trends. To the extent the nation was concerned with "Negro" problems at all, these were still conceived, at this time, as issues of civil rights in the South. The battalions that had marched with the Reverend Martin Luther King, Jr., may have been deprived, but they were not poor. Indeed, much of the impact of the civil rights demonstrations of the period surely arose from the contrast between the obvious middle-class dress, manner, and decorum of the black protesters with the red-necked vulgarity of the police and white mobs that harassed them. The profoundly different realities of the Northern Negro slum were yet to force themselves on the attention of the country (or, for that matter, of the civil rights leaders) and hence were not especially part of the political context in which the poverty program was assembled.

Yet, there was also an intellectual difficulty involved. The persons who conceived the poverty program and the somewhat different group that went on to administer it knew very little about the subject of urban Negro poverty—the issue that in one manifestation or another was soon to become our single most pressing domestic political issue. The reasons for this are varied. First, no Negro was involved in any significant way at any significant stage in planning the

Economic Opportunity Act of 1964. This is not a pleasant subject to discuss, but it is a crucial one that demands more open acknowledgment. (Nor is it merely of historical interest. Very much the same could be said of the report of The National Advisory Commission on Civil Disorders. The commission's report, issued in the spring of 1968, is almost exclusively the work of white social scientists, commentators, and writers.)

Negroes generally, and a large number of individual Negroes, have been in the "news" so much of late that it is possible for even the most perceptive persons to fail to see how little a part Negroes play in the academic and governing institutions of the nation (or business, or labor, etc.) and what little influence they would seem to have. In part, this is a matter of things that are yet to happen. Yet there are puzzling aspects as well. It is possible to argue, for example, that a Negro intellectual/academic tradition that was in full force a generation ago has somehow faltered in our time, with important consequences. Some men continue to do good work. Kenneth B. Clark continues his unique and indispensable role. But, by and large, the issues of Negro poverty in the present time have been defined and analyzed by white social scientists, and the subsequent programs have been administered by white political executives. Thus, the idea of community action in the context of opportunity theory was conceived by white social scientists, launched by white foundation executives and political activists, brought to Washington by the same, developed in the (white) President's Committee on Juvenile Delinquency and Youth Crime, sold to white economists in the Executive Office Building, and drafted into legislation by the white White House task force on poverty. It would be not inaccurate to state that the *only* Negro significantly involved in the establishment of the poverty program was Congressman Adam Clayton Powell, Chairman of the House Committee on Education and Labor, which had jurisdiction over the bill. And at best he—and his colleagues—had only the vaguest notion as to what community action or many of the other measures in the legislation were about. It does not follow that the presence of influential Negroes at any stage in this process would have brought to bear any greater insights into the issues that were to be encountered, but it might certainly have served to suggest that the enterprise was not going to be an especially simple one.

In the actual conduct of the poverty program, these factors became, if anything, more relevant. Had the program retained a large component of direct job creation for adult men, it would quite probably have acquired a more or less conservative cast, run by administrators seeking to ensure Congress and the taxpayers that an honest day's work was being had for a modest, even meager, day's pay. The net social results might have been considerable, but almost certainly—given the absence of any general economic crisis—the administrative effort would have been to keep down the noise level. But there was no adult-employment program. Further, the not inconsiderable youth-employment program, the Neighborhood Youth Corps, was from the outset administered by the Labor Department. This left OEO primarily responsible for, and interested in, the community-action programs of Title II (apart, that is, from the Job Corps in which Shriver had a special interest throughout). Community action was by definition a program that sought to bring about individual change through social change—or, rather, by definition of the white, middle-class intellectuals who conceived the program and the white middle-class activists who seized hold of it in the early days of OEO and launched it in the black ghettos of the nation. In this volume, S. M. Miller comments on the considerable discretion welfare bureaucracies exercise in the dispensing of funds and the management of their programs generally. This fact has perhaps never been so dramatically in evidence as in the community-action officials of the poverty program—a welfare bureaucracy, however much they might loathe the designation!—who sought to bring political activism and, in effect, discontent to the poor of the land, including, most visibly, the black poor of the decayed central cities of the North and West. It was OEO's tragedy that this effort had no more begun when violence broke out in those very places. From having been the passive victim of oppression or the righteous and dignified exemplar of a great and honorable tradition of peaceful protest, the Negro assumed the role of aggressor: violent, intimidating, threatening. Some of the public—or at least the Congress and, painful to state, the White House—associated the change with the poverty program, which began its community-action work at just about the time the communities involved became violent. Useless to argue that correlation does not establish causality: Things had gone wrong and blame was placed with those whose task—and promise—it had been to put them right. Almost within months of its founding, the poverty program was in trouble with the White House and the Congress, and within three years of the beginning of operations, it was severely restricted in its mission and methods, especially those

involving community action, by a punitive legislature and an acqui-
escent administration.

Had the poverty program ended there, so might the matter of its
intellectual origins and difficulties. But it did not. To the contrary,
for all the restrictions and abuse it sustained in the first session of the
90th Congress, the essential fact is that it was continued—and on a
basis that would suggest it will now become a more or less permanent
program of the federal government (although not necessarily a permanent agency). This being so, what federal administrators—and all
those involved—think to be true about matters of poverty, race, and
social change assumes an immediate programmatic importance and
does so in a political atmosphere that declares that these are the most
pressing domestic issues of the time.

THE CONCEPTUAL ORIGINS OF FAILURE

The misfortunes of the poverty program are perhaps best visualized
in terms of a downward spiral: a shaky start, followed by political
trouble, leading to underfunding, followed by still more difficulties
in performance, etc. The underfunding, however, was at least as
much associated with the war in Vietnam as with any political difficulties the War on Poverty might have caused. But if this would, in
one sense, seem a purely random influence, there is another in which
the Vietnam nightmare was closely connected. Both were efforts
largely conceived by and put into effect by the liberal thinkers and
political executives of the Kennedy era. Both attracted fierce resistance as well as strong partisans, and both came in a way to haunt
their creators. With respect to both matters, the nation tended to
polarize into two groups: one demanding de-escalation and withdrawal, the other insisting on a total national effort for "victory."
Typically, those calling for ever-greater efforts in Vietnam were most
inclined to de-escalate the War on Poverty, and vice versa. (In the
spring of 1968, before, in effect, resigning his office after finding the
conflicting pressures unmanageable, President Johnson apparently
joined the former group, calling for "austerity" at home. On the day
of Martin Luther King's funeral, across-the-board poverty-program
budget cuts were announced for northeastern cities.) Typically, the
questions were seen as interrelated, in the sense that resources in
money, men, executive energy, and something some call "moral"
leadership were limited, and choices had to be made as to which

effort would receive priority, to the exclusion if necessary (some arguing this was absolutely the case) of the other. No small matters these. As the controversies mounted and passions engaged, it became probable that the disequilibrium brought on by the apparent failure of these two great undertakings was shaking the nation in most fundamental ways. A time of the breaking of parties was at hand, of the rise and fall of dynasties, of profound reorientations.

All but unnoticed in the crash and cries and dust of battle was the curious role of contemporary social science in the initiation of these events that seemed to be ending so badly. The politicians were blaming one another, and the professors seemed content that they should do so. It was an arrangement ostensibly agreeable to all, yet not satisfactory. The role of the intellectual, especially as embodied in the academic intellectual, has changed very considerably in American life, and in a very short time. As recently as 1960, Loren Baritz, in his study *The Servants of Power,* noted: "Intellectuals in the United States have long bemoaned the assumed fact that they are unloved and unappreciated by their society." He went on to assert that while the impulse of resistance to society, to "swim against the current," was a common enough intellectual characteristic, there were nonetheless others who—*mirabile dictu!*—accepted "the main contours of American society." He described this group as "The Servants of Power," [4] meaning, for the most part, large private enterprises. That situation was to change dramatically (rather, would be seen to have changed, the process having been underway for some time). Within months of the appearance of Baritz's book, intellectuals were not only to serve power at the very center of the American national government but also to wield it. Ideas arising out of research and analysis came to have an immediately and deeply consequential impact on events. Thus, the concept of limited warfare and graduated response to Communist expansion abroad; thus, also, the "discovery" of the persistence of poverty at home and the concepts for eliminating it through a grand strategy. Both conceptions led to "war," followed, as stated, by a fairly rapid onset of disillusion and disavowal. But this disavowal was typically directed either toward the objectives of the effort or the individuals in charge of it. In neither case has there been either considerable examination of the conceptions on which the undertaking was based (or by which it was justified) or any inquiry into the degree to which the "intellectual" assumptions of the effort were internally consistent, adequately understood, and systematically put to practice, much less the degree

to which they can be considered to have been valid at the time of
their adoption and subsequently to have stood the test of events. It
would be wrong to overestimate the influence of sheer intellection in
either of these areas: The War on Poverty arose as much as anything
from the socialist tradition of men like Michael Harrington and the
political processes of the Democratic party; the war in Vietnam arose
primarily from the demands of the Cold War on an essentially imperial power such as the United States has become. But the intellectual
contribution was present in both and, on its own terms, demands
evaluation.

To do just this with respect to the intellectual assumptions on
which the War on Poverty was based is the purpose of this volume.
This was only in part the objective of the group that first met in the
spring of 1966 as the Seminar on Race and Poverty of the American
Academy of Arts and Sciences. Since a fair number of those present
had themselves participated in the conception and early implementation of the poverty program—others being even then actively associated with it—there was more than a little predisposition to get on
with the ever-pressing task of program formulation. Nothing so simplistic as a presumed dichotomy between "more studies" and "action" was involved, rather an unspoken presumption that the intellectual bases of "action" were well enough understood and agreed on
in their essentials and that, accordingly, program matters, especially
the politics of achieving program support, would be of greater interest and, what is more, would impose the greater intellectual demands. The members of the seminar were more or less deliberately
chosen for their activist concerns or their specifically activist roles, as
in the case of Joseph Kershaw and Robert A. Levine, who served,
successively, as Associate Director for Research of OEO itself. It was
thus a matter of very considerable interest and some unsettlement for
the seminar to realize, after a preliminary *tour d'horizon,* that many
persons who had been speaking the same language had nonetheless
very different meanings in mind. *There was no common understanding as to the nature of poverty or the process of deliberate social
change.* Quite divergent views existed, and according as one or another view was adopted, it seemed evident that not less divergent
policy and program implications would follow. Thus, at about the
time the poverty program was running into serious doubts and disagreements in Washington, and in the nation generally, a corresponding set of uncertainties and ambiguities arose in a gathering
not inappropriately sponsored by "The Academy." Nor did these

difficulties dissolve with further scrutiny. To the contrary, the longer the dialogue persisted, the more different positions came to be explicit, emphatic, and manifestly at odds, one with the other. Whereupon, the clear task of the seminar came to be that of explicating these differences and tracing the consequences that one, as against another, would have for public policy.

HEMINGWAY vs. FITZGERALD

It is perhaps well to state here that the widespread assertion of the "failure" of the poverty program at the present moment (just four years from the time it was presented to the Congress) could prove nothing more than a passing mood and one, moreover, that profoundly underestimates the nature and permanency of the commitment made by the Economic Opportunity Act. Gertrude Himmelfarb has pointed out that the Reform Act of 1867, while "perhaps the decisive event . . . in modern English history," was nonetheless a measure that few intended and fewer still comprehended.[5] Far from being, as G. M. Trevelyan would have it, an "orderly and gradual" accommodation to "social facts," the event was rather a jumble of responses to events of the moment that nonetheless ended with a *commitment* that was in its nature near to absolute. Professor Himmelfarb writes:

It was this act that transformed England into a democracy and made democracy not only a respectable form of government . . . but also, in the opinion of most men, the only natural and proper form of government. . . . To be sure, the Act of 1867 had to be supplemented by others before universal suffrage was attained. But once this first step was made, no one seriously doubted that the others would follow.

Is it not likely that something not dissimilar by way of a commitment was made with the launching of the War on Poverty? Indeed, the parallels with the great Victorian suffrage measure are striking, most especially in the degree to which neither was the result of any great popular agitation on behalf of the measures that were eventually adopted. The nearest thing to popular pressure that preceded the poverty program was the March on Washington for Jobs and Freedom staged by Negro leaders in the late summer of 1963, but this was generally viewed as a demand for civil rights measures, and to the degree it was concerned with problems of poverty, the demand (in wholly unspecified terms) was for a job-creation program, which the poverty legislation did not include.

The Economic Opportunity Act, at least in its specifics, was very much a manifestation of the "professionalization of reform" that was proceeding apace at this time, having resulted from the convergence of such forces as Keynesian economics, Democratic politics, a certain thaw in the Cold War, the civil rights revolution, and the emergence of social science as an influence in government.[6] Just prior to the assassination of President Kennedy, Nathan Glazer described the process:

Without benefit of anything like the Beveridge report to spark and focus public discussion and concern, the United States is passing through a stage of enormous expansion in the size and scope of what we may loosely call the social services—the public programs designed to help people adapt to an increasingly complex and unmanageable society. While Congress has been painfully and hesitantly trying to deal with two great measures—tax reform and a civil rights bill—and its deliberations on both have been closely covered by the mass media, it has also been working with much less publicity on a number of bills which will contribute at least as much to changing the shape of American society.[7]

These of course were precisely the bills incorporated in, and expanded by, the poverty program. Their origins lay to a considerable degree in presumed knowledge as to the nature of social processes and social change. Only just now does there begin what might be seen as the systematic reassessment of that presumed knowledge.

Apart from the fundamental question, Why does poverty bother us?—a question so basic as to remain unasked—the conceptual issues on which an anti-poverty program must be based come to this: In which way are the poor different from others; how did they come to be that way; what measures could be expected to bring them into a sufficient measure of conformity with the modes of the larger society that they are no longer seen as poor and different, and no longer regard themselves as such? (Whether they would wish this to be done, or whether the larger society would, is another question, the answer to which will arise more from value judgments than from anything to be described as the analysis of social processes.)

Although, as remarked earlier, a fair measure of the poverty program emerged out of concern for certain types of deviant behavior and, further, although the concept of "cultural deprivation" had won many adherents by this time, it is nonetheless the case that at the outset of the poverty program there was little emphasis on such matters. The poor were presumed to be no more than that: poor. Little heed was given the possibility that being poor might eventually lead to structural changes in personality and behavior, much as the state of being hungry can lead to a condition of malnutrition that is not to be resolved merely by the resumption of an ample diet. But the question was there nonetheless, and two factors pushed it to the fore. First was the unavoidable association of the issue of poverty with that of race and, to a lesser degree, ethnicity. Negroes (and Puerto Ricans, and Mexican-Americans, and Indians) were poor in ways other groups were not, and few could avoid the perception that such persons were viewed as different and treated differently. Second was the startling onset of black violence in the urban slums of the North and West. That this was "different" behavior none could doubt and few could explain. A paradox of sorts arose: Any number of persons grew more confident in, even more insistent on, the viability of particular strategies for relieving poverty, even as they grew more uneasy with familiar formulations of its etiology.

At the same time, it became clear that at what might be termed a descriptive level, observers of poverty had reached impressively convergent conclusions.

The existing literature reveals a considerable consensus as to the characteristics of "lower-class" persons who are more or less destitute throughout their life cycle, in contrast, that is, to "graduate-student poverty" or the poverty of persons who are disabled, or old, or otherwise living in situations quite different from those to which they were born or in which they spent significant parts of their lives. Peter Rossi and Zahava D. Blum, in Chapter 2 in this volume, summarize qualities of the group Lloyd Warner first described as "lower-lowers" to designate their place in the stratification system:

1. *Labor-Force Participation.* Long periods of unemployment and/or intermittent employment. Public assistance is frequently a major source of income for extended periods.

2. *Occupational Participation.* When employed, persons hold jobs at the lowest levels of skills, for example, domestic service, unskilled labor, menial service jobs, and farm labor.

3. *Family and Interpersonal Relations.* High rates of marital instability (desertion, divorce, separation), high incidence of households headed by females, high rates of illegitimacy; unstable and

superficial interpersonal relationships characterized by considerable suspicion of persons outside the immediate household.

4. *Community Characteristics.* Residential areas with very poorly developed voluntary associations and low levels of participation in such local voluntary associations as exist.

5. *Relationship to Larger Society.* Little interest in, or knowledge of, the larger society and its events; some degree of alienation from the larger society.

6. *Value Orientations.* A sense of helplessness and low sense of personal efficacy; dogmatism and authoritarianism in political ideology; fundamentalist religious views, with some strong inclinations toward beliefs in magical practices. Low "need achievement" and low levels of aspirations for the self.

Although several other characteristics could be added to this inventory, a review of the literature indicates that these are not only the ones about which there is most agreement but also those which tend to be stressed as critical.

But again: How has this come to be, and what might change it? While to be sure there exists a spectrum of opinion on the matter, it would be quite mistaken to imagine there to be chaos. To the contrary, on closer examination, opinions can be seen to cluster around two general positions—distinct, but not entirely incompatible. Lee Rainwater alludes to the famous exchange between Fitzgerald and Hemingway as to the peculiar ways of the rich and suggests that the question about the poor is whether they really are different or simply have less money. On the one hand, scholars such as Walter Miller and Oscar Lewis argue that there is in truth a distinctive "culture of poverty" or subculture of the poor that is not only sustained by external circumstances—poverty—but also by internal systems of values and preferences and interim personal relationships that have a validity and life of their own and that are capable of persisting well after the external circumstances have been modified or changed altogether. It is to be noted that both Miller and Lewis are anthropologists trained to perceive differences in cultures and respectful—even defensive—of those differences. Herbert Gans makes a point of this. "The behavioral conception of culture," he argues, "can be traced back to anthropological traditions and to the latent political agendas of anthropological researchers." With respect to the poor, as Myrdal reminded us a quarter century ago, this can be a risky business. From fifth-century Athens on, a literary tradition has stressed not only the validity of poverty (preferably rustic) but indeed the *superior* validity. Such fancies just possibly lend a slightly astringent air to the arguments of those who insist that the characteristics of the poor are situational rather than cultural. ". . . Poverty," writes Otis Dudley Duncan, "is not a trait but a condition." Such essentially is the view of Harold Watts and Gerald Rosenthal, both of whom, it may be noted, are economists and hence professionally more or less required to note that the state of being poor is everywhere defined as not having enough money. (And, of course, sociologists such as Hylan Lewis and Herbert Gans fervently agree.)

The difficulty with each of these general positions, as Herbert Gans argues, and as their proponents would concede, is that they require a too homogeneous view of the poverty population. People are too obviously variegated: one from another, one group from another, one region from another. (Indeed, the demonstrations by Thernstrom and Duncan of the high rates of turnover in the poverty population would seem to raise considerable difficulties for all points of view.) No one conception is likely to fit all circumstances. Moreover, to Rossi and Blum—as well as to Rainwater, Gans, and Hylan Lewis—to change the condition of poverty would lead more or less directly to behavior change. The former states, "If there is a culture of poverty or a subculture of the poor, then it is a condition which arises out of the exigencies of being relatively without resources and of being negatively evaluated by the larger society." Rainwater, while tending to accept the Parsonian and Mertonian position that there exists a common value system for Americans, such that a distinctive culture of poverty could not be said to exist, nonetheless argues that however much values may be shared, "conforming to norms requires certain kinds of social logistic support." He insists that those who are known to be poor and seen to be different in the United States have simply not received that support. Rainwater would thus argue that each successive generation can re-create the patterns of the preceding one, without there being any specifically intergenerational transfer in the process. This, he holds, is especially so in the experience of the Negro American:

The social ontogeny of each generation recapitulates the social phylogeny of Negroes in the New World *because the basic socio-economic position of the group has not changed in a direction favorable to successful achievement in terms of conventional norms.*

A historian, Stephan Thernstrom, points out that the $1.50 a day wages of the nineteenth century did not lead to the formation of a permanent class of the industrial poor; to the contrary, it sustained a high order of upward social mobility from the very lowest classes. To be sure, he argues, times have now changed and so have expectations. Then, as now, the poor got children; in those times, however, they were an economic asset, while today they are anything but. Moreover, before the mass media, or the Kennedys, or whatever, it was understood that some things took time.

While many of these families had a total combined income which hovered around the minimum subsistence budgets carefully calculated by contemporary middle-class investigators, they still managed to save. Their conception of subsistence was far more Spartan—it was potatoes! And their subculture had given them a goal which was clear and within reach—a piece of property, a piece of respectability which made all those potatoes tolerable.

Thernstrom nonetheless asserts that "those who are convinced that poverty in the U.S. is increasingly being meted out in life sentences have yet to do the homework to substantiate the claim." Save only for the Negro, whose present, persisting position at the bottom of the social order simply cannot be explained except by the not less persistent fact of racial prejudice. Marc Fried, in a study of migration of different ethnic groups in the nineteenth and twentieth centuries, concludes that the Negro experience is not notably different from that of earlier, peasant groups, but also notes the less hopeful signs of this moment and the seeming ever-present American potential for ethnic hostility. In a tour de force of sociometrics, Otis Dudley Duncan isolates and quantifies the impact of this phenomenon. This "cost of being a Negro," he argues, is in no sense a matter of "cultural" inheritance, save it is an inheritance of black skin; it is this aspect of poverty that must be the first concern of the nation. The seminar did not disagree. An essential fact of American society, Duncan writes, is that there now exist "gross discrepancies in achievements and rewards between the races" and that these simply do not disappear as "a benign fallout from conventional measures taken to enhance 'opportunity.'" S. M. Miller and Pamela Roby agree; they argue for casting the issues of poverty in terms of stratification in a status system rather than viewing it as a question of levels of income or consumption. This, they argue, leads forthwith to the issue of inequality. Which Walter Miller would accept, while denying that the inequality is all that oppressive to persons consigned to the "lower" strata by "upper" analysts. He is adamant on this point. For him the question, "In what way are the poor different from others?" ignores the logically prior question which he feels must be: "How is one to define the population seen as presenting a/the problem/problems?" It is his view that what troubles "upper" analysts and citizens in general is not that this "lower" group lacks resources (especially in the case of *urban* "lower" groups) but that it acts differently. For Miller, the term "poor" is a misleading code word for those differences in behavior.

Indeed, it is no less an authority than Shaw who reminds us in *Maxims for Revolutionists* that doing good to others can be a risky business if the others in question do not happen to share the same tastes.

Three general points emerge from this range of analysis. The first and most important is that any moderately rigorous inquiry into these issues is sooner or later, and more often sooner, stalled by an absence of data against which to check hypotheses. Again, it is not a matter of knowing nothing. An important beginning literature has come into being—much, if not indeed most, of it the work of persons represented in this volume and other members of the Academy seminar. But it is only that: a beginning. The essential fact is that our present concern for this cluster of social issues and the amount of resources being allocated to it are wholly disproportionate to our knowledge of the subject. Thus, a century after trade unions began to be organized and the appearance of industrial unemployment as a political and social issue, a half century after the founding of the *Monthly Labor Review,* almost a quarter century from the enactment of the Employment Act of 1946 and the establishment of the Council of Economic Advisers, we are still almost entirely ignorant of the effects of unemployment on individual workers. A decent beginning was made on such studies during the 1930s, but the matter was dropped and has not been heard of since.[8] Similarly, while continued references are made in this volume to the issue of income and the possibility of a "resources" strategy in the War on Poverty, there is hardly two bits worth of reliable information as to how changes in income change individual styles of life.

While this first general point will clearly be seen as fundamental, it will hardly be taken as something especially novel. The absence or insufficiency of reliable data is the common condition of social science at this time, and if academics do not overly insist on the fact, neither do they overmuch conceal it. By contrast, a second general point emerges that is not always evident in earlier discussions and even less frequently commented on. This might be described as the impact of social class on the analysis of social class. Just as poverty and race are anything but randomly distributed risks in the population, neither is concern about them nor the professional ability and/or proclivity to analyze them. So far as the social sciences are concerned, it can be laid down that literary productivity on the subject of poverty will exist in inverse ratio to the incidence of poverty in the "group" to which the social scientist happens to "belong." David Riesman is surely correct in his view of the United States as a

society only partially centralized and still radically divided along ethnic, religious, racial and class lines—but a society nevertheless with an increasingly widespread national upper-middle-class style spread by college education, the mass media, and occupational, social and geographic mobility.

This condition is, if anything, exaggerated within the intellectual-academic community, where an upper-middle-class style—the Academy seminar met amidst the Edwardian splendor of Brandegee House and did not fail to have claret and candlelight at dinner—is aggressively maintained, but where memories of a not always distant past of privation and rejection are very real indeed. Unavoidably, this affects attitudes and perceptions.

The essential fact is that one source of the continuing radical division between ethnic, religious, racial, and class lines of which Riesman speaks is that there have in fact been markedly differential rates of "success" among these groups. Moreover, contrary to what might be generally believed, there would appear to be a high correlation between success in the traditional commercial pursuits of the land and in the now not less characteristic intellectual/academic pursuits. There is no concealing failure in American society: At best, it can be translated into weakness and deployed in the manner of the weak—a female art, and typically a woman's lot, as in the confrontation of black welfare mothers and white welfare officials. Oddly, however, there is not a little concealment of success. Norman Podhoretz, rather to his disadvantage, has explained this for us: Success is to contemporary American society what sex was to the Victorian world —"the dirty little secret." Perhaps always has been. Did not William

James as far back as 1906 declare that "worship of the bitch-goddess success" was "our national disease"? Certainly it makes some persons uneasy, and not a little effort is made to cover it up; intuitively, perhaps, on the part of Jews; by habit and tradition on the part of New England Brahmins; as a deliberate tactic in a certain type of politician, especially southern ones whose constituencies are so largely comprised of "failures." In the case of "The Heathen Chinee" and their Japanese cousins, it is not clear whether it is the cunning of Ah Sin that is involved or merely a matter of caution, but the extraordinary success of these two groups is still a matter of quite limited knowledge outside a few places such as Hawaii. And if there is a general uneasiness about success, this is nowhere to be encountered in a more painful manifestation than in the literature of poverty, for it is the persisting "social fact" of this literature that it not only involves a discussion by individuals who are successful about individuals who are not, but also representatives of unusually successful *groups* dissecting unusually unsuccessful ones. In this respect, this volume is no exception. Of the fourteen authors represented, for example, just half come from Jewish backgrounds, five have white Protestant antecedents, two Catholic. This is in no way proportional to the size of the respective groups and, until recently, rather the inverse of the incidence of *urban* poverty among them. (It would appear that Protestant-Catholic differentials have about washed out now, save when to be Catholic means also to be Mexican-American, etc.)

But, on the other hand, it does quite accurately reflect the general distribution of "success" in America, certainly in the social sciences. To state that half the significant social science of the present age is the work of scholars with Jewish backgrounds is probably to underestimate; to suggest that as much as 15 per cent is the product of scholars with Catholic backgrounds is to be more generous than the spirit of ecumenicism requires. But note those not present: the Puerto Rican, the Mexican-American, the Indian-American, and, most especially, the Negro. Although Hylan Lewis played an active and important role in the seminar, the press of other commitments prevented his preparing a paper. Hence, this volume partakes of the characteristic of so many others of the present time: a discussion by whites of problems most conspicuously experienced by blacks. An inescapable fact about the current billowing literature on poverty and race relations in the United States is that while more and more it centers on the conditions of black persons in a white society, less and less is it actually the work of Negro scholars. This must be repeated: *less.* It was not always thus. A generation ago, anyone seeking to learn more of this subject would of necessity and choice have turned to the work of black authors: Frazier, Johnson, Drake, Cayton, Davis, and others almost as distinguished. But somehow that tradition, nobly begun even earlier by such as W. E. B. DuBois, declined. Myrdal's great work may have constituted a kind of overkill, at least for research by Negroes. In the mid-1950s American foundations seemingly lost interest in the subject, and white work in race relations also stopped.[9]

When interest resumed, it may be that whites took over the subject, newly *en vogue,* much as they took over the federal-style houses in Georgetown and on Capitol Hill. But for whatever reason, Negro social scientists are few and far between today; those held in the greatest respect—men such as Kenneth Clark, Hylan Lewis, John Hope Franklin, Daniel C. Thompson, Charles J. Willie, St. Clair Drake—are so overextended and in demand—those conferences and those community action programs!—as to produce less than would otherwise be the case.

It is, of course, quite an unresolved question as to whether racial, religious, class experiences, or whatever are necessarily better interpreted by persons who "belong" to the group in question. It was judged of Myrdal, for example, that one of his primary qualifications for the task he undertook in the 1930s was that he was a non-American from a nation with no colonial experience. In other words, that he had the *least* personal experience with the phenomena he undertook to analyze. On the other hand, a plain question of "data" is involved. Having lived as a Puerto Rican immigrant, for example, or an Apache, or a poor white from "a cabin in the cotton" surely gives access to knowledge as to what that condition actually involves that few outsiders can command. Not just knowledge, but also an intensity of interest and alertness to nuance that "outsiders" rarely possess. It would surely seem to be the case in social science, as it is in literature, that "insiders" write the most, if not the best, about their own group. The most that can be said at the moment is that what social science very much needs is a considerable widening of its ethnic, social, religious, and regional base. (Note for example that of the fourteen authors of this volume only two have southern backgrounds.) When social scientists observing a given milieu find that their judgments as to its qualities and characteristics are similar to, or convergent with, the judgments of other social scientists actually drawn from the milieu in question, we will be entitled to a greater order of confidence in the respective results.

Yet the problem of ethnically "representative" analysts is not merely one of the validity of interpretations. It is also one of acceptability. In a certain sense, twentieth-century social science has inherited the ambiguities and embarassments of nineteenth-century charity: its practitioners want to help and, in considerable measure, are able to do so, but they are at the same time restrained by a knowledge of the great differences along "ethnic, religious, racial, and class lines" that typically separate them from the objects of their concern and are plagued by doubts as to the validity of any prescriptions they might offer across those chasms. In its most bathetic manifestation, this concern takes the form of asking, "What right have I to impose my (corrupt, etc.) bourgeois values on these (uncorrupted, etc.) struggling folk whose values are not mine?" But the problem is present even for the most disciplined of men. What it comes to is that in a society still much given to assessing the comparative moral worth of different individuals and different modes of behavior, not at all averse by rapid calculation to adduce from the behavior of individuals the characteristics of the group to which the individuals "belong," and in which characteristic lower-class behavior is associated with quite negative moral valuations by middle-class groups, to be overexplicit about the origins and nature of that behavior is to risk seeming not merely to describe but to indict the lower-class group in question. The charge will almost automatically be raised that such analysis, howsoever well intentioned *or* accurate, by establishing the existence of behavior that can be "misinterpreted" by enemies of the group in question and used against it, more or less automatically *will be* so used, in consequence of which it must be judged that the social scientist has given "ammunition" to those enemies. If the typical social scientist open to this charge were a genuinely "objective" and "neutral" observer, such charges might be a matter of little consequence, but rarely is this the case. To the contrary, such analysts are normally much caught up with the desire to "help" those they analyze: How bitter then to be accused of having done harm. Even when such alarums concerning ever-watchful "enemies" occur largely at the level of fantasy, the attack on the social scientist is not less real nor less unsettling. The question of guilt and culpability pervades this atmosphere, to the point indeed where professional training probably had best begin taking it into account, much as psychoanalysts are trained to anticipate and to manage hostility.

It would be quite mistaken to suppose that such assaults are to be associated only with black militants hurling the charge of "racism" at 'anguished white liberals. Anything but. Not infrequently, quite the most virulent objections will come from the very "elite" circles whence they originate. Thus at one point, for example, it fell to the present author to report on the work of the poverty seminar to the 1482nd Stated Meeting of the American Academy. The report, which followed rather much the outline of this present chapter, was necessarily limited and imperfect, and nothing if not tentative. It was generally well enough received: Academicians are accustomed to hearing colleagues report that closer scrutiny of a particular subject has disclosed large areas of uncertainty, indicating the need for further research. Yet, one member present for the occasion, an astronomer, was roused to a state of considerable distress, the main elements of which were recorded in a three-page letter, of which the first paragraph might usefully be quoted.

I am writing to express my dismay and concern over the report you delivered to the American Academy of Arts and Sciences last Wednesday. I did enjoy the first twenty minutes of your talk, because I assumed I was listening to a put-on. The preposterous list of criteria for poverty, the clumsy jargon, the pathetic attempts at polysyllabic humor, and the invention of comic figures like "Miller" and "Rainwater" to act as spokesmen for hallucinatory points of view—all these seemed to be a somewhat overdone prelude to what I assumed would be a serious discussion of the problem of poverty in the United States. I still find it hard to believe that a talk that laid so much stress on the views of a man who thinks that poverty is a figment of the white liberal imagination and on interpretations of the Negro ethos by a white Mississippian was entirely lacking in humorous intent.

One cannot avoid the sheer fury of these remarks—fury that somehow the good name of the poor had been sullied—and the willing descent to a level of ad hominem disparagement of intellectual analysis that is at very least unusual. (Alas, poor Rainwater. An adult life devoted to social research and liberal politics seemingly cannot erase the stigma of birth!) Yet, it would be a fair impression that such reactions are not unrepresentative and that they have affected analyses of race and poverty in the United States.

The most conspicuous effect has been a near-obsessive concern to locate the "blame" for poverty, especially Negro poverty, on forces and institutions outside the community concerned. At different times, different factors have been in fashion—capitalism, racism, the military-industrial complex, etc.—but the tendency persists. Walter Miller (an exhilarating but rarely comic figure!) will go so far as to argue that indeed a genuine, true-believer cult has arisen in this area, a belief based on the proposition that the poor are in poverty because they are deprived of opportunity by the power structure. ". . . Simple, direct, unambiguous," he writes, "a classic theory of conspiratorial exclusionism." A certain measure of this attitude was implicit in the original poverty program of the federal government, and it came even more in evidence as "white radicals" (as they came to be perceived in the upper reaches of the Executive Office Building) gained positions of influence within OEO. Quite apart from the question of whether this position in any way corresponds to reality, this curious mind set encourages a number of singularly unhelpful tendencies of American liberalism. Foremost of these is the proclivity for seeing in the poor and dispossessed—howsoever weak and outnumbered they might be—an instrument for transforming the larger society, which at times tends to something very like indifference to the conditions of the poor as such. It has been remarked of the abolitionists, for example, that many seemed preoccupied with the souls of slaveholders but not at all interested, really, in the lives of the slaves. It was not just by chance that a large-scale program to provide employment for adult men—a traditional anti-poverty measure—was left out of the poverty program, while the quite unprecedented community-action programs were left in and, indeed, came to be the center of the program. Miller contends that while the opportunity theory on which these programs were based is inadequate, if not outright wrong, its attraction lay in the imputation of guilt on the part of the larger society. (This certainly was the message that the public received from the report of the Commission on Civil Disorders, whatever might have been the intent of the commissioners.) He states:

Opportunity is *not* a structure that people are either inside or outside of. Americans may achieve widely varying degrees of success or failure in a thousand different spheres and in a thousand different ways. Beaming to lower status people the message that one can attain "success goals" by breaching, demolishing, or otherwise forcing the "walls" that bar them from "opportunity" conveys a tragically oversimplified and misleading impression of the conditions and circumstances of success, in addition to fostering an imagery with potentially destructive consequences.

But right or wrong—men such as Thernstrom would argue that this view is quite mistaken—it is certainly the case that the apparent function of many of these programs as they actually came into being was to raise the level of perceived and validated discontent among poor persons with the social system about them, without actually improving the conditions of life of the poor in anything like a comparable degree. Can it be that this process has not somehow contributed to and validated the onset of urban violence?

But from the point of view of social science, quite the most pernicious effect of the poverty ideology has been its tendency to discourage rigorous inquiry into the social process that keeps men in poverty or leads them out of it. To blame "the system," or whatever, is not an act of analysis; it is too often the very opposite. Nor is this latter-day obscurantism confined to the study of the poor, themselves. Thus, a flaw in the otherwise powerful and moving report of the National Advisory Commission on Civil Disorders is that having declared, "White racism is essentially responsible for the explosive mixture which has been accumulating in our cities since the end of World War II," it dropped that matter then and there. No effort whatever was made, or apparently even deemed necessary, to define "white racism," to trace its etiology, to distinguish different forms and degrees of intensity, to measure its impact, to assess the counteraction it may produce in Negroes. None of this was done, nor was there any discussion even of the question of how such white racism might be diminished or eliminated altogether. The charges against the poor—rioting—had been dismissed. The guilty party—white society—had been identified. The matter need go no further.

Five months after its report was published, the Commission released a supplementary volume relating the findings of research projects which it had financed, but which evidently were not available at the time the basic document was written. The most ambitious project was a survey of public opinion in fifteen cities directed by Angus Campbell and Howard Schuman of the Survey Research Center of the University of Michigan.[10] A work of unquestioned scholarship, the survey utterly devastated the Commission's finding concerning "white racism." A bare 6 per cent of the white respondents reported attitudes that could properly be described as racist, and this was concentrated among persons over fifty years old. The overwhelming body of white opinion revealed itself as uneasy, even anxious about Negroes, but eminently reasonable in response to perceived black demands. A clear majority, for example, indicated a willingness to see their own taxes increased 10 per cent to provide better living for blacks. The man-in-the-street assessment of the situation as revealed in the Commission-sponsored survey comes through as considerably more realistic than the somewhat perfervid self-certification of the Commission report itself, with its all-too-familiar pattern of the white upper-middle class confessing the sins of the white lower-middle class. Just how much this pattern of caste disdain for the lower, but not suffering, orders contributed to the extraordinary political appeal of Presidential candidate George C. Wallace is a subject political sociologists might well look into once poverty has been conquered. Nor is it likely that whites have been the only ones affected.

One commentator, appalled by the too-eager embrace of the "white racism" verdict—an acceptance not in the least associated with an apparent national impulse to do anything about the conditions described—concluded that "all that this exercise in blame-fixing offers (the Negro) is an official nudge toward paranoia." The Commission findings, followed so shortly by the assassination of Reverend Martin Luther King, Jr., indeed gave way to a quite unprecedented display of nationwide mourning and self-indictment. Yet, the impulse to change the conditions of the life of the poor somehow lagged behind, indeed seemed hardly associated with the willingness to accept guilt for the existence of those conditions. And almost nowhere was there in evidence any apparent interest in the development of more complex and usable analyses of those conditions, nor, yet, any seeming interest in the dangers that might reside in the impulse to accept blame. The psychoanalytic doctrine that guilt turns to rage was no more heeded than William Graham Sumner's perhaps not altogether discredited notion that folkways persist.

American social science can do better, and so it ought. An honorable, and on balance honorably fulfilled, desire to be helpful has here and there succumbed to a fear of disappointing or to an alarm at contradicting. That is not the way science is done, nor in the end is it the way a republic can be governed. This volume is an effort to do what must be done: It would be presumptuous to call it a beginning effort, but not, I think, wrong to state that it appears at a time when the need for such a beginning is more widely appreciated. For there are promises to keep. In the dark hours of 1964 a bright and shining commitment was made. That commitment stands. *Pacta sunt servanda.*

Notes

1. In a column written shortly before the 1968 Democratic National Convention, Tom Wicker of *The New York Times* noted the speculation that Sargent Shriver might be Humphrey's choice as running mate, but noted also the comment of one observer that Shriver "would come with some baggage." Wicker added: "The baggage includes his service as director of Johnson's "War on Poverty," which somehow managed to wind up alienating many of the black and the poor, as well as white conservatives . . . and members of Congress. . . ." *The New York Times,* July 28, 1968.

2. See Daniel P. Moynihan, "What Is Community Action?" *The Public Interest* (Fall 1966), and *Maximum Feasible Misunderstanding: Community Action in the War on Poverty* (New York: The Free Press, 1969).

3. This section is based on the author's notes of the cabinet meeting, February 18, 1964.

4. Loren Baritz, *The Servants of Power* (Middletown, Conn.: Wesleyan University Press, 1960), p. ix.

5. Gertrude Himmelfarb, *Victorian Minds* (New York: Knopf, 1968), p. 333.

6. For an overly optimistic view, see Daniel P. Moynihan, "The Professionalization of Reform," *The Public Interest* (Fall 1965).

7. *Ibid.*

8. Samuel Stouffer and Paul F. Lazarsfeld, with the assistance of R. J. Jaffe, "Research Memorandum on the Family in the Depression," Bulletin 29 (New York, Social Science Research Council, 1937); Edward W. Bakke, *The Unemployed Worker; A Study of the Task of Making a Living Without a Job* (New Haven, Conn.: Yale University Press, 1940). Happily, in the work of Harold L. Sheppard of the Upjohn Institute for Employment Research, the long drought appears to be ending.

9. See Melvin M. Tumin, "Some Social Consequences of Research on Racial Relations," *The American Sociologist* (May 1968), 117–124.

10. Supplemental Studies for the National Advisory Commission on Civil Disorders, July 1968. "Racial Attitudes in Fifteen American Cities," Angus Campbell and Howard Schuman. Survey Research Center, Institute for Social Research, The University of Michigan, June 1968.

ꮯ *Class, Status, and Poverty*

PETER H. ROSSI and ZAHAVA D. BLUM

INTRODUCTION

The poor are different: On this, there is consensus. It is beyond this
agreement on the obvious that the critical issues in both our understanding and treatment of poverty arise: In what *ways* are the poor
different? How do these differences *arise,* and how are they *maintained?*

To provide answers, we will engage in both empirical and theoretical exercises. On the empirical side, researches on social stratification published over the past two decades will be examined to glean
fairly firm knowledge about the poor and their differences from other
layers of our society. On the theoretical side, we will attempt to
explain how these differences are generated and maintained.

Whether the poor are different qualitatively from the rest of
American society remains a moot question until we settle both the
question of how poverty is to be defined and what is meant by a
qualitative difference. For present purposes, it is sufficient to define
the poor as those who are at the bottom of our American class system.
The poor are those able-bodied adults and their dependent children [1] whose lack of income and wealth places them at the bottom-

The preparation of this chapter was supported in part by a grant from the
Russell Sage Foundation and by a Reflective Year Fellowship granted to the senior
author by the Carnegie Corporation of New York. This support is hereby gratefully acknowledged. This chapter is part of the program of research on *Education
and Social Change for Negro Americans* at the Center for the Study of Social
Organization of Schools, Johns Hopkins University.

most layer of the distributions and whose sources of income lie in either welfare payments or in unskilled and poorly paid occupations. These are the "problem" poor, those who "should be making it" in our society and who are either failing to do so or are the products of the failures of our society.[2]

The main concerns of this chapter are not merely academic. Whether one conceives of the poor as qualitatively different from the rest of society or mainly differing in degree from those above them affects social policy. A social policy based on a qualitative model of poverty tends to stress rehabilitation and retraining. A quantitative model, in contrast, underlies those policies that stress institutional changes in our society or that provide income maintenance. In the last section of this chapter, we attempt to draw out the policy implications of our empirical findings and theoretical speculations.

The main issues dealt with in this chapter have appeared in the literature on poverty in a variety of seemingly different forms. For example, there is the question of whether there exists a "culture of poverty." Or there are discussions of the alternatives of a situational versus a subcultural view of poverty, etc. It is important to bear in mind that these are all variants of the main issues of this chapter: How different are the poor and why are they different?

HOW DIFFERENT ARE THE POOR?

To answer this question, we examined the extensive, empirical social-science literature published since the end of World War II. The detailed results of our bibliographic survey are contained in the Appendix of this volume to which the interested reader may turn for a discussion of methods and detailed findings.[3] For present purposes, we will provide mainly an overview.

Our first disappointment in surveying the literature was to find that very few of the studies paid close attention to those on the very bottom of the stratification system. Systematic studies of the characteristics of the poor on an extensive basis are particularly lacking, the major exceptions being the Survey Research Center's survey of income and labor-force participation based on a national sample, augmented by oversampling of low-income households (Morgan et al., 1962).* The studies have tended mainly to make only a few

* Citations in this chapter are to articles listed in the bibliography to the Appendix of this volume.

distinctions along class lines, the favorites being "working-class/middle-class" and "blue-collar/white-collar" dichotomies. Furthermore, cutting points for the dichotomies are not consistent across studies.

Our second disappointment was to find that the major and most often-cited studies bearing directly on the characteristics of the poor were based on small samples and on qualitative observations. The poor have been studied mainly in the style of anthropological field investigations rather than in the style of large-scale systematic surveys. This is not to say that these observations are per se incorrect, but only that they are difficult to evaluate.

As a consequence of the characteristics of the research literature, we have had to fall back on a less direct strategy than would be optimally desired in answering the question of how different are the poor. Our main approach has been to assess whether the images of the poor as arising from the qualitative literature could be anticipated on the basis of extrapolation from general relationships found in the correlates of social-class position.

Although no single writer in the qualitative tradition has provided exactly the description shown below, we think it contains the essential features of most.[4] These features include:

1. *Labor-Force Participation.* Long periods of unemployment and/or intermittent employment. Public assistance is frequently a major source of income for extended periods.

2. *Occupational Participation.* When employed, persons hold jobs at the lowest levels of skills, for example, domestic service, unskilled labor, menial service jobs, and farm labor.

3. *Family and Interpersonal Relations.* High rates of marital instability (desertion, divorce, separation), high incidence of households headed by females, high rates of illegitimacy; unstable and superficial interpersonal relationships characterized by considerable suspicion of persons outside the immediate household.

4. *Community Characteristics.* Residential areas with very poorly developed voluntary associations and low levels of participation in such local voluntary associations as exist.

5. *Relationship to Larger Society.* Little interest in, or knowledge of, the larger society and its events; some degree of alienation from the larger society.

6. *Value Orientations.* A sense of helplessness and low sense of personal efficacy; dogmatism and authoritarianism in political ideology; fundamentalist religious views, with some strong inclinations toward belief in magical practices. Low "need achievement" and low levels of aspirations for the self.

Although several other characteristics could be added to this inventory, our informal content analysis of the literature indicates that these characteristics are those about which there is considerable consensus and that tend to be stressed as critical features of the poor.

Dissension among writers exists around the question of whether the poor are "happy" or not. Some writers extol the spontaneity of expression among this group; others ascribe the same phenomenon to lack of impulse control. Some see the poor as having a fine and warm sense of humor, but others regard their humor as bitter and sad. Some claim that the poor are desperately trying to change their condition, sinking into apathy when it becomes clear to them that the odds are greatly against their being able to do so; others deny that a strong desire for change exists.

A second point of disagreement arises over whether or not the "lower-lowers" have developed a contra-culture—a rejection of the core values of American society—or whether they are best characterized by what Hyman Rodman calls "value stretch," a condition in which the main values are accepted as valid by persons who, nonetheless, exempt themselves from fulfilling the requirement of norms.[5]

Our detailed findings from the survey of empirical studies are contained in the Appendix of this volume. For present purposes, it is only necessary to state that in almost every case it is clear that the alleged "special" characteristics of the poor are ones that they share generally with the "working-class" or "blue-collar" component of the labor force. In other words, the poor *are* different, but the difference appears mainly to be a matter of *degree* rather than of kind.

According to the literature reviewed, the lower the socio-economic level:

1. The higher the incidence of family disorganization: divorce, desertion, unhappiness in the marital relationship, illegitimacy, etc.
2. The greater the sense of alienation from the larger society, the poorer the knowledge concerning matters of public interest, the less participation in voting, parapolitical organizations, and associations in general.
3. The higher the incidence of symptoms of mental disorder, the higher the degree of maladjustment as evidenced on personality tests.
4. The less competence with standard English, the more likely to score poorly on tests of verbal and scholastic ability, and the more likely to drop out of school before completion.
5. The higher the rate of mortality and the incidence of physical disorders, although there is some evidence that such socio-economic differentials have been declining over time.
6. The lower the "need for achievement" and the less likely individuals are to manifest what has been called the deferred gratification pattern.[6]
7. The less likely are parents to socialize their children through the use of explanations for obedience to rules and the more likely to assert such rules without presenting rationales.
8. The higher are crime and delinquency rates (when based on arrests and convictions), although there is some evidence that law-enforcement agencies treat lower-class delinquents more harshly and that when adolescents are asked whether they have committed delinquent acts, the socio-economic differentials tend to decline.
9. The more likely to be liberal on economic issues but somewhat less liberal regarding civil liberties or toward political deviants.

In other areas of attitudes and behavior, the review of the literature did not reveal reasonable degrees of consensus concerning what is related to socio-economic status. Sometimes, contradictory patterns of findings were reported by different researchers: For example, the results in studies of child-rearing practices varied, possibly reflecting the different historical periods in which the studies were undertaken. In other cases, the data were too fragmentary or based on such small studies that, for the time being, their results were mainly suggestive. For example, studies of social-class-related linguistic differences are based on such small numbers of observations that the differences found can hardly be said to have been firmly established. Similar statements can be made about studies of value patterns or certain types of leisure activities.

A CULTURE OF POVERTY?

In its most extreme form, the position that maintains that the poor are qualitatively different is expressed in the claim that there is a distinctive culture displayed by the poor—the culture of poverty. Although our review of the literature casts considerable doubt on the distinctiveness of the poor, there are other aspects of the concept of culture of poverty that merit some examination.

The concept of "culture of poverty" is neither clear nor specific. Its popularity and its concomitant rapid diffusion into the rhetoric of the War on Poverty have helped to make the concept more important, but not clearer.

Oscar Lewis (1966), who apparently coined the term, distinguishes between "poverty per se" and poverty as "a culture or, more accurately, as a subculture with its own structure and rationale, as a way of life which is passed down from generation to generation along family lines." He then describes the characteristic features of families and individuals living in a culture of poverty.

It is not clear from this definition how distinctively different the poor must be in order to be characterized as living in the culture of poverty. Several models of class differences that might fit this definition are as follows:

A. *The "Greatest Difference" Model.* The poor differ from other socio-economic groups by displaying proportionately more of the qualities and characteristics that increasingly characterize groups as one goes down the stratification ladder. Of all low socio-economic groups, the poor show the greatest differences from the central tendencies of the society in all critical respects.

B. *The "Only Difference" Model.* The poor are the only group in the society that displays a particular characteristic, other levels of the society stratification system showing only traces of such characteristics or no such signs at all.

From Lewis's discussion, it is not clear which of these two [7] models of patterns of differences from the rest of society is meant by the phrase "a subculture with its own structure and rationale." It would seem that the concept would be of maximum utility as an explanatory tool if it had the meaning of the "only-difference" model. However, in all fairness, it should be said that the "greatest-difference" model would certainly be of some use. Hence, at least as far as class differentials are concerned, it is unclear whether the evidence from our review of the literature supports the concept. All that can be said is that there is very little, if any, support for the culture of poverty concept if by that concept is meant that the poor show unique characteristics.

The review of the literature suggests that those traits used to define the culture of poverty are manifested by the extreme poor with only somewhat greater frequency than is true of those immediately above them in socio-economic status. This is not to deny the importance of these characteristics in marking out a group that displays especially aggravated forms and degrees of disabilities, but merely to state that the poor do not display characteristics *qualitatively* different from those immediately above them in the stratification hierarchy, and so on up the ladder.

The definition of the culture of poverty contains an additional crucial element, referring to the transmission of the culture across generations. Oscar Lewis's account of an extended Puerto Rican family claims that the family has lived in the culture of poverty for at least four generations.[8]

A similar position is taken by Walter Miller [9] in his study of Roxbury, Massachusetts. Miller does not accept the concept of culture of poverty, preferring instead to refer to a "subculturally lower-class style of life." He reports the existence of such a subculture extending over a considerable period of time in Roxbury. Thus, he finds that Roxbury has included, since the eighteenth century, populations that pursued a subculturally lower-class style of life, along with other populations that did not, and that the subculture does not necessarily involve a group of specific families residing in that community for the period in question.

Some of the evidence for a culture of poverty that has been presented by its proponents concerns the continuity across generations of families on relief. For example, much has been made of statistics indicating that for some samples of families presently on AFDC (Aid to Families with Dependent Children) or public welfare, large proportions (up to 40 per cent) come from families of orientation that were themselves on the relief rolls, for example, Burgess and Price (1963).

These statements are difficult to evaluate because they are not placed in juxtaposition with statements concerning the general population. For example, Puerto Rico has been a poverty-stricken territory that, despite improvements as a commonwealth, still has a standard of living considerably below that of any state in the Union. Under those circumstances, most persons in Puerto Rico would have been descended from families who have been poor for generations. Similarly, we need to know about *all* the descendants of families living in the past in Roxbury to determine whether or not there has been a significant amount of cross-generational stability in poverty.

Data collected for Duncan and Blau [10] on intergenerational mobility indicate a considerable amount of intergenerational reshuffling of the population among major occupational groups. For example, of those sons presently (1962) listed as laborers (among whom presumably the bulk of the lower-lowers would be classified), only 12.2 per cent had fathers who were in the same occupational category. Most of the unskilled were recruited from families whose breadwinners were farm laborers (5 per cent), farmers (31.5 per cent), or operatives (15.4 per cent) .[11] Similar findings for nineteenth-century Newburyport, Massachusetts, are reported by Thernstrom (1964) .[12]

Perhaps the most persuasive argument for intergenerational transmission of characteristics comes from studies of child-rearing practices. Children in many poor households are being reared in a culturally deprived environment that is linguistically and emotionally impoverished. It is hard to imagine that considerable proportions of such children will find their way into the professional and managerial occupations. But it is not inconceivable that, despite handicaps of early childhood, large proportions will find their way higher in the "blue-collar" occupations than did their parents. If the past is any indication, then some poverty is "inherited," but life chances are reshuffled sufficiently in each generation to allow a large proportion of the children of the poor to move out.

All told, the empirical evidence from our review of the literature does not support the idea of a culture of poverty in which the poor are distinctively different from other layers of society. Nor does the evidence from intergenerational-mobility studies support the idea of a culture of poverty in the sense of the poor being composed largely of persons themselves coming from families living in poverty. That the poor are different and show higher rates of a wide variety of disabilities is seemingly well enough documented: If this is what is meant by a culture of poverty, then the concept has some validity, although perhaps little usefulness. If by the concept is meant something more, then the empirical evidence would not support such a view.

In some ways, the concept of a culture of poverty transmitted across generations would simplify the problem of how class differences in behavior are generated. If there is a subculture of the poor, then one may as easily postulate subcultures for the "working class," "middle class," or any other recognizable class group in the society, which together generate the range of socio-economic, status-related behavior summarized earlier. All that would be necessary, within such a theoretical model, would be to postulate some initial state in which class differences are generated; then, the processes of intergenerational transmission would account for the persistence of differences at any point in time thereafter. Calling into question subcultures of class differences raises the question of how class differences are generated, a topic to which we turn in the next section.

Before doing so, however, it is important to keep in mind that many of the differences among socio-economic status levels found in the literature reviewed are not very great. When correlation coefficients have been computed, it is rare for a coefficient to rise above .4; indeed, the correlation between father's and son's occupation is only .3–.4.[13] Hence, in accounting for socio-economic status differences, one is mainly concerned with explaining tendencies rather than explaining stark contrasts between class levels.

ACCOUNTING FOR SOCIO-ECONOMIC STATUS DIFFERENTIALS

Ever since empirical social scientists moved out of the classroom forty years ago to study larger social systems presenting a fuller range of socio-economic variation, it has been abundantly clear that there are small but pervasive and persistent differences among socio-economic status levels across a wide range of variables.[14] Yet, considerably more attention has been paid to the problem of defining and measuring socio-economic status than to an explanation of why socio-economic status is such an important variable.

This chapter may also be considered a contribution to a major controversy over the essential nature of social stratification. Three major conceptual positions may be distinguished: classes as subcultures defined by distinctive value patterns and differential association (Warner et al., 1949a) ; stratification as the differential distribution of resources and income; and stratification as the distribution of prestige. In empirical research, the three positions tend to converge on a common set of indicators—occupation, income, and education—indicating the extent to which the controversy has been primarily nominal. In this chapter we have used the concepts of class level and socio-economic status as roughly equivalent in meaning regardless of the variables used to index them.

Aside from Merton (1957) and Kriesberg (1963) , explanations of socio-economic status differences tend to be ad hoc or regarded as self-evident. To be sure, many such differences are self-evident in the sense that they are implied by the measurement of socio-economic status position in terms of occupation, education, or income. Thus, the concentration of business air travel in the upper socio-economic status needs no elaborate explanation: managerial and professional occupations require travel as part of occupational duties, while few blue-collar occupations require extensive travel by fast transportation. But many of the socio-economic status differences are not self-evident. Why should the lower socio-economic status levels at the same time display higher levels of economic liberalism but less support for civil liberties? Why are there quantitative and qualitative differences in reading habits? With respect to many such correlates of socio-economic status, the only thing that is self-evident is the need for the development of a systematic scheme that accounts for a wide range of socio-economic status differentials by postulating a relatively small number of generating processes.

At this stage in the evolution of sociological theory, attempts to develop generalizations by examining large amounts of empirical data tend to produce explanatory models that are complex and cumbersome. Our own attempt is no exception. The scheme described below is more complicated than one would ideally desire and as yet insufficiently well integrated to provide a clear and unequivocal set of predictions concerning what one may anticipate to be related to socio-economic status positions in either our own society or stratification systems in general. Whatever merit it may have will be mainly as an attempt to open up an area for further development.

Our starting point is to distinguish among three broad classes of processes, each of which has important, but varying, implications for the generation of socio-economic status-related behavior. First, socio-economic status levels, by definition, differ with respect to income and wealth, occupation, and education, each of which has important, but conceptually distinct, effects on behavior and attitudes. We have labeled these processes "Direct Effects of Socio-Economic Variables." Second, we distinguish processes that arise in reaction to the hierarchic and evaluational aspects of social stratification. Finally, we point out processes that tend to maintain and reinforce socio-economic status differences. These three classes of processes are probably applicable to all stratification systems that tend to be universalistic and achievement-oriented. We also consider features of the American stratification system that are peculiar to our history, in particular the ethnic and racial heterogeneity of the American population.

DIRECT EFFECTS OF SOCIO-ECONOMIC VARIABLES

Any operational definition of socio-economic status relies on occupation, income, education, or some combination of the three to place individuals and households in socio-economic status classes. Whether one regards these three variables as indicators of some more basic concept of stratification (as do Warner and Hollingshead) or as socio-economic status itself, they remain the major means by which socio-economic status is in practice determined and for that reason constitute the most obvious differences among class levels.

Obviousness is no bar to importance, however. These three variables each generate some of the differences we reviewed earlier, and it is important to point out the kinds of effects involved, at least in order to separate them from other variables to be considered later on.[15]

Because of the obvious importance of income and wealth, it is particularly disappointing that we know so little about its direct effects. The pioneering work of Morgan et al. (1962) represents the best of our efforts, but this volume is particularly meager on precisely those aspects of poverty that would most interest the sociologist and social psychologist. Because of ample amounts of market research we know most about the influence of income and wealth on consumer behavior. Differences in housing, diet, access to life experiences, etc., are all strongly conditioned by disposable income, at least in the negative sense that income and wealth determine whether certain consumer goods or life experiences are accessible to the individual, although they do not altogether determine whether the access will be used.

The influence of income and wealth on behavior is historically conditioned and very much affected by trends in household real income. Thus, thirty years ago, ownership of a telephone, a mechanical refrigerator (as opposed to an icebox), and an automobile were closely related to socio-economic status.[16] Today, diffusion of ownership of these items is so widespread that such a relationship has declined considerably. Similarly, although air travel today is restricted to a minority of the population and the upper ends of the socio-economic status ladder, one can already envisage a time when air travel will be used frequently by all.

Occupational differences, stripped of income differentials, have an effect on class-related behavior through the kinds of skills that are exercised and maintained in the activities of the occupation. Thus, part of the reason why higher socio-economic status jurors make more contributions to jury deliberations (Strodtbeck et al., 1965; James, 1964) is that higher socio-economic status occupations require the exercise and maintenance of communication and negotiation skills. Studies of the reading habits of adults indicate that white-collar workers continue reading relatively complex materials throughout adulthood, while manual workers tend to decline in their reading habits after formal schooling. The occupational activities of upper socio-economic status individuals tend to reinforce and even extend the skills acquired during formal schooling.

Whether or not entry into high status levels is becoming increasingly dependent on educational attainment, we can point to such differences among socio-economic status levels at the moment as being among the most consistent of all. As a generator of class-related behavior, education functions in two ways: First, formal education increases one's ability to handle abstract ideas and one's knowledge of the world. This relationship often makes it difficult to judge whether or not one has really tapped class differences rather than differences in ability to handle abstractions. Thus, that a much larger proportion of poorly educated respondents are unable to name the ocean that lies between the United States and Europe does not mean necessarily that lower-status persons could not find their way from Chicago to Europe. It may only mean that when asked questions of this sort, persons with more formal education understand their meaning more easily.[17]

The second way in which formal education functions is to impart to the individual a relatively standard conception of what it is to be a full member of society and what are the obligations of a citizen. Thus we find on a wide variety of measures that the better educated give answers that are more in keeping with the official values of the society. The better educated are less prejudiced on scales of attitudes toward minority groups and political deviants. They are more likely to endorse normative statements concerning participation in community affairs and to express interest in what is happening in the society and in the world. They are more likely to express opinions, even on issues of a fictitious nature.[18] The evidence up to now does not allow us to judge whether the better educated have a deeper commitment to the main value emphases of our society or whether they merely know better what those emphases are. Most likely both statements are partially true, with the critical question being which should be given more weight.

Although we have tried to make an analytic distinction here between education and occupation, in point of fact the two variables are so closely related, particularly in the upper reaches of the occupational-prestige hierarchy, that they can scarcely be empirically distinguished. High-status occupations, particularly the scientific, professional, and technical occupations, ordinarily can only be pursued by persons of high educational attainment, and the managerial occupations are being increasingly dominated by college graduates. Hence, in the empirical world, occupational differences tend to strongly reflect educational differences and vice versa, which renders separation of the effects of these two variables difficult.

REACTIONS TO CLASS POSITION

Under this heading we classify processes that involve reaction to socio-economic position. There is abundant evidence from empirical social research that there is widespread consensus both on the general outlines of the stratification system and on one's own position in the hierarchy. Studies of the prestige position of occupations in the United States and in other countries indicate very little difference between socio-economic status levels in the prestige accorded to occupations.[19] Respondents on surveys largely tend to identify their class positions according to their occupations, education, and income. Evidence from the literature reviewed shows that lower-status persons feel deprived and know they are on the bottom of the hierarchy.

Parsons (1954) views the stratification system as expressing society-wide evaluation of social positions, mainly occupational in character. To be at the bottom of the heap, then, is to be evaluated negatively. Merton (1957) emphasizes another evaluational aspect of social stratification: If the norm of the society expresses success in terms of the attainment of wealth (or of high occupational position), then those who do not attain wealth (or high occupations) have failed. Low socio-economic status is thus a position of failure, and persons in that position, argues Merton, may react to their failure in a number of ways, as indicated below.

Closely related to this argument are the explanations given by Matza (1966) and Coser (1965) for the appearance of poverty as a social problem. Both authors stress that poverty, in an objective sense, is characteristic of some groups in almost every large-scale society, but only in some societies is poverty regarded as a social problem. The process of creating the "problem poor" or poverty as a social problem is a process in which the poor are degraded by being labeled failures unworthy of full citizenship in the society. Oscar Lewis (1966) [20] takes much the same position (at least by implication) when he states that a culture of poverty can only arise in a society in which there is upward mobility and considerable unemployment, underemployment, or intermittent employment among the unskilled or poorly skilled workers. Coser and Matza argue that a particularly punishing evaluation of the poor in such societies is created through singling out this group for treatments that mark them as much less than full citizens.

The common thread running through the statements of all the writers mentioned above is the psychologically punishing situation of those on the bottom of a stratification system in a society that stresses achievement for all and universalism as a mode of selection for occupational placement. Of course, there is no reason to restrict this process only to those on the very bottom of the stratification hierarchy. While it is undoubtedly the case that for the very poor there exists the greatest gap between their position and the attainment of approbation, the punishment may be viewed as occurring, to some extent, all the way up the line, to a diminishing degree as one proceeds higher and higher. Indeed, a case might be made that although only those who have reached the very pinnacle of the occupational system may be considered a success in terms of some version of the "American dream," in fact, the experience of success probably comes at a lower level, but still somewhat above the average occupational status in the population.

The negative evaluation of the lower levels of the socio-economic-status dimension is manifested in a variety of ways. To begin with, the tone of our society is decidedly middle class. The mass media, for example, portray the American household as a middle-class household; working-class or lower-class individuals are portrayed as either problems or comics. Textbooks, mail-order catalogues, advertisements in newspapers, and novels all show much the same pattern. The positively evaluated persons—and their dress, homes, and speech—are middle class or better. At least by implication, the lower-status individual finds himself negatively evaluated because he does not see his counterparts put forth in a positive way in the institutions that set the tone of the society.

A second way in which the poor are made aware of their negatively evaluated position in the society is through the process of being designated as poor, hence a problem. The special legislation designed to provide some measure of relief for the poor in and of itself places them in a special category. It is hard to see how our treatment of the poor as a special group can do anything but compound the feeling of being less than equal.

Finally, the most extreme form of negative evaluation manifests itself as discrimination. The lower levels of the socio-economic status suffer poorer treatment at the hands of schools, stores, banks, law-enforcement agencies, medical personnel, and landlords. Some of these patterns of differential treatment have been documented in the literature reviewed. Others—for example, differential treatment in stores and government agencies—can be expected to exist and certainly can be observed readily in a qualitative way. In short, at the main points of contact with the formal organizations of our society, lower-status persons can frequently experience being treated differently and with less respect, courtesy, and efficiency.

Discrimination directed against Negroes is, of course, the most blatant of all. This is not the place to document the differential treatment accorded to Negroes in our society except to state that the psychological burden of being lower class for this group is added to (or multiplied by) being at the same time a much-discriminated-against ethnic group.

Some of the characteristics of the poor can be seen as reactions to the punishment of being judged negatively. Merton suggests that modes of reaction involve combinations of rejections of goals (mobility and wealth) and the means designated by society as legitimate ways in which such goals may be attained. Under this scheme, those who reject the goal of success but accept the means are reacting in a "ritualistic" fashion; those who accept the goal but reject the legitimate means are "deviants"; those who reject both are characterized as "retreatists"; and, finally, those who reject both and substitute alternative goals and means are characterized as "rebels."

The attraction of Merton's paradigm lies in the obvious similarity between certain characteristics of the poor and the types of reactions Merton postulated in his paradigm. The apathy and apparent withdrawal of the poor from participation in the society resemble Merton's "retreatist" reaction. The "ritualistic" reaction resembles the quiet desperation of the "poor but honest" who outwardly conform to the society while having given up any hope or desire to attain success. Perhaps the most attractive feature of the Mertonian paradigm is its explanation of "deviance" as a reaction to the structural position of the poor. This theme has been elaborated by A. K. Cohen (1955) and in modified form by Cloward and Ohlin (1960) in their theories of delinquency.

The "rebellious" reaction has been given less attention in the literature. Indeed, the events of the last three years may shift attention from "retreatism" to a concern for "rebellion." The critical issues become ascertaining the conditions under which a deprived and negatively evaluated population shifts from a posture of apathy to rioting. There is, furthermore, the question of the development of counter-ideologies. Black-nationalist movements, the adoption of African dress and hair styles, and separatist tendencies can be viewed as movements to deny the negative evaluations placed on being "black" and assert that either "black" is as good as "white," or better. In this respect, the recent shifts in Negro-leadership ideology resemble the development of nationalist feelings among European peasant immigrants to this country; the content of some pietistic sects that promise an afterlife, with either a reversed social-class system or an equalitarian one; and, more directly, political movements aimed at redistributing power, prestige, and resources.

The problems with Merton's paradigm arise from several sources: First, although it is clear that American society rewards success, it is not clear whether success is mandatory or what are the dimensions by with success is to be measured. For example, if the emphasis is on income and wealth, then entrepreneurial and managerial occupations ought to be those toward which everyone should aspire, but if the emphasis is on contributions to knowledge and culture, other occupations would be stressed. Second, Merton's paradigm remains mainly a classificatory scheme at present, with little ability to predict the appearance of one or another type of reaction for groups or individuals in different circumstances. Why does rebellion occur at this moment in the history of our urban ghettos, along with criminality, retreatist resort to drugs, etc.? To use the paradigm effectively as theory means to go beyond present formulations and to develop predictive propositions. Third, by implication, Merton's paradigm is mainly directed toward explaining working-class and lower-class behavior. It seems to the present authors that we need theoretical propositions that will cover the reactions in the full range of socio-economic status. In some sense, all but those at the very top have failed to achieve the fullest degree of achievement urged by the society. The social psychology and sociology of failure will have to be oriented toward degrees of failure and toward those devices, structural and psychological, that insulate individuals and social groups from the potentially devastating fact that only a very few achieve the most that is offered by a society at a given point in time.

It may be best, for example, to conceive of success and failure as defining two continua, rather than being at the opposite ends of the same continuum, just as it has turned out to be empirically useful to conceive of negative and positive feelings as constituting two separate and somewhat unrelated continua, both independently related to subjective feelings of happiness. (See Bradburn and Caplovitz, 1965.) If such turns out to be the case empirically, then an individual could experience neither success nor failure, or both, or combinations of more of one and less of the other. Incidentally, such a conceptualization may provide one of the clues to the mechanisms by which most members of our society do not strongly experience failure from the viewpoint of not having achieved as much as they are urged to by some level of that society. To fail may mean something more than not achieving success.

The main point to be made here is that the social-stratification system of an open society with few ascriptive bars to achievement creates a situation in which all individuals are subject to positive or negative evaluations depending on the degree of achievement. This process of evaluation is one that rewards some and punishes others, generating in turn reactive processes that underlie some of the class differences that we found in the review of the literature. It is to this source that one should probably attribute the lowered self-esteem of the poor,[21] their apathy and withdrawal from participation, their sense of helplessness and powerlessness, and the high levels of dissatisfaction with their position in life. The phenomenon of "value stretch" (Rodman, 1963), in which the poor exempt themselves from main value themes, can be seen as an attempt at accommodation to this type of evaluation.

It should be noted that these processes are ones that are to be found in any stratification system regardless of its level of living and its distribution of income.

PROCESSES THAT MAINTAIN
CLASS DIFFERENCES

We turn now to processes that tend to maintain differences among socio-economic levels. For example, there is no particularly obvious reason why child-rearing practices (especially those that do not require income expenditures) should not be uniform throughout the stratification system unless one postulates that there are barriers to the diffusion of knowledge and practice across such levels.[22] Similar statements could be made with respect to linguistic behavior— particularly dialect—class differences in food preferences, dress and cosmetic styles, etc.

Two major factors can be seen as impeding the diffusion of behavioral and attitudinal patterns across class levels. First, the different socio-economic status levels are exposed to different media and educational experiences. Studies [23] of book-reading and exposure to newspapers, magazines, radio, and television indicate that upper socio-economic status persons read, listen, and view more than lower socio-economic status persons and, furthermore, expose themselves to materials of greater complexity and difficulty. Hence, the articles in newspapers and magazines that discuss such topics as child-rearing practices or diet are more likely to be read by upper socioeconomic status persons. Obviously, this differential exposure is related to educational experiences that provide the individual with the skills to assimilate and understand such discussions. But educational experience also has a more direct effect because part of the content of formal education is instruction in speech, nutritional standards, and conceptions of citizenship that involve paying attention to the "serious" part of the mass media.

Those changing tendencies within the society that are diffused, or at least supported by reading, listening, and viewing, therefore move more slowly into the lower levels of the socio-economic status ladder.[24] Thus, some of the socio-economic status differences that may be found at a particular point in time represent differential diffusion along socio-economic status lines. Hence, some of the differences shown in the last section can be expected to disappear with time, in the same way that socio-economic status differentials in telephone ownership and the use of mechanical refrigeration have largely disappeared in the past three or four decades.

The second major mechanism maintaining socio-economic status differences involves differential association along class lines. Work groups, friendship groups, neighborhoods, and kinship groups tend to be homogeneous with respect to socio-economic status level (or at least more homogeneous than randomly selected individuals). How important such informal social supports are can be seen in studies of such diverse phenomena as voting behavior of adults and the intentions of adolescents to attend college. In the former case, a good part of the reason for class solidarity in voting behavior, despite whatever may be the political bias of the mass media, lies in the political homogeneity of informal groups. In the latter case, the class composition of high schools has an effect on intentions to go to college, modifying the influences of the class background and academic performance of the young persons involved. Adults are thus responsive to the political climates of their small groups, and adolescents are responsive to the intellectual climates of their high schools.

If we accept the general proposition that face-to-face influences are more effective and persuasive than those emanating from the mass media, then we can begin to understand how the poor manage to evade some of the more punishing aspects of being negatively evaluated by the social-stratification system and how they manage to maintain patterns of behavior regarded as deviant by the larger society. Surrounded by persons who are in much the same socio-economic situation as himself and more oriented toward obtaining approval of friends, neighbors, and kin than to the approval of the larger society, an individual can find some support for his particular style of life. We suggest that this mechanism is considerably more important to the maintenance of class differences than early childhood socialization. It is also a mechanism that helps to understand the persistence of other types of group differences along ethnic, religious, and regional lines,[25] which our review of the literature found to be as important as class differences.

It would be very easy to exaggerate the amount of socio-economic homogeneity in friendship, neighborhood, work, and kinship groups. Some types of occupations bring one into contact with a range of socio-economic status levels, for example, sales clerk, appliance repairman, etc., and kinship groups may turn out to be the most socio-economically heterogeneous of all the intimate face-to-face groups to which an individual may belong.[26] Some amount of cross-class contact continually occurs within intimate face-to-face groups, for example, enough to account for at least some part of the lack of clear-cut class differences as shown in the literature on voting behavior.

The processes commented on above are general ones that are applicable to all social-stratification systems of a universalistic-achievement type. In order to understand the stratification system of American society, however, additional features have to be taken into account. Perhaps the most important of all is the ethnic and racial heterogeneity of American society. Race and ethnicity are related to class in a complicated way that changes over time. The bottom layers of our major urban centers are at the present time heavily populated by Negro migrants from rural areas and their second-generation descendants. In the first half of this century, the same layers were occupied primarily by immigrants and their descendants from eastern Europe.

The strength of ethnic, racial, and the often accompanying religious collectivities as determinants of behavior and attitudes is considerable. For example, Jews are considerably more liberal in their political and economic ideologies than other high-status groups. Catholics tend to display standards of family and personal behavior that are, in general, more traditional than other groups: And within Catholicism, ethnic groups differ from one another. Our knowledge of American Negroes as an ethnic group is at the moment very meager since it is difficult to specify the content of ethnicity in this particular case.[27]

A major difficulty with race, religion, and ethnicity as generators of group differences in our society is that these differences tend to be particularistic and do not lend themselves to systematic treatment. The surviving cultural traits of the Germans, for example, are peculiar to that group and appear in a variety of apparently capricious ways.[28] To some extent, the class differences shown in the literature reviewed reflect the varying ethnic and racial composition of different socio-economic status levels. Which and how much of the differences can be attributed to this source of variation is not known, especially since ethnicity is not ordinarily used as a variable except in its disguised forms of race and religion. Rosen (1959), for example, finds that ethnicity and religion are as important as socio-economic status position in explaining differences in achievement motivation of young boys. Studies of presidential elections (for example, Lazarsfeld et al., 1948; Berelson et al., 1954) have found that religion was an important predictor of voting for the two sets of presidential candidates. Knowing the ethnic composition of Detroit, one wonders how different the interpretation of Miller and Swanson's (1958) findings would be if the ethnic background of individual respondents had been taken into account.

The persistence of ethnic-group differences over time can be attributed to differential association. Ethnicity, religion, and race constitute axes of interpersonal association that possibly rival class in importance. Whatever particular behavioral and attitudinal patterns different ethnic and racial groups either bring with them or develop will therefore tend to persist because of the social support provided by the ethnic and racial homogeneity of small informal groups.[29]

The main purpose of this section has been to lay out the main considerations that should comprise a theory of how class differences are generated and maintained rather than to develop such a theory in detail. Stated in another form, we have tried to decompose the concept of socio-economic status into a number of components, each of presumed importance in generating and maintaining class differences in behavior and attitudes.

To return to the initial concerns laid out in the very beginning of this chapter, the viewpoint set out in this past section has been that which is oriented toward a situational, as opposed to a subcultural, view of classes in general and of the poor in particular. With the exception of ethnicity, race, and religion, the processes stressed here whereby class differences are generated are rooted in the existential nature of social stratification. If there is a culture of poverty or a subculture of the poor, then it is a condition that arises out of the exigencies of being relatively without resources and of being negatively evaluated by the larger society. Furthermore, if there is a culture or a subculture of poverty only in this limited sense, then it is not clear what is gained, except dramatic emphasis, by the use of the term.

POLICY IMPLICATIONS

Only minor differences separate the subcultural and situational interpretations of the poor as far as empirical descriptions of their characteristics are concerned. The major disagreement centers over how these characteristics are generated and, hence, how they may be changed. The subcultural view stresses as necessary mechanisms by which behavior and attitudes are transmitted across generations, and the situational view stresses the structural features of the society that generate those characteristics without positing a necessary intergenerational transmission mechanism. Characteristically, whereas the subcultural viewpoint stresses the family, the situational viewpoint stresses the occupational system as the point to which the levers of social policy should be applied.

It is easy to exaggerate the differences between the two views as we have done in the previous paragraph. There are undoubtedly transgenerational transmission processes at work whereby the views and feelings of a parental generation are transmitted to the next, hampering or at least dampening the effects that changes in the occupational system might bring about. Similarly, subcultures can hardly be viewed as rising spontaneously without regard to the larger society. Hence, as soon as a subcultural view is pushed by the question of how such subcultures arise, then answers have to be given in terms of how such subcultures are functional to the situations of the groups involved.[30] In the long run, the two views of poverty will undoubtedly converge. In the meantime, the tactical differences, as far as social policy is concerned, will remain, the one stressing the mechanisms of socialization and the other stressing the effects of the occupational system and social stratification. Since there are better spokesmen for the subcultural view than the present authors, we will not be concerned with pursuing it any further; rather, we will seek to draw out the implications for social policy of the situational view.

According to the views outlined in the last section of this chapter, the nature of the poor is generated primarily by their positions in the occupational- and social-stratification systems. To properly draw out the policy implications of this position means to consider those elements of social stratification that are inherent in any social-class system and those that are variable and, hence, subject to change.

The immutable nature of social stratification lies in the fact that some positions in every society will be regarded as in some sense better than others. This implies that there are, and will always be, some differentials in income, life chances, prestige, deference, honor, or status. But it does not imply that the distribution is identical from society to society or from time to time in the same society. Social stratification is more a rating system than a ranking system: That is, members of a society do not each occupy a unique rank position, but many persons can share roughly the same evaluation position. This can be seen most clearly with respect to two types of stratification variables: income and prestige. Over time, the amount of income in the society, as well as its distributions, can vary. While completely equalitarian societies in terms of income have not existed on any large scale, the share of income attained by different levels of our society has changed in the last half century, along with the considerable gain in the total real income earned by the system as a whole. Similarly, with prestige: Although the distribution of the labor force has shifted, the prestige of occupations has not changed to any appreciable extent over the forty years that studies of occupational prestige (Hodge, Siegel, and Rossi, 1966) have been conducted. Compared to the 1920s, our labor force contains proportionately greater numbers in the more prestigeful occupations. In short, there have been shifts in the average amount of occupational prestige in the occupational system and shifts in the distribution of persons toward occupations with higher evaluations.

The implication of this view of social stratification is that it is not necessary to consider that we must always have some group in our society occupying positions that are highly negatively evaluated. By reorganizing the division of labor, it is possible to upgrade tasks without necessarily merely shifting the negative evaluation from one group to another. For example, among the most negatively regarded occupations in our society are those involving personal service— household help and service positions in hotels and restaurants. These are industries whose technology has remained essentially the same for a considerable period of time. It is conceivable that through technical advances the level of workers' skills can be upgraded, that the occupations can be transformed in the public view from servile to skilled trades.[31] Although it is difficult to look forward at this point in time to a period when there are no unskilled and servile occupations, it is possible to look forward to a time when the proportion of such occupations in the labor force is further considerably reduced.

The same point may be made with respect to income. A guaranteed annual income could put a floor under the consumption status of American families that would go far toward the reduction of differences in the consumption of goods and services. But an even more important function would be served by such a policy. At the moment, income supplementation in the form of welfare and relief payments can be obtained only by proving that you are in some sense unable to function normally in the society. The means test in whatever benign form is still a means test and functions to brand the poor as such. It is significant that Social Security benefits from the very beginning have not had attached to them the same negative connotation as welfare payments (Schiltz, 1968), nor have family allowances in other countries been perceived negatively. The differences are that Social Security benefits have been defined as a matter of right that goes to a group neutrally and universalistically defined, while welfare goes to a group negatively and particularistically defined.

According to the view of social stratification held by the authors, jobs would be more important to offer to the poor than income maintenance if a choice had to be made, although it might be best to provide both simultaneously, supplementing income when jobs do not provide the necessary floor for consumption.

Discriminatory practices, especially for Negroes, are another important source of negative evaluation. The effects of the punishment of discrimination at the hands of major institutions can hardly be underrated as a source of feelings of unworthiness and failure, and increasingly of anger and rebellion.

The policies suggested above have as their major aim the softening of negative evaluations in the stratification system. They are designed to produce a society in which there is a floor under household resources and a floor under individual self-respect. They are designed to remove the most invidious distinctions from our class system. Note that they are not aimed at removing all distinctions, merely those that are the most punishing.

Of course, there is more to social stratification than differential evaluation. But it is not clear that occupational and educational differences and their effects are more difficult to change than those arising out of negative evaluation. It will still be the case that college graduates will be more articulate and verbally adept than high-school graduates and that professional persons will be pursuing occupations intrinsically more interesting and satisfying than those of skilled workers. What can be done in this connection is to shorten the gaps between levels. The history of our educational efforts over the past century has indicated the extent to which progress can be made. Illiteracy has been reduced to such an extent that we no longer count (since 1930) illiterates in the Census. Our population reads more, probably reads better material, and probably has a larger vocabulary than that of fifty years ago. Putting a floor under education would help to give at least a minimum verbal adequacy to all levels of the population.

Concerning participation in decision-making, it is clear that, at the moment, the poor and lower-status persons in general are at a serious disadvantage. Our participatory institutions have not rewarded their participation, nor has their occupational and educational experience prepared them for holding their own. But we have not exhausted our ingenuity in providing organizations that make it easy for lower-class individuals to participate. Some successful examples already exist (Silberman, 1964), proving that it is possible under some circumstances to get reasonably high levels of participation from the poor.

In sum, the policy implications of our examination of the relationship between social stratification and poverty stress heavily the removal of stigmatizing processes in the occupational system and discriminatory practices of major institutions, and the provision of a floor of income and self-respect for every person in the society. While we have not indicated the specific policies that would effect these ends, they are not beyond the range of the innovative capacities of our creative society.

Notes

NOTE: Citations in this chapter are to articles listed in the bibliography to the Appendix of this volume.

1. This definition excludes those who have retired from the labor force and those who are disabled through disease or infirmity, even though their income may place them at the lowest portions of the income distribution. They are excluded because their problems could be solved by income maintenance through transfer payments of some kind.

2. Obviously this is not a definition that would be useful if one were to try to determine the number of poor people in the United States. For present purposes of reviewing a literature that does not employ standardized definitions, a flexible definition permits a wider range of materials.

3. The reader is also referred to the bibliographic review appended to this volume for all subsequent references. Spurred by the War on Poverty, additional extensive systematic researches are presently underway and can be expected to appear in the literature over the next few years, but obviously could not be reviewed here.

4. Cohen, 1964; Engel, 1966; Harrington, 1962; O. Lewis, 1966; Lockwood, 1960; Matza, 1966; S. M. Miller, 1964a, 1964b; Walter B. Miller, 1958, 1959; Pavenstedt, 1965; Riessman, 1962, 1964; and Schneiderman, 1964, 1965. Of these writers, S. M. Miller has attempted to elaborate a typology of the lower classes, distinguishing essentially between the "hopeless" poor and those who are attempting to cope with their problems.

5. As described in Rodman (1963), the concept of "value stretch" is a phenomenon not peculiar to the lower-lowers. No normative system is adhered to completely by everyone in the society, and depending on the norms in question, the latitude given for compliance can be considerable. For example, adultery has undoubtedly been widespread throughout the whole range of American social strata, although there is clear evidence from attitude surveys that legitimate sexual alliances are to be preferred over adulterous ones. If there is any reason for the concept to be applied to the lower-lowers with more force than to any other group in American society, it is that their lives (for a variety of reasons) depart from standard Americans in more areas and more dramatically.

6. Some critics have questioned the evidence for the deferred-gratification pattern, and some studies have shown that Negroes (presumably the group most likely to be among the "poor") manifest very high occupational aspirations for themselves and for their children.

7. A possible third model would be one in which the relationship between a characteristic and socio-economic status would be monotonic and nonlinear, such that the poorest group would show considerably more of a characteristic than its neighbors than would be expected on the basis of a linear relationship between socio-economic status and that characteristic. We do not consider such a model for two reasons. First, the data in the literature are too crudely studied to be able to make reasonable distinctions between linear and nonlinear relationships; second, linearity is strongly affected by which metric is used and hence can be manipulated by transformations.

8. Actually, the case histories, themselves, indicate some departure from this generalization. One of the individuals referred to her grandfather as a landowner.

9. Walter Miller, *City Gangs*, forthcoming.

10. U.S. Bureau of the Census, "Lifetime Occupational Mobility of Adult Males: March 1962," *Current Population Reports*—Technical Series P-23, No. 11 (1964). See also Ch. 4 by Duncan, in this volume.

11. Of course, not all laborers may be considered "poor," and not all the "poor" are laborers. Nevertheless, of all the occupational groups distinguished by the Census, laborers contain more of the poor by any definition. Certainly these data do not support a contention that a large number of the poor are living in "inherited poverty."

12. See also Ch. 6 by Thernstrom, in this volume.

13. These relatively low correlations are further evidence against the view of the class system as subcultures because they indicate that considerable separation between class levels does not exist.

14. Nineteenth- and early twentieth-century Censuses contained relatively meager socio-economic information, and it was difficult to relate such data to other characteristics of the population. It should be recalled that major cities began to be treated with the 1920 Census, a development that made possible ecological studies of the distribution of a variety of social phenomena. For example, ecological voting studies began in the twenties on a fine enough scale to establish clear socio-economic status differentials in voting. See Gosnell (1937) for an example of one of the earliest studies.

15. It is particularly important to do so if one is concerned with social policy.

Poverty-reduction programs that stress income maintenance need to be distinguished in their effects from policies that stress rehabilitation or retraining. The latter are based on an implicit assumption that most of the problems of the poor stem not from their lack of income but from other sources.

16. Indeed, ownership of these items was used in an index of socio-economic status in the early days of market research.

17. This problem dogs all empirical social research to the extent that one may question whether many of our most cherished findings are not merely disguised measures of educational attainment. For example, answers to the F-scale are so strongly related to education that several critics (Christie and Jahoda, 1954) feel that it is largely measuring education.

18. In an old experiment on response set, Crespi asked a sample of respondents whether or not they were in favor of the "Anti-Metallurgical Bill." Fewer of the better educated indicated that they had no opinion on this fictitious issue.

19. Hodge, Siegel, and Rossi (1966); Hodge, Treiman, and Rossi (1966).

20. Oscar Lewis also states that traditional societies that are not based on a wage economy and in which there are unilineal kinship systems have poverty, but not a culture of poverty.

21. Very dramatically portrayed in the recent study of a Washington, D.C., street-corner gang of Negro men in Liebow (1967).

22. Of course, one may also postulate that child-rearing practices are so basically a part of personality—particularly of women—that they are intractable to change, including purposeful attempts on the part of educators and the medical profession. However, if Bronfenbrenner (1966) is correct, since middle-class women have changed their child-rearing practices over the last thirty years, but working-class women have not, then we would have to postulate that working-class women have personalities that are qualitatively different from middle-class women, an assumption that is not warranted.

23. This research literature was not reviewed, except incidentally, in the previous section of this chapter. For a review of studies of book reading, see Ennis (1965). Several references to differential exposure to media are contained in Berelson and Janowitz (1966).

24. This implies that, by and large, changes in behavioral and attitudinal tendencies diffuse from the upper levels of the socio-economic status structure to the lower. There are outstanding exceptions to this pattern, for example, jazz music, certain vernacular expressions of speech, etc. David Riesman (1954), in a suggestive essay, proposes that instrumental ideas diffuse downward, but that expressive ideas diffuse upward. Whether or not he is correct, it still remains the case that some cultural items have their origins in the lower socio-economic status levels and diffuse upward from that point.

25. Although we have stressed the importance of this mechanism for the maintenance of lower socio-economic status homogeneity, obviously the same mechanism helps to account for higher socio-economic status homogeneity as well. Indeed, for some areas of behavior, for example, voting and political ideology, there is evidence that the higher levels maintain greater homogeneity than the lower. The stress is given here to the lower socio-economic status levels because their homogeneity is maintained in the face of the fact that the society, in its official institutions and in the mass media, stresses the higher socio-economic status modes of ideology and behavior as modal and model. This is a middle-class society.

26. Indeed, given the relatively low correlation between the occupational statuses of father and son, it can be anticipated that similar low correlations (of the order of .4–.6) can be found among the occupational statuses of siblings. Thus, a set of siblings and their spouses can be expected to span a range of socio-economic status greater than can be expected to be found within small work groups, for example, or perhaps greater than to be expected between adjacent neighbors.

27. The problem lies in the fact that the slavery experience fairly completely wiped out all traces of the original cultures that the Negroes brought with

them from Africa. Whatever particular cultural features of American Negroes presently exist are ones that developed within the context of American society and, hence, may be only marginally differentiated from lower-class whites in the rural South.

28. For example, among college graduates, those of German ancestry (no matter how remote) tend to be more interested in engineering and physical sciences, traits that seem sensibly related to popular conceptions of German "national character," but Irish Catholic graduates tend to be interested in medicine as a career, a pattern that appears somewhat as a surprise (Greeley, 1963).

29. We would anticipate that ethnic and racial patterns concerning family roles and interpersonal relations would persist longer than other types of ethnic differences. Those ethnic differences that would constitute a handicap in coping with the outside world of politics and economic life (for example, observance of the Sabbath) would be among the first to disappear, while those pertaining to the world of informal small groups would tend to persist longer (for example, food habits, mutual aid, expectations of friends and relatives, etc.).

30. Lewis's (1965) statement of his conception of the culture of poverty contains an analysis of the structural circumstances under which such cultures arise.

31. For example, services have been started in many of the major metropolitan areas for periodic housecleaning, employing skilled teams of workers and advanced housecleaning equipment. The servile aspects of housework are removed for the worker along with an upgrading of his skills and his wages.

Chapter 3

⊂⊇ *Poverty: Changing Social Stratification*

S. M. MILLER and PAMELA ROBY

Poverty can be viewed in many contexts. Generally neglected has been the context of social stratification. However, the limited results of poverty programs based upon subsistence standards are now forcing a realization that not pauperism but inequality is the main issue within high-income industrial societies. When we begin to discuss poverty in terms of relative deprivation and inequalities, we are posing questions about the over-all social stratification of a nation: What are considered "acceptable" gaps between the poor and other groups? What are the relevant dimensions for viewing differences among groups within the society today?

This chapter's first objective is to recast approaches to poverty in terms of stratification. A thorough poverty analysis questions the level of living of the nonpoor as well as the poor. As the late Polish sociologist Stanislaw Ossowski wrote in his brilliant analysis of social stratification, ". . . a class (is) a member of a certain system of relations. This means that the definition of any class must take into account the relation of this group to other groups in this system." [1] Not just the poor but the entire society is at issue. As yet, poverty programs have not been seen adequately as efforts to engineer changes in United States stratification.

Such a stratificational analysis implies not only viewing the poor as those who are lagging behind relative to others in society but extending the concept of poverty beyond the narrow limits of income. When poverty is viewed within the stratificational framework, we see that Max Weber and Richard Titmuss have already made major contributions to its analysis. One of Weber's outstanding contributions to social science was to untwine three components of stratification: class, status, and power.[2] The Marxian analysis centered on the economic (or class) dimensions of stratification, but Weber believed that the prestige (social honor) and political dimensions of stratification were sometimes independently important. These other dimensions could change without alteration in the economic, or they could remain stable despite changes in the economic dimension of stratification. With his widely ranging erudition, Weber illustrated his thesis by showing that, for example, a high-status group, such as the Prussian Junkers, could retain considerable political power despite its reduced economic importance. Conversely, a rising economic group, like the bourgeoisie, could have a long struggle to obtain prestige equivalent to their economic position. Weber sought not to overturn Marx's analysis but to go beyond it, to broaden its perspectives.[3]

More recently, Titmuss has further refined our tools of analysis by conceiving of income as the "command over resources over time." [4] He argues that wage-connected fringe benefits, fiscal benefits (for example, tax deductions for children that benefit the better-off more than the low-income taxpayer), and welfare (transfer) benefits must be included in any discussion of the command over *resources*.

Recently, we have suggested that a minimum approach by government in any society with significant inequalities must provide for rising minimum levels not only of incomes, assets, and basic services but also of self-respect and opportunities for social mobility and participation in many forms of decision-making.[5] To gain a better understanding of the objectives of various poverty programs and the relationships between these goals, we can look at efforts to reduce poverty in terms of (1) what aspect of poverty is the program aimed at, for example, the economic, political, educational, and social mobility, or status dimensions of stratification; and (2) what means does the program intend to employ; for example, is the program aimed at improving the social conditions of those who are poor (that is, jobs, income, housing, health, self-respect) *or* at moving some of those who are poor out of poverty into other niches in society (that is, via educational programs)? Table 3–1 may help the reader to think through these various objectives with us.

TABLE 3-1. *Governmental and Private Poverty Reduction Efforts*

PROGRAM OBJECTIVE	STRATIFICATIONAL DIMENSIONS			
	ECONOMIC: INCOMES, BASIC SERVICES, ASSETS	POLITICAL: PARTICIPATION IN DECISION-MAKING	EDUCATION AND SOCIAL MOBILITY	STATUS
Improving social conditions	Guaranteed annual income Medicare— Medicaid Social Security Concentrated employment program Housing	"Maximum feasible participation" "Black Power" "Parent participation in school decision-making"	Consumer education	Open housing Income guarantees without stigma "Black is beautiful"
Promoting social mobility	Job training Manpower programs	Negro separatist movements School integration	New careers Headstart Upward Bound	

This typology can aid social scientists in program *planning* by pointing out the diverse and frequently conflicting goals of programs and by highlighting the relatively neglected aspects of poverty. The typology may also assist in program *evaluation* by providing a framework for pinpointing the goals of programs in question and for showing the relationship among goals of various programs—first steps in any evaluation. The typology leads policy makers dealing with the poor to ask what kinds of responsibilites and burdens we wish our society to have. For example, to what extent do we wish to improve the conditions of the aged or the future conditions of today's youth? To a large extent, these are not narrow technical issues, but value issues that may be expected to produce acrimonious debate.

The second purpose of the chapter is to show that stratification theory can be refined and modernized through understanding of poverty action. The bearing that empirical research and theory have on one another has long been emphasized by Robert Merton and others.[6] Applied social science should also be a "two-way street," both drawing from, and contributing to, social theory. The many recent "applied" analyses of poverty need to be distilled and added to the general corpus of sociological theory.[7] Conceptually, the writings of Titmuss on the distribution of "command over resources" need to be connected with those of Parsons and Marshall on the meaning of citizenship.[8]

The interpretation of any particular historical period may require expanding the number of stratificational dimensions or, at least, recognizing the peculiar and changing content of each dimension. For example, Weber pointed out that, until recently, the center of class struggles had progressively shifted from consumption credit toward, first, competitive struggles in the commodity market and, second, price wars in the labor market.[9] Which dimension is of most importance may also shift.[10] In this chapter we will deal with the dimensions of economic class, status, and power, and then with a fourth dimension of education and social mobility. Weber's order will be changed to have the discussion of status, which in the long run is the basic and most difficult issue of poverty programs, follow that of "education and social mobility." We have added the "education and social mobility" dimension because over the past fifty years educational attainment and social mobility of offspring have become factors differentiating members of the working and depressed classes. Today, not only class, status, and power but educational attainment and social mobility of offspring determine persons', particularly the poor's, future standard of living. Therefore, we believe that education and social mobility have become independent stratificational dimensions and should be treated as such.

We hope that other social scientists will also attempt to relate "applied" and "theoretical" social science. We believe that doing so will enrich American social science by forcing consideration of generally neglected facts, by pressing for reconsideration of misleading or incorrect theories, by clarifying vague concepts, and by generating new theories or conceptual schemes. We are persuaded with Dahrendorf that if we as social scientists "regain the problem-consciousness which has been lost in the last decades, we cannot fail to recover the critical engagement in the realities of our social world which we need to do our job well." [11] We believe that refinement of stratification theory through analysis of applied sociology will in turn strengthen social scientists' efforts to reduce poverty.

CLASS

Weber's discussion of the class or economic dimension of stratification is built on Marx, but, as elsewhere, Weber attempted to broaden the Marxian perspective. Marx's analysis was based on the material and social relationships to the production process. Weber shifted from the sphere of production to that of the market or exchange and defined class as:

> . . . a number of people who have in common a specific causal component of their life chances insofar as this component is represented exclusively by economic interest in the possession of goods and opportunities for income, and is represented under the conditions of commodity or labor markets.[12]

The economic dimension of stratification, in Weber's conceptualization, included a great variety of explicit and implicit market relationships. As we shall discuss later, the major development today in many societies is the beginning of an important break between the market and well-being.[13]

The post-World War II era saw a proliferation of studies in which the central explanatory or classificatory variable was occupation.[14] The current concern with poverty is, by contrast, focusing on income. There are several reasons for the growth of interest in income as the definer of class position:

1. The links between occupation and income are becoming fuzzier. The range of income of incumbents of particular occupational positions appears to be getting wider.[15] The result is that a description of occupation poorly predicts income.

2. The poor are a congeries of groups who share low income in common, but frequently not many other things. While some of the poor are definable by their low-paying jobs, many other poor are outside the labor force and dependent on transfer income of various kinds.[16]

3. Government policy, growing in importance, defines groups mainly by income levels whether for purposes of income taxes or welfare assistance.

In turn, income is an inadequate indicator of economic level. Within the "welfare state," the resources that are available to individuals are a mosaic of the income derived from market activities, from the "fringe benefits" attached to various occupations and organizations, from the operation of the tax system, from various public and private transfer and pension systems, from assets whether protected or pseudo as in the case of many capital gains, and from the availability, utilization, and quality of public goods.

Weber's notion of class must be widened beyond that of property and the market. In particular, in the "welfare state," many important elements of the command over resources become available as public services. The distribution and quality of these public services affect the absolute and relative well-being of individuals.[17] Considerable inconsistency *may* exist between the income and basic services of persons or groups. While the two are fairly closely linked in the United States, poor basic services are *not* associated with low income in Sweden.[18]

A larger issue is also involved. As Marshall has argued, the welfare-state approach is to break the link between the market and well-being.[19] The role of government is tremendously increased.[20] To a growing extent, the command over resources of the individual depends on his relation to government, whether in terms of income tax, subsidies, licensing, or public services.[21] The concept of "property" has therefore to be enlarged and altered to include the perspectives of time in pension accumulations and of rights to governmental largesse and services, especially education. Property, in the more conventional sense, still remains important, but other forms of rights of determination are beginning to possess similar importance.

This broadened view of the command over resources has important political implications.[22] If government plays a major role in affecting the command over resources, then organized action will be increasingly centered on the governmental arena. When Marx wrote, the arena of action was more narrowly the workplace, the setting of production. In the United States, low-income persons have been organizing to affect their rights to welfare and to other forms of government services rather than to affect the economic market. As we shall see in our discussion of power, the relationships to government bureaucracy have become important not only for the poor but for all segments of American society.[23]

The primary point, then, in the effort to modernize the discussion of class is to become aware of the different and new elements in the command over resources over time and of the new role of the government as a direct distributor of resources. The issues of class and economics are intimately politicized as the market place and property are affected by governmental action and political formations.

POWER

Not only is the government becoming a direct dispenser or with-holder of resources, but it is also regulating, controlling, and direct-ing the economy, even in nonsocialist societies. Efforts to spur eco-nomic growth and to prevent recessions inevitably involve questions of who is to benefit, who is to pay the costs of trying to keep prices from rising rapidly, who is to be disadvantaged by economic changes. The expanding role of government means that presumed notions of market automaticity succumb to political decisions about who gains and loses.[24] These decisions are supposedly made on immutable technical grounds alone.[25] But, with greater sophistication, these decisions are found to be based on a political struggle among groups and individuals possessing different values.[26]

Consequently, political position becomes increasingly important in affecting the command over resources. The political dimension of stratification grows in significance. Political organizations are based not only on relations to the private market but to the developing "public market" in which key decisions are made.

The political dimension has its roots in the right to vote.[27] As voting becomes a widespread legal right in many societies like the United States, with important differences in intergroup voting rates, the issue becomes how to get all groups to use their vote. This means dealing with the overt and covert barriers to voting.[28] Another level connected with the interest in voting is the degree, kind, and effec-tiveness of organization of various interest positions. Currently, low-income groups are beginning to develop organizations (whether in the form of activist clubs for the aged or political associations of slum residents) that push more effectively for programs dealing with their problems.

Today, the social-stratification theorist must devote attention to political issues that go beyond voting.[29] The emergence of many institutions dispensing services and resources has meant that the well-being of individuals depends to a large extent on bureaucratic deci-sions in an immediate sense rather than political decisions in the broad sense. The bureaucracies of the welfare state have considerable discretion in the way they disperse their funds and services. Bu-reaucratic decisions having deep impact upon the well-being of both the poor and the nonpoor have been somewhat removed from accessible political processes. As a consequence, there is a growing attack on "welfare bureaucracy" as infringing upon the rights of individuals, making capricious decisions, "professionalizing" and technicizing decisions that should be political decisions.

The concern in the United States with "participatory democracy," "maximum feasible participation" in the poverty programs, and "community representation" are manifestations of the effort to deal with the growing impact of welfare-state bureaucracies and the more obvious social-control agencies, like the police, on the lives of most.[30] The ability to be relatively insulated against bureaucratic mishandling and injustice is differentially distributed in society—the better-off and better-educated groups manage more effectively than the low-income and the low-educated groups.[31]

At one level within the economic dimension, the issue is to what extent are individuals protected *against* control by bureaucratic agencies? At another level, the issue is becoming: To what extent are political processes being transformed so that recipients of government benefits become consumers and citizens with a decision-making role rather than dependents without choice or any degree of sovereignty? Both levels require the extension of traditional stratificational analysis of power to the new instruments of government, administration, and distribution of resources.

EDUCATION AND SOCIAL MOBILITY

In today's credential society, which places heavy emphasis on educational attainment for entrance into higher-level occupations, education becomes a crucial dimension in social stratification.[32] The importance of education is illustrated by Wilensky's and Duncan's findings that it is the only variable that consistently ranks all the white-collar strata above each of the manual and farm strata.[33] In addition to its economic role, educational experience affects the way individuals are treated by other people and by organizations and bureaucracies of one kind or another. An individual with inadequate education is an outsider, less able to take advantage of the opportunities that exist, and is treated less well than those with the same income but a higher education. American Negroes' great interest in education, for example, is partially due to the protection that education provides against nasty treatment.

Educational attainment of children is only a partial function of the income of parents. Below the highest IQ levels, the education of parents is more important than their income in affecting the educational experience of children. Economic position is thus not a fully adequate indicator of the educational prospects of children.

Many governmental policies are aimed at producing a break between the economic position of the child and of his parent. The aim is *inter*generational social mobility rather than improving the conditions of the poor today. For example, the emphases in the War on Poverty on job-training programs (for example, Job Corps, Manpower Development) and on education (for example, Headstart, Elementary and Secondary Education Act) are essentially programs in social mobility. The programs aimed at the young, like Headstart, obviously aim for intergenerational mobility, while those designed for older persons, like many of the Manpower Development and Training Act programs, seek *intra*generational mobility.

What is the value of casting these poverty and manpower programs in the language of mobility? In some cases, the mobility perspective points out that program goals are too low. In some job-training programs, for example, "success" is recorded if the individual secures a job, even if the job pays no more or is no less of a dead end than his previous job. Similarly, low-wage full-time employment may not be a substantial mobility step over unemployment or irregular employment.

The mobility approach may also indicate the possible importance of stratum or group mobility.[34] Important gains may be achieved not only by moving individuals out of particular low-wage occupations but by securing a substantial improvement in the occupations' relative position in terms of wages, status, and conditions.

The stratificational approach also encourages studying the factors that impede or promote mobility. Lack of education may be a less important barrier than current common sense suggests, while discrimination may continue to be significant.

As societies become increasingly future-oriented, a crucial dimension of stratification is what happens to the children of different strata. The current position of families only partially denotes future positions. Blau and Duncan found for instance that "nearly ten percent of manual sons achieve elite status in the United States, a higher proportion that in any other country." Commenting on their findings, they wrote, "The high level of popular education in the United States, perhaps reinforced by the lesser emphasis on formal distinctions of social status, has provided the disadvantaged lower strata with outstanding opportunities for long-distance upward mobility." [35] Hopefully, public policies will make sharper the break between the present of the family and the future of the child. Consequently, social mobility, an important part of Weber's concept of "life chances," should receive attention as an independent vector of stratification,

Obviously, there are important questions concerning the significant economic-political-social boundaries of high and low position. Social-stratification analysts have been slow to refine the manual/nonmanual divide. Our conclusion is that the increasingly important social divide is not between the manual and nonmanual groups, but between those with and without a college diploma—between those in professional and managerial occupations and the rest of the society. As Kolko has remarked, "Economic mobility in a technology and society enormously—and increasingly—dependent on the formally trained expert ultimately reflects the extent of equality in education." [36] Important differences obviously exist below the professional-managerial level, but the expanding "diploma elite" is becoming distinctly advantaged in society.[37] Their advantage is not only economic, but social and political as well. The diploma elite manages to achieve deference and decent treatment from governmental organizations, and at the same time—perhaps because of this—is able to organize effectively as a political voice. As the complexity of life in the United States increases, we may expect the importance of education to grow.

STATUS

Weber's discussion of the status dimension of stratification has frequently been compressed into an analysis of family or occupational prestige rankings. This reduction is an inadequate rendering of what was obviously intended to embrace the socio-psychological dimensions of stratificational systems.

Three dimensions are worth distinguishing here: "social honor," styles of life, and self-respect. In Weber's usage, "social honor" referred to the social evaluation by others of a class or political group. As we have noted earlier, a high economic class may or may not have high social prestige at any particular moment in time. This can be seen through patterns of interaction such as intermarriage among groups and classes.

Social honor is *externally* awarded on a variety of bases: income, occupation, education, family history. In the past, American sociologists probably overstressed the significance of prestige and understressed the importance of class, but prestige is again growing in importance as a dimension of stratification.[38] Because social honor significantly affects government policy, its importance grows with the increasing importance of government action affecting persons' well-being and command over resources. For example, a group that is regarded as "undeserving poor" is much less likely to be aided than "deserving poor." Prestige, then, is intimately tied to access to resources. It also, as we shall discuss later, affects self-respect.

The issues of desegregation, especially in housing, in the United States also point up the significance of prestige. Undoubtedly, much of the slowness in making it possible for blacks to have effective free choice in housing locations is due to class feelings—disturbance about "lower-class" black families. Nonetheless, a considerable part of the resistance against black mobility is directed against blacks as a status group regardless of class levels.

The development of national states accentuated the problems of ethnic minorities. These problems will probably increase again with the tide of foreign, low-level workers in many European nations. Ethnic and class factors will intertwine to make the prestige of a grouping an important factor in the way that it is treated. Alwine de Vos van Steenwijk and Père Joseph of Aide à Toute Détresse tell us that in France the way that poverty is viewed largely depends on whether the poor are thought to be of French or foreign background. In the United States, attitudes toward dealing with poverty combine with the stress on the importance of blacks as a poor group and the shifting compound of feelings about blacks.

The increased significance of government as the conveyer of the command over resources also complicates the traditional relationships between source of income and "social honor." The conclusions of yesterday were simple: Earned income is more prestigious than unearned income (unless it is very high unearned income) ; legitimate income is better than "illegitimate" income. Today, the evaluations of the different bases of income are cloudy. Income given to public-assistance clients leads to low prestige; but financial assistance to farmers in the form of money subsidies or to entrepreneurs in the form of tariffs does not.[39] Payments to the retired, which purportedly have a relationship to their contributions to a fund during their lifetime, are not stigmatized income even if the relationship of contribution and payment is indeed remote. Payments to youth who go to school are not regarded as habit-forming or character-debilitating. When made to poor families, they are often so regarded.

Thus, it is not government payments and contributions per se but their basis that is unprestigious. If the payments are connected to the operation of the production system (tariffs, agricultural subsidies) or to the future productivity of workers (education) or to previous work status, then stigma does not attach to the support.

By styles of life, the second dimension of status, we refer to the norms and values of particular groups.[40] If social honor is the way the group is regarded from without, styles of life refer to the way the group behaves. Obviously, styles of life and their interpretation affect the bestowal of social honor.[41]

The determination of styles is no easy matter; it is difficult to have a summation of a style that is not judgmental and even more difficult to have a style description that does not fall afoul of competing efforts to utilize that description in the struggle for policy choices. The significance of style of life underscores the importance of status considerations in government decisions as well as the importance of government decisions.

Because of the importance of styles of life in affecting social honor and public policy, social science becomes particularly political. Its mode of interpretation has strong reverberations. Yet, the knowledge base from which descriptions and interpretations are made is limited and controversial. In an important sense, however, this has always been true; the interpretation of the social stratification of a nation is always a most sensitive political issue. What is striking in the present is the particular importance of styles of life. The greater controversiality may be due not only to the fact of greater stakes (government is more likely to do something now than in the nineteenth century) but to the production of a larger number of fairly independent social scientists and to the politicalization of issues that provide once-neglected groups with spokesmen.

Current research on the poor is leading to the rejection of the notion of *the* one style of life among this group.[42] It is always difficult to make a historical statement, since much of the past is sentimentalized in the telling, but it does appear that life-style heterogeneity within a grouping is indeed increasing. One reason for this is the greater variety today of cross-pressures in societies that are increasingly national and in which more styles are visible through travel, the mass media, and more public life. A second reason underlines the mode of stratificational analysis proposed by Weber: Change in one dimension of life does not automatically produce change in other realms. Discontinuities often result from a rapid pace of change in which spurts and lags are pronounced.

The heterogeneity of styles is important in two ways. One has been referred to already: The receptivity to aiding particular groups, and especially the poor, depends to a large extent on their "social honor." In turn, their social honor depends largely on what purports to be their life style. Those low-income groups with more appealing life styles are much more likely to be given some aid. The second way that heterogeneity affects policy is that any given policy is likely to fit more easily into the style and condition of one section of the poor than another. The result frequently is, whether intended or not, the process of "creaming," working with the best off or most adaptable of the poor. It usually takes some time to discover that the policy left behind groups with other life styles or other class positions.

The process leads to the question of whether groups need to change their life styles in order to be able to take advantage of new opportunities in the private market or in governmental policies. Here, style of life becomes an element in the efficacy of change rather than a moral gatekeeper of whether or not a particular group should be helped.

Frequently, in the United States, life styles are discussed in terms of relatively impenetrable barriers that the culture or subculture of poverty places in the way of advance. An alternative formulation, which Riessman and Miller have attempted to develop, emphasizes those aspects of low-income life styles that must be considered in order to make public policies more effective.[43] The stress is on reducing strains, obstacles, and difficulties of policy rather than on castigating the poor or ignoring their particular outlook.

In a sense, what is important about the styles of life of groups, especially those most needful of governmental aid, is largely determined by the political culture of a nation. Whether the bases of life styles are ethnic or marginal economic circumstances, what is crucial about them is the way they interact with political values concerning who should be helped, how they should be helped, and how the behaviors of those helped should change. The style-of-life variable has become more highly charged than it was for Malthus.

Self-respect, the third dimension of status, points to the way the grouping regards itself. It is a complex admixture of economic and political conditions, social honor, and styles of life. In it, feelings of relative deprivation generally represent only a rough approximation of actual inequalities existing within a society.[44] The discussion of poverty, at least in the United States, should make us aware that only the narrowest view of poverty would make it a problem of income alone. In the spongy openness of the affluent society, poverty becomes not only a shorthand expression for inequality but also a truncated phrase for the many ways in which the poor are different in society.

One does not have to accept all the nostrums of change that are offered in the United States to recognize the importance of a feeling of dignity, of inclusion and participation in the society that goes beyond the attaining of an income above a minimum level. Obviously, rising income alone may not wipe out external stigma and internal group hate and deprecation. On the other hand, gains in group respect are unlikely if the group falls behind the rising standards of society. Between these two boundaries, many kinds of permutations are possible.

One can interpret Negroes' interest in "maximum feasible participation" in the local decision-making of the War on Poverty in many ways, but an important interpretation in terms of stratification theory is that it represents the politicalization of the issue of self-respect. One does not have to believe that the poor are the ultimate repository of all wisdom about what poverty means and what should be done about it to recognize that this politicalization recasts the search for self-respect in new ways, making a political issue out of what has appeared to be a personal struggle. Access to self-respect, despite its curious formulation, becomes one of the important dimensions of social stratification. The alienated nonpoor have had an opportunity to make a choice; not so with the poor.

CONCLUSIONS

Casting the issues of poverty in terms of stratification leads to regarding poverty as an issue of inequality. In this approach, we move away from efforts to measure poverty lines with pseudoscientific accuracy. Instead, we look at the nature and size of the differences between the bottom 20 or 10 per cent and the rest of society. Our concern becomes one of narrowing the differences between those at the bottom and the better-off in each stratification dimension.

In casting many of the issues of poverty in terms of stratification, we do not wish to imply that the poor are a fixed homogeneous group that shares a common outlook. Rather, we see the poor as those who lag behind the rest of society in terms of one dimension, or more, of life. There may be considerable turnover in these bottom groups. Although we lack data showing what proportion of persons in the bottom groups move in and out of poverty, we do know that a life-cycle pattern is of some importance, for the risk of being at the bottom is much greater for older individuals.[45] There is undoubtedly a greater turnover in the bottom 20 per cent of the population than is commonly believed by those who stress inheritance and "culture-of-poverty" theories. Even with a high turnover, however, questions concerning what size and kind of disparities are acceptable between those who fall behind and others in society remain important.

We hope that our effort to place some poverty-action issues in the context of social stratification is not merely a translation from one language of discourse to another. Therefore, we must ask what would be done differently if poverty problems were seen as issues in stratification.

First, we believe that poverty programs would aim for higher targets. Reforming the social structure so that the differences among individuals are reduced usually requires higher goals than bringing individuals up to a rather low economic standard.

Second, a stratificational approach requires constant adjustment of the targets, for as the better-off groups advance, new levels and kinds of concerns for the bottom-most should emerge. A fixed level of well-being is no longer the aim.

Third, a stratificational approach implies that economic goals are not the only important objectives. Frequently, the economic goal of raising annual incomes to a $3,000 level has been treated as though it were the only significant objective. The multidimensional concerns of stratification force attention to the noneconomic aspects of inequality.

Fourth, we see that changes and shifts in one dimension do not automatically produce changes in other dimensions. Economic gain does not ensure automatic attainment of other goals. Indeed, much of contemporary stratificational analysis is about this problem—and much of the difficulty with appraisal of poverty strategies is that little is known about the multiplier effect of each strategy.[46]

Fifth, a stratificational approach suggests that style-of-life variables may be important in the construction and conduct of programs. This statement does not suggest a culture of poverty, but an effort to make policies and programs relevant and appropriate to the life styles of their intended consumers.

Finally, we see that many programs aimed at moving youth out of poverty have neglected vital dimensions of the youths' lives. Many social-mobility programs have aimed at enhancing the prospects of youth without improving the conditions of their families. Other programs have sought to improve the education of children without improving the schools that they attend. Headstart and Job Corps, for example, have attempted to create a parallel educational system rather than change educational institutions. In these instances, the social setting of behavior has been neglected.

Conventional poverty discussions are thin because they are cast in terms of nineteenth-century concerns about pauperism and subsistence rather than in twentieth-century terms of redistribution. We are not clear about the goals of reduction of poverty and inequality because we have not forthrightly discussed our objectives. When poverty is viewed in the stratificational perspective, we see that the goal of bringing all families up to a certain income level cloaks disagreements about the relative importance of differing, often conflicting, objectives. For example, at the level of objectives of efforts to change the stratificational system, are we seeking a classless society with only minor differences among individuals; or is the goal a meritocracy in which individuals have in actuality equal access to high-level jobs that are highly rewarded; or do we seek to connect an "underclass," which does not improve its conditions as much as the rest of the society does, into the processes that will begin to make it less distinctive; or do we seek to reduce the gaps in some vital dimensions between the nonpoor and the poor? Each of these views implies a belief concerning what is important about stratificational systems, how permeable these systems are, and how other goals should be balanced against the concern with the underclasses.

The stratification perspective leads us to see that in dealing with poverty we are dealing with the *quality of life* of individuals and not just their economic positions. This means that not only individuals' relationship to government but the *quality of relationships among people* in society is important. Although governmental and organizational action is needed to diminish the economic and political inequalities separating people, we as individuals must assume responsibility for changing the quality of relationships among ourselves. Ultimately, change in the distribution of "social honor" and self-respect, the most fundamental aspects of stratification, can only be accomplished by each of us, members of society, caring about the excluded and extending our patterns of personal social interaction to include them. If poverty is about stratification, we cannot escape one another.

Notes

NOTE: This chapter is part of a series of papers. For further discussion of what is gained by putting poverty into a stratification perspective, see S. M. Miller, Martin Rein, Pamela Roby, and Bertram Gross, "Poverty, Inequality, and Conflict," *The Annals*, CCCLXXIII (September 1967), 16–52.

1. Stanislaw Ossowski, *Class Structure in the Social Consciousness* (New York: The Free Press of Glencoe, 1963), p. 133.

2. Max Weber, "Class, Status, Party," in *From Max Weber*, edited and translated by Hans Gerth and C. Wright Mills (New York: Oxford University Press, 1958).

3. See Introduction to S. M. Miller, ed., *Max Weber: Readings* (New York: Thomas Y. Crowell, 1964).

4. Richard M. Titmuss, *Income Distribution and Social Change* (London: Allen and Unwin, 1962), and *Essays on "The Welfare State"* (New Haven, Conn.: Yale University Press, 1958).

5. Miller, *op. cit.*, p. 17.

6. Robert K. Merton, *Social Theory and Social Structure*, rev. ed. (New York: The Free Press of Glencoe, 1957), pp. 85–117.

7. See the first essay by Gouldner and the concluding article by Miller in Alvin W. Gouldner and S. M. Miller, eds., *Applied Sociology* (New York: The Free Press of Glencoe, 1965). Other essays by Miller that bear on the issues of this chapter are "Poverty" in *Proceedings*, Sixth World Congress of Sociology, 1967, and "Social Change and 'The Age of Psychiatry,'" in S. M. Miller and Frank Riessman, *Social Class and Social Policy* (New York: Basic Books, 1968).

8. Talcott Parsons, "Full Citizenship for the Negro American? A Sociological Problem," *Daedalus*, XCIV, No. 2 (Fall 1965); T. H. Marshall, "Citizenship and Social Class," in *Class, Citizenship and Social Development* (New York: Anchor Books, 1965).

9. Weber, *op. cit.*, p. 185.

10. Many American sociologists had been misled into believing that society was characterized by consensus simply because conflicts centering around the workplace were considerably less violent than in the 1880s or 1900s. Rather than disappearing, conflicts have shifted from the workplace to the ghetto streets and to the campuses where rebellions are aimed at societal and governmental injustices.

11. Ralf Dahrendorf, "Out of Utopia: Toward a Reorientation of Sociological Analysis," *American Journal of Sociology*, LXIV, No. 2 (September 1958), 115–127.

12. Weber, *op. cit.*

13. Many sociologists have observed portions of this development. For example, Parsons has noted that public control of private business contributed to the inclusion of Negroes and other groups, and that government control over the value of the dollar shapes the distribution of wealth. Parsons, *op. cit.*

14. Lipset and Zetterberg maintain that, historically, occupation has been the most common indicator of stratification. S. M. Lipset and Hans Zetterberg. "A Theory of Social Mobility," in Reinhard Bendix and S. M. Lipset, eds., *Class, Status, and Power*, 2nd ed. (New York: The Free Press of Glencoe, 1966), p. 155. Great attention has been paid to the consistency with which prestige is accorded

to occupations among different nations. However, international comparative studies pose many methodological problems. These frequently appear to result in a spuriously high degree of intercountry similarity. Following the most recent comparative study of occupational prestige, Hodge et al. wrote, "It is quite possible that much genuine diversity in occupational-prestige systems not captured by our analysis is reflected in the relative placement of occupations that are not comparable across societies, or even across subsectors of any given society. In Tiryakian's study of the Philippines, only a small number of occupations could be found about which it was sensible to ask both peasants in remote villages and the residents of Manila." . . . "Invoking even so gross a distinction as the manual-nonmanual dichotomy reveals divergencies between national prestige structures which are concealed by the total correlation over all occupations. The evidence mustered not only points to dissimilarities from country to country in occupational-prestige structures but also suggests that this variation is intertwined with economic development in a way which is not fully captured by a simple 'structuralist' or simple 'culturalist' expectation of prestige differences." Robert Hodge, Donald Treiman, and Peter Rossi, "A Comparative Study of Occupational Prestige," in Bendix and Lipset, *ibid.*, pp. 318, 321. Lenski contends that "The great importance of the occupational class system is . . . indicated by the fact that one of the chief rewards distributed by most other class systems is access to favored occupations." Gerhard Lenski, *Power and Privilege* (New York: McGraw-Hill, 1966) , p. 347. We believe, however, that the importance of the occupational class system is declining as the role of government expands.

15. For instance, in only two years, the *interquartile* range of *weekly* earnings of accounting clerks increased by $2.50; of material handlers, by $8.00; and of maintenance electricians, by $12.00 in the New York S.M.S.A. U.S. Department of Labor, Bureau of Labor Statistics, *Area Wage Survey*, Bulletin No. 1530–83 (April 1967) ; U.S. Department of Labor, Bureau of Labor Statistics, *Occupational Wage Survey*, Bulletin No. 143–80 (April 1965) .

16. See Richard Hamilton, "The Income Question," Department of Sociology, University of Wisconsin, unpublished manuscript.

17. Brian Abel-Smith has contested some prevailing views of the distribution of benefits in his trenchant article "Whose Welfare State?" in Norman MacKenzie, ed., *Conviction* (London: MacGibbon and Rae, 1958) .

18. In his critique of Davis and Moore's proposition that "social stratification, the uneven distribution of material rewards and prestige, is functionally necessary," Wesolowski maintains that in Poland and Norway the range of income has been distinctly narrowed, but education and other services have been expanded. In these countries, he contends, not "material rewards" but authority (which gives one the opportunity to express his own personality) and education are viewed as "end values." In support of his thesis that occupational prestige is not an important motivational force under the Polish value system, Wesolowski cites Dr. Adam Sarapata's finding that 50 per cent of the respondents in a survey of Lodz replied, "No" when asked if some of the occupations were more important than others. Wlodzimierz Wesolowski, "Some Notes on the Functional Theory of Stratification," in Bendix and Lipset, *op. cit.*

19. T. H. Marshall, *Class, Citizenship and Social Development* (New York: Doubleday, 1964) .

20. Ossowski has noted, for instance, ". . . the experiences of recent years incline us to formulate the Marxian conception of social class in the form of a law which establishes a functional dependence: the more closely the social system approximates to the ideal type of a free and competitive capitalist society, the more are the classes determined by their relation to the means of production . . . [T]he majority of American citizens are becoming accustomed to large-scale activities planned by the central authorities . . . Hence comes the talk about the crisis facing political economics, whose laws were formerly rooted in the basic and inevitable tendencies of human behavior, but which today faces a dilemma caused by the growing influence of the government as a factor which consciously directs the country's economic life." Ossowski, *op. cit.*, p. 185.

21. The importance of government subsidy and licensing has led Charles Reich to speak of "largesse" in his seminal essay, "The New Property," *Yale Law Review*, Vol. XCIII (1964).

22. A new and neglected aspect of income is its stability. Just as the assurance of future income through pensions is an increasingly important component of well-being, the security and predictability of income within and over the years is becoming more significant. Frequently, factory workers receive more income than do white-collar employees, but the latter have a stability of income that is as yet not available to factory workers. This is true both within a year in which factories may suffer layoffs and among years in which white-collar workers can have more confidence about the drift and certainty of their incomes. As a consequence, collective-bargaining negotiations in the United States in the next years are likely to center to a large extent on the attainment of greater employment surety and income guarantees for factory workers. Obviously, the stability of income can be even more important for the poor who suffer from insecurity and unpredictable as well as inadequate income. The poor are unsure because of bureaucratic arbitrariness as well as because of unemployment and underemployment. Indeed, the War on Poverty programs, it could be argued, have increased some income uncertainties among the poor by their sudden starting up and then emergency curtailing or ending because of budgeting or political difficulties. In 1963, the unemployment rate for unskilled laborers, except farm and mine, was 12.1 per cent as compared to the national average of 5.7 per cent, 4.8 per cent for craftsmen, foremen, and kindred workers, and 1.6 per cent for managers, officials, and proprietors, except farm. In November 1967, in the midst of the Vietnam involvement, the unemployment rate for unskilled laborers (7.3 per cent) remained over three times that of craftsmen, foremen, and kindred workers (2.2 per cent) and over eight times that of managers, officials, and proprietors except farm (.9 per cent). U.S. Department of Labor, *Manpower Report of the President and a Report on Manpower Requirements, Resources, Utilization and Training*, transmitted to the Congress (March 1964), p. 25; U.S. Department of Labor, *Employment and Earnings* (December 1967).

23. Dahrendorf links class and politics even more closely when he writes, "[C]lass is about power and power is about politics." Ralf Dahrendorf, "Recent Changes in the Class Structure of European Societies," *Daedalus*, XCIII (Winter 1964). While we believe that class and power are closely related, we also believe that they remain independent stratificational dimensions.

24. Dahrendorf has observed, "Just as in a modern shoe factory, it is hard to answer the question, 'Who makes the shoes?' it is hard to tell who, in the bureaucratic administration of a modern enterprise, church, or state, holds the power." Dahrendorf, *ibid.*, p. 236.

25. See Martin Rein and S. M. Miller, "Poverty Programs and Policy Priorities," *Transaction* (September 1967).

26. For a strong attack on the "assertion that the old sources of tensions and class conflict are being progressively eliminated or rendered irrelevant" see J. H. Westergaard, "Capitalism Without Classes?," *New Left Review*, No. 26 (Summer 1964), 10–32. Also pertinent to these issues is John H. Goldthorpe's excellent essay, "Social Stratification in Industrial Society," in Bendix and Lipset, *op. cit.*, pp. 648–659.

27. See the important discussion of "citizenship" in T. H. Marshall, *op. cit.* When describing nineteenth- and twentieth-century European changes in citizenship, Dahrendorf has stated, "The slogan (political participation) points to a symptom of the development of equality of citizenship rights rather than to its entire substance. Citizenship is the social institution of the notion that all men are born equal. Its establishment requires change in virtually every sphere of social structure. Apart from universal suffrage, equality before the law is as much a part of this process as is universal education, protection from unemployment, injury, and sickness, and care for the old. Representative government, the rule of law, and the welfare state are in fact the three conditions of what I should describe as the social miracle of the emergence of the many to the light of full

social and political participation." Dahrendorf, "Recent Changes in the Class Structure of European Societies," *op. cit.,* p. 239.

28. Janowitz notes that in Great Britain, Germany, and the United States "there is a tendency for persons in the lower working classes to have a higher degree of non-party affiliation than in the other strata of society." However, he notes that the source of ineffective political participation lies not in income and education per se, but "as a series of life experiences which produces persons . . . without adequate institutional links to the political system." Furthermore, ". . . such disruption can occur at various points in the social structure, for example among elderly men and women living outside family units." Morris Janowitz and David R. Segal, "Social Cleavage and Party Affiliation: Germany, Great Britain and the United States," *American Journal of Sociology,* LXXII, No. 6 (May 1967).

29. Parsons has pointed out that inclusion ("the process by which previously excluded groups attain full citizenship or membership in the societal community") requires not a "mere statement that it is necessary for justice but that the group has the capacity to *contribute* to the larger society," . . . and as long as the group doesn't have that capacity, "the larger society needs to develop it." Because inclusion of an excluded group requires the mobilization of the entire society, Parsons suggests that it is useful to conceive of political power more broadly than usual. "Essential as government is, it does not stand alone in implementing major political changes." For example, "the political problems of integration involve all fields of organizational decision-making, especially for business firms to accept Negroes in employment, for colleges and universities to admit them for study, for trade unions to avoid discrimination." Parsons, "Full Citizenship for the Negro American?," *op. cit.*

30. Marshall's categorization of "four degrees of cooperation" is useful in the consideration of many forms of political participation as well as of the relationships between employers and employees for which it was originally intended; (1) 'information: . . . men though informed of decisions, have no share at all in the making of them"; (2) "consultation": persons "are not only informed before a decision is taken but have an opportunity to express their views on points that concern them. These views may or may not be taken into account when the decision is made; there is no transfer of authority"; (3) "delegation": persons "have been informed and consulted and their views have been taken into account in formulating a plan, then . . . small groups of them may be asked to work out the details for executing part of the plan"; (4) "joint control" exists in cases such as those in which "workers are represented in the management." Marshall, *op. cit.,* pp. 244–245.

31. After a four-year court battle, Alameda County (California) awarded $23,000 in back pay to a social-welfare worker who was fired for refusing to participate in the welfare department's "operation bedcheck." It is less likely that the female welfare recipients whose homes were invaded by welfare workers without search warrants will be recompensed. *Berkeley Barb,* August 24, 1967, p. 7.

32. See S. M. Miller, "Breaking the Credentials Barrier" (New York: The Ford Foundation, 1968). Lenski has written, "Of all the changes linked with industrialization, none has been more important than the revolution in knowledge. . . . From the standpoint of the occupational class system, this development has been highly significant. To begin with, it has been responsible for the considerable growth in size, importance, and affluence of the professional class. Second, it has caused education to become a much more valuable resource, and made educational institutions far more important in the distribution of power and privilege, than ever before in history." Gerhard Lenski, *Power and Privilege* (New York: McGraw-Hill, 1967), p. 364.

33. Otis Dudley Duncan, "Methodological Issues in the Analysis of Social Mobility," in Neil Smelser and S. M. Lipset, eds., *Social Structure and Mobility in Economic Development* (Chicago: Aldine, 1966); Harold Wilensky, "Class, Class Consciousness and American Workers," in William Haber, ed., *American Labor in a Changing World* (New York: Basic Books, 1966).

34. See S. M. Miller, "Comparative Social Mobility," *Current Sociology*, Vol. IX (1960).

35. Peter M. Blau and Otis Dudley Duncan, *The American Occupational Structure* (New York: Wiley, 1967), p. 435.

36. Gabriel Kolko, *Wealth and Power in America: An Analysis of Social Class and Income Distribution* (New York: Praeger, 1962), p. 113.

37. See Miller, "Comparative Social Mobility," *op. cit.*

38. Richard Hamilton has contended that sociologists have overstressed the blurring of status or prestige lines. He believes this has occurred because (1) although sociologists talk much about status-seeking activity, they have inadequately researched the matter; and (2) they consequently turn to income trends that they inaccurately assume to be becoming more equal and then assert that status and consumption patterns are also becoming equalized. Hamilton, *op. cit.*, p. 1.

39. Assistant Secretary of the Treasury Stanley S. Surrey has suggested that tax savings that accrue to individuals and groups from preferences or loopholes in the tax law should be reported as federal "expenditures." If this were done, the Commerce Department would show one billion dollars for aiding business in the form of special deductions. *The New York Times*, November 12, 1967. Fifty-five per cent of total 1963 government payments to farmers went to the top 11 per cent of all farmers, those with farm sales of $20,000 and over. Theodore Schultz, "Public Approaches to Minimize Poverty," in Leo Fishman, ed., *Poverty Amid Affluence* (New Haven, Conn.: Yale University Press, 1966); see also Philip M. Stern, *The Great Treasury Raid* (New York: Random House, 1964).

40. As elsewhere in this chapter, we assume that we are dealing with a group defined economically in class terms and that we are pursuing the political and social behavior components of this class group. Frequently, there is little convergence among the groups defined in class, political, or social terms.

41. The link between styles of life and their interpretation is not perfect, for as Lockwood has pointed out with regard to affluent manual employees whom he terms the "new working class," to display the life styles of those "above" and to be accepted by those "above" are two quite different things. David Lockwood, "The New Working Class," *European Journal of Sociology*, I, No. 2 (1960).

42. Other strata are also likely to be viewed as heterogeneous groupings. Cf. S. M. Miller, "The American Lower Class: A Typological Approach," *Social Research* (Spring 1964); Harold Wilensky, "Mass Society and Mass Culture," in Bernard Berenson and Morris Janowitz, eds., *Reader in Public Opinion and Communication* (New York: The Free Press of Glencoe, 1966).

43. Miller and Riessman, *Social Class and Social Policy, op. cit.*

44. Following his study of relative deprivation in England, Runciman concluded that for each stratification dimension, "the only generalization which can be confidently advanced is that the relationship between inequality and grievance only intermittently corresponds with either the extent or the degree of actual inequality." W. G. Runciman, *Relative Deprivation and Social Justice* (Berkeley: University of California Press, 1966).

45. Since the aged have different needs and consumption patterns than younger persons, it may make more sense to think in terms of stratification within the aged. Incidentally, there is a greater concentration of income among the top 20 per cent of the aged than among any other age group.

46. See Martin Rein and S. M. Miller, "Poverty, Policy, and Purpose: The Dilemmas of Choice," in Leonard H. Goodman, ed., *Economic Progress and Social Welfare* (New York: Columbia University Press, 1966).

Chapter 4

☞ *Inheritance of Poverty or Inheritance of Race?* OTIS DUDLEY DUNCAN

A recurring theme in the discussions of poverty during the 1960s has been the "cycle of poverty," the "vicious circle of poverty," the "persistence of poverty," the "legacy of poverty," or the "inheritance of poverty." There is little to choose between the official and the unofficial versions of the theme. Harrington wrote: [1]

. . . the real explanation of why the poor are where they are is that they made the mistake of being born to the wrong parents, in the wrong section of the country, in the wrong industry, or in the wrong racial or ethnic group. Once that mistake has been made, they could have been paragons of will and morality, but most of them would never even have had a chance to get out of the other America.

There are two important ways of saying this: The poor are caught in a vicious circle; or, The poor live in a culture of poverty.

The echo came back from the Council of Economic Advisers: [2]

Poverty breeds poverty. A poor individual or family has a high probability of staying poor. Low incomes carry with them high risks of illness; limitations on mobility; limited access to education, information, and training. Poor parents cannot give their children the opportunities for better health and education needed to improve their lot. Lack of motivation, hope, and incentive is a more subtle but not less powerful barrier than lack of financial means. Thus the cruel legacy of poverty is passed from parents to children.

This is a report from Project No. 5–0074 (EO–191), "Socioeconomic Background and Occupational Achievement," supported by Contract No. OE–5–85–072 with the U.S. Office of Education.

Mr. Shriver's presentation to the Congress, as it debated the Economic Opportunity Act of 1964, reiterated: [3]

Being poor . . . is a rigid way of life. It is handed down from generation to generation in a cycle of inadequate education, inadequate homes, inadequate jobs, and stunted ambitions. It is a peculiar axiom of poverty that the poor are poor because they earn little, and they also earn little because they are poor.

The President's message on the War on Poverty accordingly offered help to

young Americans who lack skills, who have not completed their education or who cannot complete it because they are too poor. The years of high school and college age are the most critical stage of a young person's life. If they are not helped then, many will be condemned to a life of poverty which they, in turn, will pass on to their children.[4]

The theme has proved to be durable. The *1965 Economic Report* (p. 170) refers to the "bonds that tie today's children to the poverty of their parents," the *1966 Report* (p. 96) to "the cycle of poverty and dependency," and the *1967 Report* (p. 142) to "the poverty cycle in which blighted environment denies poor children the skills and the attitudes they need to break out of poverty as adults." Among other administration spokesmen, Secretary McNamara has repeated the thesis: "Poverty begets poverty. It passes from generation to generation in a cruel cycle of near inevitability." [5] Examples of similar usages could be multiplied almost at will.

I have not found many attempts to test or even to call into question the assumptions of the "inheritance-of-poverty" thesis. The authors of *Income and Welfare*—one of those works that are more widely cited than read—did devote some pages to the "transmission of poverty between generations" and the "transmission of poverty to children." Their analysis is rather cursory, but still cogent enough to have justified more attention to their conclusion: "Though no sweeping generalizations can be made on the basis of these few tables, they offer little support for a theory of poverty that rests entirely on inter-generational transmission." [6] Evidently, one of the co-authors soon forgot this conclusion; without protecting himself from the logical hazards encountered in deductions from correlations, he wrote in 1964: [7]

The evidence points to the conclusion that poverty breeds poverty. Education and occupational status are correlated with economic status. The

University of Michigan study showed that low educational attainment tends to perpetuate itself between generations.

One other economist has confronted the cycle thesis head on. His calculations, based on the 1962 data on occupational mobility from the study of Occupational Changes in a Generation,[8] led Gallaway to reject

the idea that the economic status of parents is a major determinant of the economic success of offspring. . . . Data such as these certainly weaken the case for those who argue that there is a "vicious cycle of poverty." Apparently the inheritability of poverty is not nearly so great as is implied by some.[9]

This chapter is in the spirit of the suggestion that "government intervention in social processes . . . requires enthusiasm, but also intellect." [10] The notion that "people are poor because they are poor" has proved its worth in generating *enthusiasm* for a war on poverty. I am concerned, rather, with the possibility that harm may be done when we "do not insist on clarity and candor in the definition of objectives," [11] when we settle for a slogan instead of requiring analysis, when, in terms of Walter Miller's analysis (see page 260), we encumber ourselves with the ideological baggage of "code words," as when "the poor" serves as a euphemism for "Negroes."

Although a number of texts, both among those cited earlier and many not cited, could serve equally well, let me take Harrington's paragraph whole as a point of departure:

Then, poverty is a culture in the sense that the mechanism of impoverishment is fundamentally the same in every part of the system. The vicious circle is a basic pattern. It takes different forms for the unskilled workers, for the aged, for the Negroes, for the agricultural workers, but in each case the principle is the same. There are people in the affluent society who are poor because they are poor; and who stay poor because they are poor.[12]

I shall argue, in particular, that Negroes (that is, disproportionate numbers of them) are poor mainly because they are "Negroes" and are defined and treated as such by our society and that their poverty stems largely not from the legacy of poverty but from the legacy of race. I don't believe that Harrington meant to deny this, but I do believe that political as well as intellectual mischief is done when a congeries of imprecise ideas is gummed together with an ideological slogan serving as cement.

A MODEL OF THE SOCIO-ECONOMIC LIFE CYCLE

If there were any chance that the slogan makers and the policy builders would heed the implications of social research, the first lesson for them to learn would be that *poverty is not a trait but a condition.* In a work otherwise more distinguished for its rhetoric than for its contribution to knowledge, Alvin Schorr offered one insight that should become a beacon to guide our interpretations of the causes giving rise to the condition: We must "visualiz[e] poor families in the stream of life rather than as fractions of a population or at a given point in time." [13] Noting the imperfections in our present images of the flowing stream, he truly stated, "Research that will provide a sharper, truer image is badly needed." [14] Unfortunately, his own account of the "stages through which a family passes to the development of family income" is badly distorted by errors both factual and conceptual. For example, "It is a platitude of occupational research that the father's occupation determines the son's," [15] or "The first job is an excellent indication of what the last job will be," [16] or "At the close of Stage 2 (say, between twenty-five and thirty), those families who will be poor are readily recognized" [17]— all statements that are at best equivocally true[18] and fraught with the hazards of all partial truths.

Schorr's basic error—one, if I am not mistaken, that he recapitulates from studies in the culture of poverty, although he dismisses the latter as a "mystique"—is a commonplace fallacy in historical interpretations: What came to pass happened inevitably. "The choices made by people who are going to be poor may seem haphazard, but their combined effect is as accidental as the path of a trolley car." [19] But if the "choices" did include any quantum of the "haphazard," that is, if they were not fully predictable from knowledge of antecedent circumstances and choices—and Schorr himself concedes a role for "pure luck"—then their sequence is to that extent not fixed like the tracks traveled by a trolley car; rather, it bears some resemblance to Brownian motion.

The crucial questions for a life-cycle view of the genesis of poverty (or of any other position on a scale of income or level of living) are, therefore: (1) What factors, conditions, circumstances, and choices observable at one stage of the life cycle are determinative or prognostic of outcomes to be observed at later stages? (2) How predictable *are* the conditions at later stages from the information available at the earlier ones? (These are questions, obviously, that have to do with who becomes rich or poor, not with what determines the aggregate income in a society.)

The modern approach to these questions is not seeking absolute and final answers, rather it seeks models that order the available information as well as it can be ordered in the present state of knowledge. The presumption is that improvements in knowledge will result in modifications and complications of the models. Pending such improvements, questions may be put to the models with some confidence that the answers forthcoming will be somewhat more sophisticated than those vouchsafed by the analyst who is merely "well informed" but not disciplined by the methodological requirements of model construction.

I have previously suggested a conceptual paradigm for models of the socio-economic life cycle,[20] and in a collaborative study,[21] it was possible to develop in some detail the estimates needed for an actual "first-generation" model. The work to be summarized here builds on these prior contributions and offers, in effect, a "second-generation" model. From the foregoing remarks, the reader may perhaps be willing to grant that I am as alive to the defects of this work as any casual critic is likely to be. (The *constructive* critic will be one who lays down guidelines for the "third-generation" model.) Whatever these defects, I submit that the conscious strategy of model construction puts us on the way toward the "sharper, truer image" that Schorr demands.

Let Figure 4–1 be taken as a diagrammatic representation of the present model of the socio-economic life cycle. With respect to this model (though not necessarily with respect to other models one might entertain), two measures on a respondent's family of orientation are taken to be "predetermined variables"—that is, the model says nothing about how values of these variables are themselves determined. These two measures of "family background" (which term may serve as a convenient label) are the educational attainment and the occupational status of the head (normally the respondent's father) of the family of orientation. It is supposed that the size of the family of orientation, measured by the *number of siblings* of the respondent, depends on the two predetermined variables as well as on other factors that are not specified in the model and that are taken to be uncorrelated with the predetermined variables. Further, it is suggested that the respondent's *educational attainment* depends on how many siblings he has as well as on the two measures of family background and unspecified residual factors. The achieved *occupational status* of the respondent, as of the time information on him is collected, is taken to depend on prior educational attainment, on number of siblings, on family background, and on unspecified residual factors. Finally, the current money *income* of the respondent is represented as a function of his occupational status, his educational attainment, the number of siblings he has, and the two measures of family background, as well as unspecified residual factors. The "residual factors," in each case, are the closest approximation we have to

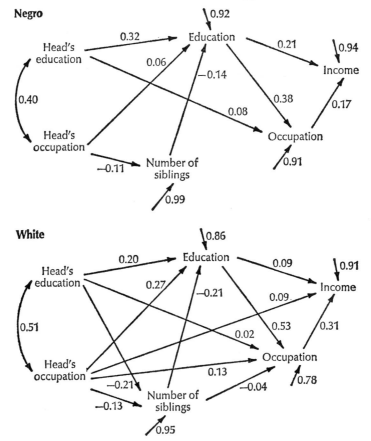

FIGURE 4–1. Path diagrams representing a model of the socio-economic life cycle in the Negro and white populations, with path coefficients estimated for native men 25 to 64 years old with nonfarm background and in the experienced civilian labor force: March 1962.
SOURCE: Computed from data summarized in Table 4–2; path is omitted when coefficient is less than its estimated standard error in absolute value.

an operational counterpart to Schorr's pure luck. To the extent that future research renders some of the presently "unspecified residual factors" specified, the apparent role of pure luck will diminish with the incorporation of additional specific factors into new models. How much the residual can be made to shrink in this fashion can only be conjectured; all experience with comparable problems suggests that models in the foreseeable future will continue to require substantially weighted terms for pure luck.

The model as described thus considers four successive outcomes for a cohort of respondents: the number of children in the families in which they grow up, their schooling, their occupational achievement, and their income levels. Each such outcome is assumed to depend, to a greater or lesser degree (the degree of dependence is to be estimated from the data), both on all the antecedent outcomes and on the predetermined variables. The model, therefore, consists of four equations, one for each dependent variable or outcome, and the equations take on what the model builders call a "simple recursive" form. In the diagrammatic representation, a straight line with an arrowhead at one end represents what is conveyed by the words "depends on" or, more explicitly, "depends *directly* on." That is, the variable at the head of the arrow depends directly on the variable at the tail. The degree of dependence is represented in the diagram by a path coefficient or, alternatively, in the tabular presentation in Table 4–1, by a regression coefficient.

Path coefficients are standardized so that there is some meaning in the comparison between different variables. Thus, for example, in the white population, income depends on occupation more heavily than it depends (directly) on education since the respective path coefficients are .31 and .09. To ascertain, concretely, the nature of the dependence, the regression coefficients in Table 4–1 are relevant: $71 of income for each point on the occupational scale and $299 for each point on the educational scale. Since occupation and education are measured on different scales, of necessity, there is no particular meaning in the fact that the latter is the larger coefficient. In using path coefficients, each variable is measured on a scale whose unit is the standard deviation of that variable in the population under study. Hence, we may conclude: For each difference of one standard deviation on the occupational scale, there is (on the average) a difference of 0.31 standard deviation on the income scale; and one standard deviation difference in education produces .09 standard deviation difference in income. In discussing how prior outcomes and

T A B L E 4 – 1 . Partial Regression Coefficients in Successive Multiple Regressions of Stratification Variables, for Native Men 25–64 Years Old, with Nonfarm Background and in the Experienced Civilian Labor Force, by Race: March 1962.

INDEPENDENT VARIABLE * AND RACE	DEPENDENT VARIABLE *			
	RESPONDENT'S INCOME (1)	RESPONDENT'S OCCUPATION (2)	RESPONDENT'S EDUCATION (3)	NUMBER OF SIBLINGS (4)
NEGRO				
(6) Family head's education	.043 †	.811	.336	−.055 †
(5) Family head's occupation	−.005 †	.005	.006	−.020
(4) Number of siblings	−.025 †	−.105 †	−.071	...
(3) Respondent's education	.249	3.653	...	...
(2) Respondent's occupation	.021	...	...	...
Constant term	2.08	4.72	3.07	5.37
(Coefficient of determination)	(.12)	(.18)	(.15)	(.01)
WHITE				
(6) Family head's education	−.008 †	.256	.181	−.334
(5) Family head's occupation	.022	.138	.019	−.017
(4) Number of siblings	−.016 †	−.365	−.117	...
(3) Respondent's education	.299	7.964	...	...
(2) Respondent's occupation	.071	...	...	...
Constant term	1.90	0.73	4.04	5.54
(Coefficient of determination)	(.17)	(.39)	(.26)	(.09)

SOURCE: Computed from data summarized in Table 4–2.

* Variable (1) measured in $1,000s. Variables (2) and (5) measured on Duncan's socio-economic index of occupational status. Variables (3) and (6) measured on transformed scale of years of school completed—o: None; 1: elementary, 1–4 years; 2: elementary, 5–7 years; 3: elementary, 8 years; 4: high school, 1–3 years; 5: high school, 4 years; 6: college, 1–3 years; 7: college, 4 years; 8: college, 5 or more years.

† Coefficient less than its estimated standard error in absolute value.

predetermined variables combine to produce their effects and in assessing "how much difference" the respective causal factors make in the outcome, the path coefficients are more convenient. In translating the effects into statements in terms of the "coin of the realm," the concrete regressions must be examined.

One more word of explanation: In the path diagram, the curved line with arrowheads at both ends does not represent dependence or causal relationship, but simply the fact that the predetermined variables are correlated for whatever reasons. The sources of this correlation are not analyzed by this particular model, although they might well be made explicit in some other model.

ESTIMATES FOR THE MODEL

Estimates of the path and regression coefficients for this model can be made separately for Negro and white (actually, all non-Negro) men as of 1962 on the basis of data collected for the study of Occupational Changes in a Generation (OCG).[22] The data used here are restricted to native men twenty-five to sixty-four years old with nonfarm background (excluding men whose fathers held farm occupations). The calculation of the estimates proceeds from the matrix of correlations for all pairs of variables in the model, supplemented by the means and standard deviations of these variables. This information is summarized in Table 4–2, to which passing reference will be made in interpreting the coefficients of the model.

A first result is that certain factors initially conceived to be causes of outcomes later in the life cycle are not sufficiently important empirically to need representation in the path diagram as *direct* influences. Thus, in the white population, occupation, education, and family head's occupation have statistically significant *direct* paths to income, while number of siblings and head's education do not. What is brought out by a path model (though it is not revealed in a conventional regression design), however, is that factors not directly influential may nevertheless have indirect influences on the dependent variable. Estimation of the indirect (or "compound") paths is accomplished by applications of the theorems of path analysis,[23] which will not be expounded here. The basic idea, however, is that of multiplication of the coefficients attached to connecting paths. For example, head's education influences respondent's income via respondent's education to the extent of $(.20)(.09) = .018$; via respond-

TABLE 4-2 . *Intercorrelations (Negro above Diagonal, White below Diagonal), Means and Standard Deviations of Stratification Variables, for Native Men 25-64 Years Old, with Nonfarm Background and in the Experienced Civilian Labor Force, by Race: March 1962.*

VARIABLE*	VARIABLE (IDENTIFIED IN STUB)						MEAN		S. D.	
	(6)	(5)	(4)	(3)	(2)	(1)	NEGRO	WHITE†	NEGRO	WHITE†
(6) Family head's education	...	.40	−.06	.36	.22	.14	6.9	8.6	3.4	3.7
(5) Family head's occupation	.51	...	−.11	.21	.12	.04	19.0	34.1	17.2	22.7
(4) Number of siblings	−.27	−.24	...	−.17	−.09	−.09	4.9	3.9	3.6	2.9
(3) Respondent's education	.39	.42	−.33	...	.41	.30	9.4	11.7	3.5	3.3
(2) Respondent's occupation, March 1962	.31	.37	−.25	.61	...	.27	19.7	43.5	16.9	24.6
(1) Respondent's income in 1961 ($1,000)	.17	.24	−.14	.31	.39	...	3.3	7.1	2.0	5.7

SOURCE: Unpublished OCG tabulations.

* Variables (6) and (3) measured in years of school completed; variables (5) and (2) measured on Duncan's scale of occupational socio-economic status.

† Includes negligible number of nonwhites other than Negroes.

ent's occupation, (.02) (.31) = .006; via respondent's education and occupation, (.20) (.53) (.31) = .033; and via number of siblings and respondent's occupation, (−.21) (−.04) (.31) = .003. The sum of these compound paths is .06. Reference to Table 4–2 indicates that the gross correlation of head's education and respondent's income amounts to .17. The difference, .17 − .06 = .11, is accounted for by the fact that head's education and head's occupation jointly influence respondent's income, but their respective contributions to this joint influence cannot be statistically separated.

The point of this arithmetical example is simply to indicate that influences of remote causes are largely indirect, but no less real on that account. A model of the type used here gives us a chance of quantifying the indirect influences of family background, while this cannot be accomplished with the usual type of cross-sectional survey and census data in which measurements of background factors are not available.

The second result to emphasize is that the estimated parameters of the model are rather different in the Negro and white populations. One reason for this is sampling variation: the Negro sample, secured as part of a national cross-section, is less than one-tenth as large as the white, so that rather small coefficients that would be statistically significant for whites are not so for Negroes. The more important reason, however, is that practically all the statistical relationships among the variables in this model are substantially weaker for Negroes than for whites. A glance at the two halves of Table 4–2 will reveal that this is true of the gross correlations as well as most of the (net) path coefficients in Figure 4–1 and the partial regression coefficients in Table 4–1. (In statistical parlance, all the variables in the model "interact" with race.)

One way of stating this finding may seem paradoxical: If, for example, the father's occupation was one of low status, this is less of a handicap for a Negro than for a white because the father's occupation makes less difference in, say, the respondent's income for Negroes than for whites. Can this be so when everyone "knows" that Negroes are handicapped by the low socio-economic levels of their families of origin? So they are; but the proposition applies to Negroes in the aggregate. What the correlations and regressions tell us is that the (relatively few) Negroes who do have favorable social origins cannot, as readily as whites, convert this advantage into occupational achievement and monetary returns thereto in the course of their own careers. The Negro family, in other words, is relatively less able than the white to pass on to the next generation any advantage that may accrue to substantial status achievement in the present generation. In one sense, stratification within the Negro population is less severe than in the white; the relatively "equalitarian" Negro structure is one that consists in a more or less equal sharing of low status and low levels of living. Those who have worried about whether American social structure is becoming too "rigid" may well ponder the question whether a little more "rigidity"—in the sense of a better developed intergenerational status transmission belt—might actually be to the advantage of the Negro population in the aggregate.

The nearest approximation to an exception to the above finding is that the intergenerational correlation of respondent's education with family head's education is very nearly as large in the Negro population as in the white. Negro families with better than average educational levels do, in general, succeed in "passing along" a comparable level of *educational* attainment to their children. But, again, the latter are less able than are white children to convert such attainment into occupational achievement and commensurate monetary returns to education.

The Negro handicap, therefore, as suggested elsewhere,[24] is a double handicap: First, the Negro begins the life cycle (typically) with characteristics that would be a disadvantage to anyone, white or Negro—specifically, in the present model, low levels of parental socioeconomic status. Second, achievements at subsequent stages of the life cycle, already lowered by the initial handicap, are further reduced when favorable circumstances (to the extent that they exist) cannot be capitalized on as readily.

One especially poignant illustration will perhaps suffice to give this situation the emphasis it deserves. Comparing the top and bottom diagrams in Figure 4–1, we see that the path coefficient from respondent's education to income is actually higher for Negroes than for whites: .21 versus .09. But the compound path, education→occupation→income, works out as $(.38) (.17) = .06$ for Negroes but $(.53)$ $(.31) = .16$ for whites. In addition, the common causes of education and income, lying back of these two variables in the model, work more powerfully for whites than for Negroes, so that in sum the gross correlation between education and income is about the same in the two populations. In terms of the magnitudes of the path coefficients, Negroes convert education into income, *holding constant occupation,* at a higher rate than whites; but whites have previously had better fortune in converting education into occupational status and occupational status into income. A lesson can be learned from all this, recalling that poverty programs, the civil rights movement, and the public relations arms of the Office of Education and Department of Labor have been saturating the media with messages to Negroes urging them to stay in school—"learn, baby, learn." What such agencies have failed to explain to Negroes is how to realize the "returns to education" that our students of "human capital" are so fond of estimating.

IMPLICATIONS OF THE MODEL

There is more to be learned from inspection of estimates of the kind discussed thus far, but to extract all their significant implications and present them verbally would be more than a little tedious. Hence, I have resolved not to dwell on the model per se any longer and, rather, to carry out one further statistical exercise whose results may be a little more accessible to the reader, whose fascination with coefficients may be somewhat less than my own. The purpose of the exercise is to represent in a rather arbitrary, but nonetheless meaningful, way the mechanisms by which the disadvantages of Negroes as measured at any one stage of the model life cycle are propagated and cumulated over subsequent stages. The arithmetic is carried out in such a fashion that both direct and indirect influences are taken into account.

Suppose that by any form of intervention whatever we could eliminate the Negro's handicap with respect to socio-economic level of the family of orientation (as represented in the model by head's education and occupation), but that disadvantages with respect to number of siblings, educational attainment, occupational achievement, and income returns, *insofar as they are not attributable directly or indirectly to Negro-white differentials in family background,* remain in effect. How much would such intervention accomplish? By how much would it reduce the gap? One meaningful answer is provided by row (*A*) of Table 4–3. This table shows that the gap amounts to 1.01 in number of siblings; eliminating the disadvantage of family background would reduce it to .47, or by .54. The gap in educational attainment is 2.3 years of school completed; eliminating background effects reduces it by 1.0, or by less than half. The gap in occupational achievement is 23.8 points on the occupational status scale used in this research; eliminating that part of it

TABLE 4-3 . Differences in Means between White (W) and Negro (N) with Respect to Number of Siblings, Educational Attainment, Occupational Status, and Income, with Components of Differences Generated by Cumulative Effects in a Model of the Socio-Economic Life Cycle, for Native Men, 25–64 Years Old, with Nonfarm Background and in the Experienced Civilian Labor Force: March 1962.

NUMBER OF SIBLINGS	YEARS OF SCHOOL COMPLETED	1962 OCCUPATION SCORE	1961 INCOME (DOLLARS)	COMPONENT *
(W) 3.85	(W) 11.7	(W) 43.5	(W) 7,070	
−.54	1.0	6.6	940	(A) [Family]
4.39	10.7	36.9	6,130	
−.47	0.1	0.6	70	(B) [Siblings]
(N) 4.86	10.6	36.3	6,060	
	1.2	4.8	520	(C) [Education]
	(N) 9.4	31.5	5,540	
		11.8	830	(D) [Occupation]
		(N) 19.7	4,710	
			1,430	(E) [Income]
			(N) 3,280	
−1.01	2.3	23.8	3,790	(T) [Total]

* Difference due to:
(A) Socio-economic level of family of origin (head's education and occupation).
(B) Number of siblings, net of family origin level.
(C) Education, net of siblings and family origin level.
(D) Occupation, net of education, siblings, and family origin level.
(E) Income, net of occupation, education, siblings, and family origin level.
(T) Total difference, (W) minus (N) = sum of components (A) through (E).

due to family background reduces it by 6.6 points, or just over one-quarter. The income gap is $3,790; family background differentials account for just one-quarter of this amount, or $940.

Assuredly, it would be worthwhile if the effects of disadvantageous social origins could be remedied to this degree. But if the remaining aspects of the structure operating to the disadvantage of the Negro were left intact, only the lesser part of the gaps in education, occupational status, and income would be bridged.

Let us proceed. For Negroes as for whites, having a large number of siblings is a handicap with respect to future achievement. Suppose that by family-planning programs, or whatever, we were able to reduce Negro family size to the extent that Negro and white families whose heads are comparable with respect to education and occupational status contained the same number of children. Such an intervention, accomplished hypothetically here by arithmetic, would reduce the educational gap by 0.1 year of school, the occupational gap by 0.6 point on the status scale, and income by $70 per annum. Even these small magnitudes are not wholly trivial, though we can hardly say whether they would be worth the cost, not knowing what the cost might be. But surely it is clear that to remedy the disadvantage of Negroes with respect to family size, except as that disadvantage grows out of their lower socio-economic levels, would not be of any great comparative benefit to the race.

The next step is to consider the hypothetical consequences of eliminating educational differences between Negro and white, except as these are produced by differences in family background and size. The previous calculation has shown that the educational difference to be eliminated amounts to 1.2 years—that part of the initial gap not accounted for by prior variables in the model. Carried over into occupational achievement, the net educational gap accounts for 4.8 points out of the 23.8 points difference between average Negro and white scores, or somewhat more than one-fifth. Translated into monetary terms, it accounts for $520 of the $3,790 difference actually observed, less than one-seventh thereof.

At this stage, our calculations have accounted for 12.0 of the 23.8-point occupational gap, thus attributing roughly half of it to educational differences, family size, and family background. The remaining 11.8 points, not otherwise "explained" by the model, one is tempted to label "occupational discrimination." It is due, literally, to the fact that Negroes equally well educated as whites (in terms of years of schooling) and originating in families of comparable size and socio-economic level do not have access to employment of equal occupational status. This disadvantage—or form of discrimination, if you will—carries over into dollar amounts of income to the extent of $830, rather more than one-fifth of the total dollar gap.

Finally, although we have attributed $830 of the Negro-white income difference to occupational discrimination, $520 to educational discrimination, $70 to net handicaps due to number of siblings, and $940 to differences in socio-economic origins, there remains the sum of $1,430 not yet accounted for. This is about three-eighths of the total gap of $3,790. Unless and until we can find other explanations for it, this must stand as an estimate of income discrimination (or of the increase in Negro income that would result from an elimination of such discrimination). Specifically, it is the difference between Negro and white incomes that cannot be attributed to differential occupational levels, differential educational attainment (for reasons given below, I do not accept the notion that allowance for "quality of education" would drastically revise the estimate), differences in size of family of origin, or differences in the socio-economic status thereof.

Handicaps have effects in producing Negro-white differences at each stage of the life cycle. Handicaps at one stage are transmitted to subsequent stages and reflected in differences there as well. In addition, at each stage, there are further substantial gaps not explained by the cumulation of prior handicaps but specific to the way the structure works at the stage itself. Thus do the model and hypothetical calculations derived from it reveal the full measure of consequences flowing from the "inheritance of race." They are far more drastic than those stemming merely from inheritance of poverty in any legitimate sense of the term. Yet, the estimates of these consequences given here are, if anything, too low. This will be apparent from the explanation, now to be given, of their derivation.

The exercise whose results have just been reviewed takes as a magnitude to be explained the "gap" between Negro and white averages on each of the variables represented as outcomes in the model of the socio-economic cycle. No doubt the nature and order of magnitude of such gaps are familiar, for information about them is widely available and commonly cited in assessments of the status and progress of the Negro minority in American society. What is accomplished by arithmetical calculations derived from the model is to break down each gap into the components that may be identified with the operation of each successive factor in the model. Operationally, the procedure is as follows, taking the income gap as an illustration. First, for the white population, compute the regression of income on family head's education and occupation (the two predetermined variables) only. Having computed the regression coefficients, substitute the Negro means on the independent variables into the regression equation for whites. This yields a calculated value of $6,130, shown as the second figure in the income column of Table 4–3. In effect, the question answered by this calculation is this: Suppose a selected group of white men had family background scores equal to the average scores for all Negroes, what would be our best estimate of their income? The calculation assumes that the remaining variables in the model operate in the fashion observed for whites.

The second calculation utilizes the white regression of income on the two family background measures and number of siblings; Negro means on these three variables are substituted into the white regression equation to produce the estimate of $6,060 shown as the third figure in the income column. The third calculation takes the white regression of income on family background, number of siblings, and years of school completed as the estimating equation, substituting the four Negro means into the equation to derive the estimate of $5,540 shown as the fourth entry in the income column. Finally, income of whites is regressed on family background scores, number of siblings, years of school completed, and 1962 occupation score. The coefficients thus obtained, when combined with the Negro means on all these variables, imply an estimate of $4,710 as shown in the fifth row of the income column. The final entry in that column is $3,280, the mean Negro income actually observed. The differences between these successive estimates have previously been discussed as components of the Negro-white income gap or as hypothetical consequences of eliminating specified forms of handicap.

Alternative estimates of these components could have been obtained, for example, by substituting white means into regressions computed for Negroes. These would have been, in general, different from the estimates shown here, reflecting a different interpretation of the notion of successively eliminating handicaps. The present calculation actually assumes that these handicaps are eliminated in two senses: First, Negro and white means on independent variables are equalized; second, the effects of the variables treated as independent are taken to be the same—contrary to the observation made earlier that Negroes actually are not as successful as whites in converting status or achievement at one stage into returns at the next. It follows, therefore, that the hypothetical calculations are to be taken to represent what would happen only if the Negro were allowed to play the same game as whites in addition to receiving a "handicap score" bonus to compensate for the effects of impediments to achievement in past generations. The estimates exhibited here are based on the hypothesis that both types of handicap are eliminated.

The model can tell us little or nothing about how this is to be done, and I believe the only honest answer one could give to the question of how to intervene is this: We must make the best guess we can, proceed accordingly, and try to estimate what difference it makes. The model does say something about what the possible returns to intervention might be, if accomplished in the fashion assumed, and thus affords some guidance as to where intervention may be most desperately needed. Thus, I suggest that for all their merit on various other grounds, family planning programs, per se, do not stand much chance of reducing socio-economic gaps between Negro and white. (Of course, it may always be urged that there are "spin-off" and "side" effects of such programs not taken into account in the model; obviously, the model cannot be used to disprove such a contention, but it would be illuminating to see a model that incorporated actual estimates of such effects. My calculation does not address the question of how many fewer Negroes would be "in poverty" if some of them had not been born, but that of what the impact of family size is on those who are born.)

One other kind of conclusion from this exercise has important implications. We have seen that the effect of family background per se, while substantial, is not large enough to explain the greater part of the Negro-white gap in income, occupational status, or educational attainment. Inheritance of poverty is of lesser consequence in the whole picture of such gaps than the aggregate of all the forms of discrimination depicted by the model—bearing in mind that the model allows fully for the indirect as well as the direct effects of differentials in family background. But if there were remedies for all these forms of discrimination, so that only the handicap of family background remained, that handicap would be materially diminished in the next generation. It would be further attenuated in successive generations under these ideal conditions, and while some persisting differential in achievement due solely to initial background handicaps would be observed for several decades, it would tend to disappear of its own accord. (There is much misunderstanding of this point on the part of analysts who have not studied Markov chains, and it would take too long a digression to explain how they are misled. The deduction stated here is, nonetheless, correct on the assumptions that have been stated.) [25] In other words, if we could eliminate the inheritance of race, in the sense of the exposure to discrimination experienced by Negroes, the inheritance of poverty in this group would take care of itself. This conclusion is "optimistic" only if one is optimistic enough to believe that we will shortly learn how to eliminate discrimination!

TINKERING WITH THE MODEL

Specialists in model construction will easily bring to mind various ways in which the present model might be altered so as to develop more interesting estimates or more cogent inferences. Analysts not so engrossed in the technicalities of model construction are likely to fix on one particular type of defect as apparently most in need of rectification: the omission of crucial variables. Since the list of candidate variables is unlimited, constructive suggestions cannot all be anticipated. Certain classes of variables, however, can be discussed in a general way in advance of the potential criticism.

It can reasonably be objected that the measurements on family background do not suffice to represent all the factors that may be implicated in the inheritance of poverty or in assaying the specific handicaps of Negroes. Actually, some considerable amount of work has been done with the earlier version of the present model to evaluate the relevance of selected additional variables and to conjecture the impact of including still others.[26] In one particular exercise, for example, the roster of family-background measures was enlarged to include the classification of families as intact or broken.[27] The estimates indicated that this factor was not a major source of variance in educational attainment (which was the only dependent variable there considered) and that estimates for the remaining measures were not greatly affected when this one was included. A general point is that inclusion of additional measures of family socio-economic status would not be expected to increase greatly the estimated impact of family background on status achievement, even though it clearly would be desirable to have at one's disposal a good measure of family income or level of living. Such a measure is not now available in a form suited to inclusion in an extended version of the present model.

There is every reason to believe, however, that the two socio-economic measures now included effectively represent most of the variance that could be attributed to such additional measures of family socio-economic levels, in view of the moderately high intercorrelation of such variables. Hence, it is not likely that the present version of the model substantially underestimates the impact of family background or substantially understates the degree of inheritance of poverty.

The discussion of race differentials in educational attainment and the consequences thereof for occupational achievement and income has been plagued by the assumption that years of schooling is an especially fallible measure of actual educational attainment for racial comparisons because of gross differences in so-called quality of schooling. On this assumption, improvement in a model of socio-economic achievement would be effected by substituting for years of schooling some index of attainment incorporating a correction for the discrepancy in quality. While the argument is attractive, it is easy to exaggerate its force. For one thing, inferior quality at any one level of the school system is likely to result in impaired chances of proceeding to the next level. Hence, school years completed has partly built into it a correlation with quality. Second, the Survey of Equality of Educational Opportunity [28] disclosed that a wide variety of more or less objective measures of school quality did not vary by race as much as most analysts had hitherto assumed. Third, there are suggestions that quality of schooling be represented by some index derived from standardized achievement tests and that such an index be substituted for years of schooling as the measure of educational attainment. It should be recognized that this would amount to a redefinition of the problem. As the present model stands—and it shares this characteristic with a great deal of related research—educational attainment really represents the respondent's investment in education, in terms of the number of years spent attending school, adjusted to the extent that a year of attendance is counted only if it results in completion of a grade. The interest in estimates from a model or in other analyses of consequences of educational attainment is then in the return to this investment, however "return" is measured. A pure index of intellectual attainment, on the other hand, would be considered as representing the factor of skill or qualifications for employment, insofar as these are academic in character. In practice, however, so-called achievement tests do not measure anything greatly different from what is ascertained by tests of general mental ability. The emphasis on quality of schooling, therefore, can be read as a proposal to supplement years of schooling with measures of mental ability in models seeking to account for variation in socio-economic achievement.

As it happens, further work with the type of model treated above has been carried out with the explicit aim of elucidating the role of mental ability in the process of status achievement. Properties and assumptions of the extended model have been discussed elsewhere [29] and will not be recapitulated here. Suffice it to say that estimates are available for a model that treats income, occupational status, and education as depending on mental test scores as well as on number of siblings and the two measures of family background. Unfortunately, these estimates pertain to a somewhat different population than that under study in the earlier part of this chapter, so that strict comparisons between the two versions of the model are not warranted. The presentation here will be confined to a tabulation of the estimates of components of Negro-white gaps, calculated in the fashion already described, inserting mental ability score into the sequence of variables following number of siblings and preceding educational attainment. The estimates are shown in Table 4–4. The reader is warned that these estimates, although they derive from what is taken to be a superior model from a conceptual standpoint, are not on quite as secure a statistical footing as those presented earlier. A variety of somewhat risky assumptions had to be made to secure the estimates, and it was necessary to combine information from several different sources that were by no means fully comparable. The tedious details are presented in the paper describing the model.

Only one such detail will be stressed at this time. This is the matter of estimating the Negro-white gap in mental test scores. Two important bodies of evidence from large-scale enterprises in data collection are relevant. (1) The previously mentioned Survey of Equality of Educational Opportunity provides mean scores by race for students in grades 1, 3, 6, 9, and 12.[30] The typical result, stated approximately, is that Negro children obtained an average score one standard deviation below the mean for white children. (2) National data from the Selective Service System have been put into a convenient form by Karpinos.[31] My calculation from his tables shows that if the score distributions are transformed to an arbitrary scale with a mean of 50 and a standard deviation of 10, white registrants have an average score of 51.2 and Negro registrants an average of 40.6. There is close agreement between the two sources. In preparing the esti-

TABLE 4-4. *Differences in Means between White (W) and Negro (N) with Respect to Number of Siblings, Mental Ability Score, Educational Attainment, Occupational Status, and Earnings, with Components of Differences Generated by Cumulative Effects in a Model of the Socio-Economic Life Cycle, for Men 25–34 Years Old: 1964*

	Number of Siblings	Mental Ability Score	Years of School Completed	1964 Occupation Score	1964 Earnings (Dollars)	Component*
	(W) 3.77	(W) 51.0	(W) 12.1	(W) 40.6	(W) 6,730	
	−.58	1.9	1.0	6.5	560	(A) [Family]
	4.35	49.1	11.1	34.1	6,170	
	−.94	0.5	0.2	1.3	100	(B) [Siblings]
	(N) 5.29	48.6	10.9	32.8	6,070	
		7.6	0.9	5.5	650	(C) [Mental Ability]
		(N) 41.0	10.0	27.3	5,420	
			0.2	0.9	70	(D) [Education]
			(N) 9.8	26.4	5,350	
				8.7	350	(E) [Occupation]
				(N) 17.7	5,000	
					1,200–1,400	(F) [Earnings]
					(N) 3,600–3,800	
	−1.52	10.0	2.3	22.9	2,930–3,130	(T) [Total]

SOURCE: Computed from regressions derived in Duncan, "Ability and Achievement," *op. cit.*

* Difference due to:

(A) Socio-economic level of family of origin (head's education and occupation).
(B) Number of siblings, net of family origin level.
(C) Mental ability, net of siblings and family-origin level.
(D) Education, net of mental ability, siblings, and family-origin level.
(E) Occupation, net of education, mental ability, siblings, and family-origin level.
(F) Earnings, net of occupation, education, mental ability, siblings, and family-origin level. [1964 mean earnings for Negro men is conjectured since there is no information available that is strictly comparable with figure for whites. Uncertainty with respect to component (F), however, does not affect estimates of preceding components.]
(T) Total difference, (W) minus (N) = sum of components (A) through (F).

mates recorded in Table 4–4, it was arbitrarily assumed that the mean scores of white and Negro men differ by exactly one standard deviation.

In a rough and qualitative sense, the estimates in Table 4–4 tend to support those offered earlier, apart from discrepancies to be expected because of differences in the specification of the populations. There are, however, some significant alterations in the inferences to be drawn that center on the consequences of including mental ability in the model. Comments will be confined to these.

In the second column, it can be seen that about one-quarter of the gap in mental ability scores is attributed to Negro-white differences in family socio-economic level and number of children. The remaining three-quarters of the gap (7.6 points on the scale being used) must be attributed to other factors, which can perhaps be summed up as "differential mental development." The model sheds no light on the causes of this differential. It has, of course, been subject to much discussion, not to say controversy. A review of the factors that have been suggested as causes is given by Pettigrew.[32] In common with most social and behavioral scientists, he contends that the explanation must lie in environmental variables, broadly construed, rather than in genetic differences between the so-called races. I share this opinion, not so much because the environmental factors adduced in such discussion are entirely plausible, but because the correct argument from genetic theory does *not* lead to the conclusion that such genetic differences are probable. Among the best of the discussions of the point at issue is that by Eckland,[33] who contributes a further illuminating point: While there is good reason to believe that part of the social-class variation in measured intelligence has a genetic basis, acceptance of this proposition does not require one to accept a similar argument with respect to racial variation.

However all this may be, the results arrayed in Table 4–4 suggest that the difference in measured or realized mental ability has important consequences. In the third column, we see that inclusion of the mental ability variable in the model allows us to come close to a complete explanation of the gap in years of school completed. Of the total gap of 2.3 years, 1.2 years are accounted for by the combination of family background and number of siblings; an additional 0.9 year by mental ability; and only 0.2 year by unspecified causes.

As a consequence of this result, most of the education component of occupational and income gaps that showed up in Table 4–3 appears in Table 4–4 as part of the mental ability component. Net of family background and size, mental ability accounts for 5.5 of the 22.9 points gap between Negro and white occupational-status scores, but education only 0.9 point. Similarly, $650 of the roughly $3,000 income gap is attributed to mental ability, but only $70 to education.

Although the introduction of mental ability into the model allows us almost fully to account for the education gap—in the sense of tracing it back to specified causal factors—the same is not true with regard to occupation and earnings. Of the 22.9 points gap in occupational-status scores, 8.7 points remain to be explained, or can be attributed, if one likes, to occupational "discrimination," specifically. Such discrimination carries over into an income differential of $350. But even the combination of occupation, education, mental ability, number of siblings, and family background leaves $1,200 to $1,400, as nearly as can be guessed, to be accounted for by other factors. Note that the "quality-of-schooling" argument has effectively been met and we are still unable, conceptually, to close the gap in incomes, except by reference to some putative mechanism of income discrimination. At least one-third of the income gap arises because Negro and white men in the same line of work, with the same amount of formal schooling, with equal ability, from families of the same size and same socio-economic level, simply do not draw the same wages and salaries. This $1,200, analogous to what Paul Siegel has called the "cost of being a Negro,"[34] is in no meaningful sense a consequence of the inheritance of poverty.

CONCLUSION

It is true, of course, that in American society one is well advised to "pick his parents" so that he begins life on a favorable socio-economic level. But the models exhibited here fully support Gallaway's conclusion that this strategy is not nearly so important as previous doctrine would seemingly have us believe. It is, however, of vital importance to choose parents of the "right" skin color if one wants to avoid a high risk of ending up at a low level on the income scale. *In general,* the supposition that the "poor are poor because they are poor" is not only an intellectual obfuscation, but also a feeble guide to policy in what is obviously the most desperate and refractory sector of the "poverty problem," that is, the "race problem."

I have no doubt that the instigators of the War on Poverty thought that it could be planned in such a way as to remedy the gross discrepancies in achievement and rewards between the races. But this just does not happen as a benign fallout from conventional measures taken to enhance "opportunity." Until we summon up the courage to distinguish between the problems of poverty and the problems of race, we shall have to reckon with the consequences of our lack of candor.

Notes

1. Michael Harrington, *The Other America: Poverty in the United States* (Baltimore: Penguin, 1963), p. 21.
2. *1964 Economic Report of the President* (Washington, D.C.: Government Printing Office, 1964), pp. 69–70.
3. *The War on Poverty*, Committee Print, Select Subcommittee on Poverty of the Committee on Labor and Public Welfare, United States Senate (Washington, D.C.: Government Printing Office, 1964), p. 35.
4. *Ibid.*, p. 2.
5. News Release, Office of Assistant Secretary of Defense (Public Affairs), Address by Robert S. McNamara, Secretary of Defense, before the Veterans of Foreign Wars, New York City, August 23, 1966, p. 3.
6. James N. Morgan, Martin H. David, Wilbur J. Cohen, and Harvey E. Brazer, *Income and Welfare in the United States* (New York: McGraw-Hill, 1962), p. 210.
7. Wilbur J. Cohen and Eugenia Sullivan, "Poverty in the United States," *Health, Education, and Welfare Indicators* (February 1964), p. xiv.
8. U.S. Bureau of the Census, "Lifetime Occupational Mobility of Adult Males, March 1962," *Current Population Reports*, Series P-23, No. 11 (May 12, 1964).
9. Lowell E. Gallaway, "On the Importance of 'Picking One's Parents,'" *Quarterly Review of Economics and Business*, VI, No. 2 (Summer 1966), 7.
10. Daniel P. Moynihan, "What is 'Community Action'?," *The Public Interest*, No. 5 (Fall 1966), 8.
11. *Ibid.*
12. Harrington, *op. cit.*, p. 157.
13. Alvin L. Schorr, *Poor Kids* (New York: Basic Books, 1966), p. 46.
14. *Ibid.*
15. *Ibid.*
16. *Ibid.*, p. 31.
17. *Ibid.*, p. 35.
18. Peter M. Blau and Otis Dudley Duncan, *The American Occupational Structure* (New York: Wiley, 1967); George Katona et al., *1961 Survey of Consumer Finances*, Monograph No. 24, Survey Research Center (Ann Arbor: University of Michigan, 1962), Chapter 5.
19. Schorr, *op. cit.*, p. 31.
20. Otis Dudley Duncan, "Discrimination Against Negroes," *Annals of the American Academy of Political and Social Science*, CCCLXXI (May 1967), 85–103.
21. Blau and Duncan, *op. cit.*
22. *Ibid.*
23. Otis Dudley Duncan, "Path Analysis: Sociological Examples," *American Journal of Sociology*, LXXII (July 1966), 1–16.
24. Duncan, "Discrimination Against Negroes," *op. cit.*

25. See Stanley Lieberson and Glenn V. Fuguitt, "Negro-White Occupational Differences in the Absence of Discrimination," *American Journal of Sociology,* LXXIII (September 1967), 188–200.

26. Blau and Duncan, *op. cit.*

27. Duncan, "Discrimination Against Negroes," *op. cit.*

28. James S. Coleman et al., *Equality of Educational Opportunity* (Washington, D.C.: Government Printing Office, 1966).

29. Otis Dudley Duncan, "Ability and Achievement," *Eugenics Quarterly,* XV (March 1968), 1–11.

30. Coleman, *op. cit.,* pp. 221–251.

31. Bernard D. Karpinos, "The Mental Qualification of American Youths for Military Service and Its Relationship to Educational Attainment," *1966 Social Statistics Section, Proceedings of the American Statistical Association,* Table 5.

32. Thomas F. Pettigrew, *A Profile of the Negro American* (Princeton, N.J.: Van Nostrand, 1964), Chapter 5.

33. Bruce K. Eckland, "Genetics and Sociology: A Reconsideration," *American Sociological Review,* XXXII (April 1967), 173–194.

34. Paul M. Siegel, "On the Cost of Being a Negro," *Sociological Inquiry,* XXXV (Winter 1965), 41–57.

☙ *Deprivation and Migration: Dilemmas of Causal Interpretation* MARC FRIED

INTRODUCTION

It has often been noted that there is a relationship between deprivation and, particularly, poverty and migration. Relatively few studies
have sought to examine or to clarify this relationship, nor has the
theme attracted great interest and attention. Historical studies of the
vast migrations that peopled the American continent have pointed
up, in a fairly general way, the great impetus to migration created by
famine and disaster or, conversely, by available land and economic
expansion. Many studies have also observed the unfortunate economic and social position of the newcomer to urban, industrial
societies. And a few economic and demographic studies have attempted to trace a bit more closely the relationship between expulsive forces in countries of origin and attractive forces in countries
of destination. Beyond these studies, which themselves offer a sad
commentary on our meager knowledge and understanding, there are
only scattered and sparse references to the relationship between deprivation and migration.

The problem arises anew in the large migrations of Negroes
from the South over the past five decades. As a social problem, the
early migration of rural Negroes, largely trained to do only routine
agricultural field jobs and with virtually insuperable impediments to
retraining as an industrial labor force by virtue of their former con-

This chapter is based on a report to the Office of Economic Opportunity in partial
fulfillment of Contract Number B89–4279.

dition of servitude, arose even before the Emancipation Proclamation. No sooner had the northern armies entered the South than hordes of Negro slaves flocked to the army camps:

They came at night, when the flickering camp-fires shone like vast unsteady stars along the black horizon; old men and thin, with gray and tufted hair; women, with frightened eyes, dragging whimpering hungry children; men and girls, stalwart and gaunt—a horde of starving vagabonds, homeless, helpless, and pitiable, in their dark distress.[1]

As the northern armies overran vast territories in the South during the Civil War and even more with the abolition of slavery, a great many former slaves became themselves an army of uprooted. However, in actual numbers, only relatively few Negroes went North or West to settle in the growing urban areas. It was not until the beginning of the twentieth century that a generation of Negroes, born free and who had, therefore, to learn about the futility of either freedom or opportunity in the South, began to migrate in increasing numbers, first to southern cities and then into the North and Midwest. And it was not until the twentieth century, World War I, and the drastic limitation of foreign immigration that large numbers of Negro migrants from the South began to reach toward the newly developing, albeit limited, chances for jobs and for a dream of dignity in urban society.

Whether we concern ourselves with the European immigration of 1830–1920 or with the Negro migration of 1900 to the present, we must deal with and be guided by fragmentary facts and partial theories. The psychological and social history of migration is even more deeply hidden behind these few statistical facts, incomplete records, selected observations, and bits of theory. In an effort to put these into perspective, we shall examine some of the data on the European migration and then turn to a comparative consideration of the Negro migration from the South. In noting some of the similarities and differences, we may better understand some of the ways in which deprivation functions as both condition and consequence, subjective and objective, of massive population redistributions.

HISTORICAL BACKGROUND

Autobiographical reports of the experience of migration usually submerge the difficulties and tribulations of entering a new society within a sense of over-all success and achievement. But the host of studies that investigate a broader range of in-migrant populations document the enormous set of problems, pitfalls, and often tragedies associated with movement from one society to another.[2] The scattered evidence suggests that these difficulties and problems beset the migrant to any urban, industrial society and not merely those who came to the United States; and, further, that the process varies relatively little whether it involves internal migration from rural to urban areas or, as in the great European migrations of the nineteenth century, emigration from the rural areas of one country to the urban areas of another.[3]

Immigration, the process of geographical and social transition from one society to another, is, at best, a drastic experience of cultural change. It requires a shift from embeddedness in the familiar to a constant confrontation with newness and unfamiliarity. More often than not, it involves a global experience of being a stranger, an alien at the mercy of an inhospitable, incomprehensible, and uncomprehending foreign population. Even under the best of circumstances when the migrant from one city to another has a relatively clear anticipation of a job or of friends or of housing conditions, migration is a highly disruptive process. Nonetheless, it seems quite clear that the degree of change required in cultural orientations and in social relationships and patterns is one of the more critical dimensions distinguishing the potential ease or difficulty of adjustment to circumstances of migration. And almost certainly intercorrelated with this and of great relevance is the possibility of anticipating, either because of prior experience, prior arrangements, or economic resources, some of the main situations and roles one will encounter in work, in social relationships, and in housing and residence.

Although many lower-status immigrants from rural areas in foreign countries to cities in the United States had some prior contact with family or friends who had already migrated, they generally had little accurate information, little basis in past experience for anticipating, and few economic or social resources for coping with these changes. Similarly, among low-status Negroes in the United States, the initial and often many subsequent contacts with the city are major transitions for which there can be only minimal preparation. But in addition to the sense of alienation and estrangement, the lack of preparation or anticipation, and the absence of fundamental resources for coping with a new environment, the reaction of host societies is almost invariably one of antagonism based on class, ethnic, and cultural differences.

American nativism and its corollary antiforeignisms waxed and waned over the course of several centuries, but there were many

rumblings of discontent about the freedom of opportunity available
to foreigners quite early in American history. By the middle of the
nineteenth century, many Americans became fearful of the ruinous
effect of newcomers on their society.[4] After the Civil War, the great
territorial and industrial expansion led to a diminution in nativist
sentiment.[5] The material need for an expanding population was
great; the same national groups, predominantly German, English,
and Irish, continued to be the dominant immigrant forces. By the
late 1870s and 1880s, however, new patterns of nativism began their
opposition to the "new immigration" only to reach a peak during
and immediately following World War I.

Viewed as a large, historical phenomenon, nativist sentiment
with its strong source in opposition to foreign competition, foreign
ideology, and foreign culture may have undergone a slow and variable progression partly modified by the pervasive sense of the United
States as both haven and melting pot. Concretely, however, most
foreign groups that entered the United States in large numbers and
differed in striking ways from Americans were subjected to extreme
difficulties. For the English, this was mitigated by the fact that, unlike most other in-migrants, they came to fill relatively skilled jobs in
specific industries. Cultural similarities also facilitated a rapid
transition.[6] For the Germans and Scandinavians, the movement toward specific regions, generally of low-population density, permitted
them to follow a path that had already been prepared and, despite
low rates of assimilation, to experience little long-term antagonism.[7]
But whether the extremely low social position, the cultural and religious distinctiveness, the competitive economic situation, or some
larger change in the society as a whole was responsible for the difference, during the latter part of the nineteenth century and the early
part of the twentieth century, the Irish, Italians, Slavs, Jews, and
others who emigrated to the United States were subjected to brutal
experiences of isolation, exploitation, and exclusion.[8] The more recent experiences of Negroes, Puerto Ricans, and Mexican-Americans
follow a well-trodden path of discrimination and segregation in the
urban, industrial areas of the United States.

CONDITIONS OF OUT-MIGRATION

Massive migrations most often occur during intolerable conditions of
economic or social crisis. They are always associated with absolute or

relative dissatisfaction with the conditions of life or with the opportunities for adaptation that are available in the country of origin.[9] The situations of deprivation, oppression, and famine that formed a background for the great migrations of Irish, Jews, Poles, and Italians and, indeed, of English and Germans and, more recently, of southern Negroes, Puerto Ricans, and Mexicans need hardly be elaborated. Only situations as severe as these can begin to account for widespread uprooting by peasants and tenant farmers whose horizons were customarily limited by the spatial environment of a small region and by the social environment of kin and neighbors.

But while these are necessary conditions for an explanation, they are not sufficient to the task. The social and economic deprivations often associated with large migratory movements were severe, but they were largely exacerbations of endemic situations rather than wholly unfamiliar catastrophes. Indeed, the currents of migration from various European countries from the middle of the nineteenth century into the beginning of the twentieth century show relatively smooth annual trends of slow increase or slow decrease only occasionally interrupted by large, temporary swings (Table 5–1). A similar over-all continuity of migration from individual countries makes it

TABLE 5–1. *Recorded Number of Immigrants to the United States from Selected Countries, 1870–1914* * *(In Thousands)*

YEAR ENDING JUNE 30	GERMANY	ENGLAND	IRELAND	SWEDEN	ITALY	AUSTRIA-HUNGARY	RUSSIA	GREECE
1870	118	61	57	13	3	4	1	†
1871	83	57	57	11	3	5	1	†
1872	141	70	69	13	4	4	1	†
1873	150	75	77	14	9	7	2	†
1874	87	51	54	6	8	9	4	†
1875	48	40	38	6	4	8	8	†
1876	32	24	20	6	3	6	5	†
1877	29	19	15	5	3	5	7	†
1878	29	18	16	5	4	5	3	†
1879	35	24	20	11	6	6	4	†

SOURCE: From Harry Jerome, *Migration and Business Cycles* (New York: National Bureau of Economic Research, 1926) Publication No. 9.

* From reports of the U.S. Immigration Commission, *Statistical Review of Immigration: 1820–1910;* and the *Annual Report of the Commissioner General of Immigration*, 1924, pp. 115–117, U.S. Bureau of Immigration. Prior to 1906, persons entering the United States were recorded by country whence they came, thereafter by country of last permanent residence.

† Less than 500 recorded immigrants.

TABLE 5 – 1 . (continued)

YEAR ENDING JUNE 30	GER-MANY	ENGLAND	IRELAND	SWEDEN	ITALY	AUSTRIA-HUNGARY	RUSSIA	GREECE
1880	85	59	72	39	12	17	5	†
1881	210	65	72	50	15	28	5	†
1882	251	82	76	65	32	29	17	†
1883	195	63	81	38	32	28	10	†
1884	180	56	63	27	17	37	13	†
1885	124	47	52	22	14	27	17	†
1886	84	50	50	28	21	29	18	†
1887	107	73	68	43	48	40	31	†
1888	110	83	74	55	52	46	33	1
1889	100	69	66	35	25	34	34	†
1890	92	57	53	30	52	56	36	1
1891	114	54	56	37	76	71	47	1
1892	119	34	51	42	62	77	82	1
1893	79	28	44	36	72	57	42	1
1894	54	18	30	18	43	39	39	1
1895	32	23	46	15	35	33	36	1
1896	32	19	40	21	68	65	51	2
1897	23	10	28	13	59	33	26	1
1898	17	10	25	12	59	40	30	2
1899	17	10	32	13	77	62	61	2
1900	19	10	36	19	100	115	91	4
1901	22	12	31	23	136	113	85	6
1902	28	14	29	31	178	172	107	8
1903	40	26	35	46	231	206	136	14
1904	46	39	36	28	193	177	145	11
1905	41	65	53	27	221	276	185	11
1906	38	49	35	23	273	265	216	19
1907	38	57	35	21	286	338	259	37
1908	32	47	31	13	129	169	157	21
1909	26	33	25	14	183	170	120	14
1910	31	47	30	24	216	259	187	26
1911	32	52	29	21	183	159	159	26
1912	28	40	26	13	157	179	162	21
1913	34	43	28	17	266	255	291	23
1914	36	36	25	15	284	278	256	36

evident that cycles of prosperity or depression, at home or abroad, can only account for relatively small proportions of the total volume of migration from any given country. More general long-term trends and policies that affect a country, a region, or a population group over many decades are necessarily implicated in these patterns that characterize the emigration from a country and distinguish it from other countries.

Ordinarily, people are reluctant to move and most reluctant to leave one society, culture, or area for another. This is ever so much more the case among pre-industrial people who are bound to long traditions and surrounded by kin and kind. Scattered reports from all over the world indicate that this holds even when the move involves departure from inadequate housing to new developments with many more conveniences only a short distance away in the same country. The data from bombed-out cities in World War II, from the reluctant departure of German Jews and Germans who were potential targets of Nazi aggression, and from the reaction of residents of planned relocation in this country and abroad further document the intense and widespread resistance to leaving home.[10] Even the vast migrations from Europe in the nineteenth and twentieth centuries appear often to have been conceived, initially, as temporary or seasonal migrations, and with a few notable exceptions, return emigration was extremely high.[11] Indeed, these vast migrations seem greater by far when the diverse streams of migration are totaled and considered as a contribution to the labor force of the United States than they do when seen as a proportion of the population from the country of origin. Taken as a proportion of population in the country of origin, the largest migration of all, that from Ireland during and immediately following the Great Famine, never rose above 3 per cent during any one year and only rarely reached this level.[12] And no other migration movement ever approached the proportions of the Irish migration during these years.

Thus, whatever the long-run effects of large-scale migration on the population in the country of origin, and no matter how severe the expulsive forces or how seductive the attractive forces, only an extremely small minority of the population in any country is willing or able to leave during any period of time. Any effort to explain large-scale migration must keep this in perspective. On the other hand, even such relatively minor rates of departure, extended over time and selected from particular regions and particular occupational and class groups, can have a considerable impact on the residual population. This is of great significance in view of population pressure as a determinant of migration. Brinley Thomas presents evidence that the single most consistent factor behind the major upswings of European migration during the nineteenth century was the cyclical increase in birth rates.[13] This appears to have been an important factor even in Ireland, which sustained an increase in population from 4,389,000 in 1788 to 8,175,000 in 1841, an increase that greatly exacerbated the severity of endemic and epidemic famines. The European population explosion led to an increasingly dangerous subdivision of small holdings that, for the peasantry of Europe, were initially barely sufficient for families of moderate size. Virtually every study of the peasantries of Europe or of emigration from European countries attributes primary responsibility for large-scale migration to these interrelated factors.[14] A similar set of phenomena appears important in explaining internal labor migrations of Italians and Poles; the large migrations of Puerto Ricans to the United States during the period from 1947 to 1960; the migration of Mexicans to the Southwest; the internal migration of Negroes from the South; and the internal migrations from the Appalachian regions to the Midwest.[15]

Population pressure and the incapacity of small land-holdings to sustain a larger population thus appear to be highly general in explaining the powerful expulsive forces that encouraged migration. And most of the large migrations consisted mainly of agricultural populations or of laborers from rural regions. At the same time, technical innovations and developments that make possible expanding employment may also displace skilled craftsmen who become potential sources of another stream of international migration. This appears to have been the case during the latter part of the nineteenth century in England when an increasing proportion of skilled laborers migrated from England to the less-developed industries of the United States where their knowledge was eagerly sought.[16] Moreover, a host of changes in agriculture itself has often led to the displacement of agricultural labor as in Germany and England. Day's analysis of United States data reveals that the vast rural-to-urban migration of the last few decades is directly associated with changes in agricultural technology, the use of fertilizer, and changes in crops farmed, all of which reduced drastically the labor requirements on farms in this country.[17]

These bare, but complex, facts provide only a rudimentary record of the source of large migrations in serious deprivation. The historical accounts capture more vividly the abject misery created by these events that culminated in the great migrations. Handlin creates an important image in his conception of the uprooted departing from their homelands all over Europe.[18] The unbelievable tragedy

of the Irish famines has been reported often enough to be patheti-
cally believable. Similar, if not quite as severe, situations obtained
both earlier and later in much of Europe. Hansen reports a relatively
early event in the migration from Germany in which the demand for
berths was so great that fares were boosted beyond the reasonable
hope of the bewildered families who had come to Amsterdam and
Rotterdam with barely enough money for minimal transportation.[19]
And Balch, describing the situation in Eastern Europe, points to the
strains as the outcome of a long history with its most immediate
antecedents in the demise of feudalism without adequate resources to
sustain an effective peasant economy.[20]

Although poverty, misery, debt, disappearing land, and expanding population stalked the peasantry of England, Ireland, Germany,
Poland, Italy, and Sweden and must be held to account for the gross
trend of out-migration, it is noteworthy that those selective factors
that clearly operated gave precedence to the able-bodied, the effective, those who could afford the costs of passage. While the evidence
for the superiority of the migrants in the European migrations leaves
much to be desired, it is widely accepted by the historians of the
European migrations. Balch reports that those districts in direst and
most settled poverty were not the major sources of emigration.[21]
Foerster reports a similar factor in the distribution of emigration
from southern Italy.[22] Walker describes the German emigration as
predominantly one of the lower-middle classes and of rural craftsmen.[23] And the data from Britain suggest that, despite strong encouragement to migrate, the paupers were highly resistant to such
moves, but that the skilled laborer, displaced by machinery, eagerly
went to the United States.[24] These views are given greater credence
by the more systematic, although fragmentary, data from the United
States that indicate the educational superiority of those individuals
who migrate compared to the persons who remain in their home
communities.[25]

Thus, deprivation provides a background, but not a specific explanation, for the great migrations from Europe. Waves of migration
from different European countries rose with increases in population
and with technical innovations or changes in crop patterns that made
men redundant or superfluous.[26] Superimposed upon these long-term
patterns, severe crises, famines, and intensified oppression created
great, if short-lived, peaks of emigration representing the direct consequences of deprivation. Withal, the strains, difficulties, and demands of migration were sufficiently great, the process sufficiently

precarious, that mainly those who could pay for passage, who could willingly look forward to back-breaking labor for the sake of better economic circumstances, who could anticipate the strain without excessive fear appear to have predominated in the migrations. It is certainly reasonable to conjecture that these were also the people most alienated from a rigidly unchanging society or most responsive to the rumors and reports of job opportunities abroad. In this respect, the selective factors involved in migration may provide a fundamental link between the conception of mass migration as a product of expulsive forces and the alternate conception of mass migration as a result of attractive forces.

Whether such selection is the essential link or not, it is important both to distinguish and to relate the several factors associated with mass migrations. The causes of migration have too often been distorted by a simplistic effort to distinguish the relative effects of "push" and "pull." But a model that views "pushes" and "pulls" as an opposition between two distinct and competing forces or a procedure that uses only data from a society or area of origin or only data from a society or area of destination is inadequate for clarifying the operation of a complex, interacting system of forces. One set of these variables may account for large-scale out-migration from a particular country or region, and a different set of factors may account for the choice of destination or the timing of migration. At the very least, it is essential to consider, for any instance of mass migration, both the expulsive and attractive forces that affect large-scale population redistribution.

CONDITIONS OF IN-MIGRATION

Looked at from the vantage point of the country of origin, the pressures of deprivation appear to be the most potent expulsive forces accounting for mass population movements. Looked at from the vantage point of the host country, the pressures of opportunity appear to be potent attractive forces that account for mass population movements.

The classic investigation of the relationship between these forces in the European immigration is the study by Harry Jerome.[27] Data for the earlier half of the century do not permit statistical analysis. Some of these earlier as well as later migration streams were markedly influenced by the availability of land and by land policies in the

United States.[28] More generally, for those periods after the Civil War in which the economic data are more adequate, the peaks and troughs of economic indicators are accompanied by rises and falls in immigration. However, while the cyclical patterns of employment and immigration were similar, the sheer volume of migration remained high through prosperity and depression and corresponded less closely to the level of employment. These patterns held not only for European immigration as a whole but also for each of the separate, large migration streams from different European countries.

Supportive evidence for the conclusion that migration is influenced by employment opportunities in the place of destination can be found in studies of internal migration within the United States. In the temporal series of interrelationships between migration and economic opportunity for the period from 1880 to 1940, Dorothy Thomas finds striking differences in migration between prosperous and depressed decades.[29] Analyzing regional displacements within the United States, she finds a trend toward higher rates of net migration among those areas of the country that have higher income levels. Lowry's analysis of migration between metropolitan areas in the United States for the period from 1955 to 1960 also provides support for the importance of economic opportunities in the place of destination.[30] Thus, just as the data from places of origin point to the importance of deprivation and expulsive forces, so do the data based on places of destination support the significance of opportunity and attractive forces in encouraging migration.[31] It is only the larger generalizations about this process that take account of the interactive nature of the process. Thus, as Vance points out, migration proceeds (a) from lower to higher per capita income areas, (b) from extractive to industrialized economies, and (c) from areas of high natural increase of population to those of low natural increase.[32] The process of migration can only be conceived, in this light, as a shift of population from conditions of disadvantage and restriction to those of relatively greater advantage and potentiality.

Migration is, of course, a continuous process through history. Mass migrations represent only one important form of population redistribution. The most intensive efforts to restrict migratory movement, exemplified in the limitation of the serf or slave to a particular plot of land or a particular master, have never served entirely to eliminate geographical and job mobility. Whether the same factors operate in accounting for the endemic process of geographical migration as those that account for mass migration is unclear. As we have indicated, even mass migrations are highly selective and represent the movement of only a minority of the population from any place. As Eisenstadt points out, the very choice of migration as a potential mass movement is itself bound up with particular social and economic settings in which the rise of autonomous economic motivation, strivings for achievement, aspirations for liberalism and universalistic orientations, and the demise of group life and community embeddedness are moderately widespread.[33] But the selective decision to migrate, whether individually or as part of a massive movement, must still be based on similar orientations and motivations impelled by the contrast between existing deprivations, expectable risks, and anticipated opportunities. And the weight of evidence suggests that the more massive migrations are more heavily influenced by deprivations at the point of origin that disrupt the entire fabric of life or of the very means of living of the vast proportion of low-status people in a country or area. It is hardly a surprising consequence that there appears to be a close association between the massiveness of emigration, the severity of deprivation and disruption, and the low-status composition of the migration stream.

Certainly, the vast majority of the immigrants to the United States during the nineteenth and twentieth centuries were relatively uneducated people from rural areas: farmers, farm laborers, unskilled or semiskilled workers, and rural or semirural craftsmen.[34] The United Kingdom, of course, provided a larger proportion of skilled workers than any other region of the world; they were also distinguished by their specific occupational interest, by the eagerness with which their services were sought, and by their continuity in occupations they had held before emigrating.[35] Between 1875 and 1910, more than half the immigrants from Wales and Scotland were listed as skilled laborers and nearly as high a proportion from England. By contrast, throughout this same period, immigrants from Ireland were preponderantly common laborers or servants and rarely numbered as many as 10 per cent skilled laborers.[36] The data for Italian immigrants suggest a picture similar to that for the Irish, with agricultural labor substituting for the servant category. The German migration seemed to draw more heavily on farmers and rural craftsmen, but nonetheless included predominantly the higher categories of low-status workers.[37]

Although there have been no thorough studies, at least in English, of the occupational histories of migrants compared to nonmigrants, there is a general consensus that low-status newcomers to an area suffer serious disadvantages compared to natives of similar status.[38] These disadvantages occur through entering the lowest-status jobs and through a high degree of job insecurity. Thus, migrants have higher levels of unemployment and among the lowest incomes in urban areas. While there almost certainly are large differences depending on educational level, urban experience, and social acceptance of different ethnic or racial groups, the phenomenally low status of migrants appears to be quite general. Vance points out that, while migrants earn less than most workers in the areas to which they move, they earn more on the average than they did before relocating.[39] Leyburn's study of Southern Appalachian migrants to Cincinnati indicates a marked disadvantage for migrants in employment rates.[40] Lipset and Bendix show evidence for marked differences in occupational status and mobility depending both on migration status and size of community of origin in several American studies as well as in Sweden and in Germany.[41] Thernstrom provides data showing the marked differences in occupational mobility of immigrants compared to natives in nineteenth-century Newburyport.[42] And Blau and Duncan's analysis of more recent data, more carefully controlled than previous studies although heavily weighted by more recent and more highly selective migrations as well as by recent periods of economic expansion, indicates an improvement in rates of occupational mobility for immigrants with a continuing disadvantage for those immigrants from the least-favored countries.[43]

THE MYTH OF SOCIAL MOBILITY AND SOCIAL ASSIMILATION

The many millions of immigrants from European countries from the middle of the nineteenth century until relatively recent decades bore the full brunt of the low-status positions accorded the newcomer, the foreign-born, the rural peasant or worker, the uneducated, and the socially ostracized. Although few studies permit us to clarify the components of background or status most clearly implicated in the demeaning occupational conditions of the immigrant, the data are unambiguous in revealing their lowly state.[44] At the extreme, immigrants from Ireland, Italy, and Poland were at the bottom of the occupational ladder and worked under conditions of unbelievable degradation and exploitation. However, even the migrants from England, Scotland, and Wales started at levels considerably below the native population.[45],[46]

A matter of more serious concern than low initial status is the slow and difficult process of mobility and assimilation. For the British, whose occupational distributions were higher than those of the native Americans by the second generation, assimilation presented no special problems.[47] For other groups like the Germans and Scandinavians, who often lived in ethnically homogeneous enclaves, the process of social mobility occurred with moderate facility.[48] Among the Jews, who have been the proverbial representatives of rapid social mobility, the process has been uneven and reveals some of the special problems of both mobility and assimilation in the face of overwhelming discrimination and restrictions.[49] And although the Chinese and Japanese, among the non-European immigrants, have achieved extremely high levels of education and occupation, their slow and painful accomplishment is hardly testimony to the open-mobility pattern or the ease of assimilation in the United States.[50]

The most recent urban migrant groups, the Negro, the Puerto Rican, and the Mexican-American have suffered severely, but many earlier immigrant groups have also experienced an extremely slow and precarious process of social mobility. This has been particularly notable among the Irish.[51] In 1870, more than twenty years after their great migration and about a half century after the beginning of a substantial migration stream, 68.6 per cent of the first generation were manual workers or servants; by 1900, it had increased to 71.6 per cent of the first-generation Irish. By contrast, the entire population of the United States, including many other low-status immigrants, contained only 45.1 per cent in these occupational categories in 1900. Moreover, progress was very slow for the second generation: In 1900, 59.7 per cent of the second-generation Irish were classified in manual work or domestic service.[52] Indeed, by 1950, the foreign-born Irish, including many who had migrated shortly after the turn of the century during the era of dwindling Irish immigration, were markedly underrepresented in white-collar occupations although they had achieved some status as semiskilled and skilled workers, managers, officials, and proprietors. The second generation, however, was moving rapidly toward parity with the native white population of native parentage.[53]

The situation of the Irish was fairly extreme and was compounded by a long history of degradation and restriction, by the rush to depart that often led them to inappropriate destinations, by the severe anti-Catholicism that met them, and by the dominance of parochial education that sheltered the second generation from the impact of American values and orientations.[54] But the Italians, arriving more recently than the Irish, were also markedly underrepresented in all higher-status occupations as late as 1950, and the second generation was moving more slowly than the Irish to an occupational distribution comparable with native whites of native parentage.[55] The Germans and the Poles had mobility rates higher than the Irish-Italian pattern but considerably lower than the English, Scotch, or Welsh. By 1910, the Germans were showing a modest level of mobility, but were still underrepresented in high-status occupations. By 1950, the first-generation Germans were close to parity with native white Americans, but the second generation was not yet equivalent to native whites of native parentage.[56] The Poles found opportunities for mobility from unskilled to skilled ranks in the major manufacturing industries. But few moved on rapidly to positions as skilled workers.[57] By 1950, however, the Poles of foreign birth had moved far and were well represented among skilled workers, managers, and officials.[58]

What these facts highlight, imperfect though they may be, is the great gap between an image of continuous and rapid mobility and the reality of slow, arduous, intragenerational and intergenerational change in status. There is no question that the process of upward mobility among immigrants has been continuous. But if, sixty to one hundred years after an ethnic group has initiated large-scale immigration into this country and much of that immigration necessarily occurred more than forty years ago, there is still such a wide discrepancy in occupational achievement from the host population, then we must alter our conceptions of the process. The rungs of the mobility ladder are wide apart for migrants to an urban, industrial society. Just as the melting pot has failed to melt and consolidate its ethnic prey, so has the mobility process failed to amalgamate its poverty-stricken, uneducated, and unskilled immigrants or their children in a vision of success. The deprived migrants of another era remain relatively disadvantaged, and their children suffer the consequences of these deprivations while slowly overcoming their effects.

At the very least, we must consider the conventional conception of mobility and assimilation of ethnic minorities in the United States a myth. Some few ethnic groups have, in fact, been highly mobile particularly if they brought scarce skills or moved into a prepared environment. Other ethnic groups, the large majority, have been slowly mobile and have had to overcome gigantic obstacles in their struggles for educational attainment, occupational status, and high income. And a few ethnic groups have struggled, virtually in vain, until a new generation, bearing fewer of the marks of ethnicity and in a different social environment, were able to confront the problem without the preformed conviction that they were doomed to failure. We must also forego any ready assumptions about the ease of social assimilation. While social mobility is often a stage in the larger assimilation of immigrants, there are large gaps in the process, and mobility achievements among immigrants, as with the Negro, Puerto Rican, and Mexican-American, have often proved necessary, but hardly sufficient, for social assimilation.

After almost a half century during which there have been no mass immigrations from Europe or Asia, the issue of the social mobility and social assimilation of the foreign-born and of their native-born children is no longer as trenchant and pressing a problem as it once was in the large cities of the United States. Although some ethnic groups have not yet reached parity with the population as a whole in education, occupation, or income, and have not yet achieved total desegregation in housing, the differences are not large. Buoyed by several periods of great prosperity that have facilitated, probably with disproportionate advantage, the mobility opportunities of immigrants, and in the context of a high standard of living in an affluent society, the problem seems academic.

However, the problem is far from academic. If these conclusions are correct, we must not only dismiss the image of rapid mobility and assimilation, but must place, in its stead, an image of a moderately restrictive and fundamentally segregationist society. Despite the absence of an overtly structured status system on the model of post feudal societies, issues of ethnicity, race, and culture have been superimposed on economic and occupational differences to provide a basis for discrimination, prejudice, and social inequality. The labor of millions of poverty-stricken immigrants was necessary for the industrial expansion of the United States, and only because of this were its doors open to indentured servants, slaves, serfs, and, as a result, to their descendants. But the people were themselves viewed as a vast and impersonal, low-status labor force to whom society owed nothing. Translations of the Elizabethan Poor Laws discouraging vagrants and the indigent and pioneering work in the development of an urban police force were our primary control mechanisms. Little attention was given to the social and personal needs of immigrants until the explosion of urban social problems made their desperate situations unavoidably evident to a few people. Even then, the society offered the immigrant with less evident needs and who was a less evident threat little or no assistance and placed great impediments in the path of establishing a meaningful and integrated life experience in the new world.

The issue is certainly neither academic nor attenuated when we confront, in this light, the situation of more recent migrants to the urban industrial environment. We shall focus particularly on the Negro experience because it highlights, in the most extreme fashion, the limits of social mobility and the gap between social mobility and social assimilation in a society characterized by severe prejudice, segregationist policies, and a casual disregard for social justice. Nonetheless, neither the misery and constraint imposed on the Negro nor the general affluence that mitigates the visibility and the most ostensible consequences of underprivilege should allow us to ignore the failures of assimilation and mobility that characterize the history of immigration to the United States. It may be here, in some of the underlying similarities rather than in the many striking differences, that the most severe problems and limitations of our society are buried but only partly concealed.

NEGRO MIGRATION IN THE UNITED STATES

The history of settlement and growth in the United States is dominated by several major trends of population movement. The large-scale movement of American Negroes, one of the most prominent streams of migration in this country since 1910, can be seen as a special case of these trends. The significance of the Negro migration is, in large part, revealed both in the similarities to and in the differences from other patterns of migration in the United States.

The consistency of over-all rates of geographical mobility in the United States over long periods of time is striking. Since at least 1850, the proportion of the native population living in states different from those in which they had been born has varied little (between approximately 20 and 25 per cent).[59] This high and stable level of population movement was characterized quite early by expanding populations along the moving western frontiers and by the slow contraction of agricultural populations and the growth of urban populations. These two trends coincided to some extent not merely in time but in the enormous rates of growth of frontier towns and cities, a frontier that gradually moved farther westward over more than a century. During several decades, these westward frontier towns and cities shifted from Pittsburgh, Cincinnati, and Lexington to St. Louis, Chicago, Denver, and San Francisco.[60] The rapid growth of towns and cities was further implemented, often to the bursting point, by the vast tides of immigration that fed the northeastern section of the country but gradually expanded to the entire country. At the same time, since 1790, there was a gradual net out-migration from rural areas and a gradual net in-migration to urban areas within the United States. In combination, these forces led to a massive change from a rural to an urban society.

One of the major regional sources of this shift from a rural to an urban society was the slow population decline in the South, a section of the country that had previously harbored the largest rural, agrarian population. From 1880 on, there was a striking transfer of population out of the southern states, a shift that was eventually to become the largest stream of out-migration in the United States. This is vividly depicted in Figure 5–1.[61] Since 1870, this movement has been dominated (and, indeed, was initiated) by the migration of Negroes out of the South to the northeastern states. After 1910, with an increasing rate of migration out of the South, the north central states began to receive a large number of Negro migrants. This monolithic and accelerating escape from the South by the large southern Negro population soon took on the appearance of a dramatic exodus through the addition of almost as large a number of white out-migrants from the South.

It is notable that, between 1950 and 1960 and even earlier, a gradual change in the character of out-migration from the South developed. While the large net out-migration of Negroes continued at only a slightly diminished pace, the net out-migration of whites decreased as a result of a reverse stream of in-migration. In particular, a reverse stream of in-migration developed through the movement of whites from the Northeast to some of the metropolitan and urban areas in the South.[62]

The difference in the destination of the white and Negro migration from the South is also clear in Figure 5–1. The overwhelming direction of population movement among whites was toward the West throughout the period from 1870 to 1950, a growth that included out-migrant whites from the northeast and the north central states as well as from the South. By contrast, the Negro out-migration from the South was initially directed almost exclusively toward the Northeast. By 1890, there was a slowly growing movement and, by 1910, a rapidly growing movement toward the north central states. The

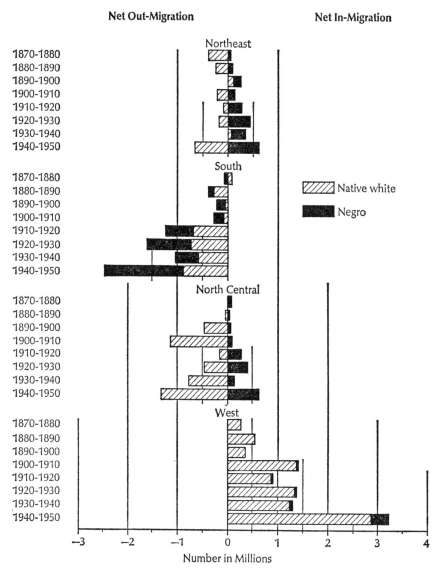

FIGURE 5–1. Net Migration of Native Whites and Negroes, by Regions, 1870–1880 to 1940–1950.

From Simon Kuznets, Dorothy Swaine Thomas, et al., *Population Distribution and Economic Growth: United States, 1870–1950* (Philadelphia: American Philosophical Society, 1964), Table 1.27.

West only slowly captured a small part of this migrant stream of Negroes from the South, a direction of movement that did not become notable until the decade 1940–1950.

Viewed only on the basis of the numbers or proportions of Negroes within large sections of the country or moving between them, it is evident that the Negro migration out of the South did not reach striking size until the decade between 1910 and 1920. Nonetheless, this was hardly the beginning of significant Negro migrations. Indeed, conceived only in terms of these regional shifts, the decade between 1900 and 1910 saw a fairly large migration. Between 1870 and 1890, the proportions of southern-born Negroes among the northern Negro population remained fairly constant at 30 per cent. This, itself, implies that the rate of in-migration to the North was proportional to the indigenous increase of northern-born Negroes.[63] By 1900, there was a small proportionate increase to 31 per cent, which grew to 40 per cent in 1910 and 50 per cent in 1920. Thus, there was almost as large a percentage increase of southern-born Negro migrants in the Negro population living in the North between 1900 and 1910 as there was in the frequently mentioned migration of the 1910–1920 decade. Other migratory movements also occurred in the period prior to 1920. While the border states were, at first, most prominent as sources of northward migration of Negroes, there was a strong trend of movement toward the southwest cotton-growing regions from other parts of the South.[64] One of the more striking migrations, although numerically small, was the "Kansas Exodus" of 1879 in which between 25,000 and 50,000 southern Negroes, disgusted with the failure of reconstruction, moved en masse to Kansas.[65]

A number of important features of the huge migration of Negroes from the southern states stand out. First and foremost is the fact that by 1960 there had been a remarkable shift of the Negro population out of the South. In 1790, 91 per cent of the Negroes in the United States lived in the South. By 1910, this was reduced only to 89 per cent. But by 1960, this proportion had dropped to 52 per cent.[66] While the movement of southern Negroes followed the gross patterns of population redistribution in the United States since 1910, the proportions of Negroes who left the South were far greater than the proportions of the numerically larger white southern population. From the vantage point of in-migration in the North, this migration was smaller in numbers than the vast European immigration from 1850 to 1910, annually or in aggregate. But it increased the proportions of the Negro population living in urban areas more dramatically than any equivalent concentration of a single ethnic group during the earlier period. At the same time, it is noteworthy that the Negro population remaining in the South is very large, and, indeed, even in 1960 a slight majority of the total Negro population of the United States lived in southern states.

A detailed analysis of the causes of the great Negro migration of the period from 1910 to 1960 is even more difficult than in the case of the European migrations of 1830 to 1920. To some extent, the situation of the southern Negro seems so self-evidently miserable that there may be little temptation to investigate it further. Whatever the manifestations of discrimination and unequal opportunities for Negroes in the North and West, objectively, discrimination is less pervasive, less extreme, and has less striking consequences for education, jobs, and incomes. This difference alone might account for the mass movement of southern Negroes even apart from the very slow progress of the South in urbanization and industrialization. Certainly the more recent and rapid growth of industry and of cities in the South, coupled with an expanding economy, has stemmed some of the tide of net out-migration by whites without appreciably affecting the out-migration of Negroes.

Although it is difficult to attribute the geographical displacement of Negroes and the trend of the Negro population out of farms and into rural nonfarm areas and cities precisely, Dorothy Thomas's data indicate that economic conditions are almost certainly involved.[67] Rates of migration, according to her analysis, are highest during periods of prosperity and are manifest largely as shifts from areas of relatively low incomes to areas of relatively high incomes. Moreover, at almost all age levels, the migration behavior of the Negro population appears to be affected more severely by cycles of prosperity and depression than are either the native white population or the foreign-born. That is, the tide of migration is more markedly diminished during depressions and more markedly augmented during prosperous periods among Negroes than among other subpopulations. The implications of these findings are not entirely clear. They may be interpreted as evidence that the Negro population of the United States is less responsive to "expulsive" forces and more responsive to "attractive" forces than native whites or foreign-born. Indeed, it is almost certainly the case that, because of discrimination, the Negro's chances of finding a job in the city during depressions are more drastically diminished than for the population as a whole; and, conversely, during periods of prosperity, when the demand for workers is great, job opportunities of Negroes increase disproportionately. Unfortunately, this does not clarify the relationship between the expulsive and attractive forces, themselves, in generating mass migrations of Negroes.

A similar problem of interpretation arises from the data on the spatial distribution of migration for Negroes and whites.[68] From Thomas's data on net in-migration, net out-migration, and economic conditions in the areas of in- and out-migration, it is evident that there is a gross movement away from low-income areas to high-income areas, with a slight tendency for the relationship between Negro migration and income differentials to be closer than for whites. Whether this is primarily a function of the expulsive pressures of low-income areas, the attractive qualities of high-income areas, or a combination of both is altogether uncertain. In view of the general principle that migration moves from lower- to higher-income areas, the relatively weak relationships and the many deviations from the expected pattern are themselves among the most interesting features of the data. Indeed, we might conclude from these results either that purely economic considerations play only a relatively minor role in the migration patterns of both Negroes and whites or that, whatever the ostensible orientation of migration patterns, they are poorly adjusted to the realities of economic circumstances. The looseness of this relationship may be quite unfortunate. In instances of massive migrations, the failure of effective correspondence between the timing or direction of movement and economic conditions can be a factor seriously exacerbating the other disruptive potentials of migrant adjustment and discrimination.

Thus, the relationship between migration and economic conditions is less finely attuned than one would hope. For Negro migrants, so much more dependent on flourishing conditions of employment that mitigate the effects of discrimination, even the somewhat greater association between migration and economic circumstances is insufficient to avoid the negative consequences of "misguided" or, more properly, "unguided" migration.

One clear relationship between Negro migration and choice of destination does stand out and appears to be a clear selection of areas with high growth potential: the striking movement of Negroes to cities. This movement toward cities is of equal importance with and as monolithic a trend as the redistribution of Negroes from the South to the North. Table 5-2 presents the percentage distribution by urban residence for Negroes and whites for the United States as a whole and by regional division into South and non-South (North, Central, and West) since 1910. The table reveals both the enormous increase in the urbanization of the American Negro since 1910 and the continuing difference between the South and other regions of the country.

TABLE 5-2. *Percentage of Negro and White Population Living in Urban Areas by Region, 1910–1960*

YEAR	UNITED STATES		SOUTH		NORTH plus WEST	
	NEGRO	WHITE	NEGRO	WHITE	NEGRO	WHITE
1910	27.4	48.7	21.2	23.2	77.5	57.3
1920	35.4	53.3	27.0	28.5	84.3	61.6
1930	43.7	57.6	31.7	35.0	88.1	65.5
1940	48.6	59.0	36.5	36.8	89.1	67.4
1950	62.4	64.3	47.7	48.9	93.5	70.1
1960	73.2	69.6	58.4	58.6	95.3	73.7

From Dorothy K. Newman, "The Negro's Journey to the City—Part I," *Monthly Labor Review*, LXXXVIII (1965), 644–649.

In the South, the urbanization of the Negro has paralleled to a remarkable degree the urbanization of the white population. By 1960, as a result of the gradual decrease in agricultural populations, the majority of both Negroes and whites in the South were living in urban areas. Indeed, comparing the data in this table for the South and for the North and West and bearing in mind the enormous migration of Negroes from the South since 1910, it becomes clear that the migration also resulted in a dramatic urbanization of the Negro population in the United States. Even in 1910, before the full swing of the great migration of Negroes from the South, more than three-quarters of the Negro population living outside the South (and predominantly in the Northeast) were living in cities. And with the growing tide of Negro migration from the South since 1910, the proportion living in urban areas has increased continuously. In this respect, the pattern of Negro migration has many similarities to the great wave of foreign immigration particularly during its last fifty years (1870 to 1920) and has resulted in a predominantly urban ethnic minority.[69] It is also notable that, while the urban trend of the white population has been quite marked throughout this period, the higher level of urbanization among the Negro population than among the white population in the North and West has been maintained during at least five decades.

The exact characteristics of this urban movement of the Negro population are not altogether clear, and the available statistics do not allow more than slightly informed conjectures. Generally speaking, rates of migration have been higher for whites than for nonwhites despite the somewhat higher rates of short-distance moves by Negroes.[70] But the huge loss of farm populations to nonfarm residences has been even greater for nonwhites than for whites and has disproportionately affected the South compared to other regions of the country.[71] By no means do these short-distance or long-distance moves represent only movement from farm to urban residence either for whites or nonwhites. Indeed, rural nonfarm residence has generally shown the greatest net in-migration rates of any residential group. However, there is some suggestion from these data, to which Figure 5–2 gives visible form, indicating a familiar pattern of migration: that the vast majority of moves are relatively short-distance moves, that these short-distance moves take place over a gradient from sparser to denser population concentrations by stages, and that the large increases in urban populations result from the vast increments due to these smaller and successive migrations.[72] With the gradual depletion of farm populations, with the large shift of the Negro population in the South from rural farm to rural nonfarm residence, to small cities, and to large cities over time, an increasing proportion of the continuing Negro migration becomes closer, both geographically and culturally, to the urban, industrial environment of the northern, central, and western regions of the country.

One final feature of the Negro migration and its effect on the Negro population of urban areas warrants attention: the attributes of migrants and the changing composition of the urban, Negro population. Although there are differences of view concerning the nature of migrant populations, the weight of evidence suggests that the great European migrations were dominated by those people from deprived areas who were most competent, with the highest occupational skills, and with some minimal financial resources to carry them through the earliest phases of migration.[73] Studies of internal migration in the United States give evidence that, indeed, migrants are of higher educational and occupational status than are nonmigrants from the same areas.[74]

To some extent, the evaluation of the attributes of migrants has been a function of the vantage point from which observation or analysis was carried out. Seen in the context of an urbanized population, migrants have often appeared to be of lower status, less competent, ill prepared for dealing with urban complexities and ambiguities. On the other hand, compared to nonmigrants who remained in the areas from which the migrants came, they have often appeared to be those with the greatest opportunity in the area of origin. As Duncan and Duncan's analysis of Chicago data reveals, both of these observations are probably correct.[75] The educational status of Negro migrants to Chicago in the decade 1940–1950 was higher than that of the states from which they mainly came, but lower than that of the resident Negro population in Chicago. However, while both Negro

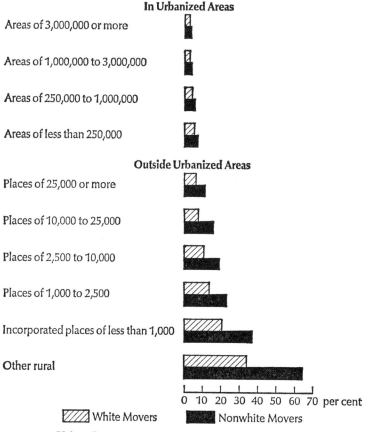

FIGURE 5–2. Urban-Rural Residence—Percentage of all movers who came from farms, for the white and nonwhite population, by size of place at destination, 1949 to 1950

From Henry S. Shryock, Jr., *Population Mobility Within the United States* (Chicago: Community and Family Study Center, 1964), p. 319.

and white migrants tend to be of higher educational level than non-migrants from the same areas, this is particularly the case for Negro migrants.[76] There is also evidence of change in the character of Negro migration that has led both to an increase in intermetropolitan migration and, corresponding to this, to an improvement in the educational and occupational composition of Negro migrants compared to the resident Negro population in the receiving metropolitan areas.[77]

Taeuber and Taeuber have given particular consideration to the changing characteristics of Negro migrants and have pointed up the fact that, over the last few decades, the urban attributes of Negro migrants have approximated ever more closely to those that characterize white migrants.[78] However, in this as in many other comparisons that permit a distinction between the South and other regions of the country, there is a marked difference between southern cities, on the one hand, and northern, midwestern, or western cities on the other. As we might expect on the basis of other information about patterns of Negro migration, a greater proportion of in-migrants to metropolitan areas in northern and border states come from other metropolitan areas than do in-migrants to southern cities. In southern metropolitan areas, nonmetropolitan in-migrants are considerably more frequent than are in-migrants from other metropolitan areas.[79] Border metropolitan areas are intermediate and show a slightly greater proportion of in-migrants from nonmetropolitan areas. In northern metropolitan areas, however, Negro in-migrants more frequently come from other metropolitan areas.

The differences in metropolitan and nonmetropolitan origins of Negro migrants into northern, border, and southern metropolitan areas, the association of metropolitan origin and educational or occupational status, and the relative significance of in-migration and out-migration account, in part, for the changing composition of the Negro population of metropolitan areas in different regions of the country. In the South, the greater proportion of nonmetropolitan in-migrants, their relatively lower educational and occupational status compared to the resident population, and the much heavier out-migration of high-status Negroes has led to declining educational and occupational status in the resident Negro population. By contrast, the increase in the migration to northern metropolitan areas of young Negro migrants of high educational and occupational status from other metropolitan areas has led to an improvement in the educational and occupational composition of the resident Negro population. Even with age controlled, the difference from previous decades is striking since, at the very least, the in-migrant population of 1955 to 1960 was equivalent to the resident population of the same ages in education and occupation. It is equally notable that, for this same period, Negro in-migrants to northern cities were equal to or of slightly higher education than the resident white population.[80] Comparing results for the 1955 to 1960 period with those for earlier periods highlights both the absolute and relative changes in the composition of the Negro migration resulting in an increase in the educational and occupational characteristics of migrants.

From the data on Negro migration in the United States, a few prominent facts stand out. While the numbers and proportions of total population involved in this migration are smaller than those of the European migration of 1830 to 1920, the Negro migration of 1910 to 1960 was vast and represented a redistribution of at least six million Negro Americans. However, the loss of Negro population sustained by the South was probably of much greater proportion than the loss of population from any country of origin during the European migrations to the United States. Thus, it is estimated that there was a loss of approximately one-third of the population of Ireland during the half century after the great famine.[81] The loss of the Negro population from the South during an equivalent period of time was almost certainly greater than one-half. Like most of the streams of European migration, the movement of Negroes out of the South was also largely a rural-to-urban transition. However, the Negro population moving into the North, Midwest, and West was even more prominently an urbanizing population, with more than 95 per cent of those Negroes outside the South living in urban areas by 1960.

In discussing the European migration of the nineteenth and early twentieth century, we considered the relative importance of expulsive and attractive forces, concluding that these are inevitably interrelated and that both pushes and pulls were essential components in accounting for the migrations. For the Negro migrations of the past half century, the data are even less adequate, but point in a similar direction. Like the situations in most of the European countries that experienced large-scale migrations, there were endemic forces that operated as continuous expulsive factors: severe poverty, a long process of subdivision of small farms, tenure-farming systems that were often duplicates of slavery or serfdom, increasing population pressure, discrimination and restriction of opportunities, widespread traditionalism opposed to change or deviation. Superimposed on these endemic forces, intensified poverty due to famine or increased discrimination and restriction often led to the marked short-term increases in migration in the European and in the southern-Negro situation alike.

It is clear that, both for the European migrations and for the migrations of Negroes from the South, there were increased rates of movement associated with periods of prosperity in the areas of destination and decreased rates of movement associated with depression or recession in the areas of destination. The endemic expulsive forces are represented, in both instances, by the continuing movement of population throughout except under the most severe economic chaos in potential host areas as exemplified by the depression of the 1930s. On the other hand, through the haze of inadequate data it appears that for most of the streams of European migration and for the Negro migration from the South, there was much misdirection. In general, the trend in both cases was for movement from areas of lower employment and income to areas of higher employment and income. But there is much evidence to indicate that the areas of destination were determined by many factors other than maximal available economic opportunities. For more recent decades, Dorothy Thomas's analysis suggests that the correspondence of migration and economic opportunity has been somewhat greater for Negroes than for either native-born or foreign-born whites suggesting the greater significance of discrimination in limiting opportunities for Negroes except under conditions of maximal demand for labor.[82]

Despite the disproportionately large number of in-migrants from other metropolitan areas with high levels of education and occupation, a substantial proportion of Negro migrants to northern cities continues to be of low status and from nonmetropolitan areas. Thus, while the Negro migration has begun to approximate the character of the white migration in some respects, there remains a substantial problem in the migration of rural, low-status Negroes to metropolitan areas, with little preparation either in choice of destination or in the adaptive necessities of life in urban, industrial societies. Moreover, it is not at all clear that the relatively high status, intermetropolitan Negro migrants do not suffer some of the consequences of migration, especially under conditions of discrimination, in the form of increased rates of unemployment and diminished occupational status opportunities.

With the extant data, it is not possible to trace these problems further. More detailed data are necessary to examine these questions more fully or with greater analytic precision. However, the patterns of migration are largely a context for inquiring into the fate of the population. While it is not entirely possible to separate issues of geographical migration and social mobility, even to the extent that this could be done with the European immigration, it is important to ask about the rates of social mobility during these decades of migration for the Negro population. We turn, thus, to a consideration of the same set of questions that we addressed about the European migrants: To what extent has there been a pattern of upward social mobility for the rapidly urbanizing Negro American, and to what extent have changes in social status entailed a marked diminution in discrimination?

SOCIAL MOBILITY AND ASSIMILATION AMONG NEGROES

In order to provide a meaningful comparison of the situation of the foreign-born immigrant to the United States and that of the Negro American whose migration patterns to urban industrial areas we have traced in gross fashion, we must now examine rates of social mobility and of social assimilation for Negroes. In examining the social mobility and assimilation of the Negro migrant, whose period of massive movement has occurred since approximately 1910 and shows only slight indications of diminution during the 1960s, we must rely heavily on recent data. Moreover, a consideration of social assimilation must depend almost exclusively on residential segregation. That there have been difficulties in both social mobility and residential segregation of Negroes long before the large-scale migrations of the past half century, however, is clear. Although several historians point to the fact that, prior to the increased immigration associated with World War II, the resident Negro population in northern cities had begun to achieve a modicum of occupational and economic advancement, these reports are based on isolated cases rather than systematic population or sample data.[83] Whatever minimal achievements the settled Negro population in northern cities experienced, residential segregation was pervasive and more severe than for other in-migrant populations.[84]

A wealth of data indicates that urban, industrial societies have quite high rates of social mobility and that this is true and has been true for some time in the United States.[85] But, apart from the technical difficulties of making even moderately precise estimates, evaluations of mobility rates as "high" or "low" are extremely subjective.[86] Thernstrom's compilation of ten different studies of occupational changes from fathers to sons covering periods from 1860 to 1956 illustrates a fairly similar pattern.[87] All of these studies vary around estimates that approximately 50 to 60 per cent (ranging from 48 to 71 per cent) of the sons of unskilled laborers were themselves either unskilled or semiskilled laborers. That the occupational progress of Negroes has been slow and halting by any criterion, however, is quite evident from the gross estimates of changes in occupational position between 1910 and 1960. Tobin, quoting Hiestand's data, shows significant improvement only during the period from 1940 to 1960, although there had been some improvement relative to whites since 1910.[88] Even these changes, which bring the occupational position of Negro males to the level of 82.1 per cent of white males by 1960, may overstate the degree of change experienced. On the other hand, most analyses of changes in education, occupation, or income of Negroes over the last few decades fail to distinguish the South from other regions of the country, which leads to another serious distortion of the results. Thus, Hare's intracohort analysis reveals that Negro rates of occupational mobility from 1930 to 1940, 1940 to 1950, and 1950 to 1960 were higher than those for whites in each age group.[89] That there was a slight decline in the rate of improvement during the decade 1950 to 1960 outside the South, coupled with a retrogression in the South during the same decade, gave the impression that the improvements of previous decades had not continued since the national figures did not distinguish regional differences.

This pattern of regional differences has been quite persistent. According to Hauser, in 1910 illiteracy was ten times greater among Negroes than among native whites.[90] However, in the South, illiteracy rates for Negroes reached 33 per cent while in the North they were only 10 per cent; that is, they were more than three times as high in the South as in the North. By 1930, Negro illiteracy rates had been cut in half, but white rates of illiteracy had regressed even more. That the South contributed disproportionately to the slow pace of change for the Negro is revealed by the fact that rates of Negro illiteracy had grown to be four times higher in the South in 1930 than in the North. Between 1940 and 1960, after the Census Bureau substituted a question on years of schooling for the question on literacy, it is possible to estimate the change in the form of grades completed. During these two decades, the difference in education between Negro and white males had diminished from 3.3 to 2.6 years, and between Negro and white females it had diminished from 2.7 to 2.5 years.[91] Moreover, these gains understate the relative educational achievement in at least one respect. Since the differentials among older age groups are considerably greater than among younger age groups (but the figures are based on median years of school completed for all age groups), they do not fully reveal the impact of the gain as a function of changes over time. Throughout, the differences between the South and other regions of the country persisted, further diminishing the over-all manifestation of educational gain.

In reviewing studies of educational, occupational, or income mobility of Negroes and whites, one is confronted by contrasting figures and contrasting conclusions that make any simple summary particularly difficult. In part, these differences are based on different sources of data; in part, they result from different statistical analyses. However, some of the most recent figures and reports appear to show greater consensus in finding a consistent improvement in the situation of Negroes relative to whites since 1960. Spady's analysis of 1964 data, for example, indicates marked educational gains for successively younger age groups among both whites and Negroes.[92] These gains are represented in the differences in educational achievement of men aged 25–34, 35–44, 45–54, and 55–64 compared to their fathers' educational achievements. In virtually all instances of relative achievements of fathers and sons the improvements among the younger age groups are consistent and relatively greater for Negroes than for whites. On the other hand, the youngest age groups among Negroes are approximately at the same educational level as the oldest age groups among the whites, suggesting a gap of more than a generation.

Although the general trend of data for earlier periods is fairly consistent in showing relatively greater occupational advances among Negroes than among whites, the most recent results show even more striking gains. Much of the occupational gain of earlier years resulted from the shift from agricultural to industrial employment. Thus, between 1910 and 1940, of those gainfully employed, the proportion of Negroes engaged in agriculture dropped from 56 to 41 per cent; during the same period, the proportion of whites engaged in agriculture diminished from 33 to 21 per cent. By 1960, only 11 per cent of the Negro labor force and 8 per cent of the white labor force was engaged in agriculture, a situation of virtual parity.[93] During the latter period from 1940 to 1960, however, other relative gains were achieved by Negro workers, and while these gains were far from what one might have hoped, they did show an increased similarity between the occupational distribution of Negroes and of whites. Moreover, the more detailed analyses available from extensive interview data suggest that, albeit at a lower level of the occupational-status scale, Negro advances are considerably greater than those among white workers.[94] But the fact remains, as with educational advances, that these gains are occurring at different levels of the occupational hierarchy; thus, Negro occupational status remains considerably behind that of the white population.

The most recent reports, based on data up to 1965, continue to present a picture of cautious optimism. Several of the higher-status-level occupations are among the occupational areas that appear to be opening up opportunities for Negroes most rapidly: professional, technical, and kindred occupations, most particularly, but also other white-collar occupations and the craftsmen and foremen occupational groups.[95] To some extent, however, some of the major gains are in occupations that are not rapidly expanding in over-all availability of positions and nonwhite gains may have to occur in different occupations to keep pace with changing patterns of industrial development and unemployment. During the expanding economy of 1962 to 1965, nonwhite workers had an even greater reduction in unemployment than white workers, but these marked gains during periods of high employment are not necessarily stable.[96] At the same time, they highlight a point that Myrdal has made, that the effects of discrimination can only be markedly diminished through maximizing over-all job opportunities.[97] During this same period between 1962 and 1965, the white-nonwhite educational differential for different occupational categories had also diminished. While this represents, in part, the same phenomenon of increased demand for workers, it does indicate greater parity in the criteria used for employing nonwhite and white workers.

The data comparing incomes of Negro and white families show much the same pattern as do the data for education and occupation and clearly reveal all of the trends previously discussed.[98] Between 1947 and 1966, the proportions of families with incomes of $7,000 per year or more rose considerably among both Negroes and whites. Indeed, they rose more sharply for Negro than for white families. Thus, two and one-half times as many white families had incomes at this

level in 1966 compared to 1947, but four times as many Negro families were in this category in 1966 as compared to 1947. Despite this
remarkable and disproportionately great gain among Negro family
incomes, the proportion of white families in this income category in
1966 was twice the proportion of Negro families. As with previous
data, the difference between the South and other regions was great.
In the South in 1966, the proportion of whites with incomes of $7,000
per year was three times that of Negroes; in other regions, the ratio
was approximately 3:2. Another feature of the data that warrants
attention is that, although the over-all gains were proportionately
greater for Negroes than for whites, recession years offered minimal
interruption to the progress of white families but seriously delayed or
retarded the gains of Negro families.

In view of the extremely high levels of discrimination and inequality of opportunity that have plagued the Negro population of
the United States and despite the many qualifications that must be
made, rates of Negro mobility in education, occupation, and income
appear quite high and considerably higher than one might have
anticipated. Certainly, the gains have not been great enough to provide any comfortable image of equality. Certainly, there may be
serious costs involved in even moderate mobility achievements in the
face of immoderate inequality of opportunity. Certainly, marked
deficits in the educational, occupational, and economic situation of
Negroes remain. And certainly, the evident consequences of current,
as well as past, discrimination appear in the discrepancies between
achievements and rewards for achievement. At each educational level,
Negro occupational status is lower than the corresponding occupational statuses of whites.[99] At each educational level, the incomes of
Negro families are lower than the corresponding incomes of white
families.[100] And at each occupational level, as well, Negroes receive
lower incomes than do corresponding white workers. As Blau and
Duncan point out, "It hardly comes as a surprise that racial discrimination in the United States is reflected in the Negro's inferior
chances of occupational success, although the extent to which Negroes with the same amount of education as whites remain behind in
the struggle for desirable occupations is striking." [101]

In stating that Negro achievements in social mobility have been
surprisingly high in light of marked inequalities of opportunity, we
find little cause for optimism. Indeed, in comparing social mobility
among foreign-born immigrants and among native Negroes, we have
slowly come to the conclusion that the assumed differences in rates of

achievement are almost certainly not so great as is usually conceived.[102] But these differences between Negroes and foreign-born whites diminish in the light of these data not because of the very high levels of manifest achievement but because both the foreign immigrants of the earlier period and the Negro migrants of the past half century have similarly fought against great obstacles and severe inequalities only to experience slow and meager gains. We have no objective way of measuring or even estimating the differences in opportunities for educational, occupational, or economic mobility for the earlier European immigrant and the more recent Negro migrant from the South. It appears almost indubitable that Negroes have experienced the most devastating forms of prejudice and limitation of opportunity. But this emerges as a serious intensification of continuing patterns of discrimination and inequality of opportunity in our society rather than as a wholly unique phenomenon.

While the earlier literature about the foreign immigrants was invariably hostile and critical and, from our present vantage point, unbelievably insulting, as early as 1890 Riis noted the more severely underprivileged and degrading situation of the Negro.[103] It may, indeed, be the case that the modest degree to which the Negro American population has achieved mobility is all the more remarkable a feat. The scattered evidence of very high levels of motivation and aspiration among Negroes, of widespread and effective community leadership in either collaboration or revolt, of outstanding achievements in numerous fields, even the fact that the most striking occupational gains of the past five years have been in the most highly skilled professional and technical pursuits, suggest that we must alter our image of the Negro in the United States. In view of the serious impediments to achievement, the level of accomplishment may well be remarkably great. And in view of the evidence for extremely slow progress among the immigrants of the great European migrations, there may be far less discrepancy in social mobility between white immigrants and Negro migrants than we ordinarily imagine.

Although we do not have any adequate measure of discrimination and the significance of inequality of opportunity as a basis for evaluating mobility achievements, measures of housing segregation do provide some basis for evaluating the role of discrimination in social assimilation. In comparing residential segregation of foreign-born immigrants and their second-generation offspring for earlier periods with the early or more recent patterns of segregation of Negroes, we have only the reports of observers. That such segregation was widespread both along ethnic and social-class divisions, however, is quite clear from the literature.[104] While the Irish, Poles, Italians, Jews, and other groups each tended to form its own little ethnic enclave, ethnic differences often merged on the basis of both social class similarities and time of arrival. Even in the earlier reports, this distinguished the Negro from other ethnic groups.[105] Negro residential areas tended to be ethnically distinctive and represented a wider range of social class positions as a consequence of pervasive discrimination in housing.

Lieberson's analysis of residential segregation from 1910 to 1950 highlights the continuities in these patterns.[106] First, he found high levels of residential segregation among all ethnic groups for all the cities studied, with little evident difference between the "old" immigration (those who predominated prior to 1880) and the "new" immigration (those who predominated between 1880 and 1920). They were quite uniformly high. Second, over time, there was a gradual dispersion, but as recently as 1950, patterns of residential segregation by ethnic group was still evident. Finally, depending on time of arrival, there is a gradual dispersion of ethnic groups both in diminished rates of segregation and in movement out of the central city. While there is some evidence in these and in other data of similar patterns among the urban Negro population, rates of residential segregation are consistently higher than for any of the immigrant ethnic groups, rates of change over time are less clear, and associations between residential dispersion and social-class achievements are less marked. Thus, although the conclusions from the analysis of social mobility suggest that Negro rates of achievement may not be so drastically different from those of other earlier ethnic minorities, the patterns of housing segregation point to far more severe discrimination as an index of opportunity for social assimilation.

The more recent analyses by Taeuber and Taeuber both confirm these findings for the Negro and clarify further the patterns of segregation that operate.[107] As they point out:

In the urban United States, there is a very high degree of segregation of the residences of whites and Negroes. This is true for cities in all regions of the country and for all types of cities large and small, industrial and commercial, metropolitan and suburban. It is true whether there are hundreds of thousands of Negro residents, or only a few thousand. Residential segregation prevails regardless of the relative economic status of the white and Negro residents. It occurs regardless of the character of local laws and policies, and regardless of the extent of other forms of segregation or discrimination.

It is quite notable that, in addition to initially high levels of segregation between 1940 and 1950, the degree of segregation increased and these increases were fairly evenly spread throughout the country. Indeed, residential segregation of the Negro was generally greater than for other of the most recent urban migrants, the Puerto Rican or Mexican-American populations. However, between 1950–1960, there was a general decrease in levels of housing segregation of Negroes in cities outside the South. As Table 5–3 indicates, the great

TABLE 5 – 3. *Changes in Indices of Housing Segregation, 1940–1950 and 1950–1960, for 109 Cities, by Region*

	1940–1950	*1950–1960*
NORTHEAST		
Decreased segregation	10	23
Increased segregation	15	2
NORTH CENTRAL		
Decreased segregation	7	21
Increased segregation	22	8
WEST		
Decreased segregation	4	10
Increased segregation	6	0
SOUTH		
Decreased segregation	5	10
Increased segregation	40	35

From Karl E. Taeuber and Alma F. Taeuber, *Negroes in Cities: Residential Segregation and Neighborhood Change* (Chicago: Aldine, 1965).

majority of cities in the northeast, north central, and western regions experienced decreases in residential segregation of Negroes between 1950 and 1960. In the South, on the other hand, the vast majority of cities continued to show increased rates of residential segregation for Negroes.

What emerges from these data is already clear. Regardless of the high and remarkably persistent forms of residential segregation of ethnic groups, many of whom had established residential patterns in these same cities more than one hundred years ago, the Negro has consistently suffered more severe discrimination in housing and has been forced into more pervasive forms of residential segregation. During the decade 1950 to 1960 there was a minor improvement in spite of the continued out-migration of whites to the suburbs, a factor that tends to increase levels of segregation although it often makes available better housing for Negroes. This improvement, however, did not occur in the South but was limited to cities in the other regions of the country. But even when there was a decrease in segregation, the levels of segregation remained extremely, unconscionably high.

Thus, even if one concludes from the analysis of social mobility that Negro achievements have been comparable to those of the white immigrants from Europe, educational, occupational, and income improvements have not markedly diminished the manifestation of discrimination in housing segregation. And while this is only one of many forms of discrimination, it is one of the better indicators of opportunities for social assimilation. Thus, social mobility for the Negro has not led to commensurate, or even reasonably modest, changes in equality of opportunity for integrated housing. While high levels of segregation in housing have existed for other ethnic groups, these appear to have been both less severe in general and more responsive to changes in social-class position than they have been for the Negro.

CONCLUSIONS

It has become conventional to point out the great gap between the achievements of the European immigrants who peopled the United States during more than a century between the end of the Napoleonic wars and the first major restrictions on immigration in 1924 and the failure of achievement, on the other hand, among Negroes whose major entrance into the urban industrial environment started around 1900 and continues apace. In the course of reviewing the extensive, albeit inadequate, data concerning social mobility and assimilation among both the European immigrants to the cities of this country and the Negro migrants from the South to the industrialized areas of the North and West, we have been forced to challenge this conclusion and to reconsider the implications of the melting pot ideology.

It is difficult to draw unambiguous conclusions about the situation of either the white or the black migrant. But the data appear to provide greater support for a reinterpretation than for the conventional conception of migratory movements and social assimilation in the United States. We have tried to show that the European immigrant most often experienced the transition from rural, pre-industrial areas and largely agricultural occupations in southern, eastern, and central Europe to the cities and low-status manual occupations in the United States as an extremely painful, difficult, and threatening process. Immigrants left and continued to leave their native homes because they could look forward to nothing but misery and a deteriorating economic and social situation. The United States offered, at the very least, the possibility of jobs, and no matter how low the wage rates, a higher income than they had previously known. Most immigrants remained in this country despite the long and often bitter struggle to maintain jobs through recurrent depressions, to retain a semblance of self-respect in the face of constant derogation of their abilities, motivation, family relationships, and their assimilability to western cultural values. Although segregated housing kept them residentially separated, they were constantly accused of separatism and ethnic clannishness.

The second generation experienced a less restrictive environment but it was far from the myth of unlimited opportunities for social mobility and assimilation. It is difficult to determine precisely how long it took and under what conditions it was possible to gain a reasonable approximation to equality of status. But for many ethnic groups, full residential assimilation had not yet been realized as late as 1950.[108] The relatively rapid social mobility of the English, Jewish, and Japanese immigrant must, in this view, be treated as one extreme of a continuum, although the Jewish and Japanese immigrant suffered a fairly typical history of severe discrimination, restriction, and ostracism. Educational and occupational mobility and cultural parity were not enough to insure social acceptance. And for the largest proportion of the immigrants, educational and occupational mobility were extremely difficult and unduly costly achievements. Thus, the idea of the United States as a melting pot emerges as a mythical elaboration of a fragmentary truth and gives way to an image of widespread inequality, racist attitudes, and ethnic segregation as the dominant reality.[109]

By contrast with contemporary views about former immigrants (but similar to former conceptions of these same European and Asiatic immigrants), the conventional view of the black population emphasizes extremely slow progress, low motivation for achievement, and an unwillingness to share in the responsibilities and concomitant rewards of an urban industrial society. Even as searching an analysis of the personal and social background of the American Negro as Frazier's emphasized primarily the historically determined limitations of the Negro in coping with the urban industrial environment.[110] Over the last few decades, a number of studies have delineated some of the other factors involved in the situation of the Negro American: the vast migration of Negroes from the pre-industrial and racist constraints of the South to the cities of the North and West and the overwhelming impact of discrimination and inequality on occupational and economic achievement among Ne-groes.[111] At the same time, the evidence for quite marked and rapid improvements in educational, occupational, and economic achieve-ment of Negroes during the last few decades has further eroded the conventional view of Negro social immobility and low motivation for achievement.[112] Indeed, one might well argue that rates of social mobility among Negroes have been remarkably high in view of the inadequate preparation of the rural southern Negro population who form a very large proportion of contemporary urban Negro Ameri-cans, the manifest inequality of opportunity, and the potency of a heritage and current experience of discrimination.

That the Negro is still far from educational, occupational, or economic equality with the white population is, of course, clear enough.[113] This is revealed both in cross-sectional comparisons with whites and in discrepancies between educational and occupational achievements or between occupational levels and income, discrepan-cies that are among the more objective stigmata of discrimination. Indeed, similar discrepancies persist for other minorities at higher levels of the status system.[114] It is thus apparent that intense discrim-ination continues to operate and is not obliterated by social mobility. Not only is each and every advance made slowly and arduously against considerable resistance and almost certainly at considerable cost, but these advances carry with them only a modest part of the rewards that might be expected.

In spite of a real discrepancy in the status achievements associ-ated with these two great rural-to-urban migrations and the more striking discrepancies in other forms of discrimination and inequal-ity, the similarities are considerable and portentous: a modern his-tory of servile status and recent emancipation that created an opportunity to migrate more readily than it provided a basis for economic or social freedom at home; rural origins in pre-industrial communities; the absence of any grounds for hope.[115] The meager opportunities in the industrialized cities of the United States were thus a marked contrast with the economic and social vacuum that stretched out before them at home. The struggle for education against overwhelming odds became a most important channel of mobility, and the episodic gains during prosperity were never wholly destroyed by periodic depressions and recessions. But discrimination, segregation, and social rejection were omnipresent for both. Massive migrations like these stem from conditions of dire deprivation. Compared to the resident population of the host society, they eventuate in new forms of deprivation and underprivilege.

But to point up the similarities is far from obliterating the differences. While it is possible to speak of the worst features of the immigrant experience in the past, the realities of the Negro experience are ever present. Certainly the relative deprivation and the potency of discrimination are far greater for the Negro than those experienced by most of the former immigrant populations. It is, moreover, not at all clear that these differences are due to a change in the economic capacity of our society to absorb newcomers.[116] Nor is there adequate evidence that the majority of the European migrants were any better prepared to deal with the demands of an urban industrial society than the more recent Negro migrants. While the demands of the economy have undoubtedly changed and a higher degree of skill is required to fill available job opportunities than was the case fifty to one hundred years ago, there is no basis for assuming that rapid upgrading of occupational skills is not entirely feasible. The fact remains, moreover, that there is a marked discrepancy between education and occupation and between occupation and income among Negroes, which indicates that opportunities are disproportionately low relative to preparedness. Thus, we can only attribute the residual problem of Negro achievement to the severity of discrimination.

The differences among European and Asian immigrant groups and the differences between these immigrants and the situation of the Negro provide a basis for subtle analyses of the conditions and processes of rural-to-urban transition. But the similarities point up certain pervasive and underlying characteristics of our society. Superimposed upon striking social class distinctions that continue to function in spite of moderately high rates of social mobility, there is a profound rejection of ethnic, cultural, and color differences in the United States. Despite the importance of social class as a primary dimension, however, and despite the marked differences in immigration experiences and social acceptance associated with social-class variations, we cannot wholly subsume other factors within this one basis for social categorization. Rather, if we use the term racism broadly to connote any sharp and pervasive discriminatory behavior toward visible and distinguishable ethnic or cultural groups, a widespread history of racism has marked the trail of the great migrations to the cities of the United States for a century and a half. The Negro is not only among the most recent but also the most visible of these minorities and has had the most severely incapacitating history of previous discrimination and caste limitation. These have served further to encourage and rationalize the fundamental inequalities of our society in their manifestation toward the Negro American.

In a different era, when foreign-born immigrants and their children were often viewed as expendable, it was possible to disregard their desperate needs for support in facilitating social mobility and assimilation. Under different economic conditions, when the economy was a captive of the business cycle and its operation less subject to deliberate manipulation, it was more difficult to create jobs, educational opportunities, or other resources for encouraging rapid change. And in an environment in which demands for equality and opportunity were more impetuously violent, more fractionated along ethnic or occupational lines, less broadly goal-directed, and in which a democratic ideology was more limited in conception, it was possible to accept police suppression and the power of the national guard or of the armed forces as an effective means of eliminating a problem by eliminating its manifest expression. All of this has changed. We have an unparalleled potential to create a situation in which rates of achievement among the Negro population can more nearly approximate overt aspirations, needs, and demands.[117] Yet, we remain relatively paralyzed in our focus on short-term goals and in our concern with such symptoms as riots rather than with those features of inequality of opportunity that lie beneath these symptoms.

In the deepest sense, our society must undergo radical institutional change in order to eliminate widespread racism and the ready rejection of ethnic and cultural differences. Our society is certainly not unique in its resistance to accepting and integrating great diversity within the province of legitimacy. But one of the cultural consequences of the transition from pre-industrial to industrial societies is precisely an increased possibility of achieving an open society. Few other nations are in so ideal a situation for realizing this potentiality. And few other major industrial powers are in so desperate a position of choice between recurrent violence, suppressive blindness, or universal democracy. Unless we appreciate the fundamental importance

of these long-term goals that the rhetoric of the great society proposes, more modest goals are likely to be too slow and too meager
to offer much hope.

At a more modest level (but, nonetheless, one requiring more
drastic change than our society appears willing to initiate), far-
reaching economic and social legislation could have a major impact.
Low-status groups have had a long and quite varied history of misery
and ostracization.[118] While the greatest depths of poverty have been
curtailed in our society and a much larger proportion of the population participates in affluence, the economic gap between the lowest
and highest income groups remains enormous and has changed little
since 1940 and perhaps since 1910.[119] Clearly, in view of the disproportionate number of Negroes in the lowest income groups, a
diminution of this discrepancy would most drastically affect the Negro population, but at the same time would go far in eliminating the
marked inequalities of economic status in the country as a whole.
Proposals for a guaranteed income move in this direction, but in
view of the large gaps in income at the low-intermediate levels, they
do not go far enough. A more basic alteration in the entire tax
structure appears to be one of the only solutions that is pervasive
enough to create a degree of economic equality commensurate with
the dream of a great society.

At the same time, in light of the diverse components of deprivation, new forms of social legislation are imperative to provide more
adequately for the aged, the ill-housed, the jobless, and the indigent.
Each and every form of deprivation more seriously affects the Negro,
and, thus, far-reaching economic and social changes most directly
benefit the Negro. But it is only by viewing these problems as societal
problems that we can hope to achieve the kind of society that is capable of dealing not only with the past but with the present and future.
While the Negro migration from the South has begun to diminish, it
is far from attrition. Thus, to the extent that the situation of the Negro is sustained by continued migration from the more severe inequalities of the South, policy must be oriented to continued efforts to
maximize opportunities and equalities in the industrialized areas of
the North and West. At the same time, only major changes at the national level are likely to reduce the severity of Negro underprivilege
in the South.

It is paradoxical that, quite often, it is the deprived, the underprivileged, and the alienated who most poignantly demonstrate the
major inadequacies of a society. There are many respects in which

the Negro social revolution of the last few decades has already pointed up central issues: the pervasiveness of discrimination, the overt and covert forms of inequality of opportunity, the changing political structure that requires greater influence from local communities, the inadequacies of our educational system except in its most privileged sectors, the need for recasting our status system and diminishing its consequences, the desperate necessity for a more searching and egalitarian ethical consciousness in our social behavior. These are problems that affect not only the black person or the individual from other minority groups in our society. But it is the black person and those from other recent minority groups who suffer most severely from these societal failures.

It is an easy escape to define the problem as if its source lay in those who experience the problem most directly and to deal with the "Negro problem," the "poverty problem," or even the "urban problem." These, however, are simply symptomatic or localized expressions of broader problems of our society. Only by shifting from transitory conceptions to long-term change, from local or focal issues to pervasive difficulties, from an expectation of perpetual progress to an appreciation of the sporadic nature of gains and the return of periodic failures, can we hope to achieve a reasonable solution even to immediate and pressing problems. These problems, symptoms though they be, are expressed most strikingly in the poverty and inequality that Negro Americans experience despite a century of individual achievements and social change. But the realistic resolution of these specific and perhaps temporary "problems" requires that our analyses and solutions transcend them and deal with the underlying injustice and restrictions that continue to characterize our society.

Notes

1. William E. B. Dubois, *The Souls of Black Folks* (New York: Avon Library, 1965).

2. Some of the more thorough reports concerning these problems in the United States can be found in John R. Commons, *Races and Immigrants in America* (New York: Macmillan, 1920); Maurice R. Davie, *World Immigration* (New York: Macmillan, 1936); Robert Ernst, *Immigrant Life in New York City, 1826–1863* (New York: Kings Crown Press, 1949); Henry Pratt Fairchild, ed., *Immigrant Backgrounds* (New York: Wiley, 1927); Oscar Handlin, *Boston's Immigrants: A Study in Acculturation*, rev. ed. (Cambridge, Mass.: Harvard University Press, 1959); Robert E. Park, *The Immigrant Press and Its Control* (New York: Harper, 1922); Robert E. Park and Herbert A. Miller, *Old World Traits Transplanted* (New York: Harper, 1921); William Carlson Smith, *Americans in the Making* (New York: Appleton-Century-Crofts, 1939); George M.

Stephenson, *A History of American Immigration, 1820–1924* (Boston: Ginn, 1926) ; Lloyd W. Warner and Leo Srole, *The Social Systems of American Ethnic Groups* (New Haven, Conn.: Yale University Press, 1964) ; Louis Wirth, "The Problem of Minority Groups," in Ralph Linton, ed., *The Science of Man in the World Crisis* (New York: Columbia University Press, 1945) .

3. For some of these contrasts, see S. N. Eisenstadt, *The Absorption of Immigrants* (London: Routledge and Kegan Paul, 1954) and Abraham A. Weinberg, *Migration and Belonging: A Study of Mental Health and Personal Adjustment in Israel* (The Hague: Martinus Nijhoff, 1961) concerning Israel; Peter Marris, *Family and Social Change in an African City* (London: Routledge and Kegan Paul, 1961) about Nigeria; Arthur Redford, *Labour Migration in England, 1800–1950*, rev. ed. (Manchester: Manchester University Press, 1964) concerning England during the Industrial Revolution; and Ronald Taft, *From Stranger to Citizen* (Nedlands: University of Western Australia Press, 1964) dealing with in-migration to Australia.

4. Commons, *op. cit.;* Oscar Handlin, *The Newcomers: Negroes and Puerto Ricans in a Changing Metropolis* (New York: Doubleday, 1959) ; John Hingham, *Strangers in the Land: Patterns of American Nativism, 1860–1925,* rev. ed. (New York: Atheneum, 1963) ; Stephenson, *op. cit.;* Stephan Thernstrom, *Poverty and Progress: Social Mobility in a Nineteenth Century City* (Cambridge, Mass.: Harvard University Press, 1964) .

5. Hingham, *op. cit.*

6. Rowland Tappan Berthoff, *British Immigrants in Industrial America, 1790–1950* (Cambridge, Mass.: Harvard University Press, 1953) .

7. Hingham, *op. cit.;* Mack Walker, *Germany and the Emigration, 1816–1885* (Cambridge, Mass.: Harvard University Press, 1964) .

8. Ernst, *op. cit.;* Oscar Handlin, *Boston's Immigrants, op. cit.;* Marcus Lee Hansen, *The American Migration, 1607–1860* (New York: Harper, 1940) ; Hingham, *op. cit.;* Samuel Joseph, *Jewish Immigration to the United States: From 1881 to 1910* (New York: Atheneum, 1963) ; Edward M. Levine, *The Irish and Irish Politicians* (Notre Dame, Ill.: University of Notre Dame Press, 1966) ; George Potter, *To the Golden Door: The Study of the Irish in Ireland and America* (Boston: Little, Brown, 1960) ; Smith, *op. cit.;* Stephenson, *op. cit.;* William Thomas and Florian Znaniecki, *The Polish Peasant in Europe and America* (Chicago: Chicago University Press, 1918; New York: Knopf, 1928) .

9. Mary Antin, *The Promised Land* (Boston: Houghton Mifflin, 1912) ; Conrad M. Arensberg and Solon T. Kimball, *Family and Community in Ireland* (Cambridge, Mass.: Harvard University Press, 1948) ; Eisenstadt, *op. cit.;* Ernst, *op. cit.;* Handlin, *The Newcomers, op. cit.;* Handlin, *Boston's Immigrants, op. cit.;* Hansen, *op. cit.;* Joseph, *op. cit.;* Park and Miller, *op. cit.;* Smith, *op. cit.;* Stephenson, *op. cit.;* Phyllis H. Williams, *South Italian Folkways in Europe and America* (New Haven, Conn.: Yale University Press, 1938) .

10. Gordon W. Allport, Jerome S. Bruner, and E. M. Jahndorf, "Personality Under Social Catastrophe," *Character and Personality,* X (1941) , 1–22; Eleanor H. Bernert and Ted C. Ikle, "Evacuation and the Cohesion of Urban Groups," *American Journal of Sociology,* LVII (1952) , 133–138. Marc Fried, "Grieving for a Lost Home," in Leonard J. Duhl, ed., *The Urban Condition* (New York: Basic Books, 1963) ; Chester Hartman, "The Housing of Relocated Families," *Journal of the American Institute of Planners,* XXX (1964) , 266–286; Lewis G. Watts, Howard E. Freeman, Helen M. Hughes, Robert Morris, and Thomas F. Pettigrew, *The Middle-Income Negro Family Faces Urban Renewal* (Waltham, Mass.: Research Center of the Florence Heller School, Brandeis University, 1964) ; Michael Young and Peter Wilmott, *Family and Kinship in East London* (London: Routledge and Kegan Paul, 1957) .

11. Robert F. Foerster, *The Italian Emigration of Our Times* (Cambridge, Mass.: Harvard University Press, 1919) ; Harry Jerome, *Migration and Business Cycles,* Publication No. 9 (New York: National Bureau of Economic Research, 1926) ; Thomas and Znaniecki, *op. cit.:* U.S. Immigration Commission, Vol. I (1911) .

12. Estimates based on tables in Brinley Thomas, *Migration and Economic Growth: A Study of Great Britain and the Atlantic Economy* (Cambridge: Cambridge University Press, 1954).

13. Thomas, *op. cit.*

14. Emily Greene Balch, *Our Slavic Fellow Citizens* (New York: Charities Publications Committee, 1910); Ernst, *op. cit.;* Foerster, *op. cit.;* Handlin, *Boston's Immigrants, op. cit.;* Oscar Handlin, *The Uprooted* (Boston: Little, Brown, 1951); Handlin, *The Newcomers, op. cit.;* Hansen, *op. cit.;* Potter, *op. cit.;* Stephenson, *op. cit.;* Thomas, *op. cit.;* Thomas and Znaniecki, *op. cit.;* Walker, *op. cit.;* Cecil Woodham-Smith, *The Great Hunger: Ireland 1845–1849* (New York: Harper, 1962).

15. Balch, *op. cit.;* Grace Leyburn, "Urban Adjustments from the Southern Appalachian Plateaus," *Social Forces,* XVI (1937), 238–246; George C. Myers, "Migration and Modernization: The Case of Puerto Rico, 1950–1960," *Sociological and Economic Studies,* XVI (1967), 425–431; Redford, *op. cit.*

16. Berthoff, *op. cit.;* Charlotte Erickson, *American Industry and the European Immigrant (1860–1885)* (Cambridge, Mass.: Harvard University Press, 1957). Redford, *op. cit.;* Thomas, *op. cit.*

17. Richard Day, "The Economics of Technological Change and the Demise of the Sharecropper," *American Economic Review,* LVII (1967), 427–449.

18. Handlin, *The Uprooted, op. cit.*

19. Hansen, *op. cit.*

20. Balch, *op. cit.*

21. *Ibid.*

22. Foerster, *op. cit.*

23. Walker, *op. cit.*

24. Berthoff, *op. cit.;* Redford, *op. cit.*

25. Rashi Fein, "Educational Patterns in Southern Migration," *Southern Economics Journal,* XXXII (1965), 106–124; C. Horace Hamilton, "Educational Selectivity of Migration from Farm to Urban and to Other Non-farm Communities," in Mildred Kantor, ed., *Mobility and Mental Health* (Springfield, Ill.: Charles C Thomas, 1965; W. Parker Mauldin, "Selective Migration from Small Towns," *American Sociological Review,* V (1940), 748–766.

26. The most systematic data and the most sophisticated analyses in support of this view are collected by Thomas, *op. cit.* The earlier study of migration and business cycles by Jerome, *op. cit.,* comes to an opposite view, but the data he provides are clearly inadequate to the burden he places on them. In particular, he tries to evaluate the conditions of emigration without adequate emigration statistics (using emigration to the United States rather than total emigration from the country of origin), without an adequate evaluation of the complex factors associated with economic expansion and deterioration other than the depression-prosperity cycle, and with far more adequate indices of these limited variables for the United States than for the countries of origin.

27. Jerome, *op. cit.*

28. Hansen, *op. cit.;* Walker, *op. cit.*

29. Simon Kuznets, Dorothy Swaine Thomas, et al., *Population Distribution and Economic Growth: United States, 1870–1950* (Philadelphia: American Philosophical Society, 1964).

30. Ira S. Lowry, *Migration and Metropolitan Growth: Two Analytic Models* (San Francisco: Chandler, 1966).

31. Jerome's *(op. cit.)* analysis does try to take account of both countries of origin and countries of destination, but does not consider migration from a country of origin to any other than the United States. As a consequence, the relative importance of economic changes in the United States is bound to weigh heavily in his statistical analysis. By contrast Thomas *(op. cit.)* more systematically considers the process of emigration from the vantage point of the country of origin and immigration from the vantage point of the country of destination and arrives at a more complex conclusion about the conditions under which either set of forces tends to predominate as a determinant of migration.

32. Rupert Vance, *Research Memorandum on Population Redistribution Within the United States* (New York: Social Science Research Council, 1938); see also Carter Goodrich, Bushwood W. Allin, and Marian Hayes, *Migration and Planes of Living, 1920–1934* (Philadelphia: University of Pennsylvania Press, 1935); for similar findings in France, see Louis Chevalier, *La Formation de la Population Parisienne au XIXᵉ Siècle* (Paris: Presses Universitaires de France, 1950).

32. Eisenstadt, *op. cit.*

33. Eisenstadt, *op. cit.*

34. Niles Carpenter, *Immigrants and Their Children, 1920* (Washington, D.C.: U.S. Government Printing Office, 1927).

35. Rowland Tappan Berthoff, *op. cit.*

36. Thomas, *op. cit.* (Tables 80 to 84). The amount of distortion in these data is unknown, and one may well anticipate some upgrading of occupations generally and the substitution of urban work categories for farmers in anticipation of occupational alterations in the United States.

37. Foerster, *op. cit.*; Walker, *op. cit.*

38. The findings of Karl E. Taeuber and Irene B. Taeuber, *Negroes in Cities: Residential Segregation and Neighborhood Change* (Chicago: Aldine, 1965) and of Peter M. Blau and Otis Dudley Duncan, *The American Occupational Structure* (New York: Wiley, 1967) reveal that this does not hold for those migrants who are of relatively high status and predominantly migrate from one city to another. But the disadvantage of migrants does hold, in these more recent data on internal migration within the United States, for migrants from nonmetropolitan areas (Taeuber and Taeuber, *ibid.*) and for migrants from farm residence (Blau and Duncan, *ibid.*).

39. Newman Arnold Tolles, "Survey of Labor Migration Between States," *Monthly Labor Review*, XLV (1937), 3–16. Vance, *op. cit.*

40. Leyburn, *op. cit.* For some striking differences in unemployment during the recession of 1961 that are associated with rural versus urban background, see Marc Fried, "The Role of Work in a Mobile Society," in Sam B. Warner, Jr., ed., *Planning for a Nation of Cities* (Cambridge, Mass.: M.I.T. Press, 1966).

41. S. M. Lipset and Reinhard Bendix, *Social Mobility in Industrial Society* (Berkeley: University of California Press, 1959).

42. Thernstrom, *op. cit.*

43. Blau and Duncan, *op. cit.* While many controls were possible for this study that could not be done with earlier data, they do not take account of changes in the occupational structure that have increased the proportion of higher status occupational positions and, thus, necessarily produce a pattern of social mobility that is built into the process of social change. Moreover, even assuming that the occupational distribution approximates an interval scale and, therefore, that occupational changes at both ends of the distribution truly represent similar degrees of mobility, an assumption to be verified, the greater variance in the occupational distributions of immigrants than of natives in their sample suggests that the rates of occupational mobility for immigrants can be more seriously affected than those of natives by differentials in occupational mobility at different levels of the occupational scale.

44. Carpenter, *op. cit.*

45. Thomas, *op. cit.* (Table 40).

46. Thomas's (*ibid.*) data and some of Lieberson's (Stanley Lieberson, *Ethnic Patterns in American Cities* [New York: The Free Press of Glencoe, 1963]) findings suggest that many migrants enter the host society at a lower level than that of their former occupations. This tends to confound any simple analysis of social mobility since, either for intragenerational or intergenerational mobility, the distance from the lower initial status of the immigrant will exaggerate mobility achievement compared with the distance from the prior, pre-immigration status.

47. Thomas, *op. cit.*; E. P. Hutchinson, *Immigrants and Their Children, 1850–1950* (New York: Wiley, 1956), Table 41a.

48. Christen Tonnes Jonassen, "Cultural Variables in the Ecology of an Ethnic Group," *American Sociological Review*, XIV (1949), 32–41.

49. Nathan Glazer and Daniel P. Moynihan, *Beyond the Melting Pot: The Negroes, Puerto Ricans, Jews, Italians and Irish of New York City* (Cambridge, Mass.: Harvard and M.I.T. Press, 1963). See Hingham, *op. cit.*, for a description of some of the recurrent waves of anti-Semitism that led to many of the quota systems, residential restrictions, and recreational exclusions during the anti-foreign outbreaks of the 1920s and have begun to diminish only during the past few decades.

50. Calvin F. Schmid and Charles E. Nobbe, "Socioeconomic Differentials Among Nonwhite Races," *American Sociological Review*, XXX (1965), 909–922.

51. Glazer and Moynihan, *op. cit.*; Handlin, *The Newcomers*, *op. cit.*

52. Thomas, *op. cit.* (Table 40).

53. Lieberson, *op. cit.* (Tables 52 and 54).

54. Glazer and Moynihan, *op. cit.*; Handlin, *Boston's Immigrants*, *op. cit.*; Potter, *op. cit.*; Thomas, *op. cit.*; Woodham-Smith, *op. cit.*

55. Lieberson, *op. cit.* (Tables 52 and 54).

56. Thomas, *op. cit.* (Table 40); Lieberson, *ibid.*

57. David Brody, *Steelworkers in America: The Nonunion Era* (Cambridge, Mass.: Harvard University Press, 1960).

58. Lieberson, *op. cit.*

59. Henry S. Shryock, Jr., *Population Mobility Within the United States* (Chicago: Community and Family Study Center, 1964).

60. Richard C. Wade, *The Urban Frontier: The Rise of Western Cities, 1790–1830* (Cambridge, Mass.: Harvard University Press, 1959).

61. Kuznets and Thomas, *op. cit.*

62. Shryock, *op. cit.*

63. Joseph A. Hill, "Recent Northward Migration of the Negro," *Monthly Labor Review*, XVIII (1924), 1–14.

64. *Ibid.*

65. Thomas Jackson Woofter, *Negro Migration: Changes in Rural Organization and Population of the Cotton Belt* (New York: Gray, 1920).

66. Philip M. Hauser, "Demographic Factors in the Integration of the Negro," *Daedalus* (Fall 1965); Conrad Taeuber and Irene B. Taeuber, *The Changing Population of the United States* (New York: Wiley, 1958) give somewhat divergent figures, suggesting a more marked decline in the Negro population of the South between 1890 and 1910.

67. Kuznets and Thomas, *op. cit.*

68. *Ibid.*

69. Taeuber and Taeuber, *The Changing Population of the United States, op. cit.*

70. Shryock, *op. cit.*

71. *Ibid.*; Taeuber and Taeuber, *The Changing Population of the United States, op. cit.*

72. Redford, *op. cit.*, demonstrates this phenomenon for Britain in the nineteenth century.

73. The classical study that postulated the greater inadequacy of migrants compared to nonmigrants as the critical selective factor leading to high rates of mental disorder among migrants is that of Ornulv Odegaard, "Emigration and Insanity: A Study of Mental Disease Among the Norwegian Born Population of Minnesota," *Acta Psychiatrica et Neurologica* (1932), Supplement 4. For more recent reinterpretations of migration and mental illness, see H. B. M. Murphy, "Migration and the Major Mental Disorders," in Kantor, *op. cit.* and Marc Fried, "Effects of Social Change on Mental Health," *American Journal of Orthopsychiatry*, XXXIV (1964), 3–28.

74. Otis Dudley Duncan and Beverly Duncan, *The Negro Population of Chicago: A Study of Racial Succession* (Chicago: University of Chicago Press, 1957); Mauldin, *op. cit.*

75. Duncan and Duncan, *ibid.*

76. Hamilton, *op. cit.;* Fein, *op. cit.*

77. Taeuber and Taeuber, *Negroes in Cities, op. cit.*

78. Karl E. Taeuber and Alma F. Taeuber, "The Changing Character of Negro Migration," *American Journal of Sociology*, LXX (1964), 429–441.

79. Taeuber and Taeuber, *Negroes in Cities, op. cit.* The cities from different regions for which the more detailed analyses are presented are: South: Atlanta, Birmingham, Memphis, New Orleans; Border: Baltimore, St. Louis, Washington; North: Cleveland, Detroit, Philadelphia.

80. Taeuber and Taeuber, *Negroes in Cities, op. cit.*

81. Arensberg and Kimball, *op. cit.*

82. Kuznets and Thomas, *op. cit.*

83. Handlin, *The Newcomers, op. cit.;* Gilbert Osofsky, *Harlem: The Making of a Ghetto* (New York: Harper, 1966).

84. St. Clair Drake and Horace R. Cayton, *Black Metropolis: A Study of Negro Life in a Northern City* (New York: Harcourt, Brace, 1945); Osofsky, *op. cit.;* Jacob A. Riis, *How the Other Half Lives* (New York: Sagamore Press, 1957).

85. Lipset and Bendix, *op. cit.;* Lloyd W. Warner and Leo Srole, *The Social Systems of American Ethnic Groups* (New Haven, Conn.: Yale University Press, 1945); Thernstrom, *op. cit.;* S. M. Miller, "Comparative Social Mobility," *Current Sociology*, IX (1960), Chapter 1; Peter M. Blau and Otis Dudley Duncan, "Some Preliminary Findings on Social Stratification in the United States," *Acta Sociologica*, IX (1965), 2–24; Sidney Goldstein, "Migration and Occupational Mobility in Norristown, Pennsylvania," *American Sociological Review*, XX (1955), 402–448.

86. Whether these rates are viewed as high or low is dependent on (a) subjective expectations or (b) the application of a linear model of mobility to a criterion population (for example, native white Americans). Both of these bases for evaluation are, at best, inadequate for a clear understanding of complex mobility patterns.

87. Thernstrom, *op. cit.*

88. James Tobin, "On Improving the Economic Status of the Negro," *Daedalus* (Fall 1965).

89. Nathan Hare, "Recent Trends in the Occupational Mobility of Negroes, 1930–1960: An Intracohort Analysis," *Social Forces*, XLIV (1965), 166–173.

90. Philip M. Hauser, "Demographic Factors in the Integration of the Negro," *Daedalus* (Fall 1965).

91. *Ibid.*

92. William G. Spady, "Educational Mobility and Access: Growth and Paradoxes," *American Journal of Sociology*, LXXIII (1967), 273–286.

93. Hauser, *op. cit.*

94. Lyle Shannon and Patricia Morgan, "The Prediction of Economic Absorption and Cultural Integration Among Mexican Americans, Negroes and Anglos in a Northern Industrial Community," *Human Organization*, XXV (1966), 154–162.

95. Joe L. Russell, "Changing Patterns of Employment of Nonwhite Workers," *Monthly Labor Review*, LXXXIX (1966), 503–509.

96. Elnar Hardin, "Full Employment and Workers' Education," *Monthly Labor Review*, XVIII (1967), 21–25; Denis F. Johnston and Harvey R. Hamel, "Educational Attainment of Workers in March 1965," *Monthly Labor Review*, LXXXIX (1966), 250–257; Russell, *op. cit.*

97. Gunnar Myrdal, *Challenge to Affluence* (New York: Pantheon, 1962).

98. U.S. Bureau of the Census, *Social and Economic Conditions of Negroes in the United States*, Current Population Reports, October 1967.

99. Rashi Fein, "An Economic and Social Profile of the American Negro," *Daedalus* (Fall 1965); Johnston and Hamel, *op. cit.*

100. Roy L. Lassiter, "The Association of Income and Education for Males by Region, Race and Age," *Southern Economics Journal*, XXXII (1965), 15–22.

101. Blau and Duncan, *op. cit.*

102. Blau and Duncan's (*op. cit.*) report that occupational mobility is similar among native-born whites and foreign-born whites and in contrast with nonwhites

does not substantially affect this conclusion. A very large proportion of the foreign-born whites who were still in the labor force in 1962, the year in which their data were collected, represented a wholly different migration from the European immigration of 1830–1920. Not only was there a different ethnic composition from the earlier migrations as a result of the immigration quotas, but the countries from which they came and the conditions under which many of them migrated involved much greater experience with urban, industrial society. In comparing the earlier immigrants with the Negro, we have been trying to assess the differences among groups with similar origins (either by birth or parentage) in rural, agricultural societies.

103. Riis, *op. cit.*

104. Handlin, *The Newcomers, op. cit.*; Riis, *op. cit.*; Robert A. Woods, *Americans in Process* (Boston: Houghton Mifflin, 1902) .

105. Osofsky, *op. cit.*; Riis, *op. cit.*

106. Lieberson, *op. cit.*

107. Taeuber and Taeuber, *Negroes in Cities, op. cit.*, p. 36.

108. Schmid and Nobbe (*op. cit.*) present interesting data for several nonwhite ethnic groups. The Chinese situation is of particular significance because Chinese immigration was more forcibly cut off (in 1882) than that of any other nationality. For the Chinese, whose immigration occurred largely between 1830 and 1882, meaningful equivalence to white American statuses in education, occupation, and income was not established until 1930–1940, one hundred years after the beginning, and fifty years after the end, of large-scale immigration.

109. For a different view of the term "racism" and its utility, see Daniel P. Moynihan, "The New Racialism," *Atlantic Monthly*, CCXXII (1968) , 35-40. Moynihan argues that the term "racialism" is more appropriate to the current situation which is largely a matter of one group's antagonism toward another group with conflicting interests.

110. E. Franklin Frazier, *The Negro Family in the United States* (Chicago: University of Chicago Press, 1939) .

111. For example, Blau and Duncan, *op. cit.*; Fein, "An Economic and Social Profile of the American Negro," *op. cit.*; Dorothy K. Newman, "The Negro's Journey to the City—Part II," *Monthly Labor Review*, LXXXVIII (1965) , 644–649.

112. Blau and Duncan, *op. cit.*; Hardin, *op. cit.*; Hare, *op. cit.*; Dorothy K. Newman, "The Negro's Journey to the City—Part I," *Monthly Labor Review*, LXXXVIII (1965) , 502–507; Russell, *op. cit.*; Spady, *op. cit.*

113. Blau and Duncan, *op. cit.*; Fein, "An Economic and Social Profile of the American Negro," *op. cit.*; Newman, "The Negro's Journey to the City—Part II," *op. cit.*

114. Schmid and Nobbe, *op. cit.*

115. It is easy to forget the fact that, for many of the countries most markedly affected by massive migrations, serfdom was abolished in the nineteenth century: Italy, Germany, Russia, Poland, Austria. While the Jews and Irish were not, literally, serfs, their servile status and the constraints imposed on their lives were perhaps even more severe.

116. National Advisory Commission on Civil Disorders, 1968; see Thernstrom (*op. cit.*) for a discussion of the "blocked mobility" hypothesis and the evidence that over-all rates of upward social mobility from the lowest ranks have probably increased over time.

117. Stanley Lieberson and Glenn V. Fuguitt, "Negro-White Occupational Differences in the Absence of Discrimination," *American Journal of Sociology*, LXXIII (1967) , 188-200, point out that, in the absence of discrimination, two generations would bring about a high level of parity in the status of Negroes and whites. In view of the high levels of aspiration and motivation among Negroes, appropriate policy might conceive this as the lowest possible limit.

118. Romuald Zaniewski, *L'Origine du Proletariat Romain et Contemporain* (Louvain: Editions Nauwelaerts, 1967) .

119. Gabriel Kolko, *Wealth and Power in America* (New York: Praeger, 1962) .

Chapter 6

☞ *Poverty in Historical Perspective*

STEPHAN THERNSTROM

In the early 1960s, Americans suddenly rediscovered poverty, and attention again turned to the unhappy lot of those eking out an existence in "the other America." But the critics who defined the issue and prodded the public conscience, certain that the situation of the contemporary poor was in many ways unprecedented, were convinced that theirs was more a discovery than a rediscovery. The poverty of the sixties was distinctive, they argued, because in the past "the immigrant saw poverty as a *temporary state* and looked forward to the day when he or his children could gain a greater access to opportunity and financial resources. The poor of today are more inclined to regard poverty as a *permanent way of life* with little hope for themselves or their children. This change in the outlook of the poor can be explained by changes in the opportunity structure." [1] You can easily fill in the rest for yourself. The poor of old had aspirations; the poor today do not. The poor of old had a culture; the poor today have only a "culture of poverty." The poor once had political machines that protected them; now they have only social workers who spy on them. And the crucial contrast, from which so much else follows: The poor were once on the lowest rungs of a ladder most of them could ultimately climb; the poor today are a fixed underclass, a permanent proletariat.

A compelling image, this, but is it *true?* One of the aims of this

This chapter was prepared for a seminar of the American Academy of Arts and Sciences, and all rights to it are reserved by the Academy. It has been published in a shorter form in the January–February 1968 issue of *Dissent* and in Jeramy Larner and Irving Howe, eds., *Poverty, a View from The Left* (New York: Morrow, 1968).

chapter is to answer that question. A related, but broader, aim is to demonstrate the necessity of examining in proper historical perspective some of the complex issues involved in current controversies over the poverty problem. Much of the literature dealing with present-day poverty bristles with large unsubstantiated assumptions about the past. Beyond that simple failure to take into account relevant portions of the historical record, there has been an error that is more difficult to describe: a failure to think about poverty in dynamic, or longitudinal, terms; a failure to conceive it as a status that people enter and leave over time, a status of which the social meaning depends, in considerable measure, on the patterns that govern entry into, persistence in, and exit from the status. Thus, a contemporary study that estimates that 10 per cent, let us say, of the citizens in a given society are living in poverty may mean that everyone in the society is impoverished for part, but only part, of his life—the graduate-student poverty model, let us call it—or it may mean that 10 per cent of the citizens are born poor, live poor, and die poor, with no one else ever experiencing deprivation. Obviously, the policy problems posed by these two extreme cases and the solutions that might make sense differ radically. As will be shown later, the massive volume of research that has been conducted on poverty in present-day America provides dismayingly little information about this crucial dimension of the phenomenon. For these reasons, it should be worthwhile to sketch what we presently know about what changes there have been over the past century in the nature, extent, and, particularly, the *permanence* of poverty for individual Americans.

We cannot examine the changing fortunes of the poor in the American past without specifying clearly what we mean by poverty, and that, as several of the chapters in this volume make clear, is no simple task. Poverty has been viewed as a state of mind, a state of the pocketbook, and a good many other related, but distinct, things. There is, however, one simplifying element for the historian. The poor left but a vague imprint on the historical record; much of what we would like to know about them is irrevocably lost. The enormous gaps in the surviving records are highly frustrating, but this defect has at least one modest compensating virtue. The problem of definition is not quite as agonizing as it would otherwise be because the choices are limited, and we must perforce content ourselves with a rough-and-ready definition appropriate to the available data. Perhaps a conception of "the culture of poverty" like that of Oscar Lewis is intellectually more satisfying than other current alternatives, perhaps not, but in any event little can be said about whether Lewis's culture of poverty is growing or shrinking, whether those who live in it today are better off or worse off than in the past, because the scanty historical record provides few clues on which to make such a judgment. Lewis and his assistants gather mountains of material in extensive interviews and describe the culture of poverty in terms of "some seventy interrelated social, economic and psychological traits" [2]; the historian of the common people must rest content with information on a few crude characteristics like occupation, ethnic background, literacy, and place of residence. But something meaningful can be said about poverty in the past even on the basis of these slender fragments. As defined in this chapter, the poor are those who occupy the lowest level of the social pyramid, as measured by occupational rank and command over economic resources, and the central question for analysis is the height and permeability of the barrier that sets them off from the rest of society.

This will become clearer if we come down to cases. By the middle of the last century the economic and social processes that shaped urban industrial America were operating; something resembling the modern city had appeared, with its factories, slums, immigrants, and other characteristic features.[3] Let us look for a moment at the situation of the poor in one of those cities, Newburyport, Massachusetts, a small textile and shoe manufacturing city.[4] After combing through census schedules, tax lists, savings bank records, and other sources that provide clues about the welfare of ordinary people, the first impression is that the entire working class lived barely above, if not actually below, the margin of subsistence. It is this that contemporary writers have in mind when they contrast the mass poverty of yesterday with the class poverty of today. Certainly if we projected backward some contemporary "poverty line"—$3,000 annual income in 1960 dollars or whatever—every workingman (and virtually all people in middle-class jobs, for that matter) would appear desperately poor.

The absurdity of this is evident. Obviously, we need a more relative and situational definition of poverty, one which divides the poor from the nonpoor according to criteria meaningful in the particular historical setting under consideration. Two such criteria are available. There was, first of all, an occupational structure that placed individuals in different social categories. Men who held nonmanual jobs—professionals, business proprietors or managers, clerks, and salesmen—were not poor in the sense in which I use the term; nor were the skilled artisans of the community, who earned much higher wages than their unskilled or semiskilled brethren, enjoyed greater job security, had solid families, characteristically owned their own homes, and so on. The size of this latter group, the skilled labor aristocracy, varied somewhat from place to place; it included half of the manual laborers in Newburyport, but was large enough to be important in every city.

Neither the skilled workers nor most white-collar employees were entirely immune from economic hardship in time of depression; at times, some were forced to turn to private or public charity for temporary assistance. Some analysts make dependency the definitive characteristic of the poor, but this is misleading. To be temporarily dependent did not relegate a man to the bottom of the social ladder; the deserving poor, the respectable poor, were not a group sharply set apart. It was the mass of unskilled and semiskilled workmen, for whom unemployment and privation were a way of life, who were seen as different and dangerous. It was the perpetuation of their way of life that William Ellery Channing had in mind when he warned of the "fatal inheritance of beggary." [5] A very useful index of the persistence of poverty in this setting, therefore, is the degree to which people on the lowest rungs of the occupational ladder actually remained fixed there over the course of their careers and the degree to which their children gravitated toward those same lowly callings. Movement into a higher ranked occupation, into a white-collar post or a skilled trade, was escape from poverty.

This is not to say that all those unskilled and semiskilled laborers who found no avenues of occupational mobility open to them were desperately and uniformly poor. There was a second key determinant of status that must be considered, for holding a lowly occupation did not impose a single style of life on all who held it. One can be a casual laborer or a garbage collector and still own one's own home, possess a savings account, go to church, and display the other traits we associate with stable working-class culture.[6] One can, and a great many workmen did in Newburyport a century or so ago. The central question to ask is not how many of the untutored newcomers who poured into the burgeoning cities of this period made it by becoming lawyers, clerks, or even carpenters; nor is it how many of their sons made it in this fashion, interesting though both of these questions are. The main issue is how many became part of stable working-class culture, an achievement that was possible without any upward occupational mobility at all.

It is not easy to provide an operational definition of stable working-class culture, not at least in terms of operations the historian can perform with the sketchy data available. But for nineteenth-century Newburyport, a satisfactory index was a family's property holdings as reflected in savings accounts and real-estate purchases. To what extent was poverty in the industrial city a century ago, as defined by occupational rank and property holdings, a permanent status? Of all of the unskilled laboring families in Newburyport, only a modest fraction either of fathers or of sons escaped into the white-collar world, and a similarly modest fraction of men from either generation succeeded in entering a skilled calling. But even though these laborers remained overwhelmingly concentrated in low-skilled occupations, with wages in the vicinity of $1.50 a day and frequent unemployment, the great preponderance of those who stayed in the city at all were able to climb into the ranks of the property-owning, stable working class. Most of them bought their own homes, most of them built up savings accounts with a few hundred dollars in them. These were people at the bottom of the occupational ladder, with unstable employment opportunities and starvation wages. But stable social patterns can exist despite unstable market conditions.

Two things that made this extraordinary achievement possible should be noted because they have an obvious bearing on the situation of the poor today. First, children were an economic asset; in the typical instance, all the children who reached the age of ten or twelve were put into the mills and their pooled earnings went to purchase the dwelling. There are some revealing figures for a statewide sample of unskilled laborers in Massachusetts in 1874; the mean annual wage of these family heads was a mere $414, but this was only 57 per cent of the mean annual income of the family unit as a whole.[7] Of course this exploitation of child labor also had important implications for the mobility prospects of the children; it virtually removed them from the competition for middle-class jobs.

The second enabling circumstance was that these people appear to have lived in a tight little island of their own, insulated from the tastes and standards of the larger community and the society as a whole. This was especially true of the Irish workingmen, who were highly visible—they had their own religious and social institutions, distinctive names, and so on—but it was to some degree true of the rural migrants from New Hampshire and Vermont as well. One indication of this is that while many of these families had a total combined income that hovered around the minimum subsistence budgets carefully calculated by contemporary middle-class investigators, they still managed to save. Their conception of subsistence was far more Spartan—it was potatoes! And their subculture had given them a goal that was clear and within reach—a piece of property, a piece of respectability that made all those potatoes tolerable.

If those who stayed in the town characteristically made it into the stable working class even without occupational gains, what of those who left the community? They, after all, were a majority; only 40 per cent of the unskilled laborers in Newburyport in 1850 were still there when the census taker made his rounds a decade later, and the comparable figures for 1860 to 1870 are 35 per cent and for 1870 to 1880, 47 per cent. These are strikingly high turnover figures, of course, and they cannot be attributed to the peculiar volatility of the Irish; breaking down out-migration rates by nativity reveals that the Yankees were a wandering breed, too, more wandering than the Irish in the last of the three decades studied.

This finding suggested the obvious possibility that relatively small industrial communities like Newburyport skimmed off certain types of people from the migratory streams that entered them— perhaps the more stable, docile, unadventuresome souls—and that in a full-fledged metropolis like Boston you might see a very different pattern. Presumably, disproportionate numbers of the highly talented and ambitious would be drawn to the metropolis and would settle down there. And the same would be true for the opposite extreme—the people least able to settle into the confining regimen of life in a small Yankee city, those who for one reason or another had failed to make a go of it in the Newburyports of America and who could huddle together in a big-city proletarian ghetto. When I began research on Boston, I was especially interested in tracking these people to their lairs, for here, if anywhere, was a culture of poverty within industrial America, here would be what David Matza calls "the dregs," the sediment from the mobility process.[8]

After tracing some eight thousand residents of Boston through census schedules, city directories, and tax records from 1880 to 1963, I now strongly doubt the existence of these permanent proles—or, more accurately, doubt their continuity in any one place over time.[9]

One expects to find that workingmen in Boston will stay put far more than they did in Newburyport, both for the reason I have mentioned (the likelihood that failures would cluster together in the big city slums) and for the additional reason that you can do a lot to satisfy an impulse to move and still remain within the boundaries of a big city—you can go from the North End of Boston to Jamaica Plain, for example, which surely is as far in social distance as the journey from Newburyport to Boston. This is a highly plausible expectation, but it turns out not to be the case, or not to be very much the case. For in the post-1880 decades on which I have comparable information, the unskilled and semiskilled workmen of Boston exhibited only a little more stability than they did in Newburyport earlier, with rates of persistence within the city approaching 50 per cent for each of these ten-year periods—higher than Newburyport, but not dramatically higher. What these figures mean is that before you even consider what happens to the people who stay around town, you must realize that they are a selection from total population you started with. If half of the people who are unskilled and impoverished in 1880 simply disappear from the universe of the study—as indeed they do—you cannot talk about the experiences of the remaining half as if they were the only people of concern.

What did happen to all these migrants who left the community? Some of them, of course, left this life altogether, but it is easy to show that death was not a prime exit for the age groups with which I was dealing. Some were lost because of errors in the sources (city directories and tax records), name changes, etc., but again these were minor influences. Most just left. Where they went, and what kind of adjustment they made there, I regret to say, cannot be discerned. The data for systematic study of these questions just do not exist.

There are, however, two general conclusions of interest to draw from these findings about population turnover. One is that it probably will be difficult to find in any American city of the past—and this, unhappily, is just about the only unit you can study until the age of national samples—a large lower-class group with high continuity of individual membership. Like Newburyport, even a great city like Boston seems to have been a Darwinian jungle in which ruthless natural selection took place. The people who remain conveniently under our microscope to be observed tend to be making it; if they weren't, they would be less likely to stay on the scene.

Second, while we don't really know what later happened to the mass of workmen who disappeared from Newburyport or Boston—it is possible that many of them fared much better elsewhere—it may be that they constituted a permanently depressed underclass, a floating body of permanent transients buffeted about from place to place until they died. I don't know that, of course; I'm not even sure about how to go about finding historical evidence that would permit us to pin down the matter. From the 1870s on, there was public discussion of the problem of the tramp, and later there were useful studies of migratory labor, the Wobblies, etc. But I have in mind a broader phenomenon, and one in which entire families participated, rather than just isolated individuals or fathers who left their families behind in the home city and made forays out into the world for temporary jobs.

It is not clear how many of the poor in America today are likewise permanent transients. There is a popular stereotype that low-status individuals tend to be rooted in one place, while professionals, managers, etc. are constantly being transferred from one community to another, but the actual situation is more complex. The very limited census data available suggest that professionals are indeed more volatile than the population as a whole, but that very low status manual laborers also display unusually high turnover rates.[10] Furthermore, recent critical work on the reliability of the census suggests substantial enumeration errors for the floating urban lower class, which may lead to an underestimation of its actual volatility.[11] In any case, the main issue is not whether the poor are a little more or a little less volatile residentially than more well-to-do Americans, for it appears that virtually all categories of American city-dwellers have a high propensity to keep moving. The point is that physical movement has different causes and consequences for different social strata and that in the lower reaches of the social order it may still have the pathological significance it appears to have had in the nineteenth century.

What of the low-skilled workmen who did remain in Boston for a decade or more, and what of their children? There are a great many ways to go about answering that question, and many complications in the patterns that I've been able to ascertain so far, but the crude generalization I would offer is that the chances of rising in the world were rather impressively high and that they remained pretty much the same between 1880 and 1963. There were some fluctuations, with the World War I decade very good and the 1930s not so good, but no clear long-term trend indicating a sharp constriction of opportunity and the appearance of a new permanent underclass.

The prospects for one important kind of mobility—intragenerational or "career" occupational mobility—can be gauged by some statistics showing the relationship between the first-known occupation and the last-known occupation of adult males in three samples—one drawn from the manuscript-census schedules for 1880, one from marriage-license records for 1910, one from 1930 birth certificates. Of the men who began as unskilled or semiskilled laborers, between 35 and 40 per cent, a very large minority, ended up higher on the occupation scale. Seventeen per cent ended as skilled craftsmen in the 1880 cohort, 11 per cent in the 1910 cohort, and 16 per cent in the 1930 cohort; the fraction entering white-collar positions was higher in each cohort—22 per cent, 28 per cent, and 20 per cent respectively. Even if occupational mobility had been the only means of climbing off the bottom and entering the stable working class or the middle class—and, as I have suggested, there were other means—you could not describe this social structure as rigid and closed.

The kind of mobility that has attracted more popular and more scholarly attention is intergenerational mobility, reflecting the old American belief that the adults can go to hell so long as you do something to rescue the kids. The figures that best give a sense of the magnitude of social mobility between generations are these. Of the sons of men holding unskilled or semiskilled jobs in Boston, 55 to 65 per cent ended up in higher status occupations, most of them middle-class occupations. The figures for entry into white-collar jobs are 40 per cent for boys coming of age around 1900, 46 per cent for those coming of age around 1920, and 38 per cent for men who were 33 in 1963. (For a variety of reasons too complicated to enumerate, it is doubtful that the drop from 46 to 38 per cent reflects a genuine trend.) In addition to this striking mobility out of the blue-collar world altogether, another substantial fraction of these youths—20 per cent, 16 per cent, and 18 per cent, respectively—ended up in a skilled trade. For the laboring families who remained in Boston, therefore—keeping in mind that an almost equally large segment of the working-class population simply disappeared from the city, and their opportunities for advancement may have been much less—there were in 1880, and there are today, very impressive chances for career mobility and even more impressive ones for upward movement between generations.

All this calls into question, to say the least, the legend of Boston as a stagnant, caste-ridden place inhabited chiefly by Cabots, Lodges, George Apleys, and surly Irish plumbers. But it would hardly be worth the effort if that were the only conclusion to be drawn. The real question is what light these findings shed on the larger question of social circulation in the United States, or at least in the American city. A good deal probably, but so little is known about mobility patterns for the first part of my period that it cannot be proved. I can only invoke the consideration that fundamental social processes like these tend to operate in broadly similar fashion in all the cities of a given society.[12]

For the period before 1900 or so my Boston findings can be generalized only on assumption, for the only comparable study of nineteenth-century mobility patterns is my Newburyport effort, and that is hardly a secure foundation for monumental comparisons. In the twentieth century, the mists begin to recede and a few more pegs on which to hang a generalization become visible. There are substantial technical difficulties entailed in comparing the highly disparate studies available, but it is sufficient to say here that there are no gross anomalies—that the little we know, and after World War II it becomes a great deal, is consistent with the general portrait that we could sketch with Boston as our only model. Less is known about career mobility than about intergenerational mobility—before 1940 there is only Norristown, Pennsylvania, as a point of comparison, while for mobility between generations there are Indianapolis and San Jose, California, for the beginning of the twentieth century and after, New Haven for the Depression decade, and several national samples for the post-World War II period.[13] All of these reveal patterns of upward mobility on a roughly comparable scale; all of them point to the conclusion, now a cliché among sociologists, but a cliché apparently unknown to authors of popular books about contemporary poverty, that the door of opportunity is not creaking shut—that it may indeed be opening a shade wider.

These remarks pertain to occupational mobility. Let us turn to the phenomenon that bulked so large in Newburyport: the presence of men who remain fixed close to the bottom of the occupational ladder but who enter the stable working class by accumulating property. There was a sizable minority, albeit a minority, of people who remained in Boston for some decades and yet experienced no notable improvement in their occupational status. To what extent may we equate this group with the dregs, the permanent proles? It is harder to judge than in the Newburyport case where property mobility was so conspicuous. This existed in Boston, too; of the fathers of sons from the 1930 birth-certificate sample who were traceable in 1963, 52 per cent of those who still held unskilled or semiskilled jobs owned some real estate. On the whole, however, property mobility of this kind was rarer in Boston after 1880 than in nineteenth-century Newburyport, and it is worth asking why. There are some difficulties with the data, too technical to expound here, that may help to account for this, and there is the further consideration that real estate is harder for a poor man to obtain in a large city where land values are higher and there are characteristically fewer single-family dwellings. In 1900, 81 per cent of the families of Boston lived in rented dwellings. (There are important variations, it should be noted, both between cities and within cities over time. The Boston rate of home ownership in 1900 was unusually low, and the rate in all major American cities has gone up precipitously since World War II, which helps to explain the 1963 figure just cited.)

It is possible that the laborer who would have put his painfully accumulated $800 into a lot and small house in Newburyport, but found fewer opportunities to do so in Boston, simply left his money in the bank there; it has not been feasible to do the tedious research necessary to answer this question.[14] It is also possible, however, that, unable to gratify his land hunger, he simply saved less and used the funds to purchase consumption goods. Did possession of these signify entry into the stable working class? It is difficult to say. Clearly a significant historical change in both the availability and the social meaning of different kinds of property has occurred some time in this century, and we will have to learn more about it than we now know to grasp the nature of contemporary poverty. At present, we can only speculate about the way in which rising per capita incomes and the custom of installment buying—which became widespread not after World War II, as has often been assumed, but in the 1920s—altered the significance of various kinds of property. It seems important that the acquisition of property in nineteenth-century Newburyport required prolonged disciplined behavior before the fact, before the desired object—a home—was obtained. The contrast should not be drawn too sharply—there were mortgages then, substantial down payments are required for certain purchases today—but clearly there has been a major historical shift in the direction of flying now and paying later. The poor today are more vulnerable to the vicissitudes of the market partly because they have made long-term financial commitments based on the most optimistic assumptions about future income and because they never developed the penny-pinching facility of their predecessors. They have more possessions, certainly, but perhaps less security comes from having the possessions.

Let us now directly confront the issue of poverty in present-day America and its allegedly unique character. Since much of the current discussion defines the poor as all those whose annual incomes fall below a certain dollar line, some initial remarks on poverty in terms of an income class would be appropriate. There has been a good deal of heated argument precisely where to draw the poverty line, but the two points of greatest significance seem to be these. One is that wherever the line is drawn—$3,000, $4,000, or wherever—an ever-smaller fraction of the American population falls below that line. The long-term trend of per capita income in this country is dramatically upward, and the way in which that income is distributed has not shifted abruptly in a direction unfavorable to those on the lower end of the scale. The rich have been getting richer, all right, but the poor have been getting richer at much the same rate.[15] (The situation of the Negro in the past decade is a partial exception; more about that later.) There has been no major increase in the proportion of the national income going to those on the bottom in recent decades, to be sure, a fact to which social commentators in the Age of Eisenhower were peculiarly oblivious. But the awkward truth that there is no pronounced trend toward more equal distribution of income in this country should not obscure the elementary fact that the disadvantaged are now receiving about the same fraction of a pie which has grown substantially larger. Admittedly they expect more, in some ways it can be said that they need more, but that it is more is of considerable consequence, however it might seem to those of us who never have to worry about the grocery bills.

A second observation is that we need to know far more than we do about whether "the poor," however defined, are an *entity* with more or less stable membership, or a mere *category* into which Americans fall and out of which they climb in rapid succession. If we assume that some fixed figure represents a minimal decent income for a family of a certain size and that all those below it are living in poverty, it is obviously crucial to know if it is pretty much the same families and the offspring of those families that fall below that line year after year as is commonly assumed by proponents of the "new poverty" thesis, or if there is a great deal of turnover in the composition of the group. Some people with desperately low incomes, after all, are graduate students. Are many of the poor temporary victims? Given the flood of publication on poverty today it is remarkable that hardly anything is known about the continuity of the group. I have been able to turn up only a few fragments of evidence which bear upon this point, and none does much to support the case of the pessimists.

One such fragment is the oft-cited statistic that about 40 per cent of the parents receiving AFDC in 1964 were themselves raised in homes where public assistance was received. This may sound impressive, but it becomes much less so when we recall that a high proportion of these parents were raised during the Great Depression, when at least a quarter, and quite possibly more, of the American population received such assistance.[16] The 40 per cent figure for AFDC parents may indicate some over-representation of the offspring of the poor of the last generation in the current group, which is hardly surprising, but the tendency is at best a modest one. And there is not the slightest reason to believe that there is anything at all new about this tendency.

No better direct evidence is available on the extent to which children born into poor households themselves end up in the low-income category for life. But a good deal is known about the extent to which sons "inherit" their fathers' occupations, and Galloway has made ingenious use of this knowledge to explore the relationship between the income position of fathers in various occupational categories and their sons' income positions.[17] Lacking information about the income of individual respondents and their fathers, he was forced to work with crude median income figures from broad occupational groups. Thus he assumes, for instance, that two individuals in the "professional, technical, and kindred workers" category, one the son of a laborer and one the son of a physician, both earned the median income for that category—i.e., $6,619 in 1960. This doubtless gives a somewhat biased estimate, since the physician's son was quite possibly a high-paid physician himself, and the laborer's son a much less well-paid laboratory technician. But Galloway's calculations are nonetheless suggestive, and the burden of proof must lie on those who claim that the problem I refer to destroys their value altogether. Galloway shows, for instance, that while the median income of professional, technical, and kindred workers was $6,619, and that of laboring fathers a shade below the $3,000 poverty line, the median income of sons of professional, technical, and kindred workers was $5,735 and that of laborers' sons $4,686. This is still a substantial gap, of course, but what is noteworthy is the pronounced covergence of the two groups, resulting from the fact that the tendency to inherit one's father's occupation is quite weak in this society. Laborers earned less than half of what professional, technical, and kindred workers earned; their sons earned more than 80 per cent of what the sons of professional, technical, and kindred workers earned.

The foregoing items pertain to the transmission of poverty from generation to generation. Equally scanty is our knowledge about the continuity of poverty from year to year and decade to decade. It is known that 69 per cent of the families with incomes below the poverty line in 1962 were in the same unhappy position in 1963 as well.[18] Is an annual rate of persistence in poverty of about two-thirds a high one or a low one? It would seem to be rather low if one could assume that remaining in the persisting group from one year to the next did not alter one's probability of escaping it in future years; 70 per cent persistence over two years would mean 49 per cent persistence over three years, 34 per cent over four years, 24 per cent over five, and so on. The assumption that, in the statistician's language, these are independent trials is obviously doubtful to some degree. The Michigan Survey Research Center study of a national sample interviewed in 1960 disclosed that of the reporting families whose 1959 incomes fell below the poverty line fully 60 per cent had never in their lifetimes earned as much as $3,000 in one year, and almost 40 per cent had never even reached $2,000.[19] This certainly suggests greater continuity in the low-income group than the simple extrapolation of the 70 per cent figure for a two-year period. But some of these respondents were of advanced age and had gone through their peak earning years at a time at which the dollar was worth considerably more than it was in 1959, so that recomputation of the data on a real dollar basis would have resulted in a lower estimate of continuity. Furthermore, the survey was made just prior to the beginning of the longest period of uninterrupted economic growth in the nation's history, so that it is quite conceivable that a comparable survey today would yield different results.

Such a study should compute persistence rates using a variety of poverty lines rather than one dollar figure; obviously it is important to know how many people depart from poverty or fall into it by earning $50 more or $50 less a year. There is the interesting finding that of the families who climbed above the line between 1962 and

1963, 2/5 remained under the $4,000 mark, 1/5 earned between $4,000 and $5,000, and 2/5 earned more than $5,000.[20] The latter families are, of course, the really impressive ones, and one would like to know much more about how many of them ever fall back and under what circumstances. Too little is known about this essential matter. At a minimum, however, one can say that those who are convinced that poverty in the United States is increasingly being meted out in life sentences have yet to do the homework to substantiate the claim.

On this question of persistence it is pertinent to note that while *low* persistence in poverty seems unambiguously desirable from the point of view of the classic American obsession with upward mobility, it is a two-edged sword. If there is considerable poverty at two points in time, and few of the impoverished at time A are still impoverished at time B, many people who previously were doing all right must have fallen into poverty. Earlier I alluded to this possibility as universal graduate-student poverty, but that was probably misleading in that it implies that everyone goes through temporary poverty at the start of his career and then escapes it permanently. Being poor would be a by-station through which everyone passes on his way out and no one returns. We know that this is not altogether the case in America today—the poverty rates broken down by age indicate that—but we have not gone very far toward developing sound actuarial knowledge about this vast problem. A promising start in this direction was made more than half a century ago by B. Seebohm Rowntree when he developed the conception of "the poverty cycle," but that was a seed which regrettably fell upon barren ground.[21] The question of the connection between poverty and the stages of the individual life cycle still cries for systematic exploration.

Another key element of the new poverty thesis is the assumption that it is now far more difficult for a low-skilled manual laborer to work his way up the occupational ladder than it once was. As already indicated, there is no reason to believe that this is in fact the case. For all of today's facile talk about the barriers against mobility growing ever higher, the fragmentary knowledge we have about the American class structure in the past and the extensive literature on current occupational mobility patterns suggests that changes in the opportunity structure over the past century have been minimal, and that those minimal changes are in the direction of greater upward mobility today. It is clear that the educational requirements for many desired jobs have been going up steadily, but the expansion of educational opportunities has kept pace with, if not outrun, this development. It may be that decisive career choices are being made earlier than they once were—that now people drop out of the race permanently when they drop out of school for certain attractive positions, positions for which there were once fewer formal requirements —but it is very doubtful that this has resulted in less recruitment from below. To some extent, it has had the opposite effect, in that the change has been part of an increasingly universalistic process of selection.

It is doubtful indeed that a new poverty has recently been created in this country because of creeping arteriosclerosis of the occupational structure. Unskilled and semi-skilled laborers still rise to a higher occupation during their lifetimes, in at least a minority of cases; the sons still make the jump more frequently than the fathers.

Impressive though it is, the evidence on rates and patterns of occupational mobility does not entirely dispose of the arguments of the pessimists. They would emphasize that the demand for unskilled labor, the capacity of the economy to absorb raw newcomers and assure them steady wages, is not what it was when the golden door was open to all. There could, in principle, be a change of this kind, a deterioration of conditions at the lowest rung of the occupational ladder, without a perceptible decline in upward occupational mobility rates. That this has indeed happened in the United States today has become an accepted truth in discussions of contemporary poverty without benefit of the slightest critical examination. Without doubt, the demand for unskilled labor is not what it used to be if we take the proportion of jobs that are classified as unskilled as our measure; indeed, discussions of this point often allude to the shrinking of the unskilled category in this century and the mushrooming of the white-collar group as if that proved something. But what about the demand relative to the supply? To say that this relationship has changed in a way unfavorable to the unskilled is to assert that the pool of unemployed or underemployed laborers—the Marxian industrial reserve army—is characteristically larger now than it was in the past, and that wage differentials between unskilled and other types of work are now larger. Neither of these propositions can be substantiated.

As to the first, we have a decent times series on average annual unemployment only back to 1900, and one broken down for specific occupational groups—which is really what we want—only since 1940.[22] But you needn't dig at all deeply into historical data to arrive at the conclusion that, however hard it may be for many people to find steady employment in our society today, it was often harder still in the past. The romantic haze through which so many commentators view the early struggles of the immigrants of old should not obscure the harsh realities. Thus in 1900 44 per cent of the unskilled laborers in the United States were unemployed at some time; of a sample of Italian workers in Chicago, for example, 57 per cent had been out of a job some time during the previous year, with the average time unemployed running over seven months.[23] These are but illustrations; systematic analysis is impossible given the paucity of data. But the fact that horror stories like these become increasingly difficult to duplicate as we approach the present, plus the mild downward trend in the over-all unemployment time series since 1900 makes me feel very skeptical about the common assumption that things are getting worse for those on the bottom. Unemployment remains a problem; it is not, at least as yet, a growing problem.

Similarly, evidence to support the claim that wage differentials are changing in a direction unfavorable to the unskilled is lacking. It is clear, indeed, that the long-term trend has been toward a diminution in wage differentials between low-skill and high-skill workmen.[24]

All this is not to deny that the unskilled labor market now offers fewer employment opportunities and rewards to certain kinds of people, and greater opportunities and rewards to others. An obvious instance of the former would be the aged, who once were free to die with their boots on and now suffer compulsory retirement. But few of them lived to reach what we now consider retirement age, so that isn't much of an argument for the good old days.

A far more important case is that of the Negro. This is a more complicated issue than is sometimes believed, but there are some grounds for pessimism here. It is painfully obvious that the labor market today, as well as the housing market, the educational system, and virtually every other American institution, is not color-blind. The disadvantaged position of the Negro vis à vis the white has been endlessly documented. Perhaps the most shocking statistic with respect to poverty is that nonwhites are 11 per cent of the population, but 20 per cent of the poor, and *40 per cent* of those who remained in poverty from 1962 to 1963, the only period for which persistence data are available.[25] But the crucial question concerns *trends;* static comparisons yield no insight into them.

There are two difficulties with the attempts which have thus far been made to examine the position of the Negro as a dynamic rather than a static problem. One is that the discussion has concentrated on very recent trends. It has been shown, for example, that in the early 1950s the Negro unemployment rate rose to double that of the white, where it has remained ever since. Similarly, the income of white families increased by 35 per cent between 1955 and 1962, while the Negro gain was only 31 per cent.[26] Dismaying as such information is, however, it would be foolish to take it as evidence of a *long-term* deterioration of the position of the Negro in this country. Systematic treatment of this question is difficult because of deficiencies in the data, but a mere glance at such books as W. E. B. Du Bois' classic *The Philadelphia Negro* (1899) or Ray Stannard Baker's *Following the Color Line* (1908) should dispel the illusion that the urban Negro was any better off at the turn of the century—quite the contrary.[27] And there is the more important objection that Negroes then were overwhelmingly concentrated on the farms of the South; it would be hard indeed to argue that the laborer in Chicago's Black Belt envied the sharecropper in Mississippi. America's Negroes voted on that proposition with their feet, and the verdict is clear.

The other main problem with the existing literature on the situation of the Negro is that the truly relevant comparison is not between Negroes and whites as a bloc, but between Negroes and earlier migrant groups at the point at which they entered the urban industrial world. An index of "white" mobility, or median income, education, or anything else is a composite figure which lumps together the illiterate Sicilian peasant or the Kentucky hillbilly just arrived in the city with the seventh-generation graduate of Harvard College and various other long-established social types. Likewise with a figure for "Negroes." Some part of the Negro's current difficulties in Roxbury or Harlem comes from the simple fact that even today a majority of the blacks in the city are newcomers to the urban industrial ways. To be able to see how many of their disabilities are specific to them rather than general concomitants of the migration process we need comparisons—not with "white society" today but with the Irish in 1850, the Irish, the Poles, the Jews, and others in 1910, and so on, and studies which compare the achievements of Negroes who are second- and third-generation city-dwellers with the achievements of those who are newcomers.[28]

Comparative statistical research of this kind has not yet been done, though Oscar Handlin's *The Newcomers* and Nathan Glazer and Daniel P. Moynihan's *Beyond the Melting Pot* pose the question properly.[29] I regret to confess, furthermore, that my own Boston study doesn't advance our knowledge in this area as much as I had hoped. It provides some of these points of comparison, but it does not, unhappily, reveal much about Boston's Negroes. They constituted such a small fraction of the population until very recently that even my large sample contained few of them, and those few had very high out-migration rates, so that few indeed remained in the city long enough to have careers that could be traced. But something can be said on the basis of the Boston data about other ethnic groups and of Blau and Duncan's comparison of the mobility patterns of non-whites and whites, divided into ethnic generations—foreign born, second generation Americans, and native-born Americans of native parentage.[30]

This evidence suggests that it is somewhat misleading to speak crudely of "the immigrant experience," for different groups had somewhat different experiences. All made some progress of the sort depicted in popular folklore, but some made much more than others over comparable periods of time. The Jews, for example, were the most dramatically mobile, and the Irish the slowest to rise as a group. (To be more precise, the Irish experienced a great deal of short-term upward mobility, but unusually high downward mobility as well; they found it especially difficult to consolidate their gains in the way that other groups did.) Negroes, however, ranked well below the average for the least successful of these groups. Many of the obvious handicaps of the Negro are those of other newcomers, it is true. Where you end up in the struggle for position is strongly influenced by your father's occupation, by your educational attainments, by your experience (or lack of experience) in urban living, and by your own initial position in the job market; on all four of these counts the Negro is in an unenviable position. But the striking and depressing thing is that in our society the Negro remains disadvantaged even when these barriers are taken into account and their effects removed by statistical controls. Not only are the fathers of Negroes exceptionally highly concentrated on the lower rungs of the occupation ladder, it is also a bigger handicap for a Negro to come from a low-status home than for a white, and similarly with low educational attainment, lack of urban experience, and poor initial start in the labor market. All groups starting at the bottom have these handicaps to overcome. The point is that these hurdles are not sufficient to account for the poor position of Negroes; there is a substantial residual factor remaining which is a measure of the distinctive prejudice which has been directed at the Negro in this society.[31]

To the extent, then, that in talking about the economic plight of "the new poor" we are really talking about the plight of the Negro there is genuine cause for alarm. The position of the Negro is by no means worse than it used to be, if that is the relevant point of comparison. But if we take the experience of preceding migrant groups as a baseline, the Negro poses a more serious problem for America than did his predecessors. In addition to the disabilities faced by all newcomers to the urban industrial world, the Negro has faced and still faces another series of obstacles which keep him down. As for the rest of the poor, however—and by none of the current definitions of poverty do Negroes constitute anything close to a majority of the group—the common assumption that the structure of the labor market has changed precipitously and disastrously seems unfounded.

There have been some changes in our society which have made things tougher for those on the bottom of the ladder and which have been responsible for some of the distress and discontent which have been mistakenly attributed to the supposed tightening of the occupational structure and the presumed glut on the unskilled labor market.

One of these has to do with the costs and rewards of having a large brood of children. We are now acutely aware that the rich get richer and the poor get children, so much so that we tend to forget that there ever was a time when kids were an economic asset. In nineteenth-century America the earnings of young children were of decisive importance in enabling laboring families to secure a property stake in the community; there is evidence that much the same sort of thing happened well into the present century. This, of course, is no longer true. The extension of compulsory school attendance has steadily narrowed the span of years in which a youth is old enough to work but too young to set up a household of his own. Furthermore, it appears that a youth who is working and yet living at home is less likely today to turn his earnings over to his father; the shift from the

CCC's practice of sending a lad's wages home to his parents to the Job Corps' practice of paying members directly is a revealing symptom of a larger social change which has weakened the economic viability of the working-class family. Having multiple wage earners, all of whom felt that what they earned was not their own but the family's, was not only a means of generating a surplus for the savings account, it was also a kind of primitive unemployment compensation scheme. Even in very hard times it was unlikely that all the family wage earners would be thrown out of work. These benefits were available in only one phase of a man's life cycle, of course—it is not very common to have a steady stream of children throughout one's entire life—but if a house could be paid for during that phase, the reduction in income that came with the departure of the children was tolerable.

A more important if less tangible change which demands attention is the steady erosion of the subcultures which defined the expectations of workingmen in the past. There were once working-class enclaves—often, but not necessarily, with ethnic boundaries—within which the mobility values of the larger society were redefined in more attainable terms. The workingmen of nineteenth-century America toiled with remarkable dedication to accumulate the funds to pay for tiny cottages of their own and were amazingly successful at it. There may be some contemporary analogues to those cottages, as books like the Middletown volumes, Chinoy's study of automobile workers, and Berger's *Working Class Suburb* suggest.[32] But everything about contemporary America conspires to make both copping out entirely and having lower aspirations than others more difficult. The unskilled laborer of today who earns $3,000 a year is prosperous indeed by nineteenth-century standards, but he probably *feels* poorer, because his expectations are formed in a very different social order. One of the clichés about the new poor is that their aspirations are lower than those of the old poor—they are a defeated bunch, living in a system "designed to be impervious to hope." [33] But the point to stress is perhaps the opposite. Many of the poor today expect more and put up with less from others in order to get it, precisely because the enclaves of old have been levelled, with all the docility and deference which they fostered. Of course one can always say that this represents a weakening of the moral fibre of the common man, that the solution to the poverty problem is to convince people that living on $3,000 isn't really living in poverty. But the point is that this weakening of the moral fibre, if you wish to call it that, is no accident; it is not a mere passing whim but the result of some large and irreversible changes in society.

It is obvious that this line of argument applies with special force to the Negro. His objective grievances are real enough, as I have stressed, but they are by no means new. They do not suffice to explain the militant mood so dramatically on the rise today. Thus, the recent insistence of the Roxbury-based Mothers for Adequate Welfare that they be given an extra welfare check to purchase turkeys for their families at Thanksgiving. "If I can't get nothing to eat on Thanksgiving," said one, "I might as well be in jail. They give you turkey in jail." [34] Demands of this kind would have been quite unimaginable in this country a century or even twenty years ago; there is every reason to believe that they will become more common in the future. The American Negro has never lived in the thrift-oriented subculture of the classic European immigrant,[35] and it is doubtful that such groups as the Muslims will be any more successful in creating one now than Booker T. Washington was earlier. Even if the wall of discrimination which has long discouraged the development of the saving ethic in the Negro community were to vanish overnight, this is no longer the nineteenth century and there is no way of isolating the ghetto from the mass media and inundating it with McGuffey's readers. Consumption expectations will probably continue to remain higher than what most Negroes can command in the labor market, even if the market becomes color-blind.

Add to this another special circumstance affecting the Negro— namely that whereas all preceding groups of newcomers were succeeded by others still more handicapped and impoverished, the Negro, along with the Puerto Rican and the Mexican, is obviously not destined to be followed by a new underclass to look down upon —and you see something of the dynamic behind the current racial crisis. Negroes are the first group in American history whose only hope of getting off the bottom is not by standing on someone else's shoulders but by eliminating the bottom altogether. They have a compelling motive to press for nothing less than the prompt attainment of a society in which no family head earns less than the median family income, a society in which there is literally an income pyramid rather than the diamond-shaped distribution we have today, with the median income (approximately $7,000 today) as the floor below which no family is permitted to fall.[36] This would, of course, be equally in the economic interest of the white poor, who are a majority of the poor, and it might even appeal to significant numbers of the affluent on the grounds of social justice.

It would be premature to claim that a truly serious War on Poverty of this kind will come to pass, or even become a lively public issue. The dominant thrust in the Negro community today is toward black control within the boundaries of the ghetto, and there is seemingly little awareness that the attainment of black power may yield no greater gains for the group than Irish power did for the Irish. There are some interesting stirrings in poor white neighborhoods, but these most often have a defensive character, as in the anti-Urban Renewal movement. And it has yet to be demonstrated that the black and white poor can effectively cooperate politically.

But to suggest that in the near future there will be growing pressure from below for the redistribution of wealth and power in American society is perhaps closer to the mark than the recent analysis by the Task Force on Economic Growth and Opportunity of the U.S. Chamber of Commerce, which concludes comfortably that the objective situation of the poor is now so encouraging that "the old socialist tradition in discussing income [distribution] is dying out. Conditions no longer call for deep-seated and widespread social change. The discussion now is on helping the poor. Expropriation of property is no longer seriously considered as a remedy." [37] It is indeed true that the economic position of the poor today has not deteriorated in the manner described by proponents of the "new poverty" thesis, but the enlightened capitalists of the Task Force are equally misguided in their belief that to disprove the law of increasing misery is to assure that no one on the bottom will ever seek to rock the boat, that the poor will remain ever grateful for the benevolent helping hand. What moves men to protest is simply more complex and elusive than that, as the ferment which has been provoked by the Johnson administration's version of "helping the poor" should make clear.

I do not, in sum, see any grounds for believing that this country is now threatened by a mass of "new poor" whose objective situations, especially their opportunities to rise out of poverty, are much worse than those of earlier generations. The "new poverty" thesis appears to have as little foundation in fact as the old pseudoscientific belief in the distinction between the "old" and "new" immigrants, which provided the intellectual rationale for the immigration restriction legislation from 1917 to 1924 and the McCarran-Walter Act of 1952.[38] The major changes I see are generally encouraging, or at least mixed.

One can be clear-headed about what is happening without being complacent about the status quo. I have never understood why so many Americans believe that to assert that things are bad you must insist that they are getting worse. I would argue that they could well be getting a little better—as the situation of the poor in America is, on the whole—and still be intolerably bad. A little less unemployment can still be too damned much unemployment in a culture in which people have become civilized enough to understand that recurrent unemployment is due not to the will of God but to the inaction of man. To conjure up a Golden Age from which to judge the present and find it wanting is quite unnecessary, and as Tocqueville pointed out long ago, it is even somewhat un-American, for the American way is to reject the achievements of the past as a standard for the present or future. Americans, he said, use the past only as a means of information, and existing facts only as a lesson used in doing otherwise and doing better.

Notes

1. Louis Ferman et al., *Poverty in America* (Ann Arbor: University of Michigan Press, 1965) , xv–xvi.

2. Oscar Lewis, *La Vida* (New York: Random House, 1965) , xliv.

3. A full analysis of poverty in the American past would begin earlier, and would examine the social structure of agrarian America. For helpful clues, see Jackson Turner Main, *The Social Structure of Revolutionary America* (Princeton, N.J.: Princeton University Press, 1965) ; Merle Curti et al., *The Making of an American Community: A Case Study of Democracy in a Frontier County* (Stanford: Stanford University Press, 1959) ; Stanley Elkins and Eric McKitrick, "A Meaning for Turner's Frontier," *Political Science Quarterly*, LXIX (1954) , 321–353, 565–602; F. L. Owsley, *Plain Folk of the Old South* (Baton Rouge: Louisiana State University Press, 1949) ; Fabian Linden, "Economic Democracy in the Slave South: An Appraisal of Some Recent Views," *Journal of Negro History*, XXXI (1946) , 140–189. But it would be a digression to pursue the issue here, for the urban frontier is the only frontier we have now, and it is to the nineteenth-century city we must look for a baseline against which to appraise contemporary poverty.

4. For details, see Stephan Thernstrom, *Poverty and Progress: Social Mobility in a 19th Century City* (Cambridge, Mass.: Harvard University Press, 1964; paperback, New York: Atheneum, 1969) .

5. William Ellery Channing, "Discourse on Tuckerman," in *Works, VI* (Boston: G. G. Channing, 1849) , 101.

6. On the crucial distinction between working-class and lower-class cultures, see S. M. Miller and Frank Reissman, "The Working Class Subculture: A New View," *Social Problems*, IX (Summer 1961) , 86–97.

7. *Report of the Massachusetts Bureau of the Statistics of Labor for 1874* (Boston, 1875) , pp. 365–370.

8. David Matza, "The Disreputable Poor," in Reinhard Bendix and S. M. Lipset, *Class, Status and Power* (rev. ed., Glencoe, Ill.: The Free Press, 1966), 289–302.

9. All comments on Boston are based on my current work in progress, which employs the techniques of the Newburyport study to examine social mobility in Boston from 1880 to 1963.

10. Donald J. Bogue, *The Population of the United States* (Glencoe, Ill.: The Free Press, 1959), 384–386.

11. Jacob S. Siegel and Melvin Zelnik, "An Evaluation of Coverage in the Census of Population by Techniques of Demographic Analysis and by Composite Methods," *Proceedings of the Social Statistics Section, 1966, American Statistical Association*, pp. 71–85; Jacob S. Siegel, "Completeness of Coverage of the Nonwhite Population in the 1960 Census and Current Estimates, and Some Implications," in David M. Heer, ed., *Social Statistics and the City* (Cambridge, Mass.: Joint Center for Urban Studies, 1968), pp. 13–54.

12. For further discussion of this point, see Thernstrom, *Poverty and Progress*, Ch. 8.

13. For citations to this literature as of 1964, see Thernstrom, *Poverty and Progress*. For the most recent contribution, and a survey of publications in the interim, see Peter M. Blau and Otis Dudley Duncan, *The American Occupational Structure* (New York: Wiley, 1967). This is a highly technical study, based on a national sample of 20,700, gathered during the Census Bureau's monthly Current Population Survey. The quantity and quality of the data presented here and the analytical ingenuity of the authors make this a work of exceptional importance.

14. Wheeler found this to be the case with the Irish of Providence, R.I., in the 1850 to 1880 period. They held little real estate, but accumulated very impressive savings; Robert Wheeler, "The Fifth-Ward Irish: Mobility at Mid-Century," unpublished seminar paper, Brown University, 1967.

15. Herman P. Miller, *Income Distribution in the United States* (Washington: United States Bureau of the Census, Government Printing Office, 1966). Miller has also prepared a most valuable survey of the evidence on "Changes in the Number and Composition of the Poor" in twentieth-century America, in Margaret S. Gordon, ed., *Poverty in America* (San Francisco: Chandler 1965), pp. 81–101.

16. M. Elaine Burgess, "Poverty and Dependency: Some Selected Characteristics," *Journal of Social Issues*, XXI (January 1965), 79–97. Burgess asserts that only 10 per cent of the American population has ever received public assistance, and that AFDC parents are accordingly dramatically over-represented. But the 10 per cent figure, taken from the Michigan Survey Research Center study, James N. Morgan et al., *Income and Welfare in the United States* (New York: McGraw-Hill, 1962), p. 144, refers to a sample of *adults* in 1960, not to a sample of persons old enough to be *grandparents* at that time. This, of course, would be the relevant point of comparison. The grandparents of the AFDC children of the early 1960s were adults back in the 1930s, when dependency rates were far higher. Precisely how much higher we do not know, regrettably. There is abundant evidence on how many aid recipients there were at any one point in time. Thus in December 1933 some 24.8 million Americans were receiving public assistance, relief, work program employment, and other emergency employment financed from federal, state, or local funds; Marietta Stevenson, *Public Welfare Administration* (New York: Macmillan 1938), p. 38. This was 20 per cent of the American population. A year later the figure was 23.5 million, or 19 per cent. But this does not tell us how many Americans *ever* turned to the government for assistance during this period. The proportion cannot be lower than 20 per cent, for 20 per cent were receiving aid at the worst moment of the depression. But the true figure is obviously above that, since it is most unlikely that all of the 23.5 million assisted in December 1934 were among the 24.8 million dependents of December 1933. About 20 per cent of the families below the poverty line in 1963, after all, had fallen into poverty after having had a higher income the preceding year; *1965 Annual Report of the President's Council of Economic Advisers* (Washing-

ton, 1965), p. 165. It seems safe to assume that in each year of the depression there were American families coming to financial grief and seeking public help for the first time. A rate for all those who ever received aid in the depression decade, therefore, would be distinctly above the rate at any one moment. It would be distinctly above 20 per cent and might even be as much as double that. If that were the case, the 40 per cent figure for the homes in which the parents of today's AFDC children were raised would indicate no tendency at all for dependency to be "handed down from generation to generation."

17. Lowell E. Galloway, "On the Importance of 'Picking One's Parents,'" *Quarterly Review of Economics and Business*, VI (Summer 1966), 7–15.

18. *1965 Report of President's Council of Economic Advisers*, pp. 164–165.

19. Morgan et al., *op. cit.*, p. 200. Table 16–7 recalculated to exclude cases in which maximum annual earnings were unknown.

20. Burton Weisbrod, *The Economics of Poverty: An American Paradox* (Englewood Cliffs, N. J.; Prentice-Hall, 1965), p. 87.

21. B. Seebohm Rowntree, *Poverty: A Study in Town Life* (London: Macmillan, 1901). Rowntree's conception was better than his execution, for his analysis of the dynamics of poverty rested on dubious inferences from static, cross-sectional data. He never appears to have contemplated the possibility that some York residents may have escaped from the vicious cycle he described, and his research technique was not suitable for discovering whether or not this ever happened.

22. Stanley Lebergott, *Manpower in Economic Growth: The American Record Since 1800* (New York: McGraw-Hill, 1964), pp. 164–190.

23. Robert Hunter, *Poverty* (New York: Macmillan, 1904), pp. 33–34.

24. Miller, *op. cit.*, Ch. 3 and the literature cited there. For other arguments against the view that the situation of the low-skilled blue-collar worker has drastically deteriorated, see Charles Silberman, *The Myths of Automation* (New York: Harper and Row, 1966), esp. Ch. 2.

25. Herman Miller, *Poverty American Style* (Belmont, Cal.: Wadsworth Publishing Co., 1966), p. 4.

26. Perhaps the most useful collection of material on the issue is Arthur M. Ross and Herbert Hill, ed., *Employment, Race and Poverty* (New York: Harcourt, Brace, 1967); the data cited are from pp. 30 and 87. Also valuable is Talcott Parsons, ed., *The Negro American* (Boston: Houghton Mifflin, 1965), esp. Rashi Fein's "An Economic and Social Profile of the Negro American," pp. 102–133.

27. W. E. B. DuBois, *The Philadelphia Negro: A Social Study* (Philadelphia: University of Pennsylvania Press, 1899); Ray Stannard Baker, *Following the Color Line* (New York: Doubleday, Page & Co., 1908). See also the excellent new historical study by Allan H. Spear, *Black Chicago: The Making of a Negro Ghetto, 1890–1920* (Chicago: University of Chicago Press, 1967).

28. This argument is developed more fully in Stephan Thernstrom, "Up from Slavery," *Perspectives in American History*, I (1967), 434–440. For data on the importance of recent migrants in the northern Negro population, see Philip M. Hauser, "Demographic Factors in the Integration of the Negro," in Parsons, *op. cit.*, pp. 71–101.

29. Oscar Handlin, *The Newcomers: Negroes and Puerto Ricans in a Changing Metropolis* (New York: Doubleday, 1959); Nathan Glazer and Daniel P. Moynihan, *Beyond the Melting Pot* (Cambridge: Harvard and MIT Press, 1963).

30. Blau and Duncan, *op. cit.*, Ch. 6.

31. This argument is strongly reinforced by the work of Professor Samuel Bowles of the Harvard Economics Department on race differentials in the returns obtained from investment in education. See "Towards Equality of Educational Opportunity?" *Harvard Educational Review*, XXXVIII (Winter 1968), 89–99. Bowles' work is based on the 1960 U.S. Census as well as a recent dissertation on returns to earnings. See G. Hanoch, "Personal Earnings and Investment in Schooling," unpublished doctoral dissertation, University of Chicago, 1965. The data indicate the appalling possibility that many Negro school dropouts are in fact behaving in an economically rational manner in that for Negroes but not for whites the income lost by remaining in school will not necessarily be made up

later. Relatively well-educated Negroes tend to earn better incomes than relatively uneducated ones, but at some educational levels short of graduate school the gap is not large enough to make up for the additional years the educated remain outside the labor market.

32. Robert and Helen Lynd, *Middletown* (New York: Harcourt Brace, 1929) and *Middletown in Transition* (New York: Harcourt Brace, 1937); Ely Chinoy, *Automobile Workers and the American Dream* (New York: Doubleday, 1955); Bennett M. Berger, *Working Class Suburb* (Berkeley: University of California Press, 1960).

33. Michael Harrington, *The Other America* (New York: Macmillan, 1962), p. 10.

34. *Boston Globe,* November 23, 1966.

35. For all of their disagreements, Booker T. Washington and W. E. B. DuBois agreed on this. See Booker T. Washington, *Up From Slavery* (New York: Doubleday, Page, 1901); paperback edn. (New York: Bantam Books, 1956), esp. pp. 62–63 and W. E. B. DuBois, *op. cit.,* pp. 185 and *passim.*

36. See the fascinating discussion of this matter in Lee Rainwater's chapter in the present volume, Ch. 9.

37. Task Force on Economic Growth and Opportunity, Chamber of Commerce of the United States, *The Concept of Poverty* (Washington, 1965), 3.

38. For an incisive critique of the old immigrant–new immigrant dichotomy, see Oscar Handlin, *Race and Nationality in American Life* (Boston: Little, Brown, 1957), Ch. 5.

Chapter 7

⊂≋ *The Culture of Poverty*

OSCAR LEWIS

As an anthropologist, I have tried to understand poverty and its associated traits as a culture or, more accurately, as a subculture [1] with its own structure and rationale, as a way of life that is passed down from generation to generation along family lines. This view directs attention to the fact that the culture of poverty in modern nations is not only a matter of economic deprivation, of disorganization, or of the absence of something. It is also something positive and provides some rewards without which the poor could hardly carry on.

In my book *Five Families: Mexican Case Studies in the Culture of Poverty*, I suggested that the culture of poverty transcends regional, rural-urban, and national differences and shows remarkable cross-national similarities in family structure, interpersonal relations, time orientation, value systems, and spending patterns. These similarities are examples of independent invention and convergence. They are common adaptations to common problems.

The culture of poverty can come into being in a variety of historical contexts. However, it tends to grow and flourish in societies with the following set of conditions: (1) a cash economy, wage labor, and production for profit; [2] (2) a persistently high rate of unemployment and underemployment for unskilled labor; (3) low wages; (4) the failure to provide social, political, and economic organization, either on a voluntary basis or by government imposition, for the low-income population; (5) the existence of a bilateral kinship system

From Oscar Lewis, *The Study of Slum Culture—Backgrounds for La Vida* (New York: Random House, 1968). © 1968 by Oscar Lewis. Reprinted by permission of Random House, Inc.

rather than a unilateral one; and finally, (6) the existence in the dominant class of a set of values that stresses the accumulation of wealth and property, the possibility of upward mobility, and thrift and that explains low economic status as the result of personal inadequacy or inferiority.

The way of life that develops among some of the poor under these conditions is the culture of poverty. It can best be studied in urban or rural slums and can be described in terms of some seventy interrelated social, economic, and psychological traits. However, the number of traits and the relationships between them may vary from society to society and from family to family. For example, in a highly literate society, illiteracy may be more diagnostic of the culture of poverty than in a society where illiteracy is widespread and where even the well-to-do may be illiterate, as in some Mexican peasant villages before the revolution.

The culture of poverty is both an adaptation and a reaction of the poor to their marginal position in a class-stratified, highly individuated, capitalistic society. It represents an effort to cope with feelings of hopelessness and despair that develop from the realization of the improbability of achieving success in terms of the values and goals of the larger society. Indeed, many of the traits of the culture of poverty can be viewed as attempts at local solutions for problems not met by existing institutions and agencies because the people are not eligible for them, cannot afford them, or are ignorant or suspicious of them. For example, unable to obtain credit from banks, they are thrown upon their own resources and organize informal credit devices without interest.

The culture of poverty, however, is not only an adaptation to a set of objective conditions of the larger society. Once it comes into existence, it tends to perpetuate itself from generation to generation because of its effect on the children. By the time slum children are age six or seven, they have usually absorbed the basic values and attitudes of their subculture and are not psychologically geared to take full advantage of the changing conditions or increased opportunities that may occur in their lifetime.

Most frequently, the culture of poverty develops when a stratified social and economic system is breaking down or is being replaced by another, as in the case of the transition from feudalism to capitalism or during periods of rapid technological change. Often the culture of poverty results from imperial conquest in which the native social and economic structure is smashed and the natives are maintained in a servile colonial status, sometimes for many generations. It can also occur in the process of detribalization, such as that now going on in Africa.

The most likely candidates for the culture of poverty are the people who come from the lower strata of a rapidly changing society and are already partially alienated from it. Thus, landless rural workers who migrate to the cities can be expected to develop a culture of poverty much more readily than migrants from stable peasant villages with a well-organized traditional culture. In this connection there is a striking contrast between Latin America, where the rural population has long ago made the transition from a tribal to a peasant society, and Africa, which is still close to its tribal heritage. The more corporate nature of many of the African tribal societies as compared to Latin American rural communities and the persistence of village ties tend to inhibit or delay the formation of a full-blown culture of poverty in many of the African towns and cities. The special conditions of apartheid in South Africa, where the migrants are segregated into separate "locations" and do not enjoy freedom of movement, create special problems. Here, the institutionalization of repression and discrimination tends to develop a greater sense of identity and group consciousness.

The culture of poverty can be studied from various points of view: the relationship between the subculture and the larger society; the nature of the slum community; the nature of the family; and the attitudes, values, and character structure of the individual.

The lack of effective participation and integration of the poor in the major institutions of the larger society is one of the crucial characteristics of the culture of poverty. This complex matter results from a variety of factors, which may include lack of economic resources, segregation and discrimination, fear, suspicion or apathy, and the development of local solutions for problems. However, participation in some of the institutions of the larger society—for example, in the jails, the army, and the public relief system—does not per se eliminate the traits of the culture of poverty. In the case of a relief system that barely keeps people alive, both the basic poverty and the sense of hopelessness are perpetuated rather than eliminated.

Low wages and chronic unemployment and underemployment lead to low income, lack of property ownership, absence of savings, absence of food reserves in the home, and a chronic shortage of cash. These conditions reduce the possibility of effective participation in the larger economic system. And as a response to these conditions we find in the culture of poverty a high incidence of pawning of personal goods, borrowing from local moneylenders at usurious interest rates, spontaneous informal credit devices organized by neighbors, use of secondhand clothing and furniture, and the pattern of frequent buying of small quantities of food many times a day as the need arises.

People with a culture of poverty produce very little wealth and receive very little in return. They have a low level of literacy and education, do not belong to labor unions, are not members of political parties, generally do not participate in the national welfare agencies, and make very little use of banks, hospitals, department stores, museums, or art galleries. They have a critical attitude toward some of the basic institutions of the dominant classes, hatred of the police, mistrust of government and those in high position, and a cynicism that extends even to the church. These factors give the culture of poverty a high potential for protest and for being used in political movements aimed against the existing social order.

People with a culture of poverty are aware of middle-class values; they talk about them and even claim some of them as their own, but on the whole they do not live by them.[3] Thus, it is important to distinguish between what they say and what they do. For example, many will tell you that marriage by law, by the church, or by both is the ideal form of marriage; but few marry. For men who have no steady jobs or other source of income, who do not own property and have no wealth to pass on to their children, who are present-time oriented and want to avoid the expense and legal difficulties involved in formal marriage and divorce, free unions or consensual marriages make a lot of sense. Women often turn down offers of marriage because they feel that it ties them down to men who are immature, punishing, and generally unreliable. Women feel that consensual union gives them a better break; it gives them some of the freedom and flexibility that men have. By not giving the fathers of their children legal status as husbands, the women have a stronger claim on their children if they decide to leave their men. It also gives women exclusive rights to a house or any other property they own.

In describing the culture of poverty on the local community level, we find poor housing conditions, crowding, gregariousness, and, above all, a minimum of organization beyond the level of the nuclear and extended family. Occasionally, there are informal temporary groupings or voluntary associations within slums. The existence of neighborhood gangs that cut across slum settlements represents a considerable advance beyond the zero point of the continuum that I have in mind. Indeed, it is the low level of organization that gives the culture of poverty its marginal and anachronistic quality in our highly complex, specialized, organized society. Most primitive peoples have achieved a higher level of socio-cultural organization than our modern urban slum dwellers.

In spite of the generally low level of organization, there may be a sense of community and *esprit de corps* in urban slums and in slum neighborhoods. This can vary within a single city or from region to region or country to country. The major factors that influence this variation are the size of the slum, its location and physical characteristics, length of residence, incidence of homeownership and land-ownership (versus squatter rights), rentals, ethnicity, kinship ties, and freedom or lack of freedom of movement. When slums are separated from the surrounding area by enclosing walls or other physical barriers, when rents are low and fixed and stability of residence is great (twenty or thirty years), when the population constitutes a distinct ethnic, racial, or language group or is bound by ties of kinship or *compadrazgo*,[4] and when there are some internal voluntary associations, then the sense of local community approaches that of a village community. In many cases, this combination of favorable conditions does not exist. However, even where internal organization and *esprit de corps* are at a bare minimum and people move around a great deal, a sense of territoriality develops that sets off the slum neighborhoods from the rest of the city. In Mexico City and San Juan, this sense of territoriality results from the unavailability of low-income housing outside of the slum areas. In South Africa, the sense of territoriality grows out of the segregation enforced by the government, which confines the rural migrants to specific locations.

On the family level the major traits of the culture of poverty are the absence of childhood as a specially prolonged and protected stage in the life cycle; early initiation into sex; free unions or consensual marriages; a relatively high incidence of the abandonment of wives and children; a trend toward female- or mother-centered families, and consequently a much greater knowledge of maternal relatives; a strong predisposition to authoritarianism; lack of privacy; verbal emphasis upon family solidarity, which is only rarely achieved because of sibling rivalry; and competition for limited goods and maternal affection.

On the level of the individual, the major characteristics are strong feelings of marginality, of helplessness, of dependence, and of inferiority. I found this to be true of slum dwellers in Mexico City and San Juan among families who do not constitute a distinct ethnic or racial group and who do not suffer from racial discrimination. In the United States, of course, the culture of poverty of the Negroes has the additional disadvantage of racial discrimination, but as I have already suggested, this additional disadvantage contains a great potential for revolutionary protest and organization that seems to be absent in the slums of Mexico City or among the poor whites in the South.

Other traits include high incidence of maternal deprivation, of orality, and of weak ego structure; confusion of sexual identification; lack of impulse control; strong present-time orientation, with relatively little ability to defer gratification and to plan for the future; sense of resignation and fatalism; widespread belief in male superiority; and high tolerance for psychological pathology of all sorts.

People with a culture of poverty are provincial and locally oriented and have very little sense of history. They know only their own troubles, their own local conditions, their own neighborhoods, their own way of life. Usually they do not have the knowledge, the vision, or the idealogy to see the similarities between their problems and those of their counterparts elsewhere in the world. They are not class conscious although they are very sensitive indeed to status distinctions.

In considering the traits discussed above, the following propositions must be kept in mind: (1) The traits fall into a number of clusters and are functionally related within each cluster. (2) Many, but not all, of the traits of different clusters are also functionally related. For example, men who have low wages and suffer chronic unemployment develop a poor self-image, become irresponsible, abandon their wives and children, and take up with other women more frequently than do men with high incomes and steady jobs. (3) None of the traits, taken individually, is distinctive per se of the subculture of poverty. It is their conjunction, their function, and their patterning that define the subculture. (4) The subculture of poverty, as defined by these traits, is a statistical profile; that is, the frequency of distribution of the traits both singly and in clusters will be greater than in the rest of the population. In other words, more of the traits will occur in combination in families with a subculture of poverty than in stable working-class, middle-class, or upper-class families. Even within a single slum there will probably be a gradient from culture of poverty families to families without a culture of poverty. (5) The profiles of the subculture of poverty will probably differ in systematic ways with the difference in the national cultural contexts of which they are a part. It is expected that some new traits will become apparent with research in different nations.

I have not yet worked out a system of weighting each of the traits, but this could probably be done and a scale could be set up for many of the traits. Traits that reflect lack of participation in the institutions of the larger society or an outright rejection—in practice, if not in theory—would be the crucial traits; for example, illiteracy, provincialism, free unions, abandonment of women and children, lack of membership in voluntary associations beyond the extended family.

When the poor become class conscious or active members of trade-union organizations or when they adopt an internationalist outlook on the world, they are no longer part of the culture of poverty although they may still be desperately poor. Any move-ment—be it religious, pacifist, or revolutionary—that organizes and gives hope to the poor and effectively promotes solidarity and a sense of identification with larger groups destroys the psychological and social core of the culture of poverty. In this connection, I suspect that the civil rights movement among the Negroes in the United States has done more to improve their self-image and self-respect than have their economic advances, although, without doubt, the two are mutually reinforcing.

The distinction between poverty and the culture of poverty is basic to the model described here. There are degrees of poverty and many kinds of poor people. The culture of poverty refers to one way of life shared by poor people in given historical and social contexts. The economic traits that I have listed for the culture of poverty are necessary but not sufficient to define the phenomena I have in mind. There are a number of historical examples of very poor segments of the population that do not have a way of life that I would describe as a subculture of poverty. Here I should like to give four examples.

1. Many of the primitive or preliterate peoples studied by an-thropologists suffer from dire poverty that is the result of poor tech-nology or poor natural resources, or both, but they do not have the traits of the subculture of poverty. Indeed, they do not constitute a subculture because their societies are not highly stratified. In spite of their poverty, they have a relatively integrated, satis-

fying, and self-sufficient culture. Even the simplest food-gathering and hunting tribes have a considerable amount of organization, including bands and band chiefs, tribal councils, and local self-government—traits that are not found in the culture of poverty.

2. In India the lower castes (the Chamars, the leather workers, and the Bhangis, the sweepers) may be desperately poor both in the villages and in the cities, but most of them are integrated into the larger society and have their own panchayat organizations, which cut across village lines and give them a considerable amount of power.[5] In addition to the caste system, which gives individuals a sense of identity and belonging, there is still another factor: the clan system. Wherever there are unilateral kinship systems or clans, one would not expect to find the culture of poverty, because a clan system gives people a sense of belonging to a corporate body that has a history and a life of its own and thereby provides a sense of continuity, a sense of a past and of a future.

3. The Jews of eastern Europe were very poor, but they did not have many of the traits of the culture of poverty because of their tradition of literacy, the great value placed upon learning, the organization of the community around the rabbi, the proliferation of local voluntary associations, and their religion, which taught that they were the chosen people.

4. My fourth example is speculative and relates to socialism. On the basis of my limited experience in one socialist country—Cuba—and on the basis of my reading, I am inclined to believe that the culture of poverty does not exist in the socialist countries. I first went to Cuba in 1947 as a visiting professor for the State Department. At that time I began a study of a sugar plantation in Melena del Sur and of a slum in Havana. After the Castro revolution, I made my second trip to Cuba as a correspondent for a major magazine, and I revisited the same slum and some of the same families. The physical aspect of the slum had changed very little, except for a beautiful new nursery school. It was clear that the people were still desperately poor, but I found much less of the feelings of despair, apathy, and hopelessness that are so diagnostic of urban slums in the culture of poverty. The people expressed great confidence in their leaders and hope for a better life in the future. The slum itself was now highly organized, with block committees, educational committees, party committees. The people had a new sense of power and importance. They were armed and were given a doctrine that glorified the lower class as the hope of humanity. (I was told by one Cuban official that

they had practically eliminated delinquency by giving arms to the delinquents!)

It is my impression that Castro, unlike Marx and Engels, did not write off the so-called *lumpenproletariat* as an inherently reactionary and anti-revolutionary force, but rather saw its revolutionary potential and tried to utilize this potential. In this connection, Frantz Fanon makes a similar evaluation of the role of the *lumpenproletariat* based on his experience in the Algerian struggle for independence:

It is within this mass of humanity, this people of the shanty towns, at the core of the *lumpenproletariat,* that the rebellion will find its urban spearhead. For the *lumpenproletariat,* that horde of starving men, uprooted from their tribe and from their clan, constitutes one of the most spontaneous and most radically revolutionary forces of a colonized people.[6]

My own studies of the urban poor in the slums of San Juan do not support the generalizations of Fanon. I have found very little revolutionary spirit or radical ideology among low-income Puerto Ricans. On the contrary, most of the families I studied were quite conservative politically, and about half of them were in favor of the Republican Statehood Party.[7] It seems to me that the revolutionary potential of people with a culture of poverty will vary considerably according to the national context and the particular historical circumstances. In a country like Algeria, which was fighting for its independence, the *lumpenproletariat* was drawn into the struggle and became a vital force. However, in countries like Puerto Rico in which the movement for independence has very little mass support and in countries like Mexico that achieved their independence a long time ago and are now in their postrevolutionary period, the *lumpenproletariat* is not a leading source of rebellion or of revolutionary spirit.

In effect, we find that in primitive societies and in caste societies the culture of poverty does not develop. In socialist, fascist, and highly developed capitalist societies with a welfare state, the culture of poverty tends to decline. I suspect that the culture of poverty flourishes in, and is generic to, the early free-enterprise stage of capitalism and that it is also endemic to colonialism.

It is important to distinguish between different profiles in the subculture of poverty, depending upon the national context in which these subcultures are found. If we think of the culture of poverty primarily in terms of integration in the larger society and a sense of identification with the great tradition of that society or with a new emerging revolutionary tradition, then we will not be surprised that some slum dwellers with a low per capita income may have moved further away from the core characteristics of the culture of poverty than others with a higher per capita income. For example, Puerto Rico has a much higher per capita income than Mexico, yet Mexicans have a deeper sense of personal and national identity. In Mexico even the poorest slum dweller has a much richer sense of the past and a deeper identification with the great Mexican tradition than do Puerto Ricans with their tradition. In both countries, I presented urban slum dwellers with the names of national figures. In Mexico City, quite a high percentage of the respondents, including those with little or no formal schooling, knew about Cuauhtémoc, Hidalgo, Father Morelos, Juárez, Díaz, Zapata, Carranza, and Cárdenas. In San Juan, the respondents showed an abysmal ignorance of Puerto Rican historical figures. The names of Ramón Power, José de Diego, Baldorioty de Castro, Ramón Betances, Nemesio Canales, and Lloréens Torres rang no bell. For the lower-income Puerto Rican slum dweller, history begins and ends with Muñoz Rivera, his Muñoz Marín, and Doña Felisa Rincón!

I have listed fatalism and a low level of aspiration as key traits of the subculture of poverty. Here, too, however, the national context makes a big difference. Certainly the level of aspiration of even the poorest sector of the population in a country like the United States with traditional ideology of upward mobility and democracy is much higher than in more backward countries like Ecuador and Peru, where both the idealogy and the actual possibilities of upward mobility are extremely limited and where authoritarian values still persist in both the urban and the rural milieu.

Because of the advanced technology, the high level of literacy, the development of mass media, and the relatively high aspiration level of all sectors of the population, especially when compared with underdeveloped nations, I believe that although there is still a great deal of poverty in the United States (estimates range from 30 to 50 million people) there is relatively little of what I would call the culture of poverty. My rough guess would be that only about 20 per cent of the population below the poverty line (from 6 to 10 million people) in the United States have characteristics that would justify classifying their way of life as that of a culture of poverty. Probably the largest sector within this group consists of very low income Negroes, Mexicans, Puerto Ricans, American Indians, and southern poor whites. The relatively small number of people in the United States with a culture of poverty is a positive factor because it is much more difficult to eliminate the culture of poverty than to eliminate poverty per se.

Middle-class people—and this would certainly include most social scientists—tend to concentrate on the negative aspects of the culture of poverty. They tend to associate negative valences to such traits as present-time orientation and concrete versus abstract orientation. I do not intend to idealize or romanticize the culture of poverty. As someone has said, "It is easier to praise poverty than to live in it"; yet some of the positive aspects that may flow from these traits must not be overlooked. Living in the present may develop a capacity for spontaneity, for the enjoyment of the sensual, for the indulgence of impulse, which is often blunted in the middle-class, future-oriented man. Perhaps it is this reality of the moment that the existentialist writers are so desperately trying to recapture but that the culture of poverty experiences as natural, everyday phenomena. The frequent use of violence certainly provides a ready outlet for hostility so that people in the culture of poverty suffer less from repression than does the middle class.

In the traditional view, anthropologists have said that culture provides human beings with a design for living, with a ready-made set of solutions for human problems so that individuals in each generation do not have to begin all over again from scratch. That is, the core of culture is its positive adaptive function. I, too, have called attention to some of the adaptive mechanisms in the culture of poverty—for example, the low aspiration level helps to reduce frustration, the legitimization of short-range hedonism makes possible spontaneity and enjoyment. Indeed, it seems that in some ways the people with a culture of poverty suffer less from alienation than do those of the middle class. However, on the whole it seems to me that it is a thin, relatively superficial culture. There is a great deal of pathos, suffering, and emptiness among those who live in the culture of poverty. It does not provide much support or satisfaction, and its encouragement of mistrust tends to magnify helplessness and isolation. Indeed, the poverty of culture is one of the crucial aspects of the culture of poverty.

The concept of the culture of poverty provides a high level of generalization that, hopefully, will unify and explain a number of phenomena that have been viewed as distinctive characteristics of racial, national, or regional groups. For example, matrifocality, a high incidence of consensual unions, and a high percentage of households headed by women, which have been thought to be distinctive characteristics of Caribbean family organization or of Negro family life in the United States, turn out to be traits of the culture of poverty and are found among diverse peoples in many parts of the world and among peoples who have had no history of slavery.

The concept of a cross-societal subculture of poverty enables us to see that many of the problems we think of as distinctively our own or as distinctively Negro problems (or as those of any other special racial or ethnic group) also exist in countries where there are no distinct ethnic minority groups. This concept also suggests that the elimination of physical poverty per se may not eliminate the culture of poverty, which is a whole way of life.

What is the future of the culture of poverty? In considering this question, one must distinguish between those countries in which it represents a relatively small segment of the population and those in which it constitutes a very large one. Obviously, the solutions will differ in these two situations. In the United States, the major solution proposed by planners and social workers in dealing with multiple-problem families and the so-called hard core of poverty has been to attempt to raise slowly their level of living and to incorporate them into the middle class. Wherever possible, there has been some reliance upon psychiatric treatment.

In the underdeveloped countries, however, where great masses of people live in the culture of poverty, a social-work solution does not seem feasible.[8] Because of the magnitude of the problem, psychiatrists can hardly begin to cope with it. They have all they can do to care for their own growing middle class. In these countries, the people with a culture of poverty may seek a more revolutionary solution. By creating basic structural changes in society, by redistributing wealth, by organizing the power and giving them a sense of belonging, of power, and of leadership, revolutions frequently succeed in abolishing some of the basic characteristics of the culture of poverty even when they do not succeed in abolishing poverty itself.

Some of my readers have misunderstood the subculture of poverty model and have failed to grasp the importance of the distinction between poverty and the subculture of poverty. In making this distinction, I have tried to document a broader generalization; namely, that it is a serious mistake to lump all poor people together, because the causes, the meaning, and the consequences of poverty vary considerably in different socio-cultural contexts. There is nothing in the concept that puts the onus of poverty on the character of the poor. Nor does the concept in any way play down the exploitation and neglect suffered by the poor. Indeed, the subculture of poverty is part of the larger culture of capitalism, whose social and economic system channels wealth into the hands of a relatively small group and thereby makes for the growth of sharp class distinctions.

I would agree that the main reasons for the persistence of the subculture are no doubt the pressures that the larger society exerts over its members and the structure of the larger society itself. However, this is not the only reason. The subculture develops mechanisms that tend to perpetuate it, especially because of what happens to the world view, aspirations, and character of the children who grow up in it. For this reason, improved economic opportunities, though absolutely essential and of the highest priority, are not sufficient to alter basically or eliminate the subculture of poverty. Moreover, elimination is a process that will take more than a single generation, even under the best of circumstances, including a socialist revolution.

Some readers have thought that I was saying, "Being poor is terrible, but having a culture of poverty is not so bad." On the contrary, I am saying that it is easier to eliminate poverty than the culture of poverty. I am also suggesting that the poor in a precapitalistic caste-ridden society like India had some advantages over modern urban slum dwellers because the people were organized in castes and panchayats and this organization gave them some sense of identity and some strength and power. Perhaps Gandhi had the urban slums of the West in mind when he wrote that the caste system was one of the greatest inventions of mankind. Similarly, I have argued that the poor Jews of eastern Europe, with their strong tradition of literacy and community organization, were better off than people with the culture of poverty. On the other hand, I would argue that people with the culture of poverty, with their strong sense of resignation and fatalism, are less driven and less anxious than the striving lower-middle class, who are still trying to make it in the face of the greatest odds.

Notes

1. Although the term "subculture of poverty" is technically more accurate, I shall use "culture of poverty" as a shorter form.
2. Although the model presented here is concerned with conditions in con-

temporary urban slums, I find remarkable similarities between the culture of poverty and the way of life of Negro slaves in the antebellum South of the United States.

3. In terms of Hyman Rodman's concept of "The Lower-Class Value Stretch," *Social Forces*, XLII, No. 2 (December 1963), I would say that the culture of poverty exists where this value stretch is at a minimum, that is, where the belief in middle-class values is at a minimum.

4. *Compadrazgo* is a system of relationships and obligations between godparents (*padrinos*) and godchildren (*ahijados*) and between godparents and parents, who are *compadres*.

5. It may be that in the slums of Calcutta and Bombay an incipient culture of poverty is developing. It would be highly desirable to do family studies there as a crucial test of the culture of poverty hypothesis.

6. Frantz Fanon, *The Wretched of the Earth* (New York: Grove Press, 1965), p. 103.

7. "The present Partido Estadista Republicano (PER) is the inheritor of the coalition Republican Union Party of the thirties and early forties. As such it is deeply committed to the continuance of the juridical presence of the United States in Puerto Rico; but this commitment has only recently been expressed exclusively in terms of statehood. . . .

". . . The Partido Estadista Republicano, unlike the Partido Popular Democratico, is formally affiliated with one of the national parties of the United States. The affiliation of the mainland and insular Republican parties dates from 1903, and with the exception of a brief interlude between 1916 and 1919, during which the bonds were formally dissolved, the affiliation has continued uninterrupted to the present day. Federal patronage jobs in Puerto Rico now consist of only the customs collector, the United States attorney for the Puerto Rico district, two assistant federal attorneys, the federal marshal, the director of the Caribbean area office of the Production and Marketing Administration, and when vacancies occur, postmasters and two federal district judges." From Robert W. Anderson, *Party Politics in Puerto Rico* (Stanford, Calif.: Stanford University Press, 1965), pp. 81, 91.

8. Indeed, it is doubtful how successful the social-work solution can be in the United States!

Chapter 8

☙ *Culture and Class in the Study of Poverty: An Approach to Anti-Poverty Research* HERBERT J. GANS

I. THE MORAL ASSUMPTIONS OF POVERTY RESEARCH

Poverty research, like all social research, is suffused with the cultural and political assumptions of the researcher. Consequently, perhaps the most significant fact about poverty research is that it is being carried out entirely by middle-class researchers who differ—in class, culture, and political power—from the people they are studying. Such researchers—and I am one of them—are members of an affluent society, who, however marginal they may feel themselves to be, are investigating an aggregate that is excluded from that society. Whatever the researcher's political beliefs—and students of poverty span the political spectrum—this difference in class position affects his perspective, particularly at present when the new social-science literature on poverty is little more than impressionistic. Consequently, the researcher's perspective is often built on random ob-

This chapter was prepared for a seminar of the American Academy of Arts and Sciences, and all rights to it are reserved by the Academy. The paper was stimulated by Walter Miller's oral presentation at that seminar. A preliminary version, "Poverty and Culture," was prepared for the International Seminar on Poverty, University of Essex, April 1967, which drew in part on an earlier paper, "Some Unanswered Questions in the Study of the Lower Class," written in 1963. All versions are indebted to the work of Hylan Lewis, particularly his "Culture, Class and the Behavior of Low Income Families," reprinted in *Culture, Class and Poverty* (Washington: Cross-Tell, 1967), pp. 13–42. I would like to thank Dr. Moynihan and the Academy for allowing me to include the paper as Chapter 22 of my *People and Plans: Essays on Urban Problems and Solutions* (New York: Basic Books, Inc., 1968) pp. 321–346, prior to its publication in this volume.

servations and untested assumptions and may include inaccurate folklore about the poor that he has unconsciously picked up as a middle-class person. As a result, "social science views (of poverty) inevitably grow out of the more common sense views." [1]

Moreover, poverty researchers, like other affluent Americans, have had to grapple with the question of how to explain the existence of an underclass in their society. In a fascinating paper, Rainwater has recently described five explanatory perspectives that, as he puts it, "neutralize the disinherited" by considering them either immoral, pathological, biologically inferior, culturally different, or heroic. As his terms indicate, these "explanations" are by no means all negative, but they enable the explainers to resolve their anxiety about the poor by viewing them as different or unreal. [2]

Rainwater's list is a sophisticated and updated version of an older, more familiar, explanatory perspective that judges the poor as *deserving* or *undeserving*. This dichotomy still persists today, albeit with different terminologies, for it poses the basic political question of what to do about poverty. If the poor are deserving, they are obviously entitled to admittance into the affluent society as equals with all the economic, social, and political redistribution this entails; if they are undeserving, they need not be admitted, or at least not until they have been made or have made themselves deserving.

The history of American poverty research can be described in terms of this moral dichotomy. Most of the lay researchers of the nineteenth century felt the poor were personally and politically immoral and therefore undeserving. [3] Although some researchers understood that the moral lapses of the poor stemmed from economic deprivation and related causes, most offered a cultural explanation, indicting the non-Puritan subcultures of the Irish and Eastern and Southern European immigrants. [4] These high-born observers, who were struggling to maintain the cultural and political dominance of the Protestant middle and upper classes against the flood of newcomers, proposed that poverty could be dealt with by ending the European immigration and by Americanizing and bourgeoisifying the immigrants who had already come. [5]

Social scientists took up the study of poverty in the twentieth century without an explicit political agenda and also changed the terminology. They saw the poor as suffering from individual pathology or from social disorganization; they treated them as deficient rather than undeserving, but there was often the implication that the deficiencies had to be corrected before the poor were deserving of help.

This conception of the poor spawned a generation of countervailing research that identified positive elements in their social structure and culture.[6] Although many of the studies were done among the working class populations, the findings suggested or implied that because the poor were not disorganized, socially or individually, they were therefore deserving.

At the present time, the debate over the moral quality of the poor is most intense among the practitioners of public welfare and anti-poverty programs. Today's advocates of undeservingness see the poor as deficient in basic skills and attitudes. Educators who share this view describe them as culturally deprived; social workers and clinical psychologists find them weak in ego strength, and community organizers view them as apathetic. Professionals who believe the poor to be deserving argue that the poor are not deficient but deprived; they need jobs, higher incomes, better schools, and "maximum feasible participation"; "resource strategy equalization" in Lee Rainwater's terms, rather than just services, such as training and counseling in skills and ways of living that lead to cultural change.[7]

Today's social scientists have debated an only slightly different version of the same argument. Some feel that the poor share the values and aspirations of the affluent society, and if they can be provided with decent jobs and other resources, they will cease to suffer from the pathological and related deprivational consequences of poverty. According to Beck's review of the recent poverty literature, however, many more social scientists share the feeling that the poor are deficient.[8] Yet, others, particularly anthropologists, suggest that poverty and the lowly position of the poor have resulted in the creation of a separate lower-class culture or a culture of poverty, which makes it impossible for poor people to develop the behavior patterns and values that would enable them to participate in the affluent society.

Although few social scientists would think of characterizing the poor as deserving or undeserving, at least explicitly, those who argue that the poor share the values of the affluent obviously consider them as ready and able to share in the blessings of the affluent society, whereas those who consider them deficient or culturally different imply that the poor are not able to enter affluent society until they change themselves or are changed. Walter Miller argues that the poor do not even want to enter the affluent society, at least culturally, and his analysis implies that the poor are deserving precisely because they have their own culture. Even so, those who see the poor as deficient or culturally different often favor resource-oriented anti-poverty programs, just as those who feel that the poor share the values of the affluent society recognize the existence of cultural factors that block the escape from poverty.

The ghetto rebellions have, however, encouraged a popular revival of the old moral terminology. The Negro poor, at least, are now seen by many whites as undeserving; they have rioted despite the passage of civil rights legislation and the War on Poverty and should not be rewarded for their ungrateful behavior.[9] Observers who feel the Negro poor are deserving, on the other hand, claim that the rebellions stem from the failure of white society to grant the economic, political, and social equality it has long promised and that rioting and looting are only desperate attempts by the poor to obtain the satisfactions that the affluent society has denied them.

THE POOR: NEITHER DESERVING NOR UNDESERVING

Because of its fundamental political implications and its moral tone, the debate about whether the poor are deserving or undeserving will undoubtedly continue as long as there are poor people in America. Nevertheless, I feel that the debate, however conceptualized, is irrelevant and undesirable. The researcher ought to look at poverty and the poor from a perspective that avoids a moral judgment, for it is ultimately impossible to prove that the poor are more or less deserving than the affluent. Enough is now known about the economic and social determinants of pathology to reject explanations of pathology as a moral lapse. Moreover, since there is some evidence that people's legal or illegal practices are a function of their opportunity to earn a livelihood in legal ways, one cannot know whether the poor are as law-abiding or moral as the middle class until they have achieved the same opportunities—and then, the issue will be irrelevant.[10]

It is also undesirable to view the poor as deserving or undeserving, for any judgment must be based on the judge's definition of deservingness, and who has the ability to formulate a definition that is not class-bound? Such judgments are almost always made by people who are trying to prevent the mobility of a population group that is threatening their own position, so that the aristocracy finds the *nouveau riche* undeserving of being admitted to the upper class; the cultural elite believes the middle classes to be undeserving partakers of "culture"; and many working-class people feel that people who do not labor with their hands do not deserve to be considered workers. Still, almost everyone gangs up on the poor; they are judged as undeserving by all income groups, becoming victims of a no-win moral game in which they are expected to live by moral and legal standards that few middle-class people are capable of upholding. Deservingness is thus not an absolute moral concept but a means of preventing one group's access to the rights and resources of another.

The only proper research perspective, I believe, is to look at the poor as an economically and politically deprived population whose behavior, values—and pathologies—are adaptations to their existential situation, just as the behavior, values, and pathologies of the affluent are adaptations to *their* existential situation. In both instances, adaptation results in a mixture of moral and immoral, legal and illegal practices, but the nature of the mix is a function of the existential situation. Since the standards of law—and even of morality—of an affluent society are determined by the affluent members of that society, the poor are, by definition, less law-abiding and less moral, but only because they are less affluent and must therefore adapt to different existential circumstances.

If the poor are expected to live up to the moral and legal standards of the affluent society, however, the only justifiable anti-poverty strategy is to give them the same access to resources now held by the affluent, and to let them use and spend these resources with the same freedom of choice that is now reserved to the affluent.

The remainder of the chapter will elaborate this perspective, particularly around the debate over class and culture among the poor, spelling out some of the implications for both social-science theory and anti-poverty policy. I should note that when referring to "the poor," I shall refer principally to those people who have presumably been poor long enough to develop cultural patterns associated with poverty and are permanently rather than temporarily poor.

II. POVERTY AND CULTURE

The argument between those who think that poverty can best be eliminated by providing jobs and other resources and those who feel that cultural obstacles and psychological deficiencies must be overcome as well is ultimately an argument about social change, about the psychological readiness of people to respond to change, and about the role of culture in change. The advocates of resources are not concerned explicitly with culture, but they do make a cultural assumption: Whatever the culture of the poor, it will not interfere in people's ability to take advantage of better opportunities for obtaining economic resources. They take a *situational* view of social change and of personality: that people respond to the situations—and opportunities—available to them and change their behavior accordingly. Those who call attention to cultural (and psychological) obstacles, however, are taking a *cultural* view of social change, which suggests that people react to change in terms of prior values and behavior patterns and adopt only those changes that are congruent with their culture.[11]

Since academicians have been caught up in the debate over deservingness and undeservingness as much as the rest of American society, the situational and cultural views of change have frequently been described as polar opposites, and theorists have battled over the data to find support for one pole or the other. Clearly, the truth lies somewhere in between, but at present, neither the data nor the conceptual framework to find that truth is as yet available.

The situational view is obviously too simple; people are not automatons who respond either in the same way or with the same speed to a common stimulus. Despite a middle-class inclination on the part of researchers to view the poor as homogeneous, all available studies indicate that there is as much variety among them as among the affluent. Some have been poor for generations, others are poor only periodically; some are downwardly mobile; others are upwardly mobile. Many share middle-class values, others embrace working-class values; some have become so used to the defense mechanisms they have learned for coping with deprivation that they have difficulty in adapting to new opportunities; and some are beset by physical or emotional illness, poverty having created pathologies that now block the ability to adapt to nonpathological situations.[12] Sad to say, there is as yet no research to show, quantitatively, what proportion of poor people fit into each of these categories.

THE SHORTCOMINGS OF THE CULTURAL VIEW OF CHANGE

The cultural view of social and personal change is also deficient. First, it uses an overly behavioral definition of culture that ignores the existence of values that conflict with behavior; second, it sees culture as a holistic system whose parts are intricately related, so that any individual element of a culture cannot be changed without system-wide reverberations.

The behavioral definition identifies culture in terms of how people act; it views values as *behavioral norms* that are metaphysical and moral guidelines to behavior, and are deduced from behavior. For example, Walter Miller sees values as "focal concerns" that stem from, express, and ultimately maintain behavior. As he puts it, "the concept 'focal concern' . . . reflects actual behavior, whereas 'value' tends to wash out intracultural differences since it is colored by notions of the 'official' ideal." [13] This definition, useful as it is, pays little or no attention to *aspirations,* values that express the desire for alternative forms of behavior.

The behavioral conception of culture can be traced back to anthropological traditions and to the latent political agendas of anthropological researchers. The fieldworker who studied a strange culture began by gathering artifacts, and as anthropology matured, he also collected behavior patterns. The cultural relativist, who wanted to defend these cultures against involuntary change, sought to show that the behavior patterns were functional to the survival of the group, and how people felt about their behavior did not interest him unduly. He noted that infanticide was functional for the survival of a hunting tribe, but he did not devote much attention to how people felt about the desirability of infanticide or about less deadly patterns of culture.

His approach may have been valid at its time; it was in part a reaction against nineteenth-century idealism that identified culture solely with aspirations and was not interested in how people really behaved. The behavioral view of culture was also a useful tool to fight the advocates of colonialism who viewed all cultures in terms of the aspirations of their own western society and were ready to alter any culture they encountered to achieve their aspirations. Moreover, the approach was perhaps empirically valid; it may have fit the preliterate group whose culture had developed around a limited and homogeneous economy and ecology. Tribes who devoted themselves exclusively to agriculture or hunting developed cultures that fit such single-minded economies. Such cultures gave their people little, if any, choice; they bred fatalists who did not know that alternative ways of behaving were possible, usually because they were not possible, and thus left no room for diverging aspirations.

But such a definition of culture is not applicable to contemporary western society. Many poor people in our society are also fatalists not because they are unable to conceive of alternative conditions but because they have been frustrated in the realization of alternatives. Unlike preliterate people—or at least the classic version of the ideal type of preliterate—they are unhappy with their state; they have aspirations that diverge from the focal concerns underlying their behavior. Of course, they can justify to themselves and to others the behavioral choices they make and must make, and Walter Miller's insightful analysis of focal concerns indicates clearly how they "support and maintain the basic features of the lower class way of life." [14] Even so, people who are forced to create values and justifications for what they must do may also be well aware of alternatives that they would prefer under different conditions.

For generations, researchers made no distinction between norms and aspirations, and most research emphasis was placed on the former. Lay observers and practitioners were only willing to judge; they saw the behavioral norms of the poor that diverged from their own and bade the poor behave like middle-class people. In reaction, social scientists who had done empirical work among the poor defended their behavioral norms as adaptations to their existential situation or as an independent culture but paid little attention to aspirations diverging from these norms. Walter Miller has taken perhaps the most extreme position; he implies that lower-class aspirations, as well as norms, are different from those of the rest of society, and if poor people express middle-class values, they do so only because they are expected to endorse the "official" ideals.[15] Their real aspirations, he seems to suggest, are those of their own lower-class culture.

Recent research has, however, begun to distinguish between aspirations and behavioral norms. Starting with a debate among anthropologists over whether Caribbean lower-class couples in "living" or consensual relationships preferred formal marriage, several studies have shown that poor people share many of the aspirations of the affluent society but also develop norms that justify their actual behavior. Rodman conceptualizes the divergence between aspirations and norms as lower-class value stretch; Rainwater argues that poor people share the aspirations of the larger society, which he calls conventional norms. Knowing that they cannot live up to them, however, they develop other norms that fit the existential conditions to which they must adapt.[16]

At present, there are only enough data to affirm the existence of a divergence between aspirations and behavioral norms and to underline the need for more research, particularly in areas of life other than marriage. In a heterogeneous or pluralistic society, such divergence is almost built in; when a variety of cultures or subcultures co-exist, aspirations diffuse freely. Among affluent people, the gap be-tween aspirations and behavioral norms is probably narrower than among poor people; the former can more often achieve what they want. Even if they cannot satisfy occupational aspirations, they are able to satisfy other aspirations, for example, for family life. The poor have fewer options. Lacking the income and the economic security to achieve their aspirations, they must develop diverging behavioral norms in almost all areas of life. Nevertheless, they still retain aspira-tions, and many are those of the affluent society.

Consequently, research on the culture of the poor must include both behavioral norms and aspirations. The norms must be studied because they indicate how people react to their present existence, but limiting the analysis to them can lead to the assumption that behav-ior would remain the same under different conditions when there is no reliable evidence, pro or con, to justify such an assumption today. As Hylan Lewis puts it, "It is important not to confuse basic life chances and actual behavior with basic cultural values and prefer-ences." [17] Cultural analysis must also look at aspirations, determin-ing their content, the intensity with which they are held, and above all, whether they would be translated into behavioral norms if eco-nomic conditions made it possible.

The second deficiency of the cultural view of change is the conception of culture as holistic and systemic. When a behavior pat-tern is identified as part of a larger and interrelated cultural system and when the causes of the pattern are ascribed to "the culture," there is a tendency to see the behavior pattern and its supporting norms as resistant to change and as persisting simply because they are cultural, although there is no real evidence that culture is as un-changing as assumed. This conception of culture is also ahistorical, for it ignores the origin of behavior patterns and norms. As a result, too little attention is paid to the conditions that bring a behavior pattern into being—or to the conditions that may alter it. Culture becomes its own cause, and change is possible only if the culture as a whole is somehow changed.

This conceptualization is, once more, a survival of a now inap-propiate intellectual tradition. Anthropologists started out by study-ing small and simple societies that may have been characterized by a cultural system whose elements were interrelated. Whether or not this was the case, the desire to preserve preliterate cultures en-couraged fieldworkers toward holistic functionalism, for if they could argue that any given behavior pattern was an integral part of the system and that the entire system might well collapse if one pattern was changed, they could oppose the colonialists who wanted to change a tribe's work habits or its religion.

Sociology used much the same conceptual apparatus; it became enamored of such terms as *Gemeinschaft* and community, viewing these as organic wholes that could only be changed with dire results, that is, the creation of a *Gesellschaft* and the city, which were described as atomized, impersonal, and dehumanized groupings. Like the anthropological concept of folk culture, *Gemeinschaft* and the organic community bore little relation to real societies, and although these terms were formulated as ideal types rather than descriptive concepts, they were nevertheless largely romantic fictions generated by nostalgia for the past and by the opposition of earlier sociologists and anthropologists to urbanization and industrialization.[18] It is very doubtful whether any past society ever came close to being a folk culture or a *Gemeinschaft* or whether any modern society is principally a *Gesellschaft*.

The systemic concept of culture is also inappropriate. Modern societies are pluralist; whether developed or developing, they consist of a diverse set of cultures living side by side, and researchers studying them have had to develop such terms as subculture, class culture, and contra-culture to describe the diversity.[19] Holistic functionalism is irrelevant, too; no culture is sufficiently integrated so that its parts can be described as elements in a system. In modern sociology and anthropology, functionalism can only survive by identifying dysfunctions as well as functions and by showing that cultural patterns that are functional for one group may well be dysfunctional for another.

An ahistorical conception of culture is equally inapplicable to modern societies. In such societies, some behavior patterns are persistent, but others are not; they change when economic and other conditions change, although we do not yet know which patterns are persistent—and for how long—and which are not. More important, culture is a response to economic and other conditions; it is itself situational in origin and changes as situations change. Behavior patterns, norms, and aspirations develop as responses to situations to which people must adapt, and culture originates out of such responses. Changes in economic and social opportunities give rise to new behavioral solutions, which then become recurring patterns, are later complemented by norms that justify them, and which are eventually overthrown by new existential conditions. Some behavioral norms are more persistent than others, but over the long run, all of the norms and aspirations by which people live are nonpersistent; they rise and fall with changes in situations.[20]

These observations are not intended to question the validity of the concept of culture, for not all behavior is a response to a present situation, and not all—and perhaps not even most—behavior patterns change immediately with a change in a situation. A new situation will initially be met with available norms; only when these norms turn out to be inapplicable or damaging will people change; first, their behavior, and then the norms upholding that behavior. Nevertheless, the lag between a change in existential conditions and the change of norms does not mean that norms are immutable.

AN ALTERNATIVE CONCEPTION OF CULTURE

Behavior is thus a mixture of situational responses and cultural patterns, that is, behavioral norms and aspirations. Some situational responses are strictly ad hoc reactions to a current situation; they exist because of that situation and will disappear if it changes or disappears. Other situational responses are internalized and become behavior norms that are an intrinsic part of the person and of the groups in which he moves, and are thus less subject to change with changes in situation. The intensity of internalization varies; at one extreme, there are norms that are not much deeper than lip service; at the other, there are norms that are built into the basic personality structure, and a generation or more of living in a new situation may not dislodge them. They become culture, and people may adhere to them even if they are no longer appropriate, paying all kinds of economic and emotional costs to maintain them.

The southern white reaction to racial integration offers many examples of such intensely internalized norms, although it also offers examples of norms that were thought to be persistent but that crumbled as soon as the civil rights movement or the federal government applied pressure to eliminate them. Indeed, there are probably many norms that can be toppled by a threat to exert power or to withdraw rewards; the many cultural compromises that first- and second-generation ethnics make to retain the affection of their children are a good example. Conversely, some norms are maintained simply because they have become political symbols, and people are unwilling to give them up because this would be interpreted as a loss of power. Thus, acculturated ethnic groups often preserve ethnic cultural traits in order to justify the maintenance of ethnically based political influence. The role of power in culture, culture change, and acculturation deserves much more attention than it has so far received.

Not all behavioral norms are necessarily conservative; some may make people especially adaptable to change and may even encourage change. Despite what has been written about the ravages of slavery on the southern Negro, he went to work readily during World War II when jobs were plentiful. Similarly, the southern businessman operates with behavioral norms that make him readier to accept racial change than others; he cannot adhere with intensity to any beliefs that will cut into profit.

To sum up: I have argued that behavior results initially from an adaptation to the existential situation. Much of that behavior is no more than a situational response that exists only because of the situation and changes with a change in situation. Other behavior patterns become behavioral norms that are internalized and are then held with varying degrees of intensity and persistence. If they persist with a change in situation, they may then be considered patterns of *behavioral culture,* and such norms may become causes of behavior. Other norms can encourage change. In addition, adaptation to a situation is affected by aspirations, which also exist in various degrees of intensity and persistence, and form an *aspirational culture.* Culture, then, is that mix of behavioral norms and aspirations that causes behavior, maintains present behavior, or encourages future behavior, independently of situational incentives and restraints.

CULTURE AND POVERTY

This view of culture has important implications for studying the poor. It rejects a concept that emphasizes tradition and obstacles to change and sees norms and aspirations within a milieu of situations against which the norms and aspirations are constantly tested. Moreover, it enables the researcher to analyze, or at least to estimate, what happens to norms under alternative situations and thus to guess at how poor people would adapt to new opportunities.

With such a perspective, one can—and must—ask constantly: To what situation, to what set of opportunities and restraints do the present behavioral norms and aspirations respond, and how intensely are they held; how much are they internalized, if at all, and to what extent would they persist or change if the significant opportunities and restraints underwent change? To put it another way, if culture is learned, one must ask how quickly and easily various behavioral norms could be unlearned once the existential situation from which they sprang had changed?

Moreover, supposing this change took place and opportunities, for example, for decent jobs and incomes were made available to poor people, what behavioral norms, if any, are so deeply internalized that they interfere, say, with taking a good job? Answers to this question lead directly to policy considerations. One alternative is to seek a change in norms; another is to design the job in such a fashion that it can be accepted without requiring an immediate change in strongly persisting norms. Since such norms are not easily changed, it may be more desirable to tailor the opportunity to fit the norm rather than the other way around. For example, if the inability to plan, often ascribed to the poor, is actually a persisting behavioral norm that will interfere in their being employable, rather than just an ad hoc response to an uncertain future, it would be wrong to expect people to learn to plan at once just because jobs are now available. The better solution would be to fit the jobs to this inability and to make sure that the adults, once having some degree of economic security, will learn to plan or will be able to teach their children how to do so.

The prime issue in the area of culture and poverty, then, is to discover how soon poor people will change their behavior, given new opportunities, and what restraints or obstacles, good or bad, come from that reaction to past situations we call culture. To put it another way, the primary problem is to determine what opportunities have to be created to eliminate poverty, how poor people can be encouraged to adapt to those opportunities that conflict with persistent cultural patterns, and how they can retain the persisting patterns that do not conflict with other aspirations.

Because of the considerable divergence between behavioral norms and aspirations, it is clearly impossible to think of a holistic lower-class culture. It is perhaps possible to describe a *behavioral lower-class culture,* consisting of the behavioral norms with which people adapt to being poor and lower class. There is, however, no *aspirational lower-class culture,* for much evidence suggests that poor people's aspirations are similar to those of more affluent Americans. My hypothesis is that many and perhaps most poor people share the aspirations of the working class; others, those of the white-collar lower-middle class; and yet others, those of the professional and managerial upper-middle class, although most poor people probably aspire to the behavioral norms of these groups—to the ways they are living now—rather than to their aspirations.

Under present conditions, the aspirations that poor people hold may not be fulfilled, but this does not invalidate them, for their existence—and the intensity with which they are held—can only be tested when economic and other conditions are favorable to their realization. If and when poor people obtain the resources for which they are clamoring, much of the behavioral lower-class culture will disappear. Only those poor people who cannot accept alternative opportunities because they cannot give up their present behavioral norms can be considered adherents to a lower-class culture.

In short, such conceptions of lower-class culture as Walter Miller's describe only part of the total reality. If Miller's lower-class culture were really an independent culture with its own set of aspirations, its practitioners would presumably be satisfied with their way of life. If they are not satisfied, however, if they only adapt to necessity, but want something different, then ascribing their adaptation to a lower-class culture is inaccurate. It is also politically undesirable, for the judgment that behavior is cultural lends itself to an argument against change. But if data are not available for that judgment, the researcher indulges in conceptual conservatism.[21]

Miller does not indicate specifically whether the adolescents he studied adhered to both a behavioral and aspirational lower-class culture. He suggests that "the motivation of 'delinquent' behavior engaged in by members of lower-class corner groups involves a *positive* [italics mine] effort to achieve states, conditions or qualities valued within the actor's most significant cultural milieu," [22] that is, that the adolescents valued the behavior norms for which they were rewarded by their reference groups.

Perhaps the Roxbury adolescents did not share the aspirations of the larger society; they were, after all, delinquents, youngsters who had been caught in an illegal act and who might be cynical about such aspirations. Moreover, the hippies and other "youth cultures" should remind us that adolescents do not always endorse the aspirations of an adult society. The crucial question, then, is how did lower-class adults in Roxbury feel? I would suspect that they were less positive than the adolescents about their youngsters' delinquent activities, partly because they are more sensitive to what Miller classes "official ideals," but partly because they do adhere to a non-lower-class aspirational culture.

My definition of culture also suggests a somewhat different interpretation of a culture of poverty than Oscar Lewis's concept. If culture is viewed as a causal factor, and particularly as those norms and aspirations that resist change, then a culture of poverty would consist of those specifically cultural or nonsituational factors that help to keep people poor, especially when alternative opportunities beckon.

Lewis's concept of the culture of poverty puts more emphasis on the behavior patterns and feelings that result from lack of opportunity and the inability to achieve aspirations. According to Lewis,

The culture of poverty is both an adaptation and a reaction of the poor to their marginal position in a class-stratified, highly individuated society. It represents an effort to cope with feelings of hopelessness and despair which develop from the realization of the improbability of achieving success in terms of the values and goals of the larger society.[23]

His conception thus stresses the defense mechanisms by which people cope with deprivation, frustration, and alienation, rather than with poverty alone; it is closer to a culture of alienation than to a culture of poverty. In fact, Lewis distinguishes between poor people with and without a culture of poverty, and in indicating that people can be poor without feeling hopeless, he seems to suggest that the culture of poverty is partly responsible for feelings of hopelessness. Moreover, if poor people can overcome their malaise and resort to political action —or if they live in a socialist society like Cuba, in which they are presumably considered part of the society—they give up the culture of poverty. "When the poor become class-conscious or active members of trade-union organizations, or when they adopt an internationalist outlook on the world, they are no longer part of the culture of poverty, although they may still be desperately poor." [24]

Lewis's distinction between poverty and the culture of poverty is important, for it aims to separate different kinds of poverty and adaptations to poverty. His emphasis on alienation suggests, however, that his concept pertains more to belonging to an underclass than to being poor, while his identification of the culture of poverty with class-stratified, highly individuated societies suggests that, for him, the culture is an effect rather than a cause of membership in an underclass even though he considers the culture of poverty to be a causal concept. The various traits of the culture of poverty that he describes are partly socio-psychological consequences, partly situational responses, and partly behavioral norms associated with underclass membership, but the major causal factor is the class-stratified, highly individuated society. From a causal perspective, Lewis's concept is thus less concerned with culture than with the situational factors that bring about culture; it is less a culture of poverty than a sociology of the underclass.

Whether or not the families who tell their life histories in Lewis's books adhere to a culture that is a direct or indirect cause of their remaining in poverty is hard to say, for one would have to know how they would react to better economic conditions. Since such data are almost impossible to gather, it is difficult to tell how the Sanchez and Rios families might respond, for example, if Mexico and Puerto Rico offered the men a steady supply of decent and secure jobs. Since almost all the members of the families aspire to something better, my hunch is that their behavioral and aspirational cultures would change under improved circumstances; their culture is probably not a cause of their poverty.

As I use the term culture of poverty, then, it would apply to people who have internalized behavioral norms that cause or perpetuate poverty and who lack aspirations for a better way of life, particularly people whose societies have not let them know change is possible—the peasants and the urbanites who have so far been left out of the revolution of rising expectations. The only virtue of this definition is its emphasis on culture as a causal factor, thus enabling the policy-oriented researcher to separate the situational and cultural processes responsible for poverty.

If the culture of poverty is defined as those cultural patterns that keep people poor, it would be necessary to also include in the term the persisting cultural patterns among the affluent that, deliberately or not, keep their fellow citizens poor. When the concept of a culture of poverty is applied only to the poor, the onus for change falls too much on them, when in reality the prime obstacles to the elimination of poverty lie in an economic, political, and social structure that operates to protect and increase the wealth of the already affluent.

CULTURE AND CLASS

My definition of culture also has implications for the cultural aspects of social stratification. Class may be defined sociologically to describe how people stand in the socio-economic hierarchy with respect to occupation, income, education, and other variables having to do with the resources they have obtained, but it is often also defined culturally, in terms of their class-bound ways of life, that is, as class culture. Generally speaking, descriptions of class cultures pay little attention to the distinction between behavioral and aspirational culture on the one hand and situational responses on the other hand. Analyses that define class position on the basis of situational responses, but ascribe it to culture, make ad hoc behavior seem permanent and may assign people to long-term class positions on the basis of data which in fact describe their short-run response to a situation.[25] For example, if poor people's inability to plan is a situational response rather than a behavioral norm, it cannot be used as a criterion of lower-class culture, although it might be considered a pattern associated with lower-class position. Class, like culture, should be determined on the basis of norms that restrain or encourage people in adapting to new conditions.

Class-cultural descriptions must therefore focus on behavioral norms, on the intensity with which they are held, and on people's ability to adapt to new situations. Morever, if culture is defined to include aspirations, assignments of class position would have to take people's aspirations into account. Since these aspirations may be for working-class, lower-middle-class, or upper-middle-class ways of life, it becomes difficult to assign poor people to a single lower-class culture. In addition, if the previous criterion of ability to adapt is also included, those who can adapt to change would have to be classified further on the basis of whether their aspirations are for one or another of the "higher" classes. The resulting classification would be quite complex, but would indicate more accurately the diversity within the poverty-stricken population than do current concepts of lower-class culture. More important, the number who are, culturally speaking, permanently and inevitably lower class is much smaller than sometimes imagined, for that group would include only those whose aspirations are lower class and whose behavioral culture prevents easy adaptation to change.

This approach would of course limit the use of current typologies of class. Dichotomies such as working class and lower class, or upper-lower and lower-lower class can be used to describe the existential condition in which people find themselves and the situational responses which they make, that is, as *sociological* typologies of class, but they cannot be used as *cultural* typologies, for people who share the same existential situation may respond with different behavioral norms and aspirations.[26] Combining sociological and cultural criteria into a single holistic category not only underestimates the diversity of people but also implies that they are satisfied with or resigned to being lower class. Class culture is thus used to explain why poor people remain lower class when in reality their being poor and members of an underclass is responsible. No doubt cultural patterns do play a causal role in class culture, but they must be determined empirically. Any other approach would reify the concept of class culture and give it a conservative political bias that suggests the poor are happy with or resigned to their lot.

Moreover, dichotomies such as working and lower class are in many ways only a sociological version of the distinction between the deserving and undeserving poor, even if their formulators had no such invidious distinction in mind. These labels are also too formalistic; they only chart the social and economic distances between people on a hierarchical scale. The terms lower or middle class are positional; they do not describe people's behavioral or aspirational culture. In fact, they really refer only to the economic, behavioral, and status deviations of poor people from the middle classes, for most current models of the class system are based on the amount of deviation from middle-class norms and aspirations.

Ideally, definitions and labels of class should include substantive elements that refer to the major themes of each class culture and that indicate the real differences of culture, if any, between the classes. If the data for a thematic cultural analysis were available, we might discover that there is no distinctive lower-class culture; there are only tendencies toward distinctiveness, many of which are but functions of the situations with which people must cope and that might disappear altogether once situations were changed.

Sociologists cannot ignore present situations, however, even if they are undesirable, and despite my reservations about the concepts of class and culture, ultimately I would agree with Lee Rainwater when he writes:

If, then, we take subculture to refer to a distinctive pattern of existential and evaluative elements, a pattern distinctive to a particular group in a larger collectivity and consequential for the way their behavior differs from that of others in the collectivity, it seems to me that there is no doubt that the concept of lower class subculture is useful.[27]

I would add only that I am skeptical of the existence of lower-class evaluative elements, or what I have called aspirational culture.

III. AN OUTLINE OF BASIC RESEARCH AND POLICY QUESTIONS

The remainder of this chapter attempts to apply the frame of reference I have outlined by suggesting some of the questions that ought to be asked by researchers and by indicating the methodological implications of the approach.

Studies of the poor should give up the notion of culture as largely behavioral (with little concern about divergent aspirations), as holistic, and as a persistent causal factor in behavior. Instead, insofar as poverty research should focus on the poor at all—a point I will consider below—it should deal with behavior patterns, norms, and aspirations on an individual basis, relate them to their situational origin, and determine how much the behavioral norms related to poverty would persist under changing situations. Whether or not there is a persisting and holistic culture (or set of subcultures) among the poor should be an empirical question.

In studying behavioral norms and aspirations among the poor, the following questions are most important: Does a given behavioral pattern block a potential escape from poverty, and, if so, how? Conversely, are there aspirations related to this behavioral pattern and do they diverge from behavior? If so, are they held intensively enough to provide the motivation for an escape from poverty when economic and other opportunities are available? Are there behavioral norms that encourage this escape?

In analyzing the behavior patterns that do block the escape from poverty, one must look for the social and cultural sources of that behavior. Is the behavior a situational response that would change readily with a change in situation, or is it internalized? If it is internalized, how does it become internalized (and at what age), what agents and institutions encourage the internalization, and how intensive is it? How long would a given behavioral norm persist if opportunities changed, and what are the forces that encourage its persistence?

Similar questions must be asked about aspirations: What are their sources, how are they internalized, and how intensely are they held? How responsive are they to changes in situation, and can they enable people to give up poverty-related behavior once economic opportunities are available? And what kinds of noneconomic helping agents and institutions are needed to aid poor people in implementing their aspirations?

Equally important questions must be addressed to the affluent members of society. Indeed, if the prime purpose of research is the elimination of poverty, studies of the poor are not the first order of business; they are much less important than studies of the economy that relegate many people to underemployment and unemployment and nonmembers of the labor force to welfare dependency. They are also less important than studies of the political, social, and cultural factors that enable and encourage the affluent population to permit the existence of a poverty-stricken underclass. In the final analysis, poverty exists because it has many positive functions for the affluent society, for example, by providing a labor force to do the "dirty" work of that society.

Consequently, assuming that lower-class culture is less pervasive than has been thought and that poor people are able and willing to change their behavior if economic opportunities are made available to them, one must ask what kinds of changes have to take place in the economic system, the power structure, the status order, and in the behavioral norms and aspirations of the affluent members of society for them to permit the incorporation of the poor into that society? Which of the functions of poverty for the affluent population can be eliminated, which can be translated into functional alternatives that do not require the existence of poverty, and which functions absolutely require the existence of either a deprived or a despised class, or both?

In addition, one must ask questions about the affluent society's attitudes toward behavior associated with poverty. Many behavior patterns may be the result of poverty, but they do not necessarily block the escape from poverty. They do, however, violate working- and middle-class values and thus irritate, and even threaten, working- and middle-class people. For example, the drinking bouts and extramarital sexual adventures that have been found prevalent among lower-class people may be correlated with poverty, but they do not cause it and probably do not block the escape from poverty.

They might persist if people had secure jobs and higher incomes, or they might not, or they might take place in more private surroundings as they do in the middle class. But since they shock the middle class, one must also ask which behavior patterns must be given up or hidden as the price of being allowed to enter the affluent society. This question must be asked of affluent people, but one would also have to determine the impact of changing or hiding the behavior on poor people. In short, one must ask: What changes are *really* required of the lower class, which ones are absolutely essential to the escape from poverty and the move into the larger society, and which are less important? [28]

These rather abstract questions can perhaps be made more concrete by applying them to a specific situation, the set of behavioral norms around the female-based or "broken" family. The first question, of course, is: Does this family structure block the escape from poverty? Assuming that the answer could be yes, how does it happen? Is it because a mother with several children and without a husband or a permanently available man cannot work? Or is the female-based family per se at fault? Does it create boys who do poorly in school and on the job and girls who perpetuate the family type when they reach adulthood? If so, is the matriarchal dominance to blame (perhaps by "emasculating" boys), or is it the absence of a father? Or is it just the absence of a male role-model? If so, could surrogate models be provided through schools, settlement houses, and other institutions? Or are there deeper, dynamic forces at work that require the presence of a stable father figure? Or is the failure of a boy due to the mother's lack of income, that is, a result of her being poor and lower class? Or does their failure stem from the feelings of dependency and apathy associated with being on welfare? Or is their failure a result of lack of education of the mother that makes it difficult for them to implement their aspirations for raising their children to a better life? (But lack of income and education is not restricted to the female-based family.)

Next, what are the social, economic, political—and cultural—sources and causes of the female-based family, and to what situations, past and present, does this institutional array of behavioral norms respond? Moreover, how persistent are the norms that uphold this family type, and what aspirations exist that would alter or eliminate it if conditions changed? If the female-based family is an adaptive response to frequent and continuing male unemployment or underemployment, as I suspect it is, one must then ask whether the family structure is a situational response that would disappear once jobs were available. But if the norms that underlie this family have been internalized and would persist even with full employment, one would then need to ask: Where, when, and how are these norms internalized? Do the men themselves begin to lose hope and become so used to economic insecurity that they are unable to hold a good job if it becomes available? Do the women develop norms and even aspirations for independence, so that, doubting that men can function as husbands and breadwinners, they become unable to accept them if they are employed?

Are such attitudes transmitted to the children of female-based families, and if so, by whom, with what intensity, and at what age? Do the boys learn from their mothers that men are unreliable, or do they conclude this from the male adults they see around them? At what age does such learning take place, and how deeply is it internalized? If children learn the norm of male unreliability during the first six years of their life, would they have difficulty in shedding their beliefs under more favorable economic conditions? If they learn it when they are somewhat older, perhaps six to nine, would they be less likely to internalize it? If they learn this norm from their mothers, is it more persistent than if they learn it later from their peers and the male adults they see on the street? And at what age does the boy begin to model himself on these male adults?

It may be that the entire set of norms underlying the female-based family are much less persistent than the questions in the previous paragraph assume. Whether or not they are persistent, however, one would have to go on to ask: Under what conditions is it possible for people, adults and children, to give up the norms of the female-based family? Would it follow quickly after full employment, or would adults who have become accustomed to economic insecurity and female-based families pass on these norms to their children even if they achieved economic security at some time in their lives? If so, the female-based family might persist for another generation. Or are there helping institutions that could aid parents and children to give up irrelevant norms and speed up the transition to the two-parent family? And, if it were impossible to help adults to change, how about eighteen-year-olds, or thirteen-year-olds, or six-year-olds?

Moreover, what aspirations exist among the poor for a two-parent family? Do lower-class Negro women really "want" a two-parent family, and are their aspirations intense enough to overcome the behavioral norms that have developed to make them matriarchs?

In addition, one must also ask what functions the female-based family performs for the affluent members of society, and what obstacles the latter might put in the way of eliminating this family type. How quickly could they overcome their belief that Negro family life is often characterized by instability, illegitimacy, and matriarchy? Would they permit public policies to eliminate male unemployment and to provide higher and more dignified income grants to those who cannot work? And most important, would they permit the changes in the structure of rewards and in the distribution of income, status, and power that such policies entail?

If these kinds of questions were asked about every phase of life among the poor, it would be possible to begin to determine which of the behavioral norms of poor people are causally associated with poverty. I suspect that the answers to such questions would show what Hylan Lewis found among the people he studied: "The behaviors of the bulk of the low income families appear as pragmatic adjustments to external and internal stresses and deprivations experienced in the quest for essentially common values." [29]

STRUCTURING NEW OPPORTUNITIES

If the ultimate aim of research is to eliminate poverty, one would also have to ask questions about how to structure new economic and noneconomic opportunities to include incentives that will overcome the restraints of persisting behavioral norms, which might otherwise prevent the poor from accepting these opportunities. Current experiments providing job training and even jobs to the unemployed have encountered enough failure to indicate quite clearly that giving unemployed men any kind of job training or any kind of job is not enough. Since unemployed youths do not have lower-class aspirations, but want the kinds of jobs that considered decent, dignified, and status-bearing in working- and middle-class cultures, the new opportunities must be designed accordingly.

The first policy question is: What kinds of opportunities have highest priority, economic or noneconomic? Assuming that the first priority is for economic opportunity, what is most important for whom, a job or an income grant? And what types of jobs and income grants are most desirable? What type of job would actually be considered an opportunity by poor people, unemployed or underemployed, and what type would be considered inferior to present methods of obtaining an income, for example, welfare payments, illicit employment provided by the numbers racket, or various forms of male and female hustling?

To answer this kind of question for policy guidance would require an analysis both of job aspirations and of persistent behavioral norms that interfere with holding a job. What elements of a decent job are most important to poor people: The wage or salary, the security of the job, physical working conditions, the social character-istics of the work situation, the relationship to the boss, the skills required, the opportunities for self-improvement and promotion, or the status of the job—and in what order of priority?

Which behavioral norms function as incentives to holding a job? And what are the obstacles: The lack of skills; the unwillingness to work every day, or an eight-hour day; the pressures to associate with the peer group; or the inability or unwillingness to adapt to the non-work requirements of the job, for example, dress, decorum, or sub-mission to impersonal authority? What kinds of incentives, monetary and otherwise, can overcome these obstacles, and what kinds of train-ing programs, job guarantees and social groupings on the job would be necessary to "acculturate" people who have never or rarely held a full-time job into the society of workers?

Similarly, what kinds of income grants would provide the best means for a permanent escape from poverty for those who cannot work and particularly for their children? Is the amount of income alone important? If not, how important is the release from stig-matization and identification as poor that would be provided by a family allowance in contrast to welfare payments or a negative income-tax grant? What forms of payment will provide the least discouragement and the most encouragement to work for people who want to be in the labor force? Would across-the-board grants be more desirable than a set of categorical grants, such as a family allowance, rent supplements, and Medicaid?

Also, what kinds of noneconomic opportunities are necessary or desirable? Would jobs and income grants replace the need for social casework, or would people be more likely to ask for help from social workers once they no longer depended on them for welfare pay-ments? And what helping milieu is most effective? Should services be provided in special institutions for the poor, or should the poor be given grants so that they can buy the same services as affluent people? Would poor people prefer to go to a private physician whom they pay like everyone else, or to a superior clinic or group practice that is set up especially for them? Which alternatives would be most com-patible with the behavioral norms and aspirations of different kinds of poor people? And what are the benefits and costs of grants for the use of private medical and other services compared with the benefits and costs of improved services provided expressly for the poor?

Finally, how long must special opportunities be made available before poor people can truly be on their own? How much security, economic and other, must be provided for how long before people can take the risk of grasping at new opportunities and be able to give up present behavioral norms and associations?

Other questions must be asked of the affluent society, for example, of employers and employees who will be working alongside the newly employed poor. Yet other questions arise because many of the poor are nonwhite and their poverty is a result of segregation. Eventually, questions must also be asked of the voters to estimate the political feasibility of instituting the needed programs in order to determine what program designs have the greatest chance of political acceptance. In the last analysis, the shape of an effective anti-poverty program probably depends more on the willingness of affluent voters to accept such a program than on the economic and cultural needs of the poor.

IV. SOME METHODOLOGICAL IMPLICATIONS: THE NEED FOR SOCIAL EXPERIMENTS

Many of the questions I have raised about the culture of the poor can be investigated through a combination of presently available empirical research methods: participant-observation; the mixture of ethnological techniques, participant-observation and life-history collection used by Oscar Lewis; intensive or depth interviewing; and extensive interviewing of large samples by social surveys.

Yet none of these methods is able to get at the prime question about the culture of the poor: What behavioral norms will and will not persist under changed economic and noneconomic conditions? *This question can best be answered by altering the conditions and seeing how people respond.* Consequently, the most desirable method of anti-poverty research is inducing social change and observing the results, for example, by eliminating poverty-inducing conditions.

Researchers lack the power and the funds to undertake social change on a large scale, but they can do it on a small scale—as social experimentation. The best technique is the field experiment, which would enable a sample of poor people to live under improved conditions in order to determine whether or not this led to a change in behavior and in the degree to which they implemented their aspirations. Such experiments can illustrate the effect of a variety of new opportunities on poverty-related behavioral norms, such as family structure, mental health, physical health, work and work performance, school attendance and school performance, and political participation.

A wide range of experiments is needed to determine (and compare) the response of poor people to different kinds of new opportunities, economic and noneconomic: secure and well-paying jobs, a guaranteed income without employment, income derived from public welfare, the negative income tax or a family allowance, superior education for children, better housing for families, and others. Alternative policies for eliminating poverty must be tested among various kinds of poor people, with control groups established wherever possible, to measure the impact of the specific policy or policies being tested. Such experiments are already coming into being; as this is written, the Office of Economic Opportunity has begun an experiment to test the impact of the negative income tax on work incentives and other behavior and attitude patterns; the Department of Health, Education and Welfare and the Ford Foundation are considering tests of the effects of alternative types of income grants such as the family allowance. Other experiments are needed to study various employment, job-training, and noneconomic programs.

Most experiments must be set up *de novo*, but others can treat existing social processes as experiments. One approach is historical: analyzing the experience of the European immigrants in America and their descendants in order to measure, however imperfectly, the impact of stable jobs and decent incomes on the cultural patterns that they brought with them from Europe. More useful studies could be conducted among people, white and nonwhite, who have recently been able to move out of the slums of American cities, to determine what opportunities were available to them, how they took hold of these opportunities, and what changes in behavior followed. A comparison of an experimental group that escaped from a ghetto and a control group that did not might yield some useful preliminary answers to the questions raised in this chapter.[30]

In addition, it is possible to analyze the various anti-poverty programs and demonstration projects now going on all over the United States as experiments, to see how the participants reacted to the opportunities they were offered. Such studies would focus on program elements on the one hand and on the behavioral norms and aspirations of participants on the other to determine which program elements and cultural factors were responsible for success and which for failure.

The great need is for more experiments. Most social experiments can only be initiated by the government or by well-endowed private foundations, but they can only be undertaken if social scientists are willing to design them in the first place. If social science is to serve the ends of policy, and particularly to help eliminate poverty, it must place less emphasis on the study of existing conditions and more on experimentation with improved conditions. Such an approach would also be fruitful for social-science theory, for it would answer more reliably than current research methods whether there is a culture of poverty and a lower-class way of life.

Notes

1. Lee Rainwater, "Neutralizing the Disinherited: Some Psychological Aspects of Understanding the Poor," Pruitt-Igoe Occasional Paper No. 30 (St. Louis: Washington University, June 1967—mimeographed) , p. 2.

2. *Ibid., passim.*

3. See, for example, David Matza, "The Disreputable Poor," in Reinhard Bendix and S. M. Lipset, eds., *Class, Status and Power,* 2nd ed. (New York: The Free Press of Glencoe, 1966) , pp. 289–303.

4. For a useful review of these writings, see Robert H. Bremmer, *From the Depths* (New York: New York University Press, 1956) .

5. See, for example, Barbara Solomon, *Ancestors and Immigrants* (Cambridge, Mass.: Harvard University Press, 1956) .

6. William F. Whyte, Jr., *Street Corner Gang* (Chicago: University of Chicago Press, 1943) ; Michael Young and Peter Willmott, *Family and Kinship in East London* (London: Routledge and Kegan Paul, 1957); Walter Miller, "Lower Class Culture as a Generating Milieu of Gang Delinquency," *Journal of Social Issues,* XIV (1958), 5–19; Oscar Lewis, *The Children of Sanchez* (New York: Random House, 1961) ; Oscar Lewis, *La Vida* (New York: Random House, 1966) ; Herbert J. Gans, *The Urban Villagers* (New York: The Free Press of Glencoe, 1962) ; Hylan Lewis, "Culture, Class and the Behavior of Low Income Families," *Culture, Class and Poverty* (Washington: Cross-Tell, 1967) . Elliott Liebow, *Tally's Corner* (Boston: Little, Brown, 1967) ; Lee Rainwater, this volume, Ch. 9.

7. Lee Rainwater, this volume, Ch. 9.

8. Bernard Beck, "Bedbugs, Stench, Dampness and Immorality: A Review Essay on Recent Literature about Poverty," *Social Problems,* XV (Summer 1967) , 101–114.

9. Some writers have even resurrected Karl Marx's pejorative *lumpenproletariat* to describe participants in the rebellions, ironically forgetting that Marx applied the term to people who did not share his revolutionary aims. Still, it is interesting that Marx, who apotheosized the working class, nevertheless felt the poor were undeserving, although his pejorative refers to political, rather than moral, lapses. Conversely, nineteenth-century American observers felt the poor were politically immoral for the opposite reason, because they were drawn to socialist and Communist movements.

10. See, for example, Jerome Carlin, *Lawyers' Ethics* (New York: Russell Sage Foundation, 1966) .

11. See, for example, Louis Kriesberg, "The Relationship between Socio-Economic Rank and Behavior," *Social Problems,* X (Spring 1963) , 334–353.

12. Hylan Lewis, *op. cit.,* pp. 17–18.

13. Miller, *op. cit.,* p. 7.

14. *Ibid.,* p. 19.

15. *Ibid.*, p. 7.

16. Hyman Rodman, "The Lower-Class Value Stretch," *Social Forces*, XLII (December 1963), 205–215; Lee Rainwater, this volume, Ch. 9.

17. Hylan Lewis, *op. cit.*, pp. 38–39.

18. See Robert A. Nisbet, *The Sociological Tradition* (New York: Basic Books, 1967).

19. For more extreme examples of the use of the term *culture* see Hylan Lewis, *op. cit.*, pp. 14–15. See also Jack Roach and Orville R. Gurselin, "An Evaluation of the 'Culture of Poverty' Thesis," *Social Forces*, XLV (March 1967), 383–392.

20. For a persuasive illustration see Margaret Mead, *New Lives for Old* (New York: Morrow, 1956).

21. For some illustrations of the policy implications of conceptual conservatism, see Frederick S. Jaffe, "Family Planning and Public Policy: Is the 'Culture of Poverty' Concept the New Cop-Out?", paper presented to the December 1967 meeting of the American Sociological Association, San Francisco, California.

22. Miller, *op. cit.*, p. 18.

23. Oscar Lewis, *La Vida*, p. xliv.

24. *Ibid.*, p. xlviii.

25. See, for example, Kriesberg, *op. cit.*

26. For excellent discussions of this point, see S. M. Miller, "The American Lower Classes: A Typological Approach," and S. M. Miller and Frank Reissman, "The Working Class Subculture: A New View," in Arthur B. Shostak and William Gomberg, eds., *Blue-Collar World* (Englewood Cliffs, N.J.: Prentice-Hall, 1964), pp. 9–23, 24–35.

27. Lee Rainwater, this volume, Ch. 9.

28. See S. M. Miller, *op. cit.*, p. 20.

29. Hylan Lewis, *op. cit.*, p. 38.

30. Zahava Blum has suggested studies of American Indians who received large cash payments from the government for their reservations to determine how they spent these funds and what successes and failures they encountered in escaping from the poverty of reservation life.

Chapter 9

☞ *The Problem of Lower-Class Culture and Poverty-War Strategy*

LEE RAINWATER

As long as there have been poor people there have been commentators on their lot. Since the Industrial Revolution, such commentary has assumed an important place in political dialogue concerning the causes of poverty, the cures of poverty, and social-welfare policy generally. As David Matza has shown, there has been a succession of fashions in the concepts brought to bear for understanding "the disreputable poor," and these fashions have in turn been highly consequential for the ways in which the larger society has dealt with poor people.[1]

LOWER-CLASS CULTURE AS AN EXPLANATORY CONCEPT

THE POOR ARE DIFFERENT FROM YOU AND ME

The concept of a lower-class subculture has been one of the recent mainstays of professional attempts to comprehend the life, the motivations, the problems, of the least-well-off portion of the population. In the sociological and anthropological literature of the past thirty

I have benefited greatly from comments on an earlier draft of this chapter by Alvin W. Gouldner and Norman F. Whitten. Some of the ideas about the lower-class subculture as a conceptual issue stem from conversations with Marc J. Swartz. The substantive issues dealt with derive in large part from Pruitt-Igoe field work (NIMH Grant Number MH09189) and analysis carried out by Boone Hammond, Joyce Ladner, David Schulz, and William Yancey. I have also profited from criticism and comments by Herbert J. Gans, S. M. Miller, Hyman P. Minsky, Hyman Rodman, Corinne S. Schelling, and Harold W. Watts.

years, two rather different views have been advanced about the distinctiveness of lower-class norms and values vis-à-vis the larger "conventional" society. One of these views, fathered most directly by Allison Davis and further developed by Walter Miller, holds that there is a distinctive culture that characterizes those who are brought up in the lower-class world:

Now a child cannot learn his mores, social drives, and values—his basic culture—from books. He can learn a particular culture and a particular moral system only from those people who know this behavior and who exhibit it in frequent association with the learner. If a child associates intimately with no one but slum adults and children, he will learn only slum culture. Thus the pivotal meaning of social classes to the student of behavior is that they limit and pattern the learning environment; they structure the social maze in which the child learns his habits and meanings.

In the slum, as elsewhere, the human group evolves solutions to the basic problems of group life . . . Because the slum individual usually is responding to a different physical, economic and cultural reality from that in which the middle class individual is trained, the slum individual's habits and values also must be different if they are to be realistic. The behavior which we regard as "delinquent" or "shiftless" or "unmotivated" in slum groups is usually a perfectly realistic, adaptive, and—in slum life—respectable response to reality.[2]

By the time, some ten years later, that Walter Miller applied these same views to the understanding of gang delinquency, the assertion of a distinctive lower-class culture was even more sharply drawn:

There is a substantial segment of present day American society whose way of life, values, and characteristic patterns of behavior are the product of a distinctive cultural system which may be termed "lower class." Evidence indicates that this cultural system is becoming increasingly distinctive, and that the size of the group which shares this tradition is increasing . . . the standards of lower class culture cannot be seen merely as a reverse function of middle class culture—as middle class standards "turned upside down": lower class culture is a distinctive tradition, many centuries old with an integrity of its own.[3]

Ranged in apparent opposition to this view are the views of such more general theorists as Parsons and Merton who have seemed to maintain that American society possesses a single more or less integrated system of values, that "it" is "morally integrated" because basic moral sentiments tend to be shared by different actors "in the sense that they approve the same basic normative patterns of conduct." [4] The contrary view concerning the lack of distinctiveness of lower-class culture compared to the rest of society was developed by Merton in his essay on social structure and anomie:

> Our egalitarian ideology denies by implication the existence of non-competing individuals and groups in the pursuit of pecuniary success. Instead the same body of success symbols is held to apply for them all. Goals are held to transcend class lines, not be bounded by them, yet the actual social organization is such that there exist class differentials in accessibility of the goals. . . . "Poverty" is not an isolated variable which operates in precisely the same fashion wherever found: it is only one in a complex of identifiably interdependent social and cultural variables. . . . When poverty and associated disadvantages in competing for the cultural values approved for all members of the society are linked with a cultural emphasis on pecuniary success as the dominant goal, high rates of criminal behavior are the normal outcome. . . . When we consider the full configuration—poverty, limited opportunity and the assignment of cultural goals—there appears some basis for explaining the higher correlation between poverty and crime in our society than in others where rigidified class structure is coupled with *differential class symbols of success*.[5]

If one wishes, one can construct out of the writings of men such as Davis and Miller, on the one hand, and Parsons and Merton, on the other, a counterpart of the classic exchange between F. Scott Fitzgerald and Ernest Hemingway. For Fitzgerald, "The rich are different from you and me." Hemingway retorted, "Yes, they have more money." The advocate of a distinctive lower-class culture will argue the counterpart to Fitzgerald's notion, "The poor are different from you and me." And the advocate of the universality of societal values will argue, "Yes, they have less money."

It is an interesting issue, yet its status in sociological and anthropological writings is a curious one. Neither of the two sets of scholars whose views I have presented really dwelled on the conceptual problems of maintaining that there does or does not exist a distinctive lower-class culture.[6] The relatively offhand way in which the competition between these two concepts developed—with Davis and Miller using the concept of lower-class culture merely as preface to the presentation of field research concerning lower-class behavior, and Merton using his ideas about the dominance of a common "success goal" in American society merely to illustrate his more general theory concerning social structure and anomie—has meant that the dialectic between these two views has never been fully explored or adequately tested against existing and developing empirical research concerning lower-class behavior.

The result has been that the unthinking application of each of these paradigms by subsequent commentators on lower-class behavior has sometimes made lower-class persons appear as "conceptual boobs," to use an expression coined by Harold Garfinkel. To date, perhaps the most successful self-conscious attempt to deal with these issues has been Hyman Rodman's concept of the "lower class value stretch," an adaptive mechanism by which

the lower class person, without abandoning the general values of the society, develops an alternative set of values . . . (so that lower-class people) have a wider range of values than others within the society. They share the general values of the society . . . but in addition they have stretched these values or developed alternative values, which help them to adjust to their deprived circumstances.[7]

Rodman's formulation avoids the pitfall of making lower-class persons out as "conceptual boobs" by not implying that (1) they are ignorant of or indifferent to conventional norms and values, or that (2) they persist in maintaining full-fledged allegiance to conventional norms despite their inability to achieve satisfactorily in terms of them.

Since I believe that much of the unclarity and artificial character of these two conceptions of the situation of lower-class people stems from insufficient attention to the actual exigencies of day-to-day life and to the patterned processes of growing up in the group, I want to shift now from these larger questions of over-all cultural or subcultural systems to a closer examination of social and cultural factors operating in connection with one particular aspect of lower-class life: The question of the regulation of sexual and procreative activities; specifically, the question of the normative status of marriage and having children.

THE STABILITY OF HETEROSEXUAL RELATIONS
IN A LOWER-CLASS NEGRO COMMUNITY

I will draw on data from one particular lower-class Negro community. This particular community is the Pruitt-Igoe public housing project of St. Louis, a complex of some thirty high-rise buildings with a population of about ten thousand persons. Although it is a public housing project and one that tends, by default, to be inhabited by the least well-off and most damaged families of the Negro lower class (for example, over half the families are supported by public assistance and over half are headed by women), our limited field work in private slum-housing areas outside of the project suggests that the patterns we see are not distinctive to the project but are merely exaggerations of much more widespread lower-class patterns. Therefore, for purposes of illustration, I will speak of our findings as representative of lower-class Negro life, representative in pattern if not in proportion.

From extensive participant observation by a large staff of researchers and from surveys, it is possible to piece together a portrait of normative and existential views held by this lower-class group. In several earlier papers, Pruitt-Igoe staff members have presented some tentative formulations of views concerning marriage, sexual behavior, and procreation.[8]

In this chapter, I want to present data from a questionnaire survey of adult project residents carried out in the summer of 1965. The survey data, bearing particularly on questions of attitudes, beliefs, and normative considerations, add another dimension to some of the material covered in the earlier papers that were concerned primarily with an analysis of behavior patterns in the community.

First, let us examine the question of the normative status of premarital sexual relations. We asked a random sample of approximately fifty men and women in Pruitt-Igoe whether they felt that "it matters much if a girl has sexual relations with boys but doesn't get pregnant?" and followed that by asking how important it is "that a girl be a virgin when she gets married?" The first question suggests a considerable amount of sexual freedom, while the second allows the respondent to define a girl who is not a virgin in a more restricted way, perhaps as having sexual relations only with a man whom she eventually marries.

In both cases, about half of the men we asked felt that it was not important or did not matter much whether a girl was sexually active or not, but the responses of the women were somewhat different. Half of the women felt that it is important for a girl to be a virgin, and half of them did not. However, 80 per cent of the women felt that it does matter if a girl is more freely involved in sex with boys even though she does not get pregnant. Why they feel this way is perhaps more intriguing than the answers themselves. It is often felt to be immoral for girls to have sex with boys. Quite aside from the individual's own moral views, it is felt that it is likely to affect her reputation and ultimately her chances for establishing a stable marriage relationship. Besides, eventually she is going to get pregnant. There is much more frequent support for the view that virginity per se is not necessary, that perhaps it is a good idea for a girl to see if she is sexually compatible with the man before she marries him. On the other hand, a great many of the women feel that even moderate sexual activity with potential husbands represents a danger to the girl. They say that the man will not trust her, that he will feel "if she does it with him, she'll do it with others." However, adherence to the desirability of virginity is considerably attenuated by the belief that it is a very rare commodity; as one woman commented: "You can't hardly find a virgin anymore unless she's five or six."

What about premarital pregnancy? We asked our sample whether it matters much if a girl gets pregnant but isn't married. Ninety per cent of the women and 60 per cent of the men said that it does matter if a girl gets pregnant before marriage, and most were able to give compelling reasons why it matters. If marriage takes place subsequent to the pregnancy, it is often felt that the marriage is unfortunate in that it is much more likely to break up as the couple discovers that they are not really compatible. If marriage does not take place, the child represents a burden to the girl and to her family and is believed to weaken her chances for marriage to another man. One woman wrapped up the whole issue by saying, "It matters because she's got to explain."

Illegitimacy is much too frequent for the people in our sample to express horror or great condemnation of it, but getting pregnant before marriage significantly exposes the girl and the child to potential stigmatization—"she's got to explain."

Although premarital pregnancy means "serious trouble," it is also regarded as a very frequent occurrence. Every one of our respondents could tell us of situations they knew about in which girls had gotten pregnant before marriage. In a rating test in which we asked how frequent having a child before marriage is, almost three-quarters of the men and women characterized premarital pregnancy as very frequent in the community. On the sexual histories that were part of our survey, 45 per cent of the women reported a premarital pregnancy, 27 per cent of them indicating that the pregnancy was also terminated premaritally.

When we asked how the boys who impregnate girls premaritally feel about this we found a very striking indication of the belief that men have the primary role in sustaining the high degree of non-marital sexual activity. A minority of the respondents said that the boys are sorry, feel responsible, feel inclined to marry the girl, but the majority indicated that boys either do not care and are indifferent to the fact that their girlfriends are pregnant, or with surprising frequency, that they feel proud because making a girl pregnant shows that you are a man! "Some of them be proud. They think they are a man when this happens."

It is apparent that there is a tremendous disjunction between behavior and norms about the way things should be. It is apparent also that violation of these norms is believed to put girls at least in jeopardy in terms of their chances for stable marital relations with men. A history of known sexual activity, and particularly a history of one or more pregnancies outside of marriage, marks a girl someone a man may not trust, a burden as a potential wife.

In such a situation, all kinds of contending beliefs, some of them more grounded in reality than others, grow up to provide operating codes for the world as it is and not as it should be. The effect of these codes is to justify, if they do not fully legitimize, sexual activity outside marriage and illegitimacy.

One of the most striking, because of its divergence from conventional norms, is the view advanced to participant observers by a good many men and women that "it's all right if a husband or wife each step out by themselves sometimes and have a girlfriend or boyfriend on the side as long as the other one doesn't know about it." In our survey, we asked respondents whether they thought this happens very often and discovered that over 85 per cent of them believed that it does. Then we asked whether or not they believed that "many people" feel this way; 70 per cent of them agreed that many people do indeed feel this way. (On both of these counts there were no differences in the responses from men and women, and no differences between the responses of women who were currently married and women whose marriages were disrupted.) However, when we asked whether the respondents believed that it is actually true that "everything usually works out all right as long as neither one knows about it," we found that although some people support the deviant norm, the great majority believe that such institutionalized infidelity inevitably causes trouble. A good many believe that even if the infidelity is not discovered it will repercuss in other ways on the couple's relationship; an even larger number assert that sooner or later the infidelity will be discovered and that when this happens it will inevitably make trouble between husband and wife: " (Won't work) because somebody is missing something somewhere. You can't take care of two women or two men. They'll come across each other sooner or later."

Thus, the "rebellion" that is apparent in the assertion of this counter-norm appears much more a rationalization or a wish than a viable alternative norm because in a pinch it is not really supported even by those who assert it.

Because of this permanent availability of men and women, it is believed that marriages in the community are highly unstable. We asked the survey respondents, "Out of every ten couples around here who get married, how many do you suppose break up, separate, or divorce sooner or later?" The mean estimate was that 5.8 marriages out of 10 eventually break up.

When we asked why these marriages break up, we discovered that sex rears its ugly head as the most common reason. Slightly over 40 per cent of the respondents, both men and women, gave as at least one of the reasons for breaking up, often as the only reason, a complex of sexual references that included "running in the streets," "jealousy," and more directly "having another lover."

It should not be supposed that these responses mean that the respondents believe that the spouses *in fact* are unfaithful, since it is also often believed that unfounded jealousy breaks up marriages or that unfounded jealousy encourages infidelity. (What the actual facts are concerning infidelity in marriage is unclear to us. In the sexual histories of the women in our sample, only 8 per cent of the women who were currently married admitted having extramarital affairs, but 31 per cent of those who were no longer married did so.)

When the focus is shifted from the abstract—"Why do marriages break up?"—to the concrete—"Why did your marriage break up?"—the same pattern is apparent. Sixty marriages among the women in our sample had been disrupted by divorce or separation. The distribution of reasons given for the disruptions is as follows:

TABLE 9–1. *Cause of Marital Disruption*

	PERCENTAGE
Sexual infidelity	40
Husband wouldn't support her; wouldn't work	27
Husband lost job and couldn't find another	3
One of the partners was immature (too attached to parents, too young)	17
Husband drank excessively	15
Husband cruel, beat her	15
Husband gambled too much	7
Husband in jail	3
Unspecified incompatibility	22
Husband just deserted, no reason given	8

It is apparent that the most common reason given for marital disruption is sexual infidelity. (This was almost always on the part of the man since the woman is telling her side of the story; if we could talk to the departed husbands, they would probably also have some accusations to make.) The women are, in general, rather uncharitable toward their ex-husbands—even with the issue of support all but a few of the women seem to feel that the husband was *unwilling* to support them ("he wouldn't work," "he wouldn't give me enough money") rather than *unable* in the sense that he could not get a job or earn enough money for the family.

Obviously, then, lower-class Negroes see their world as one in which there are a great many threats to the stability of marriage, threats that precede marriage, in the form of a sexual activity that does not bode well for the trustworthiness or respectability of the husband or wife, and that continue in marriage in the form of economic instability and the ever-present threat of seduction by "the street." Once the marriage is broken the prospects for a second try are even worse since both economic instability and "fidelity instability" are enhanced.

From the analysis of participant-observation data reported in previous papers and from the questionnaire material discussed above, it is possible to piece together a portrait of how the world appears to the Negro lower-class men and women who live in Pruitt-Igoe. Shifting now from the way Pruitt-Igoeans express their understandings of the world and their norms to a language more appropriate to a concern with conceptual problems of norms, existential views, and deviance from norms, the following would seem to be the essential elements of Pruitt-Igoe views concerning marriage, sexual behavior, and procreation:

1. Lifelong marriage is the only really desirable way of living if one has the opportunity, if one can manage it. A person fully vested with the proper social and cultural characteristics should be able to contract and maintain such a marriage provided he can find a partner who is similarly vested.

2. In the same way, children should be born only in marriage relationships; to procreate outside of marriage is to fall importantly short of the way things ought to be.

3. Any kind of sexual relationship outside of marriage is a dangerous thing, although it is also a very attractive possibility. A double standard applies in the realm of ideals at least, in that

sex outside of marriage is much more dangerous for a woman than for a man.

4. In short, there is a little ambiguity about the norms concerning sex and procreation as these apply to how good people will behave in a good world. Sexual and procreative events outside of the context of marriage are not normative, and they do involve costs.

5. But, and this is still from the perspective of Pruitt-Igoeans, reality makes it extremely difficult to live up to these norms. Reality must be taken to include not only the individual's chances in the instrumental opportunity structure (his ability to make out in the larger world, to get enough education, to hold a job, etc.), but also his chances of resisting the pressures toward deviance from his peer group—as he grows up he experiences such pressures from other boys and girls, men and women, *and* he learns the competing attraction of the "high-life" world.

6. Therefore, if one does not have very strong resistance, deviance from sexual and procreative norms is seen as an almost necessary result of participating in the peer-group society. Resistance is weakened when one does not possess attributes and abilities that allow him to make out in more conventional ways—when one does not manage to get enough education, hold a job, etc.

7. Therefore, deviance from these norms is *tolerable*. The great discovery that lower-class people make, which middle- and working-class people find so hard to understand, is that it is possible to live a life that departs very significantly from the way you think life ought to be lived without ceasing to exist, without feeling totally degraded, without giving up all self-esteem.

8. Once one learns that such a life is tolerable it is possible for individuals to engage in "rebellion" à la Merton. One can call into question both the cultural goals and the institutionalized means for achieving them, and seek to put in their place contrary goals and means that bring action and norms more closely in line *and* thus reduce cognitive dissonance. However, it is important to remember that rebellion is not revolution, that the pull of the old norms is great, and that very few lower-class individuals end up defining their own interests as lying ideally in the support of the deviant norms rather than the conventional ones.

9. With respect to the central importance of marriage, the compromise solution most frequently adopted in the Negro lower

class is to marry fairly quickly, particularly in response to the pressures of pregnancy or extensive sexual activity that begins to look promiscuous, and to hope against hope that the marriage will work out and last so that one may achieve conventional status. Therefore, lower-class Negro Americans tend to marry fairly early rather than to go through a series of mating unions (including domiciliary ones) and crown their sexual careers with marriage, as in the Caribbean. The corollary of this difference, however, is that among urban lower-class Negroes in the United States, first marriages very often break up (indeed, a majority probably do), whereas in the Caribbean legal marriage tends to be much more stable.[9]

10. Expectations concerning widespread sexual activity continue throughout life to pose a constant threat to the stability of relationships in which people try to "do right," to maintain stable relationships. The Negro lower class conforms with a vengeance to Bernard Farber's model of permanent availability of all men and women as mates.[10] Men are seen as the main carriers of this tradition, but women are also active participants. Although the double standard is seen as representing a more ideal state of affairs than equality in sexual relations, it is believed that women are almost as likely to be "disloyal" to their mates (either maritally or nonmaritally) as are men. There is evidence, however, that to a considerable extent the sexual freedom that women claim is reactive to a conception of men as so likely to transgress that a woman is a "fool" for being single-minded in her loyalty.

We can conclude this examination of the Pruitt-Igoe data by saying that it seems that lower-class Negro Americans (and lower-class Negroes in the Caribbean) share a set of problems in connection with bringing their behavior in line with norms concerning sexual and procreative activities, and that much of the characteristic behavior of the group can be understood as their cultural adaptations to these problems. The norms support legal marriage and legitimate birth as the only really proper way to establish families (but women are more dedicated to these norms than men, although both sexes recognize their legitimacy) ; yet, the more impersonal socio-economic forces and the intimate interpersonal forces of the community militate against living up to these norms, and the majority of the population does not indeed live up to them.

The result is that a set of more or less institutionalized alternatives have developed historically for adapting to the actual pressures under which men and women live, but these adaptations are not basically satisfactory to those who make use of them both because of the pains, frustrations, and tensions built into these ways of living and because of the vulnerability people feel to attributions of having somehow fallen short of full moral status, attributions that are made both by oneself and by others.

Let us turn now to a consideration of the implications of these data for the argument that there exists a distinctive lower-class culture.

IS THERE A LOWER-CLASS SUBCULTURE?
WHAT IS DISTINCTIVE ABOUT IT?

Evocative definitions of culture usually define the concept as referring to "a way of life" or "a design for living." Culture is social heredity, transmitted by one generation, learned by another, and shared in the particular collectivity that possesses it. More conceptually, culture is a system of symbols that orders experience and guides behavior.

*Sub*culture suggests that within a larger collectivity possessing an over-all culture, there are sufficient variations in designs for living that it is worth the trouble of trying to specify several different subdesigns because of the consequences these are presumed to have. Since the social scientist discovers this culture or subculture by abstraction from the behavior of persons in a group, the decision to define subcultures is to a certain extent an arbitrary one. Its arbitrariness is reduced only by the possiblity of demonstrating that the differences one believes exist are sufficiently consequential to be of use in understanding behavioral variation within the larger collectivity.

Culture as social heredity, as transmitted symbol system, involves two main dimensions. It involves certain existential predications about the world, and it involves an evaluative component specifying what is good, not so good, or bad about that which is said to exist. In other words, culture involves an "is" component and an "ought" component. These components are compounded in the inventory of elements traditionally said to comprise culture—knowledge, belief, technology, values, and norms. As Clyde Kluckhohn [11] observed, the existential propositions in a culture always carry implicit in them certain evaluation overtones, and equally (for our purposes more) important the evaluative elements of culture (values and norms) always carry implicit in them certain necessary existential concommitants.

If, then, we take subculture to refer to a distinctive pattern of existential and evaluative elements, a pattern distinctive to a particular group in a larger collectivity and consequential for the way their behavior differs from that of others in the collectivity, it seems to me that the concept of lower-class subculture is useful. All who have studied lower-class people, whether under the influence of the Mertonian emphasis on general cultural norms, like Cloward and Ohlin, or under the influence of strong proponents of class subculture, like Allison Davis and Walter Miller, have produced findings concerning lower-class behavior and belief that clearly suggest a distinctive patterning.[12] *The distinctive pattern consists of elements that are shared with the larger culture and ones that are peculiar to the group*—it is the configuration of *both* kinds of elements that is distinctive to the lower class. The argument comes not so much in whether a lower-class subculture can be said to exist, but in what its content is and how it should be characterized.

About the distinctiveness of the existential perspective of lower-class people there is relatively little disagreement. All investigators who have studied lower-class groups seem to come up with compatible findings to the general effect that the lower-class world view involves conceptions of the world as a hostile and relatively chaotic place in which you have to be always on guard, a place in which one must be careful about trusting others, in which the reward for effort expended is always problematic, in which good intentions net very little. I am not suggesting that one can find neatly organized in one place an exhaustive description of the existential perspectives of lower-class persons, but I think one can say that the various ways in which different investigators have described this aspect of lower-class culture are not in any kind of essential conflict.

The issue with respect to the evaluative aspect of lower-class culture, with respect to values and norms, is a much more complex one, as we have seen. As Rodman implies, the issue is in some respects a false one that derives basically from the unrealism of separating the normative from the existential. Every norm predicates several existential conditions. These conditions are more often implied than clearly stated, but careful observation of concrete social behavior suggests that these existential conditioners of norms are central to any understanding of behavior that has reference to norms. The existential predications come most clearly to the surface when people seek to justify their own deviance from norms. Then it becomes apparent that all people take the position that they will live up to the norms of their group if they possibly can. That is, conforming to norms requires certain kinds of social logistic support. (This is apparent not only to social scientists but also to the members of a society!) Although people are most sensitive to the necessity for certain kinds of resources for living up to norms with respect to their own behavior and tend to blind themselves to this aspect of the situation when they evaluate other people's behavior, individuals who find themselves in the same boat in lacking resources generally develop some understanding tolerance for each other's deviance.

Norms with their existential concomitants are perhaps best regarded as rules for playing a particular game. That game represents one kind of adaptation to the environmental situation in which a group finds itself. Individuals in a group negotiate with significant others to be allowed to play the normative game—to get into the game and to have the resources that will allow them to play it. If the individual is not allowed in the game (for example, Negro slaves under slavery), or if he cannot get the resources to play the game successfully and thus experiences constant failure at it, he is not "conceptual boob" enough to continue knocking his head against a stone wall—he withdraws from the game. Instead, he will try to find another game to play, either one that is already existing and at hand or one that he himself invents.[13] Merton's well-known adaptations to anomie suggest several different kinds of attempts to create new games out of the wreckage of failure to gain admission to and succeed at conventional games.

But what if a good many people cannot play the normative game, are in constant communication with each other, and there is generational continuity among them? In that case, the stage is set for the invention and diffusion of substitute games of a wide variety. In the case of New World Negroes, these substitute gains have been worked out long ago and subjected to some modification by each generation depending on the situation (urban or rural, their labor in demand or not in demand, etc.) in which they find themselves. Thus, though in the abstract one can analyze synchronically the situation of a deprived group vis-à-vis the larger society and its norms, in reality each generation learns the substitute games at the same time that it learns the normative ones. To some extent, the substitute adaptations of each generation condition the possibilities subsequent generations have of adapting in terms of the requirements of the normative games.

Nevertheless, in the American context at least it is clear that each generation of Negroes has a strong desire to be able to perform successfully in terms of the norms of the larger society and makes efforts in this direction. The inadequacies of the opportunity structure doom many to failure to achieve in terms of their own desires and therefore facilitate the adoption of the readily available alternatives. In this way, the social ontogeny of each generation recapitulates the social phylogeny of Negroes in the New World *because the basic socio-economic position of the group has not changed in a direction favorable to successful achievement in terms of conventional norms.*

If a group by some means becomes totally isolated from the dominant group whose games its members can't play, they may succeed in establishing normative games of their own. But if they continue to some extent under the influence of the dominant group, their substitute games cannot acquire full normative character. Instead, the games may become pseudonormative; the players assert to each other that their new game has full moral justification, but careful observation of actual behavior belies that fact, as Matza has shown, for juvenile delinquents, who sometimes manage to develop ideologies that seem to legitimate delinquent activity as normative, but in which as a matter of fact the delinquents themselves do not really believe.[14]

In short, those segments of the over-all society who control the normative game are in a position to arrange conditions so that it is very difficult to have a competing game with a normative cachet. Though the competing games may have to be tolerated because of unwillingness or inability to provide everyone with the resources to play the normative game, as long as the keepers of the normative game have sufficient power, they are able to frustrate the success of efforts to declare the competing games normative.

Given this power of conventional society, members of the lower class are likely to be socialized in such a way that they recognize the normative status of conventional games even though they eventually discover that their own best bets, given the world as it is and as they see it, lie with substitute games. As Goffman observes:

The stigmatized individual tends to hold the same beliefs about identity that we do . . . the standards he has incorporated from the wider society equip him to be intimately alive to what others see as his failing, inevitably causing him, if only for moments, to agree that he does indeed fall short of what he really ought to be. Shame becomes a central possibility, arising from the individual's perception of one of his own attributes as being a defiling thing to possess, and one he can readily see himself as not possessing.[15]

Though the substitute games developed in the lower-class world have as perhaps their most important function the insulation of the individual from a full and sharp awareness of these facts and of the shame that goes with this awareness, careful observation reveals that the stigmatizing standards are nevertheless internalized and have their effects.

These substitute games involve a structure of rules appropriate to them, but the rules tend to have a purely operating character. It is very difficult for their players to fully institutionalize the rules as normative except in a way that acknowledges their character as substitutes. For example, there are rules about how to make a life that retains some sense of self-esteem even though one is the mother of illegitimate children. One girl commented that her mother reacted in this way to her pregnancy: "She cried, she was hurt. And she told me that because I made one mistake, don't wallow."

HOW DOMINANT SOCIETY'S NORMS ARE MAINTAINED IN THE LOWER CLASS

The argument in this chapter has sought to support the view that conventional society manages somehow to inculcate its norms even in those persons who are not able to achieve successfully in terms of them and to prevent any efforts to redefine norms within the lower-class subculture in such a way that contrary views acquire full normative status. To the extent that this can be demonstrated to be true, it raises further very intriguing issues that are only touched on here. By what processes is it possible to persuade lower-class people to accept norms that are highly punishing to them and to accept the label of deviant or stigmatized persons?

One of the primary reasons that it is impossible for the lower class to institutionalize its own norms is that all individuals in the group, to some extent and under some circumstances, will assert the validity of conventional norms and the invalidity of substitute norms. Even in Jamaica, in which nonlegal unions are in the majority, 20 per cent of all first unions, and a somewhat higher proportion of the first domiciliary unions, involve legal marriage. There are, in short, too many "squares" around to interfere with efforts to negate the conventional norms. These individuals to some extent counter the existential challenge to the norms by demonstrating that it is possible to live up to them even with very few resources. In addition, they acquire a vested interest in derogating and demeaning those around them who do not live up to the norms. To the extent that such persons have power and prestige in the informal social networks of the lower-class community, they are able to operate against an overthrow of the norms.

The sliding scale of leniency in evaluating deviation for "me," "thou," and "the other fellow" means that even individuals who are themselves involved in playing deviant games will, on occasion, particularly when angry and in a mood to degrade the status of others, assert the validity of the norm even as this behavior, because it reinforces existential beliefs about the difficulty of living up to the norm, reinforces deviance.

The aging process also has something to do with sustaining the validity of conventional norms. The older people become in a lower-class community, the more conventional their views tend to become and probably the less deviant their behavior is likely to be (at least in terms of frequency). This means that in their contest with younger persons for the right to define what is and should be, and to control the social and perhaps economic resources of the group, they acquire a vested interest in supporting conventional norms against younger persons who are more likely to challenge them. Thus, not only is there conflict between men and women, with women upholding conventional norms more readily than men, but there is also conflict between young and old. While women and older persons have to accept a great deal of behavior that is deviant from conventional norms, they do not have to like it when they feel that it costs them in terms of life chances and respect.

These conflicts at the interpersonal level are given expression in certain indigenous lower-class institutions that tend to be organized (at least in part) around the support of conventional norms. In the Negro community, the church is particularly important here since most of the *verbal* content of church sermons and Christian religiosity is solidly in support of conventional norms. The conflict is, however, built into the church no less than informal social relations by the counter-message conveyed by church music and ecstatic behavior during church services.

Finally, almost all of the external institutions with which lower-class people come into contact are fairly solidly ranged in support of conventional norms. These institutions can sometimes punish lower-class people directly for not living up to conventional standards, and (perhaps more important) functionaries of these institutions are constantly engaged in demeaning and derogating the status of lower-class people, being especially sensitive to indications that lower-class people are not "respectable" in their behavior and attitudes. It seems very likely that the major power sustaining the salience of conventional norms comes from this kind of day-to-day contact with conventional functionaries in schools, stores, work places, public agencies, and the like. What comes across most clearly to the lower-class person in these settings is that he would be much better off if he were able to live in a conventional way because other people would not "bug him" so much.

In short, I am suggesting that the key to understanding how conventional society manages to maintain its norms lies in understanding the concerted effects of the operation of those who sustain the norms within the community (family and neighbors) and of those outside the community who sustain them by effectively punishing (and perhaps sometimes rewarding).

FUNCTIONAL AUTONOMY AND ADAPTIVE
LOWER-CLASS CULTURE

The end result of these various processes is the development and maintenance of a lower-class subculture that is distinctive yet never free of the heavy hand of conventional culture and its norms. Lower-class subculture acquires *limited functional autonomy* from conventional culture just as the social life of the lower class has a kind of limited functional autonomy vis-à-vis the rest of society. As Gouldner has observed, the phenomenon of functional autonomy in a social system arises in situations in which the demands of full functional integration are too great for the resources available in the system.[16] A compromise solution is for subunits of the system to pull apart, to survive more on their own since they cannot survive together in the one big happy family of a functionally integrated society.

This functional autonomy of the lower class is in the interest of both the larger society and of the lower class. The lower class requires breathing room free from the oppressive eye of conventional society and therefore from the oppressive application of conventional norms. Conventional society is freed from the necessity of facing up to the pain and suffering that it has wrought; conventional culture is relieved of the necessity of confronting the fact that norms are constantly flaunted and that the social control mechanisms that are supposed to ensure observance of the norms cannot operate effectively.

Lower-class subculture, then, can be regarded as the historical creation of persons who are disinherited by their society, persons who have adapted to the twin realities of disinheritance and limited functional autonomy for their group by developing existential perspectives on social reality (including the norms and practices of the large society) that allow them to stay alive and not lose their minds, that allow them some modicum of hope about a reasonably gratifying life, and that preserve for many the slim hope that somehow they may be able to find admittance for themselves or their children to the larger society. In line with these existential perspectives, lower-class culture has developed as the repository of a set of survival techniques for functioning in the world of the disinherited. Over time, these survival techniques take on the character of substitute games, with their own rules guiding behavior. But, as has been suggested above, these operating rules seldom sustain a lasting challenge to the validity of the larger society's norms governing interpersonal relations and the basic social statuses involved in marriage, parent-child relations, and the like.

Discussions of lower-class culture in isolation from the social, economic, and ecological setting to which that culture is an adaptation will generally prove to be misleading (and, with respect to policy, pernicious). The dynamic adaptational quality of any culture must be at the center of attention if social process and social change are to be understood. In the case of planned social change directed to solving problems of American poverty, this means that an appreciation of lower-class culture as an element of lower-class life requires *pari passu* a systematic examination of the day-in-day-out social situation for which that culture provides the tools for folk understanding, evaluation, and adaptation.

The lower-class world is defined by two tough facts of life as it is experienced from day to day and from birth to death: deprivation and exclusion. The lower class is deprived because it is excluded from the ordinary run of average American working- and middle-class life, and it is excluded because it is deprived of the resources necessary to function in the institutions of the mainstream (which is after all working, and not middle, class) of American life. The most basic deprivation is, of course, low family income, but from this deprivation flows the sense so characteristic of lower-class groups of not having the price of admission to participation in the many different kinds of rewards that ordinary society offers; some of these cost money, but a good many others (education, for example) do not.

In short, those who grow up in the worlds of poverty learn that they are not able to find enough money to live in what they, and everyone else, would regard as the average American way. Because of inability to find work or very low pay, they learn that the best that they can hope for if they are "sensible" is despised housing, an inferior diet, and a very few of the available pleasures. Because of their economic disadvantage, they are constrained to live among other individuals similarly situated, individuals who, the experience of their daily lives teaches them, are dangerous, difficult, out to exploit or hurt them in petty or significant ways. And they learn that in their communities they can expect only inferior service and protection from such institutions as the police, the courts, the schools, the sanitation department, the landlords, and the merchants. In short, they live in a society that is structured to make life livable for average people, and they learn that people with incomes significantly below average simply cannot move around freely and confidently in such a society. By their very peers and even more by their "superiors," lower-class people are deprived of a right that even the most uncivilized and primitive people that anthropologists have studied routinely accord their members. That is, the right to consider oneself and to be considered by others a worthwhile and valid representative of the human race.

The ways of living that lower-class people work out represent adaptations to this disjunction between the demands society makes for average functioning and the resources they are able to command in their own day-to-day lives.

POLICY IMPLICATION OF LOWER-CLASS CULTURE AND ADAPTATION

If, then, the situation of the lower class is defined most basically by social and economic exclusion and by an anomic and threatening world that grows up in response to that exclusion, we can begin to see some of the ways in which change in the situation of lower-class people might be brought about on a major scale instead of on a merely palliative and individual rescue-operation scale.

Each of the contrasting views of the situation of the lower class discussed above tends toward different and distinctive sets of policy implications in terms of strategy for dealing with problems of poverty. The third view, the adaptational view of lower-class culture, which is an effort to bring about some synthesis of these two views, also tends toward a distinctive set of social policy guidelines for an effective program to deal with problems of poverty.

If one takes the extreme, common-American-culture point of view as represented most clearly by Merton and his students, one is led toward policies that emphasize "opportunity" rather than more radical alterations in the socio-economic system. That is, it is argued that the lower class are basically ordinary Americans who happen to be caught in an unfavorable situation for achieving their common American desires. It is necessary only to provide them with the ordinary means to the achievement of these desires, for example, with such things as job-training programs, more thoughtful and seriously undertaken education programs to replace the poorly equipped and staffed schools that are available to them, perhaps some counseling to make them aware of the opportunities that are available to them in the outside world, etc. In other words, the intervention that is required is basically the fairly superficial one of providing realistic access to means of achieving the level of income and other kinds of functioning that are necessary to be part of regular society. In pursuing an opportunity strategy, however, one becomes aware of all of the many obstacles to making opportunities realistically available that exist in the elaborate private and public bureaucracies that provide jobs, welfare services, educational services, and the like. Therefore, the opportunity strategy will tend eventually to focus one's attention on the failures and incompetence of the institutional framework that theoretically has the task of furthering equality of opportunity.

This is the perspective that informed much of the war on poverty as it was initiated. The goal of the war was not to directly provide resources that would cancel out poverty, but to provide opportunities so that people could achieve their own escape from poverty. But to the extent that the common-American-culture point of view is not a valid one, the opportunity programs, "means" programs, will not make a major dent in poverty because lower-class adaptations to the actual situation of deprivation exist and interfere with the means program by making them unattractive, meaningless, or distrusted.

If, on the other hand, one pursues the lower-class subculture point of view and attempts to derive a strategy from an appreciation of the distinctive characteristics of lower-class subcultural values, techniques for coping with the world, and personality characteristics that go along with those, then policy implications are likely to stress the necessity for culture and personality change as prerequisites for a solution to the problem of poverty. One seeks means to interrupt the transmission of lower-class culture from one generation to another, and instead to arrange to transmit cultural elements that will enable lower-class people to function in stable working- or middle-class ways. One popular version of this view (apparently not held by many serious social scientists) is simply to remove children from their lower-class homes and to provide in the form of American *kibbutzim* an environment in which conventional culture is transmitted and in which lower-class culture is not available. Less horrifying versions would involve special educational programs to remedy cultural deprivation and disadvantage, preschool programs like Head Start, and adult-education programs oriented to bringing about cultural change through instruction such as consumer education programs, prevocational training oriented to etiquette, dress, speech, and the like.

But from the standpoint of anthropological theory, there is one glaring fallacy in such strategies. We view culture as an adaptation to the social and ecological situation in which peoples find themselves. Anthropologists are fascinated with unraveling the varied ways in which culture represents an adaptation to the existential realities of tribes and peasants in all parts of the world and, increasingly, of those who dwell in urban industrial societies. Now, if culture is an adaptation to life situations, if it is transmitted as the accumulated knowledge of the group about how to adapt, and if the learning of that culture is systematically reinforced by the experiences that individuals have as they grow up and go about their daily lives making their own individual adaptation to their own individual social and ecological situation, then one can predict that any effort to change lower-class culture directly by outside educational intervention is doomed to failure. Lower-class people will have no incentive to change their culture (indeed they would suffer if they tried), unless there is some significant change in their situation. Anthropologists, in short, have tremendous respect for culture as a way of coping with the stresses of human life; it follows that they have to respect the problem-solving ability of lower-class culture and the tenacity of lower-class human beings who have worked out adaptations that, to some extent at least, minimize their problems (no matter how far these adaptations fall short of "perfect" ones) .

And, also, any realistic assessment of the likelihood of either an opportunity or a cultural-change strategy paying off must include an assessment of the middle-class caretaker culture as well as the culture of lower-class people. As Herbert Gans points out in Chapter 8, a proper definition of the "culture of poverty" ought also to include those cultural characteristics of conventional society that serve to sustain and militate against any change in the lower-class culture. In short, middle-class culture forms part of the social and ecological situation of lower-class people to which they adapt by developing their own subculture. Central to the caretaker culture is the apparent inability of large-scale public institutions to change in ways that allow them to serve lower-class populations without also demeaning them, or to obligate the tremendous resources that would be necessary to carry out culture change (or opportunity programs) that might prove effective. The central characteristic of the middle-class component of the culture of poverty is the almost total unwillingness of conventional society to admit its complicity in the suffering and exclusion that lower-class people experience. Anthropologists have been traditionally distrustful of the culture-change potential of missionaries; it is not difficult for them to see the analogous situation involved in many community-action, guided self-help, and education-for-the-disadvantaged programs.

This line of analysis then leads one to the view that if lower-class culture is to be changed and lower-class people are eventually to be enabled to take advantage of "opportunities" to participate in conventional society and to earn their own way in it, *this change can only come about through a change in the social and ecological situation to which lower-class people must adapt.*

A strategy, then, to change the situation of lower-class people so that whatever negative consequences issue from their distinctive culture also change requires an understanding of what it is about those situations that fosters lower-class cultural adaptations. If, as has been argued here, lower-class culture is an adaptation not to an absolute deprivation of living below some minimum standard, but to the relative deprivation of being so far removed from the average American standard that the lower-class individual cannot feel himself part of his society, then the policy implications point clearly to the necessity for developing programs that allocate sufficient resources to lower-class people to correct their situation of relative deprivation. If the common-American-culture point of view encourages an "opportunity" strategy and the distinctive lower-class culture point of view suggests a "culture change" strategy, the adaptational view argued here points toward a "resource equalization strategy."

EQUALIZING INCOME, THE KEY RESOURCE

What little we know about what most Americans think about poverty, deprivation, and discrimination suggests that Americans want a society in which there is no class of people below "the average man" in terms of prestige, income, or other advantages. The lowest man on the totem pole, in their minds, should be able to hold up his head as an "average American." So much do Americans cleave to this ideal that 80 per cent of them will call themselves middle class (rather than upper or lower) and very, very few will admit to the label lower class. Although a denial of reality, this behavior suggests that for Americans the good society is one in which each man and woman can earn the right to an average standard of living. While Americans do not like the idea that average-man resources should be handed to anyone on a silver platter, they do believe that a successful American society would be one in which each person does indeed *earn* such a standard of living because of the opportunity and security that are available to him.

Today's political challenge is to so govern the society that these ideals are realized. But in order to realize them, they must first be consciously faced. The ideal that every family have at least the average American standard of living has simply not been fully articulated in modern times. Instead, to the extent that the issue has been dealt with at all, it has been in terms of "minimum standards of living" rather than average standards of living. The perspective implicit in the various poverty standards that have received widespread attention since the beginning of the War on Poverty represents a kind of compromise with the American ideal that beleaguered liberal politicians and welfare workers have accepted and established because they have so little hope that anything can be done to achieve the ideal of a nation of average men. Poverty standards are part of a kind of desperate view of the world in which only a little bit of assistance ("not too much health, education, and welfare") is possible or allowed. Liberals, particularly as they are incorporated into the political and welfare establishment, have become so used to this notion that it is hard for them to imagine political programs that go beyond improving slightly the welfare measures now in existence. And the new radicals seem equally wedded to such an ungenerous conception of what American society might be, given some political imagination, because it confirms their pessimistic view of the world and their cataclysmic preferences for a revolution that somehow is going to come tomorrow.

Yet, there have been times in American history when we have not been content with such limited vision, and government action has been directed not so much to goals of "subsistence" as to the goal of providing opportunities for a larger and larger group of Americans to enjoy the going level of average affluence. One of the most dramatic examples is the Homestead Act of the nineteenth century, which aimed at a nation of free, self-sufficient, and average, not subsistence, farmers. However ineffective and piecemeal such programs may have been, their aim at least was high compared to any of the poverty programs we accept today as representing the best we can offer.

The emphasis on minimum standards, on "poverty lines," which informs so much of our thinking today, is subject to a very real embarrassment. The embarrassment is that as the nation becomes more affluent the poverty line seems to creep up.[17] That is, each decade, the "subsistence package" seems to involve a little bit more in the way of goods and services than it did the decade before. The implicit or explicit model used in most definitions of minimum standards revolves around the problem of inadequate diet and is therefore supposed to reflect a line that separates life and death, or at least sickness and health. The standard in a very real sense is concerned with man as an animal and with keeping him alive. Yet, even so, this standard seems to creep up imperceptibly with the decades. Why should this be so? Perhaps it is because the inventors of the standards do not really believe that an animal standard is meaningful, because they do believe that in order to even subsist as a *person*, individuals and families must somehow approximate the average standard of living. Wouldn't we be better off if we admitted that this is our standard and then explored ways of pursuing it vigorously; if we stopped talking as if our aspirations are so modest as simply to want to keep people from starving or being in poor health because they are not adequately sheltered and clothed?

There is a real congruence here between the implicit view of a great many Americans and the findings of much social-science research on problems of poverty and deprivation. As outlined above, what causes the various lower-class pathologies that disturb us— "apathy," "poor educational performance," "crime and delinquency," the various forms of striking out at those around you and those who are better off—is not the *absolute deprivation* of living below some minimum standard, but the *relative deprivation* of being so far removed from the average American standard that one cannot feel himself part of his society.

For all of these reasons it seems unlikely that we will succeed in our effort to eradicate poverty unless we can succeed in engineering a radical shift in the national income distribution in the direction of greater income equality for the lower half of the population. It is possible to indicate sign posts along the way to that goal by which progress can be assessed. The view presented here is that income equity represents a floor on family incomes such that no family falls below that floor—*a floor phrased not in terms of an absolute amount but relative to the median income for the nation,* that is, to the incomes of other families. Such a standard is dynamic in that it takes account of the upward movement of median income as GNP increases.

We are concerned here with changes in the *shape* of the distribution of families by income and are less concerned with the absolute amount of the minimum income not only because an absolute amount (even taking into account cost-of-living increases) will tend to lag behind the more rapidly rising median family income but also because, with the exception of a tiny proportion of families who receive truly subsistence incomes, the real problem is relative deprivation.

We will further assume that income equalization should be pursued in terms of the equalization of incomes of heads of families and not the family income as a whole. That is, an equitable society would not require a certain proportion of its families to achieve average-income status by forcing the wife, for example, to enter the labor market. Americans want a society in which the average standard of living can be achieved by heads of families. Whether or not the wives or older children also work should be considered a personal option balanced against the gains and losses of not working. If families want their wives or older children to work, that should be possible, too, but the society should not tie itself to equalization on that basis.

Another factor that should be considered a personal option is that of family size. Assuming that birth-control services are widely available, the number of children a couple has is popularly regarded as a kind of consumer choice. Some people prefer to have more children than others and spend their money on the additional children; others prefer to have fewer children and spend their money in other ways. (As long as we are confronted with a situation in which birth-control services are not widely available, special measures may be needed to provide reasonable incomes for very large families.) When the target of policy is a minimum-subsistence income, the size of family becomes a very important variable, but when the target of policy is achieving average-income status for all families, then the size of family becomes less of an issue.

The goal, then, is to change the shape of the distribution of families by income. The present distribution is diamond-shaped. Using 1965 family income as an example, about 30 per cent of the population are in income classes that are $2,000 or more below the median and a similar proportion are that far above the median, leaving about 40 per cent of the families in a broad, middle-income band of $5,000 to $9,000.

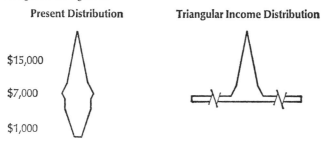

FIGURE 9–1. Present and More Equal Income Distribution (Using 1965 Non-farm Income Distribution for Illustration)

Let us mark off two stages along the way toward the goal of having the lowest-income class also be in the median-income class, the situation that most fully meets the criterion that no family has an income that is below the average for all families (see Figure 9–1, which uses the sociological convention of representing the hierarchy of families—in this case by income—by an appropriate geometric figure).

The first-stage goal should be to increase the income of those at the bottom of the distribution in such a way that the distribution assumes the shape of a triangle rather than a diamond. This goal is met when (a) the median-income class is the bottom-income class and (b) there are fewer people at each successive higher income level. Such an income distribution preserves the deeply felt American desire that it should be possible to strive for success and excellence and that such striving should be materially rewarded, but begins to do away with the present situation in which some families are so far out of the society that the questions of motivation for achievement become really meaningless.

Using 1965 as an example, this first-stage triangulation of the income distribution would mean that the income floor would have been at $5,000 and that 40 per cent of the nonfarm families would have been in the $5,000 to $5,999 income class. Thirty per cent of the families would have had to have their incomes increased by an average of about $2,000 a year to achieve this.

The second stage would then be to broaden the base of the income-distribution triangle by moving the floor up one income class. If this had been true in 1965, this second stage floor would have been $6,000. In this case 49 per cent of the nonfarm families would have been in the lowest income class.

It must be emphasized that the goals offered here are derived from the sociological analysis presented earlier in the chapter. That analysis suggested that any serious program to eliminate poverty would have to ensure that resources are made directly available to poor families, and not secondhand through training programs, Head Start programs, community-action programs, and the like. Income is the most straightforward resource, as well as the most directly measurable indicator of achieving the goal of the elimination of poverty. However, this analysis cannot consider the feasibility of achieving these goals, nor for this purpose is that necessary. If the analysis is correct, then political leaders, with the technical assistance of economists and others, will have to work out the ways of achieving the goal of a changed-income distribution. If that is not possible, then this analysis suggests it is not possible to eliminate poverty.

Economists are becoming increasingly sophisticated in simulating a variety of socio-economic conditions. In their work, they have generally taken the income distribution more or less for granted. The argument in this chapter recommends that the income distribution itself be taken as problematic and that theoretical and empirical efforts be directed toward discovering the economic measures by which the distribution of families by income could be changed.

Obviously, the particular measures used to achieve income equality would have important effects in and of themselves. A major emphasis on employment both through aggregate stimulation and public employment programs would have one set of effects. A major emphasis on income maintenance programs would have a different set of effects, and even the different possible varieties of income-maintenance programs (negative income tax, family allowance, more liberal welfare payments, etc.) would have varied impacts. There are excellent sociological reasons to suggest that the major emphasis should be on employment programs, with income maintenance approaches used only when employment programs fail to provide reasonable incomes. But all such issues of specific programs and their effects will obviously require a great deal of scholarly effort before their effects can be predicted with any reliability.

Just as obviously, a change in the shape of the income distribution will have major effects on other economic factors—national product, productivity, balance of payments, the rate of inflation, incentives to work, etc. It seems likely that awareness of these many ramifications has so far discouraged economic policy makers from even examining thoroughly the ways in which income distribution might be changed. But the results to date of a war on poverty in which economic approaches have seemed almost irrelevant suggests that these issues cannot be avoided.

CONCLUSION

The goal described here involves an approach that equalizes income from bottom up. Such a goal could probably be attained over a ten-year period by a marked redistribution of annual increases in national income toward the lowest income groups. A plan that redistributes only the *increases* in national income and does not make inroads into current income avoids the problems of direct confrontation involved in the older model of "soaking the rich to give to the poor." If the proper economic planning skills were brought to bear, it should be possible to achieve such a redistribution without provoking entrenched opposition from the higher income groups, particularly since we have every reason to believe that a move toward income equalization would result in much larger increases in gross national product and therefore in national income than are now envisioned.[18]

Notes

1. David Matza, "The Disreputable Poor," in Reinhard Bendix and Seymour M. Lipset, eds., *Class, Status and Power*, rev. edn. (New York: The Free Press of Glencoe, 1966).

2. Allison Davis, *Social Class Influence Upon Learning* (Cambridge, Mass.: Harvard University Press, 1952), pp. 10–11.

3. Walter B. Miller, "Focal Concerns of Lower Class Culture," in Louis A. Ferman et al., *Poverty in America*. (Ann Arbor: University of Michigan Press, 1965), pp. 261, 270.

4. Talcott Parsons, "An Analytical Approach to the Theory of Social Stratification," in Talcott Parsons, *Essays in Sociological Theory* (Glencoe, Ill.: The Free Press, 1954), p. 72.

5. Robert K. Merton, *Social Theory and Social Structure* (Glencoe, Ill.: The Free Press, 1957), pp. 146–147.

6. Interestingly, for both Merton and Davis, whose differing views were worked out at about the same time, their approach to lower-class behavior represented a polemic against biological determinism. For Davis, lower-class culture demonstrated the primacy of environment over heredity, of nurture over nature, in explaining the behavior of its members; Merton's views concerning anomie (the disjunction of culturally prescribed goals and institutionalized means for their achievement) served as a polemic against the view that lays responsibility for the faulty operation of social structures to failure of social control over man's imperious biological drives. The biology they were against, however, was slightly different. Davis polemicized against race or class biological inferiority, Merton against Freud's biological drive. Davis, a psychologically-oriented learning theorist, preserved a common human biology as an important element in his theories, while Merton sought to eschew, or at least "hold constant," biology.

7. Hyman Rodman, "The Lower-Class Value Stretch." *Social Forces* (December 1963).

8. Boone Hammond, "The Contest System: A Survival Technique," Masters Honors Essay, Washington University, 1965; Joyce A. Ladner, "On Becoming a Woman in the Ghetto," unpublished doctoral dissertation, Washington University, 1968; Lee Rainwater, "Crucible of Identity: The Negro Lower Class Family," *Daedalus* (Winter 1966); Lee Rainwater, "Work and Identity in the Lower Class," in *Planning for a Nation of Cities* (Cambridge, Mass.: MIT Press, 1966); David Schultz, "The Lower Class Negro Family: Some Reality Behind the Statistics," presented to the Department of Sociology, Rochester University, 1966. David A. Schultz, *Coming Up Black: Patterns of Ghetto Socialization* (Englewood Cliffs, N.J.: Prentice-Hall, 1969).

9. For discussions of various Caribbean mating and family patterns, see Judith Blake, *Family Structure in Jamaica* (New York: The Free Press of Glencoe, 1961); William Goode, "Illegitimacy in the Caribbean Social Structure," *American Sociological Review*, XXV (February 1960), 21–30; William Goode, "Note on Problems in Theory and Method: The New World," *American Anthropologist*, LXVIII, No. 2, Part 1 (April 1966); Fernando Henriques, *Family and Color in Jamaica* (London: Eyre and Spottiswoode, 1953); Keith F. Otterbein, "Caribbean Family Organization: A Comparative Analysis," in Talcott Parsons, ed., *Essays in Sociological Theory* (New York: The Free Press of Glencoe, 1954); Hyman Rodman, "Illegitimacy in the Caribbean Social Structure: A Reconsideration," *American Sociological Review*, XXXI (October 1966), 673–683; M. G. Smith, *West Indian Family Structure* (Washington: University of Washington Press, 1962); Raymond T. Smith, "Culture and Social Structure in the Caribbean: Some Recent Work on Family and Kinship Studies," *Comparative Studies in Society and History*, VI, No. 1 (October 1963), 24–46; Nancy L. Solien de Gonzalez, "Family

Organization in Five Types of Migratory Wage Labor," *American Anthropologist,* LXIII, No. 6 (December 1961) ; J. Mayone Stycos and Kurt W. Back, *The Control of Human Fertility in Jamaica* (Ithaca, N.Y.: Cornell University Press, 1964) .

10. Bernard Farber, *Family: Organization and Interaction* (San Francisco: Chandler, 1964) .

11. Clyde Kluckhohn, "Values and Value Orientations in the Theory of Action," in Talcott Parsons and Edward A. Shils, eds., *Toward a General Theory of Action* (New York: Harper, 1951) .

12. William L. Yancey, "The Culture of Poverty: Not So Much Parsimony," unpublished paper, Social Science Institute, Washington University, 1964.

13. Albert J. Cohen, *Delinquent Boys* (New York: The Free Press of Glencoe, 1955) .

14. David Matza, *Delinquency and Drift* (New York: Wiley, 1964) .

15. Erving Goffman, *Stigma* (Englewood Cliffs, N.J.: Prentice-Hall, 1965) .

16. Alvin W. Gouldner, "Reciprocity and Autonomy in Functional Theory," in Llewellyn Gross, ed., *Symposium on Sociological Theory* (Philadelphia: Row Peterson, 1958) .

17. Oscar Ornati, *Poverty Amid Affluence* (New York: Twentieth Century Fund, 1966) ; Victor Fuchs, "Redefining Poverty and Redistributing Income," *The Public Interest* (Summer 1967) , pp. 88–95.

18. After a broad-based triangular-shaped income distribution has been achieved, it would then be possible to begin to raise the question about how equitable is the distance from the top of the distribution to the median, that is, to raise the question about whether the rich are overly rewarded for their contributions. But this is an issue that is likely not to have the same explosive social and political implications that the present highly inequitable and extremely tenacious distribution has. Given the levels of affluence likely to be enjoyed in a highly productive society with a triangular income distribution, this kind of question is likely to seem relatively unimportant, both because everyone will have so much and because the rewards of achievement will become increasingly intrinsic ones as the extrinsic rewards of being able to live decently are taken more and more for granted.

Chapter 10

⊂⊅ *The Elimination of the American Lower Class as National Policy: A Critique of the Ideology of the Poverty Movement of the 1960s* WALTER MILLER

> Persons responsible for [governmental] programs who do not insist on clarity and candor in the definition of objectives and the means for obtaining them . . . do not much serve the public interest.
>
> DANIEL P. MOYNIHAN

> Values appear in disguised form in our "factual" analyses and bipartisan or nonpartisan discussions.
>
> S. M. MILLER

> . . . it is the essential peculiarity of ideologies that they do not simply prescribe ends but also insistently propose prefabricated interpretations of existing social realities . . . that bitterly resist . . . revision.
>
> IRVING KRISTOL

THE URBAN LOW-SKILLED LABORING CLASS AS A SOCIAL PROBLEM

That portion of the population of the United States of America whose customary occupational pursuits center on low-skilled labor currently presents a perplexing problem for public officials whose responsibilities include domestic policy. As it has for many centuries in large economically differentiated societies, the way of life associated with low-skilled manual labor involves a characteristic set of life conditions and customary behavioral practices. Ten of these are:

1. A pattern of work involvement entailing predominantly non-specialized physical labor at low-skill levels and incorporating

varying degrees of recurrent intermittency as demands for low-skilled labor of different kinds wax and wane with changes in the seasons and/or the supply-and-demand circumstances of the market.

2. A pattern of educational involvement characterized by little formal schooling or relatively short periods thereof, with primary emphasis on more generalized social and occupational skills rather than advanced and/or specialized training.

3. A level of monetary and/or nonmonetary recompense generally commensurate with low levels of occupational skill, based on a societal reward system that grants higher levels of reward to those whose occupations involve higher levels of skill and responsibility.

4. A pattern of income acquisition that is versatile rather than constricted and that involves an expectation of the provision of some portion of one's income by private superordinates or agencies of the state on the basis of considerations other than occupational performance as such.

5. A set of arrangements for producing and rearing children whose viability is not predicated on the consistent presence in the household of an adult male acting in the role of husband and father, facilitating flexibility of male participation in the occupational sphere, with mating unions often instituted without recourse to a formal religious and/or legal ceremony.

6. A mode of rearing children organized so as to minimize the duration of necessary in-household socialization, facilitate early participation in the work world, and provide for both male and female offspring the learning of important elements of sex role and related forms of behavior through the medium of extra-household peer groups and/or local adults.

7. The allocation of limited portions of one's material resources and physical energies to enterprises involving the ownership, maintenance, and adornment of residential structures and their environs.

8. A set of attitudes and practices with regard to authority and formal organization involving special skills and techniques for performing subordinate roles, an expectation that major responsibility for exercising superordinate authority will be assumed by those at higher levels of skill and training, and a low level of participation in a particular set of formally organized economic and political enterprises whose conduct and administra-

tion constitute a major focus of concern and involvement for those at higher status levels.

9. A characteristic set of pursuits outside the occupational sphere that provide direct and immediate emotional and/or physical gratification and the quest for stimulating inner experiences; for example, recurrent use of ingested stimulants, following and participating in high-risk games and contests, forms of entertainment and diversion that provide high-intensity drama and excitement.

10. Customary engagement in forms of behavior that violate the legal statutes of relevant political jurisdictions, often involving violence, but most commonly comprising theft by males, particularly adolescents.

Couched in these terms, these practices and conditions can be conceived with little difficulty as mutually interrelated features of a particular way of life geared to the circumstances of low-skilled labor. While the nature of these relationships cannot be developed here, brief consideration of each feature with reference to the question, "How does this feature arise from or contribute to the circumstances of low-skilled labor?" will indicate the nature and extent of mutual coherence.[1] From this perspective, the degree of concordance among the several features appears greater than the degree of discordance, and the way of life as a whole can be conceived with little difficulty as making an important contribution, albeit only one of many contributions, to the social and economic viability of our society. Moreover, conceptualization in these terms lays the groundwork for a formulation of problematic aspects of the circumstances of low-skilled laboring populations that is based on consideration of their present and future role with respect to the total economy, and in particular the impact on this role of technological changes and large-scale population movements.

If one grants the possibility of characterizing this way of life in relatively moderate descriptive terms, how then is one to account for the fact that most current characterizations of the low-skilled laboring class—particularly the urban portion thereof—resound with frantic alarm? Urban lower-class communities are depicted as dismal ghettos swarming with victimized inhabitants at once tragically apathetic and monstrously violent, somehow enduring an unendurable existence permeated with pathology, wracked with desperation, ominously sowing the bitter seeds of the gigantic cataclysm that will destroy us all. One clue is provided by directing attention to the *language* customarily applied to the ten conditions cited above.

The low-skilled laboring population itself is characterized in terms such as "the underclass," "the *lumpenproletariat,*" "the underprivileged," and "the culturally disadvantaged." Common terms for the cited features are "marginal labor," "unskilled labor," "chronic unemployment," "poor job skills," "unorganized jobs," "underemployment" (low occupational skill, intermittency) ; "cultural deprivation," "undereducation," "school dropouts," "functional illiteracy" (low formal education) ; "chronic dependency," "welfare dependency," "slave mentality" (income supplementation) ; "broken homes," "broken families," "family instability," "wife desertion," "illegitimacy" (female-based households) ; "child neglect," "parental indifference," "premature independence" (early independence socialization) ; "urban blight," "deterioration," "substandard housing," "dilapidation and decay" (low housing investment) ; "political apathy," "alienation," "anomie," "political marginality," "disenfranchisement," "apoliticality," "dependency" (low organizational participation, subordinacy) ; "defective impulse control," "primitive inhibitory control," "self-indulgence" (immediate-gratification recreation) ; "crime and violence in the streets," "collapse of law and order," "epidemic lawlessness" (violative behavior) .

All of these terms, widely used to characterize low-skilled laboring populations and major features of their subculture, share a common element; they are heavily infused with value. It is not their function to provide a basis for objective description, but rather to indicate with minimum ambiguity a particular set of value judgments. Practices and conditions are formulated in such a way as to make it impossible to speak of organization or consistency, and terms of reference are chosen that forcefully convey a sense of disapproval.[2]

It will be the thesis of this chapter that these and related terms are products of a distinctive and pervasive ideology—an ideology that has profoundly conditioned prevalent modes of perceiving and conceiving the life circumstances of low-status populations, profoundly influenced the formulation of policy objectives, profoundly affected the capacity of planners to develop effective programs. The chapter will contend, further, that this ideology has assumed the quality of the sacred dogma of a cult movement and has become so deeply and unconsciously ingrained as to critically restrict consideration of policy options. It will propose, finally, that an essential prerequisite to new and more effective policy is the deliberate abandonment of the current ideological apparatus and the substitution of a sophisticated and well-conceived conceptual rationale.

This chapter will use the term the "Movement" to designate that category of persons who customarily conceptualize the circumstances of American low-skilled laboring populations in terms such as "poverty," "the poor," "deprivation," "relative deprivation," "denial of opportunity," "the power structure," "apathy," "alienation," and "the ghetto." Like all broad social categories, this one includes persons who may differ substantially with respect to other characteristics —ignoring, for example, the distinction between scholarly analysts and avowed social reformers. The argument will proceed through a discussion of four of the key terms of the Poverty Ideology along with several closely related concepts. A final section will consider briefly some policy implications of the analysis.[3]

KEY CONCEPTS OF THE POVERTY IDEOLOGY

The ideology of any social movement incorporates a set of words or phrases with particular characteristics. They are limited in number; they indicate major areas of concern and acceptable attitudes toward them; they ascribe virtue and blame; they are heavily evaluative. Each key term, in addition, has at least two sets of meanings: a more generally understood or explicit connotation and one or more code-word connotations, which convey a different meaning or meanings to those in a position to understand them. A special requirement of key-ideology terms in the United States is that they have the simplicity, catchiness, and popular appeal of a successful advertising slogan. Following sections will discuss four of the key terms of the "Poverty Ideology"—"The Poor," "Poverty," "Deprivation," and "Opportunity," along with several other related concepts such as "the poverty line," "the culture of poverty," "relative deprivation," "the power structure," and "the ghetto."

POVERTY

The terms "The Poor" and "Poverty," central concepts of the Ideology, represent simple prepackaged solutions to two highly complicated problems: How is the population under consideration to be identified and defined? What is it about this population that is problematic? Age-old semantic overtones of the term "poverty" imply that

it is a concrete and readily identifiable condition and that it is piti-
fully rather than reprehensibly bad. The term thus effectively serves
the Public Relations purposes of the Movement, but at a formidable
cost. The cost is massive confusion.

At the root of the confusion is the failure to distinguish in any
explicit or consistent fashion between the "absolute" and "relative"
senses of the term and a continual shifting between the two. Poverty,
in the absolute sense, refers to a condition of acute physical want—
starvation, near starvation, or a diet conducive to malnutrition and
disease; lack of clothing or shelter necessary for protection from elements; absence of minimal medical services. This is the condition of
some populations in India and Africa. Poverty in the relative sense is
very different. It may be attributed quite freely to a wide range of
populations whose income or other circumstances are adjudged to be
lower or worse than those of other populations, specified or unspecified. Poverty in this sense may be applied to populations that are
healthy, adequately fed, and adequately housed.[4] The essential element here is not the objective circumstances of the lower income
group, but an *awareness* on their part of differences between their lot
and that of others, an awareness centering on the experience of envy.
This aspect of "relative" poverty will be discussed further under the
concept "deprivation."

The existence of poverty in the absolute sense indicates directly
and with little ambiguity, to persons reared in a democratic tradition, the need for ameliorative action and the kinds of action needed,
thus providing a solid basis for national policy. In the United States,
however, there is a major drawback to the use of this concept as a
justification for public programs; poverty in the absolute sense is
virtually nonexistent. When, from time to time, some diligent in-
vestigator discovers a family on the edge of starvation or a southern
community with grave subsistence problems, the event is sufficiently
noteworthy to make national headlines.

The fact is that innovative and broad-ranging social legislation
in the 1930s laid the basis for an extensive network of public health
and welfare organizations whose services and resources, universally
available by law, make it virtually impossible for any substantial
portion of our population to be denied necessary food, shelter, clothing, or health care for any extended period. It would be foolish to
maintain that this system is so efficient, so evenly administered, and
so well-financed as to effectively satisfy the subsistence needs and
desires of all persons at all times; "pockets" of poverty in the absolute

sense do appear from time to time and place to place. Professional social workers, however, like to pretend that there exist in this country vast numbers of needy persons who are so isolated, so uninformed, so "unreached" that they cannot avail themselves of resources to which they are entitled. This is a myth. Investigators working assiduously to uncover this vast reservoir of "unreached" Americans have repeatedly failed to discover any substantial numbers of persons truly beyond the reach of local, state, or federal health and welfare services.

Given, then, the fact that poverty in the absolute sense is virtually nonexistent in the United States or, at best, sufficiently rare as to provide scant justification for the allocation of billions to its eradication, the ideologists have been constrained, upon rejecting the obvious alternative of scrapping the term entirely, to resort to the concept of "relative" poverty as the prime justification for the Movement. In so doing, they have opened up a Pandora's box of unsolved and insoluble problems. Since the essential criteria of relative poverty, as conceived by the ideologists, are certain subjective experiences, the principal order of evidence for its existence must be some reliable measure of these experiences. Such a measure is, however, beyond the scope of our most advanced investigative techniques, although expressions of discontent are quite easy to elicit from most people under the proper circumstances. The existence of the determining criteria of relative poverty, then, must be *deduced* by the Ideologists on the basis of considerations other than findings of reliable empirical investigation.[5]

What are these considerations? They are, as S. M. Miller has pointedly indicated, a set of value judgments of the most abstruse and intricate kind, involving such philosophical classics as the relative happiness of persons at higher- and lower-status levels, the kinds and degrees of justice and injustice involved in the uneven distribution of societal resources, the relative value of "personal happiness" and "societal welfare," the desirability or undesirability of social-status differentiation, the social consequences of subjectively experienced envy or discontent, and many others. Whatever the ultimate resolution of these perennial issues, the current inclinations of partisans of one view or another provide dubious support for a central justificational concept of a mammoth public enterprise.

The abstract speculations that underlie the concept of relative poverty are sufficiently dubious as to make many public officials most uncomfortable. Moreover, key concepts of an Ideology, to be effective, should present the appearance of hard and immutable truths. Sensing these difficulties, the Ideologists have undertaken a series of maneuvers in an attempt to impart some semblance of absolute meaning to a thoroughly relativistic concept. Nowhere is this better seen than in the extraordinary gyrations on that giddy tightrope, the "Poverty Line." Initial formulations, centering on the uncomplicated notion that a family of two or more with an annual cash income of $3,000 or less was "In Poverty" and one with more than $3,000 was not, were so patently untenable as to impel the Ideologists into a series of acrobatics that have produced a set of abstruse definitions such as the decision that the Poverty Line is $1,710 for a farm family with two children, but $5,135 for a nonfarm family with six.[6]

Poverty in the absolute sense, then, cannot be used as a valid justification for federal programs because of its rarity, and in the relative sense because it is impossible to adduce nonevaluative empirical evidence for its existence. Why, then, is the concept so tenaciously retained? A major clue is provided if one assumes that Poverty is in fact a code word for something else, and that the "something else" is the total pattern of life of low-skilled laboring populations, a pattern in which low income as such is only one element. The "problem" is not that low income permits little education resulting in low-skilled jobs producing low income, but that low income is only one feature of a complex and ramified life style whose component characteristics, many of which are defined as "problematic" ("dependency," "illegitimacy," "instability," and so on), evince an order of mutual coherence that is not merely the regrettable consequence of a "vicious cycle of Poverty," but that derives instead from the particular and complicated role played by the low-skilled laboring population with respect to the total social and economic order.

The concept of Poverty cannot be abandoned by the Ideologists because its code-word meaning provides them a way of more accurately representing the condition of low-status populations without at the same time conspicuously contradicting those Ideological tenets that deny validity to the code-word meaning. This explains their extreme ambivalence to the "Culture of Poverty" concept, which they cannot live with and cannot live without. While many are well aware of the ambiguities and inconsistencies of this position ("that vague and misleading potpourri of tastes and judgments": S. M. Miller), they cannot nonetheless afford to reject it because it provides an illusion of salvage for the ill-fated absolute-relative dilemma. The Culture of

Poverty concept, while it does imply a degree of ordered relationship among the elements of the "culture" that is anathema to the Ideologists, is in most other respects highly compatible with the Ideology, in that it conceptualizes its major elements in a fashion congenial to ideological tenets, couches its explanational dynamic in essentially the same terms ("Pathology," "Deprivation," "The Power Structure"), provides a desperately needed semblance of cross-cultural validation to the "cycle-of-poverty" idea, and shores up the trembling foundations of "relative poverty" with seemingly solid anthropological sandbags.

The Movement's choice of the term "poverty" as their code word for the subculture of low-skilled laboring populations provides an excellent example of the process whereby measures undertaken to further the purposes of a movement serve to frustrate other purposes, such as achieving clarity in the formulation of objectives. If the "elimination of poverty" is indeed the true purpose of the Movement, the question immediately arises, Why not just give them more money? This could be accomplished quite readily through any one of a number of economic measures currently being proposed: a negative income tax, guaranteed annual incomes, family allowances, and so on. Why, then, all the tortured debates about alternative strategies,[7] and why the intensive efforts involving schooling, training, jobs, citizen action groups, political participation, and all the rest?

The answer is, of course, that the "elimination of poverty" is not the objective of the Movement at all. It is, rather, the elimination of the whole subcultural complex for which Poverty is a code word—work practices, educational involvement, child-rearing arrangements, housing practices, political behavior, attitudes toward authority and responsibility—the well-established way of life indicated by the ten features cited earlier. It is very difficult to imagine how the simple expedient of seeing to it that people receive enough additional money to raise their annual incomes above one or another of the various poverty lines could have anything more than a very limited impact on this complex. The subculture of contemporary low-skilled laboring populations has repeatedly proved to be highly resistant to a wide variety of directed change efforts, some of which have been far more sophisticated and ingeniously contrived than the proposal for raising incomes. If people follow a lower-class way of life because they have little money, then more money should alter that way of life; if, on the other hand, they have little money because they follow a lower-class way of life, the situation is far more complicated.

It confronts the Ideologists with the arduous task of facing up to the nature and implications of their objectives, a task that the easy formulation "the elimination of poverty" enables them to avoid.

THE POOR

The choice of the term "The Poor" to designate the population taken by the Movement as their object of concern is particularly unfortunate. In the United States, the selection of a term to refer to low-status populations is never easy, due primarily to an egalitarian ideology that virtually enjoins reference to low social status except in certain oblique ways. Most commonly used terms fall into one of four categories. The first selects one out of the many related characteristics of low-skilled laboring-class life, couches it in evaluative terms, and uses it to represent the totality. Examples are The Impoverished (low income), The Underclass (subordinacy), and The Dependent (Income Supplementation). The second characterizes the population with reference to a valued characteristic of an unspecified comparison population. Examples are The Underprivileged (fewer privileges than ?), The Disadvantaged (fewer advantages than ?), and The Deprived (of?). The third is predicated on a judgment that low-status people are "outsiders" with reference to a postulated "inside" society; examples are The Dispossessed, The Rejects, The Disowned, The Disenfranchised. The fourth category represents simple expressions of value centering around worthlessness, lack of merit, contemptibility; examples are Riff-raff, Trash, The *Lumpenproletariat*.

The term "The Poor" falls into the first, or metonymic, category. All metonymic characterizations involve logical problems, but the choice of low income as a primary class-defining criterion raises particularly troublesome ones. A major logical difficulty inheres in the fact that the various income-level definitions commonly used to delineate "The Poor" catch up in the same net millions of people whose "problems" are very different from those of the population at issue. Little careful work has been done by the Ideologists to develop typologies of the masses of persons included within the various "poverty-line" definitions, but even their own figures suggest that at least half, and most probably more, of those designated as "Poor" under the widely used $3,000 yearly income criterion are *not* those taken by the Movement as its primary object of concern.

As used by the Ideologists, the term "The Poor" elicits images of physically capable persons in their middle years whose low income is a consequence of their participation in the labor market, or lack thereof. In point of fact, 1960 Census figures indicate that just about half of all persons categorized as "poor" by the $3,000 "poverty-line" criterion (about five million families and four million "unrelated individuals") received their income in the form of Dividends, Interest, Rents, Royalties, Veterans' Payments, Social Security, and Pensions of various kinds.[8] The majority of these people are elderly couples, widows or widowers living on pensions and/or Social Security; others include disabled veterans, persons with work disability pensions, and retired servicemen. The lives of all these people involve "problems," as do those of any category of persons one can delineate, but they are not those implied by the term "The Poor" as used in the Movement. A very substantial proportion of those categorized as "poor" under the various income-level criteria—in some cases a majority—do *not* present the kinds of problems to which the Ideology of the Movement is geared.

A second major difficulty with the concept "The Poor" is that an income-level definition involves the same morass of slippery relativistic judgments as in the case of "Poverty." The process of delineating a sector of the population whose income level supports a reasonably valid characterization as "poor" entails consideration of a large number of highly complex variables, including differences in dollar value at different times and in different areas, amounts and kinds of non-money income, differences in life circumstances of "individuals" and "families," rural versus urban living conditions, changing conceptions of "adequate" or "minimal" incomes, and many others. The availability of so many variables provides a wide latitude of choice in the selection of criteria for designating people as "poor" or "nonpoor"—choices that are heavily and inevitably influenced by subjective values.

In the face of so wide a latitude in choosing criteria for a definition of "The Poor" that will best suit the aims of the Movement, it is all the more striking how little success has been achieved in doing so. The "urgent-crisis" component of the Ideology Message would be best served by a definition that would show the numbers of The Poor to be large and growing rapidly larger. Available statistics, in fact, appear most readily to indicate the opposite. Even a cursory examination of income figures reveals that the proportion of persons at the lowest income levels is growing steadily smaller, their share in the total income growing larger, and even that their absolute numbers are decreasing in the face of substantial population increases. One of the most respected of the population statisticians, Herman Miller, concludes an intensive examination of family and nonfamily income with the statement that "there has been a very sharp drop in the proportions of persons living at near-subsistence levels, and that . . . for millions of people *absolute* want has been eliminated." Miller documents "a precipitous drop" in the proportions of families and unrelated individuals with annual incomes under $2,000; in the 1930s, the proportion was 3 in 4; in 1941, 3 in 5; in 1950, 1 in 4; in 1960, only 1 in 8.[9]

Statistics of this kind severely tax the capacity of the Ideologists to infuse some semblance of "absolute" validity into the concept "The Poor," and at the same time make more imperative their obligation to do so. Ornati, led by his calculations to the realization that "poverty-line" definitions of even the recent past delineate a strikingly small number of present-day "Poor," remarks, "By taking past standards that go back far enough, we are bound to find that there are no poor today, which is a patent absurdity." The statement "there are no poor today" might perhaps be seen as rather less absurd than the manipulations required to adduce evidence for worsening conditions out of statistics that most readily indicate improvements.[10]

With all these inconsistencies and ambiguities, why does the Movement continue to use "The Poor" as its principal term for denoting the population at issue? In American society, there is obvious public-relations value in a term that uses a single and simple criterion—money—to define the class. But there is more than this. This ancient term strikes a deep and responsive chord in all those raised in the Protestant, Catholic, or Jewish religious traditions, for it designates a solidly traditional and thoroughly virtuous vehicle for achieving one's personal salvation through works of Charity. These overtones are of particular value in enlisting the support and even the active participation of middle-class people. The increasing secularization in recent times of middle-class belief systems has blunted the effectiveness of the more obviously religious appeals to Charity for its own sake, but the Movement has substituted a patina of scientific validation, a superficially rational ideology, and a comfortable orbit of organizational operations that provides a thoroughly modern rationale for the traditional pursuit of Good Works.[11]

The very qualities of ambiguity and inconsistency which make the term "The Poor" so unsatisfactory as a basis for sound policy render it eminently suitable as a code word. Code-word meanings may be varied to suit the purposes of the moment. On a broad and general level the term refers, of course, not merely to those with little money, but to that whole population that manifests the subculture of low-skilled labor—a population whose income circumstances may vary considerably. On a more restricted level and for somewhat different purposes, the term refers to the urban portion of that population, and on a still more restricted level to the negro portion of the latter. The code word use of the "The Poor" to mean "low-status urban Negroes" has become increasingly prevalent as the behavior of this group has moved further into the forefront of national attention.

DEPRIVATION

The term "Deprivation" serves as a multipurpose conceptual workhorse for the Ideology. As a critical link in a causational formula whose other terms (poverty, the poor, opportunity) are conceptually weak and ambiguous, it bears a special burden; unless the concept of deprivation can be shown to be particularly strong—logically, empirically, or both—the fundamental operating rationale of the entire Movement remains open to very serious question.

As used outside the Ideology, the term "deprivation" generally connotes objectively evident conditions wherein people lack the basic elements necessary to life and well-being. General usage also incorporates two additional connotations. First, while the elements whose absence results in "deprivation" are seen primarily as physical or material (food, clothing, shelter), usage admits the possibility that nonmaterial elements may also be involved. Second, by comparison with more passive terms such as "want" or "need," the term implies an active agent that is doing the depriving—a connotation to be discussed under "Opportunity."

The proposition that "The Poor" experience "deprivation" constitutes an essential justification for the existence and activities of the Movement. But as already shown in the discussions of The Poor and Poverty, deprivation in its non-Movement sense of the absence of material elements necessary to sustain life and physical well-being is virtually nonexistent in the United States. To preserve the capacity of the concept to justify the Movement, the Ideologists have been constrained to resort to two logical shifts: from absolute to relative, and from material to nonmaterial.

The shift to a relative level when validity in an absolute sense proves insupportable is, as has been seen, the classical, logical maneuver of the Movement. In the case of Deprivation, this maneuver takes the form of the proposition that the essence of this condition is not what people have or don't have in any concrete or absolute sense, but what they have or don't have *relative* to other people. The shift from the material to the nonmaterial sense of the term involves, in its turn, two additional shifts: the locus of the condition shifts from objective social and economic characteristics of populations to subjective states of individuals; and the elements necessary to life and well-being shift from material resources to inner psychological responses. These transmutations thus make it possible to adduce the existence of "Deprivation" when a designated population is perceived to experience disturbing subjective responses with reference to the perceived conditions of another population. The following paragraphs will examine first the logical and then the empirical supportability of these contentions.

The concept of Relative Deprivation is the logical keystone of the Poverty Ideology and serves to justify the entire Movement. Since the number of persons in the United States who are "deprived" in any objective sense is so small, the Ideologists are impelled to project a series of theoretical postulates that will enable them to deduce widespread Deprivation. These are: (1) The United States of America has a single-standard social order wherein all citizens continually judge themselves with respect to commonly accepted and clearly defined criteria of success, adequacy, excellence, respectability, and the like. (2) Those whose life circumstances diverge from this standard weigh themselves and find themselves wanting, producing a "self-image" centering on the absence of characteristics such as "self-respect," "dignity," "a sense of personal worth," "adequacy," "decency," "manhood," and the like. (3) The subjective discontent engendered by this self-evaluation is in itself highly detrimental, and, in addition, engenders passive withdrawal ("resignation," "alienation," "anomie," "retreatism," and "apathy") or Frustration that produces Aggression that produces Violence; the ideology is not specific as to which of these logically opposed consequences will result.[12]

Even more. Relative Deprivation not only explains the genesis of The Problem of The Poor, but its dynamics as well. The Crisis of Our Times by no means requires that there be any significant worsening in the objective material circumstances of low-status populations; these may stay the same or even improve, so long as the circumstances of higher-status populations are improving *faster*. This logical maneuver enables the Ideologists to speak of an ominous deterioration in the circumstances of The Poor in the face of evidence showing little change or even improvements.

How adequate is the concept of Relative Deprivation, its underlying premises, and postulated consequences? The concept owes much of its current popularity to a social-psychological inquiry into military morale during World War II. A major conclusion of this study was that morale was determined by relative, rather than actual, circumstances. Soldiers under punishing combat conditions remained cheerful in the face of minimal rations, inadequate shelter, physical discomfort, and constant danger; soldiers in garrisons were discontented, complaining that the officers' steaks or movies were better than theirs or that civilians had all the women and lush jobs.[13] The relative-deprivation interpretation of these findings (which, of course, admit of other equally plausible interpretations) was later extended to a wide range of situational differences, including differences in social status. This basic idea—that people become unhappy whatever their lot if confronted with visible evidence that the lot of others is better—permeates much current thinking and underlies such concepts as "The Revolution of Rising Expectations," popularized by Walt Rostow.

There is obviously some truth in the concept of Relative Deprivation. As the contemporary social-science rendering of the ancient homily "Envy Breeds Discontent," it bears the credentials of a well-respected piece of traditional wisdom. There is little doubt that the requisite conditions of the paradigm are in evidence in contemporary United States; given a society with high valuation of material goods and a system of mass communication that exposes all sectors of the society to the spectacle of abundant and increasing wealth, it would be astonishing if many of those who felt they were not getting "a piece of the action" were not envious.

Granting the plausibility of this argument, the question still remains as to whether the logical validity of Relative Deprivation has been sufficiently well established as to serve as the keystone of a cause-and-effect argument that justifies the expenditure of federal millions. It would seem not. Beneath the surface appearance of plausibility lies a perfect jungle of the most intricate, abstruse, and thoroughly speculative philosophical issues. A few of these are: In what sense is it possible to grant validity to the contention that there is a "common value system" in the United States? To what degree is the experience of status discontent or envy unique to low-status populations? How does its *intensity* compare to that of other populations? Does this intensity remain fairly constant, or does it wax and wane under different circumstances? If so, what kinds of circumstances? Is the quality or substance of this experience significantly different from that of other populations? If so, how? Is the experience more likely to induce responsive action or the failure to take action? If action, what kinds and under what circumstances? If a failure to act, in what areas and under what circumstances? It is impossible within the compass of this essay even to scratch the surface of this enormously problematic subject. The following paragraphs touch briefly on a very few of the more debatable issues.

It would appear, first, that status discontent is universal. Every category of persons one can think of manifests dissatisfaction of varying kinds and intensity with respect to some of the conditions associated with that status. Highly patterned sets of complaints, for example, are customarily manifested by members of such status categories as graduate students, college professors, high school teachers, adolescents, housewives, nurses, Catholics, urbanites, skilled union craftsmen and so on. Insofar as the bases of their expressed discontent (overly heavy work loads, too little personal attention, overly restrictive sets of rules, etc.) represent divergences from ideal conceptions or the perceived circumstances of others, the preconditions for Relative Deprivation are present. But what are the *consequences* of discontent in each of these cases, and to what degree do they constitute major social problems? A strong case for Deprivation can be made for middle-class housewives in their middle years. The assertion that all such persons experience serious discontent because they feel they are not getting enough love is coordinate with the assertion that all persons at the lowest status level experience serious discontent because they feel they are not getting enough valued resources. The love-deprivation experience of middle-class housewives is not trivial; it can engender profound unhappiness. But what does the housewife *do* as the result of this experience? She makes recurrent appeals to her husband to devote more of his time and attention to her and the family; she may consider affairs with other men and perhaps undertake one or more of greater or lesser seriousness; she will complain to and commiserate with status mates with similar difficulties. More important is what she does not do. Except in the rarest instances, she does *not* relinquish her role as mother and abandon her children; only rarely does she leave her husband for another man or no man, and then as a last extreme. She does not band with others to stage demonstrations and make demands of public agencies. She does not burn buildings and loot stores. Status discontent, in and of itself, no matter how prevalent or acute, does *not* provide a sufficient motivational basis for generalized social protest, nor a sufficient logical basis for explaining the behavior of low-status populations. The question remains: Under what circumstances does status discontent engender socially problematic responses and under what does it not?

A second major issue also concerns the consequences of status discontent. On the basis of certain social-psychological theories and an acceptance of the American value conception of the primacy of "happiness," the Ideologists have placed almost exclusive emphasis on the detrimental consequences of discontent. According to the Ideology, lower-status persons make invidious comparisons between themselves and those of higher status, producing discontent that produces frustration that produces aggression, expressed or repressed, against others or oneself. Earlier generations entertained rather more flexible notions as to the consequences of discontent, one of them expressed in the homily "a man's reach should exceed his grasp, else what's a heaven for?" Even in the recent past the experience of status discontent, far from being held responsible for social unrest and all sorts of other ills, was seen as a prime moving force in the American success story. The lowly immigrant, farm boy, or city urchin, consumed with envy and discontent upon beholding the spectacle of wealth and power around him, was fired with an iron resolve to emulate the objects of his envy, and embarked on a life of dedicated and energetic productivity.

Behind the simplifications of this stereotype lies an important element of validity; status discontent experienced by millions of American English, Irish, Italians, Jews—yes, and Africans—has provided a vital force behind achievements of great value to our society. The Ideologists admit only the possibility of detrimental consequences and regard such reasoning as reactionary. Discontent can engender detrimental, or beneficial, or other kinds of consequences. The question remains, What circumstances produce what kinds of consequences?

A third question concerns that ancient issue, the relation of wealth and happiness. The Ideologists take as an axiom the proposition that low income and unhappiness are inextricably associated; they are fond of making assertions such as "the poor are desperately unhappy," and using the eradication of this postulated unhappiness as a major justification for the Movement. As is the case for other major premises of the "relative-deprivation" hypothesis, this contention can claim little substantial support on either logical or empirical grounds. A long and respectable philosophical tradition argues that there is no direct relation between poverty and unhappiness, and eminent thinkers have even argued the opposite relation. Among these are ancient Jewish and Christian theologians, and more recently in the United States, Henry Thoreau.[14]

The logical argument for the proposition that low income in the United States produces misery leans heavily on the "envy" and "invidious self-comparison" notions. Granting that Jesus or Thoreau, in other times or contexts, could maintain that a paucity of material possessions is more virtuous or more gratifying or both, such a contention, it is claimed, could not possibly apply in contemporary America for reasons already suggested. Leaving aside at this point the knotty problem of what "happiness" might be (there has been notably little success in developing either logically acceptable or empirically testable definitions), the question then evolves on the key issue of the relative degree of unhappiness of persons at higher and lower status levels. Few would maintain flatly that the wealthy are happy and the poor miserable, nor deny that there are sources of discontent arising directly from the conditions of both lower- and middle-class life. However, for the "low income produces misery" contention to serve as an adequate supporting proposition for the "relative-deprivation" hypothesis, the argument must clearly establish that the balance of unhappiness lies unequivocally with low-status populations. This it fails to do.

The establishment of this proposition would require valid information as to the nature, intensity, and prevalence of both happiness and unhappiness at both lower and higher status levels. Such information might suggest that along with the highly publicized sources of unhappiness in the lives of those at lower levels (dirt, rats, financial difficulties, vulnerability to envy) there are also seldom-publicized sources of gratification that are less available to middle-class adults. Among these are a greater capacity to derive pleasure from immediate experience, more gratifying involvement in the affairs of parochial locality groups, less guilt over inadequate work performance, greater capacity to enjoy varied recreational experiences without reference to beneficial consequences, and greater freedom from a sense of responsibility for the welfare of larger collectivities. Against these one would have to balance the numerous sources of unhappiness associated with adult middle-class life, such as guilt over not accomplishing enough of real significance, conflicts over the scope of one's work, social and organizational obligations, dissatisfaction with the seemingly superficial nature of most interpersonal relationships and the rarity of true intimacy, and chronic concern over perceived or anticipated failures in the enterprise of rearing one's children. In the absence of adequate evidence, it is most likely, as discussed shortly, that the attribution by middle-class observers of acute unhappiness to low-status populations is based neither on logical nor empirical grounds, rather on personal projection. This is reflected in the words of Lee Rainwater: "If *I* had to live under these conditions, *I* would be miserable." This is undoubtedly true, but it is not evidence, and it enables the Ideologists to evade the responsibility of demonstrating that the balance of unhappiness sufficiently favors the low status as to support the "deprivation" hypothesis.[15]

On logical grounds, then, the status of the concept of Deprivation is weak. In the course of shifting its meaning from an objective paucity of material essentials to a subjective experience of discontent relative to others, the set of propositions needed to support the concept has become increasingly conjectural and dependent on unexamined assumptions. The element of truth in the proposition that envy breeds discontent is not sufficient to support the conclusion that Relative Deprivation lies at the root of The Problem of The Poor. Status discontent has very different consequences under different circumstances and cannot be regarded as a sufficient precondition for Deprivation. The concept must be regarded as legitimately arguable at best and clearly untenable at worst.

However shaky the logical status of the concept of Deprivation, it might still help to justify the Movement if it were supported by reliable empirical findings. Through what kinds of evidence do the Ideologists attempt to establish the existence of Deprivation? They have facilitated their task by delineating at least four different kinds of Deprivation: absolute material, absolute nonmaterial, relative material, and relative nonmaterial. Techniques for measuring material deprivation in the absolute sense (e.g., malnutrition and disease resulting from overexposure), while not without problems, are probably the most reliable. However, as has been shown, the amount of deprivation thus demonstrable is far too little to justify the Movement. Such justification is predicated on the existence of widespread nonmaterial deprivation in the relative sense, as evinced by subjectively perceived deficiencies in certain personal states or conditions relative to perceived states or conditions of others.

Adducing evidence for such criteria poses formidable methodological problems. Empirical indicators of Deprivation include the lack or relative absence of entities such as dignity, decency, self-respect, a sense of personal worth, meaningful work experiences, and the like. Difficulties in deriving reliable operational indexes to and data-collection methods for such entities are enormous. Currently, major techniques center around information elicited from informants by interviewers. This procedure yields results ranging from fair to good in certain informational areas (date of birth, residence locale, years of schooling) ; in other areas, particularly those involving value preferences, emotional responses, or subjective states, the validity of results is subject to the most profound question. This technique is probably least reliable in situations in which questioner and respondent are of different social statuses and in which topics at issue have class-relevant value implications. Of particular relevance to interactional situations of this kind is that many lower-status persons regard the expression of sentiments concerning unhappiness, injustice, and misfortune as a routinely expected aspect of certain types of interaction with higher status persons.[16]

Even more damaging to the case for the empirical validity of Deprivation is the probability that many of the higher-status adherents of the Movement base their convictions on a form of evidence even weaker than interview-elicited sentiments—their own subjective reactions to their perceptions of the life-circumstances of low-status populations. An eloquent statement is provided by Lee Rainwater:

For the individual who cannot avoid knowing about poverty and how the poor cope with their lives, there is at the most personal level a profound sense of *perplexity and anxiety* [sic] that arises when the *regular person* confronts his observations of how the poor live . . . The evidence available to regular people leads to a deeply felt belief that "I would not live that way; I could not live that way." The basic *human* response . . . leads to a *common sense judgment* . . . that the . . . way of life is "unlivable" . . . a perception of the situation as somehow *unreal* [italics, other than first, added].[17]

This is extremly revealing. It suggests that for many people the belief that The Poor are Deprived has very little to do with objective evidence of any kind, but is rather a manifestation of the familiar phenomenon whereby persons perceive and evaluate the traditions of another culture or subculture in terms of their own. Measured according to the perceptual framework and evaluative standards of one's own class or subculture, which are perceived as absolute and universal ("the regular people," "basic human responses," "common-sense judgments"), the way of life of other classes or subcultures frequently appears as disorganized, distasteful, distressing ("perplexity," "anxiety," "unlivable," "unreal"). This suggests that some of the most fundamental tenets of the Ideology derive to a greater degree from subjective responses such as the classic ethnocentric reaction than from evidence of any kind.[18]

It is clear, in summary, that the concept of Deprivation fails to achieve the degree of adequacy its central position in the Ideology requires. Faced with the fact that deprivation in an objective sense is too rare in the United States to justify the scope of the Movement, the Ideologists have attempted to enhance its justifying capacity by means of a logical argument whereby the essence of deprivation lies not in objectively determinable physical circumstances, but in subjective reactions to the circumstances of others. The validity of the concept must thus rest on the logical adequacy of the argument and the empirical supportability of its constituent premises. Neither is adequate. The major premises of the argument can scarcely be considered as established; all are arguable, some highly dubious. With respect to empirical validation, basic concepts are either formulated so as to render empirical testing difficult or impossible, or rest on kinds of evidence that are highly questionable on methodological grounds. Failing acceptable logical or empirical support, many Ideologists maintain their adherence to this concept essentially without reference to questions of evidence, but on the basis of deep and generally unconscious cultural or subcultural values.

OPPORTUNITY

Each of the terms thus far discussed provides the Movement with one essential element of its basic formula. The problem is "poverty"; those subject to it are "the poor"; its basis is "deprivation." It remains for the concept of "opportunity" to provide the guide to program, or what to do about the problem. The basic diagnostic statement provided by these terms is that The Poor are in Poverty because they are Deprived of Opportunity. The indicated course of action is thus clear; *provide* them the Opportunity they are Deprived of. This would appear to wrap up the rationale behind program development except for a few loose ends. Among these are the questions, "Just what is this 'Opportunity' The Poor are Deprived of?"

and "How did they get to be Deprived of it?" The effort to tidy up these loose ends reveals that the Opportunity package is not quite as substantial as it first appears.

Nothing could be more impeccably American than the concept of Opportunity. No true patriot could fail to endorse opportunity and decry its absence any more than he could fail to endorse mom's apple pie or decry moral collapse. But this concept must be approached with great care, for within the glowing lure of Opportunity as proffered by the Ideologists, there lies concealed a set of hooks— barbed and sharply pointed. It is inevitable that so broad a term as opportunity be susceptible to widely varying interpretations, but code-word connotations in this case show a relation to apparent meanings that is unique among the concepts thus far considered. Code-word meanings of terms such as The Poor represent modifications or specifications within the same general sphere, but in the case of Opportunity, major code-word connotations contrast sharply with apparent meanings.

This term, as it appears in such time-tested phrases as "the land of opportunity," refers to a kind of social order wherein a set of basic rights and privileges, including suffrage, occupational choice, residential choice, mate selection, legal and juridical rights, and many others are made equally available to all citizens whatever their status with respect to certain major forms of intrasocietal differentiation— principally sex, race, religion, region, national ancestry, and, to some extent, age. In those documents that define national ideological principles (Declaration of Independence, Constitution, Bill of Rights, relevant Supreme Court rulings), the concept applies primarily, though not exclusively, to *legal* rights. In recent years, however, it has come increasingly to apply to the abridgement of rights through *custom* as well. The granting of suffrage to non-property-owners, ex-slaves, and women all represent steps toward an ideal of a society wherein no important rights are withheld from citizens either by law (restriction of franchise by sex, segregation of public facilities by race) or by custom (restrictive housing covenants, sex-preferential hiring, religion of elected officials).

Few Americans who have given serious thought to the essential character of the American polity would fail to support this ideal of opportunity or to oppose attempts at its frustration. It is most dubious, however, that such support would extend as well to a major code-word conceptualization of Opportunity. This formulation is an amalgam of disparate elements, including a traditional homily, a theory of social deviance, an analysis of southern urban leadership, and classical early Marxism. Its major tenets are as follows:

1. In the United States, with its single-standard social order, there is a common and unitary conception of The Good Life, whose major components ("success" and "achievement") are conceived as a semisolid package of valued resources.
2. The term "Opportunity" applies sometimes to the package itself, sometimes to the means to obtain it.
3. "Access" to this Opportunity is controlled by a group called "The Power Structure," composed of variously specified members of the nonpoor.
4. The power, affluence and prestige of this group rests directly on maintaining The Poor in a condition of powerlessness, poverty, and stigmatization; they are *victimized* and *exploited*.
5. Well-entrenched, tightly organized, and highly sensitive to their own interests, The Power Structure has a massive investment in the status quo and vigorously resists efforts to alter the distribution of social and economic resources on which its power rests.
6. It thus pursues a concerted policy of Denial of Opportunity to The Poor, wherein the requirements of power always supersede those of justice.
7. The only way to effect vitally needed social reforms is to set up *competing power structures* to conduct programs centering on active social protest.
8. While violence is not a necessary component of such programs, it should be remembered that violence is often the only "language" The Power Structure will listen to and thus must be recognized as a necessary cost of vitally needed social reform.[19]

By what process did the concept of opportunity come to represent a set of tenets so divergent from traditional American political philosophies? As in the case of Deprivation, the concept as used by the Movement is based on a traditional homily modified through the concept-building process of social science. The notion that the rich get rich at the expense of the poor is hardly novel, nor is the Marxian concept of the class struggle, but it took the creative intellectual efforts of a group of academic sociologists to remold these ideas into a modernized and Americanized form that has exerted great influence on many persons in government and out who have never heard their names. While part of a continuous intellectual stream in which the names of Emile Durkheim and Robert Merton figure prominently, the persons most responsible for the contemporary transmutation of the Opportunity concept are Richard Cloward and Floyd Hunter.

In 1958, before juvenile gangs and gang delinquency had become passé as a national issue, a young prison social worker named Richard Cloward wrote a brief essay in which he proposed that in the criminal world as well as the noncriminal, the road to success can be pretty rocky if you don't have the right attributes—personal and social.[20] A short time later, in collaboration with another influential criminological sociologist, Lloyd Ohlin, Cloward developed and expanded this set of ideas to apply to a much larger range of phenomena—including, among other things, why boys join gangs instead of going to college and what kinds of gangs they join.[21]

It is of direct significance to its future career that the meteoric rise of the concept of Opportunity was given impetus by Cloward's observation that the big bosses of what later came to be known as the Cosa Nostra pursued a stringently discriminatory policy as to whom they would let into the Syndicate, and particularly into its top jobs. Among others, they discriminated against (and still discriminate against) non-Italians, nonmales, and nonrelatives.[22] This basic formulation—that "access" to "opportunity" is "denied" those who lack certain social characteristics—while it underwent modifications before ending up as an axiom of the Poverty Ideology, nevertheless retained the marks of its origins. If one takes the formula, "Syndicate bosses exclude people from favored positions in the Syndicate on the basis of certain social characteristics," and substitutes "The Power Structure" for "Syndicate bosses" and "The Larger Society" for "The Syndicate," the Opportunity formula emerges in pristine form. It is instructive to consider the impact on policy of an analysis of the United States and its leadership modeled in part on an image of Syndicate bosses ruthlessly excluding those who fail to meet a set of rigid membership requirements.

Collaboration with Ohlin both expanded the scope and blunted the sharpness of Cloward's earlier formulations. *Delinquency and Opportunity* is quite vague as to who or what is doing the denying of Opportunity. It would appear that the primary agency of Opportunity–denial is "The Society"—a generalized and impersonal entity rather than any particular subsector thereof.[23] For example, the discussion of "Structural Barriers to Legitimate Opportunity" is devoted largely to making the point that lower-class youth can't go to college because they have to quit school early to go to work to make money their families need. This is called an "economic barrier" to the primary avenue to Opportunity (or perhaps the Opportunity itself) —education. This commonsense argument out of the cycle-of-poverty tradition appears to assign responsibility to "the system" itself, with its "socially structured deprivations." [24]

It is immediately obvious that the requirements of the Movement are poorly served by assigning responsibility for Denial of Access to Opportunity to an impersonal social system with its "socially structured deprivations," no matter how cruel and unjust that system may be in firing up its members with lofty aspirations without providing the means to achieve them. Concretistic and moralistic, the Movement needs villains—specific, visible, tangible—to serve as the malign and personalized agents of denial. This vital element was provided by the concept of Power Structure, popularized in the mid-1950s by Floyd Hunter's book on community leaders in a southern city.[25] From a careful study, Hunter drew the conclusion that beneath a façade of democratic process, basic decisions concerning major public issues (schools, housing, voting) were in fact made by a small and nonrepresentative clique he called "The Power Structure." The affairs of the local Negro community also were regulated by a black power structure, whose form and ideology paralleled that of the whites.

The addition to the Ideology of a personalized villain, compounded of various aspects of discriminatory Cosa Nostra bosses, repressive prison officials, exploiting business tycoons, and southern segregationists, completed the major elements of the basic causational formula of the Movement: The Poor are In Poverty because they are Deprived of Opportunity by The Power Structure. This formulation is simple, direct, unambiguous—a classic theory of conspiratorial exclusionism. In the course of their passage from the pages of Cloward, Ohlin, and Hunter to the flaming banners of the Great Crusade against Poverty of the 1960s, the concepts of Opportunity and Power Structure acquired a host of accretions, emotional and semantic, that depart substantially from the careful and qualified statements of their scholarly antecedents. It is clear that these developments are well beyond the control of the original authors, but it is equally clear that it was their writings that seeded and watered the soil in which they flourished.

The Movement has its villain. It is now clear how The Poor became Deprived. A powerful and collusive Power Structure deliberately conspires, out of bigotry and narrow self-interest, to keep them down. The major device by which they Victimize and Exploit The Poor is to deny them access to those resources on which their own success is founded: advanced education, well-paying jobs, sound housing, political influence. Only through the effective application of counter-power can the iron grip of the slum lords and establishment politicians be loosened and the rightful heritage of the dispossessed be realized. The smooth flow of this liturgy is, however, somewhat disturbed if one turns to consider in greater detail the actual identity of the villains themselves. Just who is, or are, The Power Structure?

In the classic Marxist version of this morality play, all is clear. There is a major hero, the Noble Working Class, a major villain, the Capitalist Exploiters, a minor hero, the far-seeing and altruistic Intellectuals, and a minor villain, the lowly *Lumpenproletariat,* that rock-bottom group too degraded to pursue revolutionary objectives. The Movement version of this cast of characters holds some surprises. Who are its principal villains? They are monopolistic labor unions rigidly excluding minority groups; sadistic policemen brutally inciting explosive violence; greedy local politicians diverting for their own uses funds meant for The Poor; bigoted Mrs. Murphys refusing to rent their modest quarters to the objects of their bigotry; rural sheriffs who are not above murder to curb threats to their power; blue-collar homeowners zealously guarding their residential communities from incursions by the unwanted and undertaking precipitous flight to the suburbs when such incursion occurs.

This roster of villains at once suggests that a dramatic change has occurred in the traditional assignment of roles; with some exceptions, the bulk of those included in the Movement's cast of villains find their origins in what is generally called "the working class"— that very same group serving the Marxian drama as its major hero! While some of the villains may have either working- or middle-class backgrounds (gouging local merchants, rat-tolerating slum lords, patronage-hungry mayors), the background of the Movement's modal villain is unmistakable working class.

What, then, of its heroes? That very group so despised of the classic Marxists, the *Lumpenproletariat,* is now depicted in heroic proportions. It is they who have provided, now these many centuries, the sweat and sacrifice that have made this country great, and it is upon their prostrate backs that The Power Structure has climbed to the lofty heights of power and affluence they now occupy. It is long past time to redress this most grievous injustice and to give back to

The Poor—not a pitiful handout to buy them off, but their own fair share of the wealth they did so much to create, at last to return what is rightfully owing to them by virtue of centuries of exploitation.

And what of that arch-villain—the grasping monopolistic capitalist? Again, surprises. While not entirely purged of evil, his villainy has been substantially diluted. He may even be moving to occupy the role of minor hero, now being vacated by the intellectual. Many of these powerful captains of industry, far from resisting efforts to grant to The Poor what is rightfully theirs, actually take the lead in organizing and financing substantial Programs for The Poor through their giant foundations; in adopting policies not only of nondiscrimination but of actually seeking out minority-group employees if at all qualified; in relocating their plants in the slums and setting up training programs for the least qualified of the slum dwellers. Not only that. The wives of the rich hold meetings to plan programs for bringing The Poor to the affluent suburbs for inspirational visits, to attend school, or even to live; their children serve gladly as unpaid or low-paid volunteers, working quietly but doggedly to do what they can to readmit the Dispossessed into The Larger Society.[26]

This remarkable reshuffling of role assignments must certainly be seen as a major contribution of the Ideology to traditional modes of allocating blame for The Plight of The Poor. The reassignment process is, to be sure, incomplete. Some of the Bourgeoisie and their lackeys are still clearly villainous; the pro-poor activities of the Capitalists are not quite free of suspicion of being attempts to patch up the system by stopgap measures so as to forestall radical change; the heroic image of The Poor is still adulterated by other images that present them as pitiable objects of compassion or lacking in self-esteem.[27] Withal, the shift has been great enough to astound an early twentieth-century socialist.

The Power Structure, The Poor, and their associated rosters of heroes and villains provide for the War on Poverty a basic essential of a genuine movement—clear and concrete objects of love and hate. Woe betide the unfortunate who dares question the virtue of the heroes or the iniquity of the villains; he, too, is vilified. The most celebrated instance, in the middle 1960s, of the elevation of a public figure to the official position of Enemy of the Movement is known as the Moynihan Affair. In 1965, D. P. Moynihan, a young political scientist working as an assistant secretary in the U.S. Department of Labor, circulated a brief report on the Negro family, intended for limited intragovernmental distribution. Moynihan documented with charts and tables the familiar thesis that child-rearing arrangements among low-status Negroes tend to take the form of the female-based household (see low-status life condition number 5, page 261) and argued that this characteristic, which he saw as a central, sustaining feature of lower-class life, was becoming increasingly prevalent, particularly among urban Negroes.[28] Through a series of complicated events, the Moynihan report became known to devotees of the Movement as a major departure from Ideological orthodoxy authored by a person who had the ear of the President.[29]

What is the Moynihan issue? Outside the Movement and its special objectives, few informed persons would dispute the generalization that the life circumstances of any major sector of the population (for example, females, children, Catholics) derive in some part from characteristics of that population itself and in some part from the way in which they are regarded and treated by other sectors (for example, males, adults, Protestants). For example, the relative scarcity of female corporation executives is due in some measure to male attitudes toward female executives and in some measure to the fact that most women are more interested in being wives and mothers than executives. It is obvious that a formulation along these lines would be quite unacceptable when applied to The Plight of The Poor since it does not make an unambiguous attribution of blame to one group and blamelessness to another.

Moynihan's unforgivable crime was not that he impugned the sex morality of Negro adults, denied "togetherness" to Negro child-rearing units, or ascribed criminality to the products of broken black homes; his crime, in fact, bore only an oblique relationship to the character of the Negro family as such. The crux of his heresy lay in the implication that some part of the cause for the circumstances of low-status populations can be located in the characteristics of *these populations* themselves—whatever the influence on these characteristics one may attribute to other populations—as well as in the bigotry and exploitative policies of The Power Structure.

A critical test for the authenticity of a cult movement lies in the intensity of anger evinced by the faithful when a basic tenet of the ideology is called into question by someone who cannot easily be ignored. The bitterness and virulence of Movement attacks on the Moynihan report leave no doubt as to the genuineness of The Poverty Movement. What makes the intensity of the castigation all the more striking is the *elaborate* care taken by Moynihan to avoid even the tiniest implication that he was blaming the heroes of the Movement; to the contrary, he insisted repeatedly that their plight was an absolutely predictable consequence of prevalent policies of the dominant society—its selfish support of slavery, its racial bigotry, its criminal neglect of the newly urbanized. Alas. All to no avail. However elaborately qualified, the merest suggestion that some part of The Problem of The Poor might be attributable to causes other than Power-Structure villainy was enough to make the word "Moynihan" the Movement code word for this grievous heresy.[30]

But even more. It is for the apostate that the cult reserves its bitterest enmity. The faithful can readily identify their conventional villains because they customarily attribute to The Poor a set of stereotyped characteristics such as laziness, irresponsibility, disorder, sexual looseness, lack of ambition, and so on. In strong contrast, the language and conceptual framework of the Moynihan report are precisely that of the orthodox Ideology, with its references to barriers to opportunity, tangles of pathology, unstable family structures, cycles of poverty, deprivation, alienation, deterioration, social breakdown, and all the rest. *Here* is the reason for the intensity of the hatred; it is one of *us* who now nourishes the enemy by providing him with new and potent ammunition. Moynihan himself, seeing his work as a contribution to and not a negation of the Ideology, was astonished at the vigor of the attacks, and only dimly understanding their basis, hurt and angry.

The concept of Opportunity clearly has done yeoman service for the Movement. It raised the stars and stripes at the head of the columns of Poverty Warriors; it furnished the basic rationale for its programs of action; it provided a name for the federal agency charged with major responsibility for Poverty; it produced the scenario and delineated the heroes and villains for the starkly simple drama of The Poor; it ascribed perfidy and virtue, blame and innocence. Surely it is uncharitable to ask even more of a concept that has already given so much, but one is compelled to press one further question: How adequately does Opportunity provide a logical and explicit conceptual basis for policy? It would appear, alas, that it serves this latter purpose rather less well. Among its inadequacies in this respect are conceptual ambiguity, concealment of major objectives, misleading reliance on spatial imagery, and recourse to blame in lieu of analysis.

For a concept that serves, along with its other functions, as the basic guide to the action programs of the Movement, the meaning of Opportunity is surprisingly elusive. Turning to the works of Cloward and Ohlin which provide the basic charter for the concept as used by the Movement, one is at once struck by the fact that nowhere is the definition of Opportunity addressed directly. In contrast to the careful attention devoted to its coordinate concept "delinquency" in *Delinquency and Opportunity*, Opportunity remains in these works as it does for the Movement, a "primitive" or undefined concept.[31] To discover what it *is* intended to mean one must examine its use in the various contexts in which it appears. This reveals not only that the meanings of Opportunity shift around within the same work, but that the concept as a whole undergoes a fascinating transmutation between earlier and later formulations.

It is never quite clear, in the first place, whether Opportunity is a means to an end or an end in itself. In phrases such as "access to," "barriers to," or "denial of" Opportunity, it appears to be the actual objective to be achieved. Elsewhere, in analyses of "means" to "success goals" or in analogies to "avenues," it appears as a means to a further objective. The former implication is probably due in large part to the "solid-structure" imagery to be discussed shortly, and since the latter usage is clearly more prevalent, discussion will be confined to a consideration of Opportunity as means.

What is the end or ends to which Opportunity is the means? In Cloward's earlier paper as well as in *Delinquency and Opportunity* it would appear to be "success" (called "success goals" or "success values"). Two distinct conceptions of "success" appear: One is that common and uniform criteria for success hold for the whole society and for all social classes; the other, that there are different conceptions of success at different social levels. While the theoretical argument of *Delinquency and Opportunity* is predicated on the validity of the first conception, the second plays a prominent role in Cloward's earlier paper and parts of the book written with Ohlin. At least three different varieties of success are distinguished: legitimate lower class (boxer, night-club entertainer), illegitimate lower class (racketeer, pimp), and legitimate middle class (schoolteacher, banker).[32] The fourth logical type, illegitimate middle class (embezzler, real-estate swindler), is not explicitly treated. This formulation readily permits the concept of Opportunity to apply to success as a numbers runner or syndicate boss, as seen earlier. In fact, Cloward maintains at one point that the Opportunity theory applies primarily to success in lower-class terms—to slum youth who want to be successful "within their own cultural milieu"—that is, to make lots of money but not to adopt middle-class forms of behavior.[33]

By the time the concept appears as the major guide to the programs of Mobilization for Youth, a lineal precursor of the Office of Economic Opportunity, it has undergone a significant change. The "success" to which Opportunity is a means has become restricted almost entirely to one of the earlier four types—legitimate middle class. While traces of the earlier usage are still in evidence,[34] the developed theoretical rationale has essentially abandoned the idea that "access to opportunity" can apply to success as a boxing champion, let alone a syndicate boss. This constriction is signaled by the increasing use of the term "conformity" in place of "success" to denote the end for which Opportunity is a means.[35]

While the concept of conformity, in common with that of Opportunity, assumes different means in different contexts (in some places it appears in opposition to "deviancy" to denote law-abiding behavior), a major usage clearly indicates that what conformists conform to is the idealized standards of middle-class life, or some amalgam of middle- and "stable working"-class life. Thus, one achieves conformity if of lower-class origins not by adhering to the customary practices of one's class, as one does if middle class, but by an active effort to *deviate* from these practices by engaging in what is called "upward social mobility" by the social scientists and "social climbing" by the socially ensconced. Thus, in the course of its evolution, Opportunity starts out as a concept for explaining impediments to becoming a successful racketeer or prison inmate and ends up as the Movement code word for an old, familiar friend—the process of elevating one's social position.

If, then, when the Ideologists say that a primary goal of the Movement is the "enhancement of opportunity," what they really mean is "the movement of lower-class persons toward middle-class status," the requirements of policy would be far better served if this were stated plainly and directly. It would then be possible to subject *this particular objective* to a rational and methodical examination—something that is quite impossible so long as it appears only in its cryptic code-word disguise. Some questions might be: How feasible is the objective of elevating social status? For what numbers of persons? For what categories of persons? How *desirable* is it? For what numbers? For what categories? How far in the social scale are lower-status persons to rise? What periods of time is elevation of various distances expected to take? What are possible consequences of varying degrees of success? Of limited success? Of extensive success? Are there possibly undesirable side-effects, and if so, what are they? Should those who do not now wish to change their status be persuaded to do so, and if so, how? Questions of this kind, while far from simple, are at least susceptible to systematic examination, and the objective as a whole can be compared to others as one in a range of possible objectives. Such consideration cannot be directed to an objective phrased as "the enhancement of opportunity," since, in the United States, as shown earlier, the worth of opportunity is as unchallengeable as its meaning is vague.[36]

The concept of Opportunity renders still another disservice. Present discussion has referred to this concept in the form "opportunity," but in the works of Cloward and Ohlin, as well as in many derived Ideological writings, it appears more frequently in the form "the opportunity structure," coordinate with its companion concept, "the power structure." The presence of the words "the" and "structure" is hardly of incidental significance. This usage derives from and reflects a dominant characteristic of the Movement—the use of a "solid-structure" imagery that is so deeply ingrained and pervasive as to be virtually unconscious.

As is the case for other major usages, the Movement is indebted for the solid-structure imagery to academic social science, in which this usage has been endemic for years, often for similar reasons. The word "structure" is appended to a wide range of terms with varying justification. Sometimes it is used to impart an aura of scientific substantiality to highly abstract constructs (ego structure, the structure of action) ; sometimes it signals a special technical meaning for a word in common lay usage (social structure, personality structure) ; sometimes it signifies a more extended field of concern than is implied by the unmodified term (kinship structure) ; often it serves all three purposes, and others. While there is obviously some legitimacy in each of these usages (in some more than others), there is a great temptation to apply the term indiscriminately, particularly when social scientists feel insecure about the unstructured base concept. One might speculate that the greater the insecurity, the more likely the use of the word "structure."

It is immediately obvious that the term "structure" comes as a Godsend to the Movement. Faced with the contradiction between a need for concepts that give an impression of solidity, and the reality of concepts that are for the most part ephemeral and insubstantial, the use of the term "structure" appears inevitable. "The Structure of Poverty" [37] is, of course, completely predictable; "The Structure of Deprivation," rather surprisingly, is not yet current, but the advent of "The Structure of Discontent" [38] would suggest it might be on its way. The urge to further harden up relatively "hard" concepts is reflected in usages such as "The Structure of Community Organization" [39] creating a precedent for "The Structure of Social Structure," or possibly "The Structure of Structure."

The solid-structure mode of conceptualization, of which the ubiquitous affixation of "structure" is only one manifestation, proceeds in a characteristic fashion. One first represents complex processes or abstract relational systems as concrete objects or physical structures and then proceeds to treat the original phenomena as if they had the properties of their analogues. This is clearly illustrated in the devices used by the Movement to refer to low-status residential communities. Two major metaphorical conventions appear in the works of Cloward and Ohlin and in corresponding parts of The Ideology: The first constructs an imagery of being walled out; the second of being walled in.

The walled-out imagery depicts "opportunity" or "the larger society" as a glorious castle or mansion whose lush environs are surrounded by high fences or walls that the excluded Poor are intently determined to breach and the entrenched Rich as intently determined to defend. This imagery explains otherwise puzzling usages such as "barriers to," "access to," "obstacles to," or "avenues to" Opportunity or Success Goals. The "walled-in" imagery pictures the Affluent as constructing walls around the communities of The Poor instead of (or perhaps in addition to) around their own; thence terms such as "the prison" or "the ghetto." It would appear that the walled-out imagery was more popular during earlier phases of the Movement, with the walled-in version moving rapidly to the forefront during later phases. Representing low-status communities as "ghettos" was perhaps the single most successful merchandising venture of the entire Movement. [40] The "prison" imagery (quite predictable since both Cloward and Ohlin developed basic concepts out of their prison studies) also continues to flourish, as witness such fanciful constructs as "patterns which block the escape from poverty." [41]

But after all, what harm is done? Expression in English is next to impossible without some use of metaphor, and all these images and analogies might be seen merely as devices for adding a little color to otherwise rather drab concepts. Moreover, this general approach has produced useful predictive models in fields such as economics (fiscal structure) and physics (wave theory). As applied by the Ideologists to problems of low-status populations, however, it is neither harmless nor productive of useful models.

The representation of complex social processes and systems of relationships as solid blocks of matter provides a dramatic illustration of the conflicting requirements of a movement and those of sound policy formulation. However distasteful to those committed to rapid social reform, the hard reality is that the circumstances of low-status populations, the character of their communities and their relations to other sectors of the society, are enormously complex, and knowledge as to effective modes of change is exceedingly primitive. A movement demands simplicity, concreteness, unambiguity, both of diagnosis and prescription. The image of a monolithic Power Structure depriving The Poor of Access to The Larger Society through Barriers of Opportunity is simple and satisfying: as a basis for sound policy, however, it is misleading at best and dangerous at worst.

Even more serious. The conversion of complex processes and relational systems into concrete objects like power structures and opportunity structures and ghettos and prisons creates an illusion of manipulability that is bound to produce disillusionment. Building blocks can be carted around, walls can be raised or lowered, structures can be built, renovated, demolished, with relative ease. Modes of exercising authority or relations between sectors of a society cannot. The pervasive and often unconscious influence of the solid-structure conceptualization creates an unrealistic impression of the ease with which fundamental forms of social change can be effected. Having bought the walls-and-barriers imagery, people are terribly disappointed when an easing of legal or custom-based restrictions fails to produce an easy and ecstatic passage out of the Ghetto and into the Mansion. The illusion of manipulability is further fostered by the importation of inappropriate metaphors from economics. One reads, for example, of the "redistribution of opportunity," as if it could be sliced up and parceled out.[42] Money and tangible commodities can be distributed and redistributed; opportunity, an abstract concept, cannot.

Opportunity is *not* a structure that people are either inside or outside of. Americans may achieve widely varying degrees of success or failure in a thousand different spheres and in a thousand different ways.[43] Beaming to lower-status people the message than one can attain "success goals" by breaching, demolishing, or otherwise forcing the "walls" that bar them from "opportunity" conveys a tragically oversimplified and misleading impression of the conditions and circumstances of success, in addition to fostering an imagery with potentially destructive consequences.

Society-wide decision-making in the United States is *not* invested in a "power structure," let alone "the" power structure. The agencies of authority are enormously diverse, exercising power, authority and influence of widely varying degrees in thousands of different spheres of social, political, and economic endeavor. While a substantial degree of mutual agreement and concerted action must obviously obtain among different agencies of this vast system at different times and under different circumstances, to represent the exercise of power in the United States as the prerogative of a monolithic and collusive power structure is terribly misleading, fostering in lower-status persons the hope that their problems will be solved if only they can somehow induce "the power structure" to listen and act.

Lower-class residential areas are *not* ghettos in which homogeneous populations are confined by state-supported force. While many urban slums are predominantly Negro (as many are predominantly white), the average lower-class district contains a mixture of different races, religions, national backgrounds, and status levels within the lower class. The question of why people live in slums rather than elsewhere is far more complicated than is implied by the simple analogy to walled-in districts of medieval cities in which persons of divergent religious beliefs were compelled, by state fiat, to reside. Of course, race prejudice can restrict one's choice of housing in "better" residential areas, but by picturing slum residents as helpless pawns of Power Structure exclusionism, the Ideology entirely ignores those influences that attract people *to* these areas, stressing only those that keep them from others.[44]

Urban lower-class communities are not prisons, nor are governmental officials prison guards. Prisons are peopled by society's most serious lawbreakers who are assigned to particular institutions with no personal choice and confined therein by state-supported force; slums are peopled by citizens whose choice of particular communities is essentially their own. Such communities show high rates of residential movement, both within and between neighborhoods, and the daily life of the average resident is just as free of official supervision, if not freer, than that of middle-class persons. Those whose political power may affect such communities, through federal, state, or local office, have no power to dictate residence locale nor to determine who may move in or out. However strong the temptation to indulge in fanciful metaphors like the iron bars of prejudice and patterns that block the escape from Poverty, or to equate slum riots with prison riots, the whole prison imagery, like the rest of the Ideology's solid-structure imagery, represents an abdication of the responsibility to base policy formulation on careful examination of the actual character of lower-class life.

The concept of Opportunity, finally, seriously impedes the task of developing satisfactory answers to a vital question: How can one account for the circumstances of the present-day lower class? The Opportunity frame of reference, with its villains and heroes, evil Power Structure and noble Poor, theories of conspiratorial exclusionism, and all the rest, embodies an approach whose major thrust is not the development of useful explanations but the attribution of blame. A major participant in the Moynihan controversy put his position in these words: "The real issue is: Who is to blame?" [45] This is precisely what the real issue is not. The Opportunity thesis, as used by the Movement, has fostered a tragic confusion of explanation and recrimination.

The "Who is to blame?" response is not at all unusual. Attribution of blame is, in fact, the "normal" method used by most humans to account for most human troubles. Evil beings, natural or super-natural, are generally regarded as responsible for the majority of human problems. Classic modern examples are found in explanations for juvenile delinquency (the fault of bad, neglecting parents) and prostitution (victimization by exploiting males). It is precisely because blame attribution is so natural that those responsible for explanations that guide policy must be particularly on guard against it.[46] Unfortunately, this habit of thinking is quite characteristic of many of the scholars who have contributed to the rationale for the Movement, although their ascriptions of blame are generally muted through the conventional locutions of scholarly discourse.

Negro leaders, by contrast, have little compunction about using the word "blame" and designating villains directly.

The real issue is: Who is to blame? Is it the Negro . . . born into a miserable vermin-infested apartment . . . not really taught to read, write, or count . . . educated in the street? The disorder, the alienation, the violence of the ghetto . . . are imposed.[47]

Once we admit that Negroes are in no way to blame for their predicament, the minimum consequence would be respect for persons of color and persons who are poor; (they are in this predicament) because racism runs rampant through our institutional structure.[48]

By laying the primary blame for present-day inequalities on the pathological condition of the Negro family and community, Moynihan has provided a massive cop-out . . . It has been the fatal error of American society to ultimately blame the roots of poverty and violence . . . upon Negroes themselves.[49]

Scholars generally tend to avoid the word "blame," but manage to communicate the same idea.

The explanations (of Negro life) almost always focus on the supposed defects of the Negro victim as if these, and not the racist structure of American society, were the cause of all the woes . . . If we are to believe the new ideologies, we must conclude that segregation and discrimination are not the terrible villains we thought they were.[50]

Both the white and Negro middle class—not to mention the white lower class—have a considerable investment in the status quo which condemns the poor Negro to membership in a powerless, deprived underclass . . . most whites are more driven to revenge than reform when Negro deprivation does reach into their lives.[51]

If one applies the culture of poverty to the poor, the onus for change falls too much on the poor, when, in reality, the prime obstacles to the elimination of poverty lie in an economic system which is dedicated to the maintenance and increase of wealth among the already affluent.[52]

The culture of poverty is both an adaptation and reaction of the poor to their marginal position in a class-stratified, highly individuated, capitalistic society. (Their problems are) not met by existing institutions and agencies . . . Often (the culture of poverty) results from imperial conquest in which the native social and economic structure is smashed.[53]

Among the objects of blame designated or implied in the above quotations are the racist structure of American society, the white middle class, the Negro middle class, the white lower class, the affluent, a class-stratified capitalistic society, and social-structure-smashing imperialists. Probably the most popular villain of the Movement is a stereotyped bigot who stereotypes lower-class people ("lazy," "dependent," "aggressive," "destructive"). Some authors choose to scapegoat these scapegoaters with a "look who's talking" approach.

The middle classes, of course, have their *own* faults. They . . . use their verbal facility . . . to make themselves comfortable about their generally undeserved positions of affluence . . . in which they manage to obtain the most pay and security for doing easy and interesting kinds of work.[54]

This blaming-the-blamers tactic, along with that of the Negro leaders —"You say *we're* to blame but we say *you're* to blame"—assumes the form of the classic dialogue between eight-year-olds, "It's your fault!" "No, it's your fault," with about as much profit.

Are there any alternatives? Is it possible for humans to develop explanations for highly charged, highly problematic social situations without taking sides or invoking devils? Such explanations have been forwarded for particular social problems, but it is probably safe to say that the attempt to develop a comprehensive and blame-free explanation for the life circumstances of the American low-skilled laboring class has never been seriously undertaken.[55] Such an enterprise would have to incorporate several assumptions. It would take as a premise, first of all, that no broad category of persons is any more or less virtuous, or any more or less villainous, than any other—men or women, adults or adolescents, whites or blacks, upper class, middle class, or lower class, northerners or southerners, employers or employees, professionals or laborers.

It would assume, further, that each of these categories of persons has a set of *class interests* that are directly related to the general welfare of that particular category or class; that these class interests arise logically and understandably from the conditions of existence of each class and the kinds of tasks its members customarily pursue; that there is in large differentiated societies a complex division of labor whereby each societal class performs different kinds of tasks and serves different functions, each making some important contribution to the welfare of the total society. It would assume that in no society is it possible to maximize all these class interests at the same time, so that there will always exist *true* conflicts of interest among the several classes that arise from their differing circumstances and operating requirements.

It would also assume that attempts by particular classes, given circumstances of limited resources, to maximize their own class interests at the expense of impinging classes are natural and expectable and may be animated by motives other than greed and selfishness; it would hope, if not assume, that policy makers at the highest levels could take as their *own* class interest the collective welfare of the entire set of classes and remain as nonpartisan as possible as to the virtue or villainy of any or all of the many scores of classes, each striving to further its own interests.

Such an explanation, evidently, would be too complicated, too inclusive, too neutral, to serve the true-believer purposes of the Movement. But the complexity and intellectual difficulty of this enterprise are not, in all probability, the major reason it has not been undertaken. One of the most delicious gratifications known to man is that of luxuriating in righteous indignation at the prospect of an absolutely unequivocal case of social injustice. Scholars of society, in general, have not distinguished themselves in the degree to which they are willing to forego this pleasure. It is, in fact, a principal incentive for many in a field in which, heaven knows, gratifications are few enough, and the wisdom of depriving them of this opportunity would have to be considered with great care. However, this indulgence, like all indulgences, has its cost, and the cost in this case is a tragic shortage of the kind of detailed, balanced, and objective knowledge that is the *sine qua non* of effective policy. This cost, swept in on the wide and surging tide of the opportunity formulation, has been great.

LOW-STATUS POPULATIONS, THE POVERTY IDEOLOGY, AND FEDERAL POLICY

On the face of it, the rationale and major objective of the federal anti-poverty programs of the 1960s seem clear and unambiguous. It became apparent in the 1950s that the United States was experiencing the highest level of material prosperity in its history and probably the highest ever experienced by any nation. And yet, in the face of this unprecedented wealth, there still remained "pockets of poverty," certain urban and rural communities whose residents were not sharing the general bounty, and who, in fact, continued to pursue an age-old mode of existence characterized by low income, low education, sporadic involvement in low-skilled occupations, sporadic paternal participation in home life, inelegant residential facilities, and all the rest. Surely it should be within the power of this mighty nation, at the peak of its material success, to eradicate these pockets and to achieve for the first time in human history the ancient dream of the elimination of poverty. While the exact means for achieving this objective were not immediately evident, it did appear that a principal approach involved a relatively simple matter of redistribution—spreading out the vast wealth of the nation so as to reduce pronounced discrepancies between the very rich and the very poor.

In the late 1960s, as this is being written, this dream had faded. The apparent simplicity of the problem and its indicated solution has burgeoned into a thousand complex fragments; optimism that the nation controlled the power and resources to solve this problem has turned to pessimism. It is too early to pronounce as a failure the 1960s phase of the nation's attempt to cope with the problems of its low-skilled laboring class, but it is quite clear that it cannot be pronounced a success. Many of the programs set up in accordance with the Poverty-Deprivation-Opportunity formulation are simply not amenable to reliable evaluation, and it is unlikely that anyone will ever know what they have accomplished or failed to accomplish. Evidence for the effectiveness of those programs for which evaluation has been undertaken is highly ambiguous—even on the basis of research conducted by the admittedly partisan staffs of the operating agencies themselves. Despite strong incentives to demonstrate success, this research has had great difficulty in adducing evidence for the achievement of even the immediate goals of the several sub-programs of the Poverty effort (for example, youth employment training, educational programs), let alone its major goal of eliminating, or even significantly reducing, "poverty." [56]

One apparently clear-cut indicator of success or failure—the amount and intensity of large-scale domestic violence—is in fact susceptible to highly divergent interpretations. The gross trend itself is clear; the scope and intensity of citizen violence in the urban slums of the United States between the years 1964 and 1967 increased in direct proportion with the increase in the scope and intensity of the federal Poverty programs. Moreover, some of the cities experiencing the most intensive rioting were those with the most intensive programs. The apparent relationship—the more Poverty-program activity, the more violence, and a possible conclusion that Poverty activity was one major *cause* of the rioting—cannot be used as evidence for the failure of the Poverty movement.[57] It could be so used only if the prevention or inhibition of urban violence were taken by the Movement as an explicit objective, and this is by no means the case. In fact, a principal tenet of the Opportunity formulation, as shown on page 282, is that it is impossible to "reach" The Power Structure except by forceful methods, with physical violence by no means foreclosed. Moreover, the "rising-expectations" thesis postulates that people sunk in the depths of Apathy and Deprivation are far too passive to do anything as energetic as rioting, but that once they have been sufficiently helped by public programs to improve their circumstances so that their energies are no longer totally consumed by the simple struggle for survival, and also to better appreciate the degree of injustice inhering in their condition, revolt is both possible and expectable. On the basis of this argument, the increase of citizen violence in the United States can be taken as direct evidence of the success of the Movement, and the more violence, the more success.

For many adherents of the Movement, the major reason for its lack of success was simple and directly evident. Barely underway on the War on Poverty, and devoting to it only a fraction of what it required, the nation became heavily involved in an ill-advised, immoral war in Asia, thus bringing to a halt the allocation of resources needed to advance the domestic War, or, at best, limiting it to a holding action. The hopes of the downtrodden having been raised only to be cruelly crushed, it would be amazing if they did *not* react out of frustration and despair. Thus, in perfect accord with the spirit of The Ideology, The Plight of The War on Poverty is laid to very specific villains—the evil Political Administration—just as The Plight of The Poor is laid to the evil Power Structure.

This chapter has focused on a very different kind of reason for ineffectiveness of the national effort. It contends that a central cause, although by no means the only cause, lies in the inadequacy of its underlying conceptual rationale. The enterprise at issue—whether described as a "war on poverty" or as attempts to accommodate contemporary problems of the low-skilled laboring class and its relation to the rest of society—is of enormous complexity and scope. Simple common sense would indicate the need for a conceptual rationale of commensurate scope. This vital need was not met. The basic elements of the ideological rationale that guided the federal War on Poverty were taken over in a curiously casual fashion from a doomed enterprise in a related area.[58] Infused with unexamined values, riddled with empirically unsupported assumptions, hobbled by internal inconsistencies and contradictory directives [59] peppered with oblique and deceptive code words, permeated with oversimplified imagery and misleading analogy, confounding means and ends, absolute and relative, explanation and recrimination—the emergence of effective policy from this ideology would have been little short of miraculous.

It is of the most direct significance that some of those who were most active in shaping federal policy would counter the assertion that its underlying conceptual rationale was inadequate by the claim that there was in fact *no* conceptual rationale, but that program proposals were guided largely by pragmatic, ad hoc considerations such as the availability of particular programs, interests of relevant governmental agencies, and simple happenstance.[60] This contention is striking in the face of the extraordinary consistency of language used by these men, with terms such as barriers to opportunity, escape from poverty, the poor, deprivation, alienation, apathy, the power structure, and all the rest appearing repeatedly in their speech and writings. This terminology, it should now be evident, derives from and reflects one very particular and highly distinctive conceptual framework. The classic manifestation of a deep-rooted and pervasive belief system lies in the conviction by believers that their perceptions are not the product of a "belief system" at all, but, like the air they breathe, simply the *way things are,* the substance of reality. The very fact that the frame of reference that in fact guided the poverty programs was so unconsciously taken for granted is powerful evidence for the conclusion that it was never examined or evaluated in any explicit or systematic fashion.

However well the Poverty Ideology may serve the purposes of a cult movement, it is critically inadequate as a basis of effective policy formulation. Many of its deficiencies have been indicated in previous sections; two others, treated in greater detail in the expanded version of this chapter, will be mentioned briefly. The first concerns the phenomenon of the definition-generated objective. The kinds of solutions seen as appropriate to any problem bear a critical relation to the way in which the problem is defined in the first place.[61] Nazi Germany's "final solution to the Jewish problem" was essentially predetermined by the way the "problem" was defined; just so the movement's solution to "The Problem of Lower-Class Culture" [62] is implicit in its definitions. Pathological, disorganized, deprived, alienated, excluded, apathetic, violent, victimized, exploited—The Poor of The Poverty Movement can be accorded only one possible future. Their way of life must be liquidated, and they themselves transformed into something different as rapidly and as efficiently as possible. The inevitability with which this prescription flows from the diagnosis radically restricts the range of options open to policy makers. An enterprise less rigidly restrained by its ideology could entertain a range of differing diagnoses, greatly expanding its chances for developing other, and potentially more effective, prescriptions.

A second additional difficulty with the Poverty Ideology relates to its potential for engendering costly reactions. Two useful concepts of social science concern "unintended side-effects" of directed action and the "self-fulfilling prophecy"; both are relevant to the relation between the Ideology and urban violence in the 1960s. As already mentioned, the causes of a phenomenon as widespread and consistently patterned as the urban riots must be multiple and complex, and it would be foolish to attribute exclusive or even primary causative influence to any single element. Within this complex, however, the role of the Poverty Ideology itself has generally been granted considerably less attention than other influences such as unemployment, public welfare policies, police practices, and so on.

Central tenets of the Opportunity formulation, as shown, ascribe the circumstances of low-status populations to deliberate policies of evil men, represent The Poor as victims of injustice and exploitation, and suggest that modification of Power-Structure policy requires forceful measures. The primary-intended audience of this message, insistently and effectively beamed by the Movement, was the alleged authors of these evils, with the intention of inducing them, in part through appeals to justice and in part through predictions of violence, to change their ways. Partly as a consequence of the Movement's image of The Poor as passive and apathetic, the impact of this message on the intended beneficiaries of these changes was not carefully considered. Screened through the perceptions of a subculture that is scarcely apathetic with respect to matters such as aggression and revenge,[63] this message, promulgated by persons of high position and influence, constituted not only a suggestion but an authorization for violence. The constant and ominous statements that "unless ——— is done at once, this summer will be longer and hotter than the last . . ." embody the classic characteristics of the self-fulfilling prophecy.

The contention of the Opportunity theorists that violence can be a cost of necessary reform cannot be ignored, and there is little doubt that some benefits accrued and will accrue from the rioting. If, however, the evocation of violent action is to be undertaken as an instrument of domestic policy by federal or federally supported agencies, it should be done only after the most deliberate and careful weighing of potential benefits against potential costs. The tragedy of the urban riots of the 1960s is that they were in some measure an unintended by-product of policies aimed at quite different objectives, involving serious miscalculations as to the impact of certain major tactics of the Movement, and virtually no calculations of benefits relative to costs.

A PROPOSAL FOR A NEW
CONCEPTUAL RATIONALE

The 1960s phase of the national attempt to accommodate contemporary problems of its low-status populations was marked by curiously contradictory orientations with respect to a guiding rationale. On the one hand, there were assertions that the problem was so clear, the objectives so evident, and the need so urgent that any substantial allocation of resources to the development of a guiding rationale was unwise, unnecessary, or both. Some even converted the lack of an explicit rationale into a virtue by claiming that systematically developed justifications for policy are largely irrelevant, since programming is determined largely by political considerations anyway, and this is all to the good.[64] On the other hand, as has been shown, the actual conduct of governmental activities was guided by a very specific and pervasive ideology. Some accommodated this contradiction by denying the existence of any ideology and following it unconsciously, thus making it all the more influential.

This chapter has contended that the failure to devote explicit attention to the rationale for the federal anti-poverty programs was a major reason for their lack of success. The policy implications of this contention are clear. It is folly to conduct an enterprise of this magnitude without devoting the most direct and explicit attention to the matter of a guiding rationale. Such a failure not only seriously weakens the possibility of developing effective measures, but entails grave risks of engendering unanticipated consequences quite at variance with explicit aims. The major proposal of this chapter also follows directly: A principal requirement of the next phase of this enterprise is that the Ideology of The Poverty Movement of the 1960s be replaced by a comprehensive, systematically developed, deliberately formulated conceptual rationale.

It has not been the purpose of this chapter to develop such a rationale. This would be well beyond its scope and in all probability well beyond the capacity of any one person—particularly someone accustomed to viewing the problem primarily in terms of any one of the several competing positions. Rather its purposes have been to show that there *is* a guiding ideology behind the "war on poverty," to delineate some of its major characteristics, and to create a sense of dissatisfaction with its capacity to serve as a basis of effective policy.

Two proposals are presented: one for immediate implementation, the other as a long-term undertaking.

The immediate proposal is this: that all federal agencies, and all agencies within the orbit of federal influence, be advised forthwith to terminate the practice of using, in speech, reports, legislative proposals, and all other documents, the major terms of the Poverty Ideology—particularly such terms as "the poor," "the power structure," "the ghetto," "denial of opportunity," "deprivation," and "alienation." This proposal assumes first that the conceptualization underlying these terms provides a major incentive for domestic violence in that it justifies a policy of revenge for past and present injustices, and second that it promotes a dangerously divisive image of the United States as comprising two irreconcilably warring camps: the exploited and the exploiters. Even those who remain unconvinced of the validity of these assumptions might see fit to support this measure on the grounds that it can be implemented at little cost relative to the benefits that could accrue if the assumptions are valid.

The long-term proposal is that an appropriate and adequately supported agency, in or out of government, deliberately and systematically undertake the development of a conceptual formulation that can serve as a sound basis for national policy with respect to low-status populations in the United States. As already mentioned, many feel that the diversion of national attention and resources to Asian warfare has seriously impeded efforts to accommodate pressing domestic problems; this diversion could be turned to advantage if it were conceived as a temporary lull that provides an opportunity to prepare the groundwork for a revitalized postwar renewal of these efforts. Most important, it affords an opportunity to remedy one of the most critical defects of the War on Poverty—the absence of an adequate conceptual rationale.

What should be the characteristics of such a rationale? The first requirement is that it be developed with the aim of maximizing conceptual adequacy. This means that primacy be granted considerations such as internal consistency (does one part contradict others?), explanational efficiency (how well does it account for the phenomenon at issue?), and empirical supportability (to what degree does available evidence accord with included propositions?). In recent years, a position has gained currency with respect to scholarly formulations of relevance to public policy that maintains that primacy be granted to considerations of implementation potential—ease and practicality of conversion into "action" programs, degree of political acceptability, and so on. Some have even gone so far as to propose that some of the most fundamental concepts of social science be conceived and utilized *primarily* as instruments of social reform rather than as vehicles of understanding.[65]

The present proposal is based on a diametrically opposed assumption—that the best explanation is that which explains best, quite independent of its potential for public acceptance or conversion into program. Implicit in this assumption is the notion that there is a legitimate division of function between the process of formulation and that of execution and that the maintenance of this separation—using appropriate specialists in each sphere and equally specialized "bridge" personnel or agencies to maintain communication between them—will ultimately produce far more effective programs than attempts to optimize conceptual and program considerations at the same time. Such a division would also reduce the danger of assuming that since no abstractly "pure" formulation can ever be converted directly into practical programs that one is thereby relieved of the responsibility of considering them at all.

A particular problem in developing an adequate rationale for policy relative to low-status populations is that there are now current several formulations that not only differ substantially but conflict directly with respect to basic issues both of substance and interpretation. Two broad alternatives present themselves. The first involves the delineation, in as "pure" a form as possible, of three, four, five or more of the basic diagnostic positions, each developed with an eye to maximal explanational adequacy. Each of these could be subjected to a systems-analysis type of process wherein the different program implications of each were developed, "simulations" made of implementational procedures, the several alternatives compared, and choices made on the basis of cost-benefit types of considerations. Alternatively, starting from the same initial steps, an attempt could be made to derive from the several formulations those elements they share in common, thus producing a "consensus" model as a basis for policy. Either of these procedures, or others of similar character, would substitute rational procedures for the hazy and haphazard process by which the Poverty Ideology was adopted.[66]

The second requirement of the new rationale is that it be as free as possible of unexamined values. It has become fashionable to assert that we now realize, in contrast to earlier and more ingenuous scholars, that a value-free science of human behavior is quite impossible, and that one must proceed on the assumption that the impact of values on all propositions about human behavior is deep and inevitable. Some have even moved to a position that sees built-in value premises as desirable as well as inevitable; from this perspective, the term "objective description" comes close to a pejorative. This assertion represents a rationalization for a failure to pursue an ideal that is extremely difficult and highly uncongenial to many. The choice is not between a formulation that is totally value-free and one that is totally value-laden, but between one that is 10 per cent value-free and another that is 20 per cent, with the difference of great importance. The formulation or set of formulations that provide the basis for national policy cannot be, and should not be, free of values: This very proposal for a less-value-laden formulation derives from very specific values. What is strongly urged is that it be as free *as possible* from *unexamined* values. Each formulation, or a possibly synthesized formulation, should be subjected to the most searching and exacting analysis, with the aim of disclosing the major value premises it incorporates or assumes and making each of these as explicit as possible. In this way, it should be possible to avoid much of the conflict and confusion attending divergent interpretations of the many hidden-value code words of the Poverty Ideology.

Of particular importance to the enterprise of delineating hidden values are those that relate to differing political philosophies. Such values command the most powerful and personalized emotional investment and, as such, are particularly resistant to deliberate examination. Two among the more volatile of the numerous issues in this area relate to desired rates and mechanisms of societal change, and the allocation of societal resources to the various age, sex, social status, racial, and other societal classes. One of the most important of the implicit political values of the Poverty Ideology involves a conception of "compensatory" justice that represents a significant departure from the more traditional American concept of "equal" justice. Certain of those societal classes that are seen in the past to have been less favored than others with respect to political power, prestige, wealth, and so on, are henceforth to be granted commensurately more of these advantages as a kind of balancing-out mechanism. Evaluative conceptions of this kind must be made as explicit as possible so that their implications for policy can be considered with the greatest of care.

A third requirement of the new rationale relates to its utility from the point of view of popular appeal, political palatability, and sales value in the broad sense. Some proponents of the Poverty Ideology claim to be perfectly well aware of its conceptual deficiencies, but defend them as necessary in a world in which the possibility of implementing policy depends in large measure on its capacity to command public and legislative support. This argument is applied, for example, to the fanciful "warfare" imagery that pervades the Ideology.[67] The argument asserts further that clarity and conceptual precision may actually be detrimental in areas in which there are marked differences of outlook, in that a principal device for securing the consensus necessary to policy implementation is a terminology sufficiently ambiguous and imprecise to allow persons with divergent views to believe they in fact are similar. Moreover, the argument maintains, a formulation couched in the dry and intricate terminology of scholarship (for example, "low-status populations" instead of "the poor") would not only fail to achieve public understanding but would offend public sentiment.

One must grant a measure of validity to these arguments; the viability of a democratic government requires effective communication with a broad range of public and legislative audiences of widely varying levels of sophistication. However, the argument for the deliberate use of conceptual looseness and merchandising language would be much more convincing if one found that the Ideologists customarily employed at least two modes of discourse: one for public-relations purposes and the other for serious deliberation. This is not the case. Virtually all of the examples of Ideology terminology presented here —slogans, code words, value-laden concepts—were taken not from legislative proposals, public-relations releases, or speeches to lay audiences, but from scholarly articles intended primarily for professional colleagues. The Ideologists have so confused the purposes of salesmanship and scholarship that the two have become one.

The formulation of a new rationale must maintain a strict distinction between the requirements of conceptual adequacy and those of sales potential. It must focus directly on logical consistency, theoretical adequacy, and explanational efficiency. The execution of this task is difficult enough in itself, without assuming at the same time the responsibility for ensuring public acceptability. This vital consideration can be accommodated *after* the formulation has been developed. Surely it is not beyond the capacity of competent thinkers to render a difficult and complex set of ideas in simpler form, using perhaps three or four levels of simplification to accommodate different audiences. But such translation can only follow the development of the basic formulation; it cannot precede or substitute for it. The conduct of effective policy requires that there exist somewhere, in as sophisticated a form as the talents of this nation can arrange, a sound and well-conceived explanation for the circumstances of low-status populations.

Those Americans who realize that effective national policy is impossible in the absence of a set of abstractly formulated guiding principles have been strangely intimidated by vocal activists who proclaim that the problem is clear, the goals are clear, that what is needed is action, and massive action, not more abstract theories. The experience of the Poverty Movement of the 1960s should have made it abundantly evident that neither problem nor goals are at all clear. Effective action requires as clear a conception as possible of what the ends of action are to be; this conception, in turn, must be derived from an informed and accurate diagnostic statement.[68] Action for the sake of acting can create an illusion of progress, but the cost of nourishing this illusion, the 1960s have shown, can be enormous. Statements of objectives such as "the enhancement of opportunity" or "escape from the ghetto" actually vitiate the possibility of effective action since their ambiguity supports divergent and often conflicting interpretations. Efforts to meet the problems of the American low-skilled laboring class in the absence of a well-conceived conceptual rationale are like the actions of men groping blindly in the dark in pursuit of unknown and unperceived goals.

Notes

1. Analyses of the relation of these features, along with others not cited here, to one another and the subculture as a whole are contained in Walter Miller, *City Gangs,* forthcoming.

2. Chapter 1 by Peter Rossi and Zahava Blum in this volume includes a brief citation of six features of a population designated as "the poor" that is freer of evaluative connotations than most such citations but still reflects the evaluative approach in the use of terms such as "unskilled labor," "menial jobs," "instability," "superficial relationships," "alienation," and "dogmatism."

3. This chapter is a shorter version of a more extended treatment. The longer version includes a discussion of a fifth key term, civil rights, which treats the confusion between race and class in Movement formulations. It also contains two additional major sections. The first examines some of the epistemological bases of the ideology under the topics "cultural absolutism," "reform activism," and "sentiment as reality"; the second, some of its consequences under the topics "a constriction of choice" and "a spur to violence." (Unpublished manuscript; Cambridge, Mass.: Harvard–MIT Joint Center for Urban Studies.)

4. See discussions of the absolute-relative issue in Herman P. Miller, *Income Distribution in the United States,* U.S. Bureau of the Census (Washington: Government Printing Office, 1947), pp. 29–32, and Martin Rein and S.M. Miller, "Poverty, Policy and Purpose: The Dilemmas of Choice" (Washington: Bureau of Social Science Research, 1965), pp. 5–8.

5. This issue is discussed further under the topics "relative deprivation" and "sentiment as reality." A discussion of "status discontent," and the function for lower-status persons of expressions of discontent to higher-status persons is included in Walter Miller, "A Comparison of the Status-Discontent and Subcultural Generation Approaches to Juvenile Delinquency," Seminar on Delinquency and Deviant Behavior (University of Chicago, School of Social Service Administration, March 1960).

6. Office of Economic Opportunity, *Dimensions of Poverty in 1964* (rev. December 1965), October 1965. The authors of this report are uncomfortably aware of the relativistic basis of their formulations, as evidenced by phrases such as, "The poor (must choose) among hard alternatives, which needs may be endured and which must be satisfied." They also characterize their definitions as "arbitrary," but justify them on the basis of "usefulness" for unspecified purposes. The appeal of this kind of numbers game became, under the spell of the Movement, so irresistible as to involve even highly reputable and conscientious scholars. Charles Willie, for example, based an extensive study on the assumption that Washington families with annual incomes of $4,500 or less were in poverty and those with over $4,500 were affluent. Charles V. Willie, "The Relative Contribution of Family Status and Economic Status to Juvenile Delinquency," *Social Problems*, XIV, No. 3 (Winter 1967).

7. See "Origins of the War on Poverty," in Vol. II, this series: James L. Sundquist, ed., *On Fighting Poverty* (New York: Basic Books, 1969).

8. Herman Miller, *op. cit.*, Table 2-3, p. 43.

9. Herman Miller, *op. cit.*

10. Ornati first suspected that figures showing decreases in the proportion of the poor were due to applying "poverty-line" definitions from one era to another, so he recalculated the data using 1947 "poverty-line" definitions for 1947 and 1960 definitions for 1960. On this basis, he still found decreases, and that the larger decreases occurred at the lower levels. At the lowest level there was not only a decrease in the percentage of the population (15 to 11 per cent) but even a decrease in absolute numbers (21 to 20 million), during a period when the national population grew by 35 million. Oscar Ornati, "Poverty in America," in L. Ferman et al., eds., *Poverty in America* (Ann Arbor: University of Michigan Press, 1965), pp. 25–27.

11. The primary movement-approved attitude toward the poor is "compassion."

12. An explanation for "retreat" or "conflict" as alternative responses to status discontent is contained in one of the major sources of the conceptual content of the ideology (R. A. Cloward and L. E. Ohlin, *Delinquency and Opportunity: A Theory of Delinquent Gangs* [New York: The Free Press of Glencoe, 1960], but the movement has not stressed this distinction; see the later discussion of "opportunity."

13. S. A. Stouffer et al., eds., *The American Soldier* (Princeton, N.J.: Princeton University Press, 1949).

14. It is not surprising that the "poverty-brings-happiness" position has few vocal exponents in contemporary money-minded America; occasionally, however, one is reminded that proponents of this position not only exist but also act on their principles. Poverty-movement-era newspapers quoted the sentiments of a skid-row resident who refused $20,000 from the sale of a filling station he had abandoned fifteen years before. "What a time us winos have had the past ten years. What a time! No worries, free as a bird. No taxes. No rush to work. All I want out of life is a loaf of bread, a piece of bologna, a hunk of cheese, good health. I've got all that here. I'm at peace with the world." (Los Angeles *Times*– Washington *Post*, February 12, 1968.)

15. One of the few "hard" indicators of subjective discontent is suicide rates; the act of committing suicide provides as direct an order of evidence as is available of acute unhappiness. The data do not support the contention that lower-status persons are more unhappy; to the contrary "(suicide rates) are higher in the upper socio-economic classes than in the lower." (Dr. Norman L. Farberow, **Los**

Angeles Suicide Prevention Center; quoted in *The New York Times,* September 1967.)

16. The methodological issue of the validity of self-reported information is very basic and very complex and is discussed in greater detail in the expanded version of this chapter under the heading "sentiment as reality."

17. Lee Rainwater, "Neutralizing the Disinherited: Some Psychological Aspects of Understanding the Poor," Pruitt-Igoe Occasional Paper No. 30 (June 1967), 6. Rainwater is perhaps only the most eloquent representative of a genre wherein middle-class persons describe their inner reactions to encounters with lower-class conditions. See, for example, Joseph Himes's description of his initial responses to a conventional lower-class work milieu: "I can still remember vividly how alien and unprepared I felt the first days in . . . the factory. The overwhelming and incessant racket, the inescapable glaring lights, the sense of frantic perpetual motion distracted and terrified me. Everything and everyone was strange . . ." Joseph S. Himes, "Some Work-Related Cultural Deprivations of Lower-Class Negro Youths," *Journal of Marriage and the Family* (November 1964). Note that both Rainwater and Himes stress the emotional response of "anxiety" or "terror."

18. The role of culture-centrism in the epistemology of the ideology is discussed further in the expanded version of this chapter under the heading "cultural absolutism."

19. It is instructive to compare the image of the United States underlying these propositions with what Morton Schwartz calls the "classical Marxist image" of the United States—"an economic system dominated by a small group of powerful monopolies whose great wealth is the product of a system of ruthless profiteering at the expense of American labor . . . a social system in which each citizen's position in life is determined by his relationship to the system of class exploitation, either as its master or its victim. In the orthodox view, there are only two kinds of Americans; those who prey and those who are preyed on," Morton Schwartz, "What Moscow's Washington-Watchers See," *The New York Times Magazine,* October 8, 1967. According to Schwartz the present generation of Soviet Washingtonologists has long since given up this "crude" stereotype.

20. Richard Cloward, "On the Concept of Illegitimate Means: A Contribution to the Theory of Anomie and Deviant Behavior" (New York School of Social Work, Columbia University, October 1968). Later published as "Illegitimate Means, Anomie, and Deviant Behavior," *American Sociological Review,* XXIV, No. 2 (April 1959).

21. Cloward and Ohlin, *op. cit.*

22. Cloward, "On the Concept of Illegitimate Means: A Contribution to the Theory of Anomie and Deviant Behavior," *op. cit.,* pp. 19–20. These ideas resemble similar notions of Daniel Bell. According to Lloyd Ohlin the opportunity concept owes more to the prison than the syndicate; the concept of differential opportunity was enunciated prior to Cloward's analyses of organized crime as part of an explanation of differences between two prisons—one of which afforded more "legitimate opportunity" than the other (Lloyd Ohlin, personal communication). The impact of these prison analogies is discussed later.

23. Cloward's earlier paper contains precedents for both the personalized and impersonalized renditions of the agencies of opportunity-denial. This paper, along with its Cosa Nostra analogies, contains some unexpectedly balanced statements as to the determinants of opportunity; for example, "All manner of forces intervene to determine who shall succeed and who shall fail in the competitive world of business and industry, as well as in the whole of the conventional occupational structure." Cloward, "On the Concept of Illegitimate Means: A Contribution to the Theory of Anomie and Deviant Behavior," *op. cit.,* p. 11.

24. Cloward and Ohlin, *op. cit.,* pp. 101–103.

25. Floyd Hunter, *Community Power Structure; A Study of Decision Makers* (Chapel Hill: University of North Carolina Press, 1953).

26. Traditionalists will be comforted to learn that the classic capitalistic villain has not been made entirely obsolete by the combined impact of the new technology and the new ideology. For example, in 1965, ". . . new patterns of cor-

porate consolidation . . . invest some corporate structures with an inordinate degree of influence in establishing market conditions that are detrimental to the reduction of poverty . . . in a climate where the prime consideration is profit-motivated actions . . ." Ferman et al., *op. cit.*, p. 137.

27. The process of transmuting the *lumpenproletariat* from villain to hero would lead one to suspect that some ideologists would be making serious efforts to unadulterate the still adulterated heroic quality of The Poor by casting as virtues even those attributes conventionally regarded as disabilities and by representing characteristics difficult to so transmute (for example, crime and sexual mores) as inevitable consequences of the evils of others, and thus not blameworthy. Prominent among those engaged in this enterprise are Frank Riessman ("Lower Income Culture: The Strengths of the Poor," *Journal of Marriage and the Family*, XXVI, No. 4 [November 1964], 417–421) and Robert Coles (*Children of Crisis: A Study of Courage and Fear* [Boston: Atlantic, Little, Brown, 1967]). These authors face contradictions between the requirements of representing the poor as sufficiently unflawed as to meet the requirements of the hero role and as sufficiently flawed as to serve the help-is-urgently-needed message of the Movement.

28. U.S. Department of Labor, *The Negro Family: The Case for National Action,* March 1965.

29. The nature of these events, along with a sophisticated analysis of their bases and consequences, is presented in a well-organized and balanced report by Lee Rainwater and W. Yancey, *The Moynihan Report and the Politics of Controversy* (Cambridge, Mass.: MIT Press, 1967).

30. Some suggestion of the anger aroused by the report is conveyed by published comments included in Rainwater and Yancey, *ibid.* For example, "Enormous conclusions based on tiny scraps of evidence . . . irresponsible nonsense . . . narrow and wholly inadequate framework . . . painful as well as fallacious . . . damnable inaccurate simplicity. As the murderer pleads guilty to manslaughter . . . liberal America is pleading guilty to savagery and oppression . . . to escape trial for the crimes of today." William Ryan, p. 461 *passim*, "I'm angry . . . really angry . . . we are sick unto death of being analyzed, mesmerized, bought, sold, and slobbered over while . . . the ingredients of our oppression go unattended . . . The fatal error of American society . . . to blame the roots of poverty and violence upon Negroes themselves . . . is here again, in its most vicious form . . . insulting the intelligence of black men and women everywhere . . . the most serious threat to the ultimate freedom of American Negroes to appear in print in recent memory." James Farmer, p. 409 *passim,* ". . . the Moynihan thesis is a one-sided presentation . . . to emphasize one-sidedly the limiting aspects and presumed pathology . . . is to do the Negro a deep injustice . . . It is most inappropriate to attempt to involve people in change by emphasizing some alleged weaknesses in their make-up . . ." Frank Riessman, p. 474 *passim.*

31. Cloward and Ohlin, *op. cit.,* pp. 2–5, 69. Subsequent work by Ohlin, as yet unpublished, addresses this issue directly. His definitions, involving concepts such as "the structure of rules and norm" and "gatekeepers" to various systems, lean heavily on the spatial and solid-structure imagery criticized in later sections. Lloyd Ohlin, personal communication.

32. *Ibid.*, pp. 104, 162.

33. *Ibid.*, p. 96.

34. See Mobilization for Youth, Inc. *A Proposal for the Prevention and Control of Delinquency by Expanding Opportunities,* New York, December 9, 1961, p. 49.

35. See for example, *ibid.*, p. 43, sections entitled "Expanding Opportunities for Conformity" and "Barriers to Opportunity."

36. A classic case of the disastrous consequences of the adoption of a policy objective phrased so ambiguously that it permits a wide range of divergent interpretations is presented in Daniel P. Moynihan, "Maximum Feasible Misunderstanding: Community Action in the War on Poverty," Sanford Lecture on Local Government, May 1967.

37. Ferman et al., *op. cit.*, p. xv.

38. Raymond J. Murphy and J. Watson, *The Structure of Discontent*, UCLA Institute of Government and Public Affairs, June 1967.

39. George Brager, "Organizing the Unaffiliated in a Low-Income Area," in Ferman et al., *op. cit.*, p. 393. James Sundquist, "The Structure of a Subculture," in volume 2 in this series is also a step in this direction.

40. The concept "ghetto" probably did more to shape the policies of the movement during later periods than the concept "poverty." Like "opportunity," "ghetto," in most movement usages, is a primitive or undefined concept. One of the few published attempts at a definition appears as a footnote in President Johnson's Riot Commission Report. This definition is confusing and imprecise; it is a direct product of the ideology ("poverty," "social disorganization"), and its key phrase "involuntary segregation" is highly controversial, with little evidence to support the "involuntary" assumption. *Report of the National Advisory Commission on Civil Disorders* (New York: Bantam, 1968), p. 12.

41. Herbert Gans, "Culture and Class in the Study of Poverty," this volume, Ch. 8.

42. See, for example, Leon Keyserling, "Planning a Long-Range Balanced Effort," in Ferman et al., *op. cit.*, p. 435. Other examples of this usage are "the redistribution of privilege" (Gans, "Culture and Class in the Study of Poverty," *op. cit.*) and "the differential distribution of positive feelings about oneself," which nicely combines the solid-structure imagery and the imputation of subjective states (S. M. Miller et al. "Poverty, Inequality and Conflict," *The Annals of the American Academy of Political and Social Science*, CCCLXXIII (September 1967), p. 50.

43. See Cloward, quotation from "On the Concept of Illegitimate Means," *op. cit.*

44. For slum heterogeneity see John R. Seeley, "The Slum: Its Nature, Use, and Users," *Journal of the American Institute of Planners*, XXV, No. 1 (February 1959), 7–14. One among several good discussions of "centripetal" forces attracting people to slums is contained in David Caplowitz, "The Merchant and the Low Income Consumer," in Ferman et al., *op. cit.*, p. 197, an excellent analysis of how intricately and directly the commercial organs of low-status communities are geared to the credit status of local consumers.

45. Bayard Rustin, "Why Don't Negroes . . ." in Rainwater, *op. cit.*, p. 419.

46. Evidence of this thesis might be found in the fact that the present essay ascribes blame for ill-advised policy to those who persist in using the "blame" approach.

47. Rustin, *op. cit.*, p. 419.

48. Martin Luther King, "A Bill of Rights for the Disadvantaged," *The New York Times*, November 12, 1967.

49. James Farmer, "The Controversial Moynihan Report," in Rainwater, *op. cit.*, p. 409.

50. Ryan, *op. cit.*, pp. 463, 464. (See note 30 above.)

51. Herbert Gans, "The Negro Family: Reflections on the Moynihan Report," in Rainwater, *op. cit.*, p. 467.

52. Herbert Gans, "Poverty and Culture: Some Basic Questions about Methods of Studying Life Styles of the Poor," paper to International Seminar on Poverty, April 1967 (unpublished).

53. Oscar Lewis, *La Vida* (New York: Random House, 1965), p. xlv.

54. Warren C. Haggstrom, "The Power of the Poor," in Ferman et al., *op. cit.*, p. 315.

55. One preliminary piece of this task, using a primarily historical approach and analyzing the persistence of a lower-class community in terms of relationships among technology, labor supply, market conditions, immigration and emigration, residence patterns, and similar factors, is presented in Walter Miller, "The Evolution of an Urban Lower Class Community," *City Gangs, op. cit.*, Ch. 2. This chapter includes a discussion of the "blame" frame of reference that forms the basis of parts of the present chapter. It also forms one basis of the thoughtful

essay by Lee Rainwater on different modes of conceptualizing low-status populations ("Neutralizing the Disinherited," *op. cit.*).

56. Robert A. Levine, "Evaluating the War on Poverty," in Vol. II, this series: James L. Sundquist, ed., *On Fighting Poverty* (New York: Basic Books, 1969), Ch. 9.

The bulk of this conscientious overview is devoted to discussions of why particular programs are difficult or impossible to evaluate. Levine distinguishes four categories of program—Manpower, Individual Improvement, Community Betterment, and Income Maintenance. The second and third are said to be either not amenable to evaluation or to show highly ambiguous results. Income Maintenance programs are not supported by Office of Economic Opportunity (OEO) funds. This leaves Manpower programs. For only one of these, Job Corps, is careful evaluation reported; others, such as the Neighborhood Youth Corps, Work Experience Program, and Concentrated Employment Program, are characterized either as difficult to evaluate or as having a "low success rate and other flaws." With the Job Corps thus bearing the major burden for the research-evaluated success or failure of the War on Poverty, through the process of elimination, the "hardest" evidence of success presented is a modest cost-benefit ratio of 1.2. The "benefit" calculations, moreover, are not based on any direct measurement of work experience but on theoretical speculations derived from scores on "educational" tests. Thus, even the "hardest" evidence of the effects of one of the very few programs seen as susceptible to evaluation is based on theoretical speculations derived from a "proxy" measure. Measures based on rather less abstract indicators, such as crime and welfare rates, show no impact of poverty programs. A major trend with respect to a measure of central importance, income levels, shows a decrease from 34.1 (1964) to 29.7 (1966) million in the number of persons below one of the several (here unspecified) "poverty lines." This trend cannot be attributed to the War on Poverty, since the research fails to handle the critical problem of separating the influence of poverty programs from the weighty influence of many other national-level factors such as wage levels and production-related employment rates.

57. The phenomenon of urban violence is highly complex. An adequate analysis of the urban riots of the 1960s would require the delineation of a fairly large number of contributing influences (police behavior, lower-class male-adolescent subculture, intensity and impact of hostility between whites and blacks, incidence and causes of "normal" volume of violent and appropriative crimes among low-status populations, etc.), categorizing these as more "proximate" and more "generic," and assigning different weights to the range of delineated variables. This task is obviously beyond the scope of this essay, but the issue is relevant here because it reveals with great clarity the powerful influence of the Ideology on contemporary explanations. One excellent example is found in the report of President Johnson's Riot Commission (*Report of the National Commission of Civil Disorders, op. cit.,* pp. 203–281). This treatment is of very little value as an explanation, but of great value as an illustration of the capacity of the Ideology to impede the development of adequate explanations. In particular, this treatment, in common with other Ideology-influenced explanations, completely ignores the causative role of the Movement itself. The process whereby the Movement and its activities provide one major incentive for the rioting is discussed under the heading "A Spur to Violence" in the expanded version of this chapter. Sound conclusions as to the contribution of the movement to the rioting would require careful measures of the amount and intensity of violence in the several cities and of Poverty-Movement activity, and measures of association between the two.

58. The role of the President's Committee on Juvenile Delinquency and Youth Crime (PCJD) as a major predecessor of the poverty programs, and the OEO in particular, has received very little detailed attention. This lack is made up in part by several of the chapters in Vol. II of this work that cite the PCJD, stressing in general continuities between the two enterprises. (See in particular papers by Sundquist, Yarmolinsky, and Kravitz). Less attention is paid the

manner in which the PCJD served the authors of the Poverty programs as an object lesson in what not to do. The PCJD was conceived as a "demonstration," with the testing of particular theories of delinquency-causation through action programs as a major objective. In practice, since Lloyd Ohlin was playing an important role at the level of federal granting agencies, virtually all programs were based on Cloward and Ohlin's Opportunity Theory. The process of articulating the basic tenets of the theory, developing relevant action programs, and arranging their implementation and evaluation was very difficult and quite time-consuming when measured on a political-administration-tenure time scale. These features of the enterprise aroused the ire of influential elected officials for whom "action programs" can be a political asset, and "testing the validity of causational theories" a matter of indifference, if not a liability. The politically-sophisticated authors of the poverty programs considered PCJD personnel as politically naïve and were determined to avoid such difficulties. They therefore plunged directly into action programs with only the briefest consideration of the theoretical reasons for undertaking them. Paradoxically, however, having rejected the political style of the PCJD, they embraced uncritically and with enthusiasm the identical theoretical rationale the PCJD had failed to test. The evidence that *was* available at the time (and which was strengthened by later evidence) indicated that the opportunity theory was proving quite inadequate as a basis for programs aimed at the relatively limited problem of juvenile delinquency; the experience of the PCJD provided no basis whatever for supposing it would prove any more effective as the basic rationale for a far more comprehensive undertaking—the wholesale alteration of the over-all life style of low-status populations.

59. An acute analysis of the contradictory policy directives inherent in the poverty ideology is contained in Rein and Miller, "Poverty, Policy and Purpose, *op. cit.*

60. Adam Yarmolinsky, "The Beginnings of OEO," in Vol. II, this series: James L. Sundquist, ed., *On Fighting Poverty* (New York: Basic Books, 1969), pp. 34–51.

61. See John R. Seeley, "The Problem of Social Problems," in John R. Seeley, ed., *The Americanization of the Unconscious* (Philadelphia: Lippincott, 1967), pp. 142–148.

62. This is Lee Rainwater's phrasing. Lee Rainwater, "The Problem of Lower Class Culture" (*op. cit.*) prepared for Sociology Department Colloquium, University of Wisconsin, September 23, 1966.

63. See Walter Miller, "Lower Class Culture as a Generating Milieu of Gang Delinquency," *Journal of Social Issues*, XIV, No. 3 (1958); Walter Miller, H. Geertz, and H. Cutter, "Aggression in a Boys' Street Corner Gang," *Psychiatry*, XXV, No. 3 (August 1962); Walter Miller, "Violent Crimes in City Gangs," *The Annals of the American Academy of Political and Social Science*, CCCLXIV (March 1966).

64. See, for example, Levine, *op. cit.*

65. See, for example, the discussion in Gans, *op. cit.* and this volume, Ch. 8.

66. These ideas as to procedure are intended as broad and general suggestions rather than specific proposals; the proposed course of action involves difficult problems on both theoretical and practical levels. In particular, the citation of "cost-benefit-type" analyses refers to the spirit rather than the letter of the method; the limitations of this currently fashionable procedure, particularly in areas where values are heavily and inevitably involved, are pointed up in an excellent analysis by Rein and Miller, "Poverty, Policy and Purpose," *op. cit.* Also unattended here are practical implementational matters such as the organization, auspices, and financing of such enterprises. Some of these are discussed briefly in a short memorandum: Walter Miller, "Proposal for the Establishment of an Office of Conceptual Formation" (Cambridge, Mass.: Harvard-MIT, Joint Center for Urban Studies, January 1968).

67. Space limitations preclude a fuller treatment of the "warfare" imagery which is carried to surprising lengths in some writings. Sundquist, for example, in a single essay (which contains the wise statement that "words and concepts

determine programs"), uses the terms "declare war," "unconditional war," "mobilizing," "under the banner," "massive coordinated attack," "strategy," "assault," "combating," "skirmishing," "weapons," "arsenal." (James Sundquist, "Origins of the War on Poverty," *op. cit.*) That mature scholars choose in all seriousness to invest in full military trappings an enterprise centering on efforts to alter the life conditions of low-status populations attests once more to the enormous influence of public-relations thinking. It also reflects the great prestige, during this period, of the military, particularly of the Defense Department and certain of its analytic techniques (for example, the Program Planning and Budgeting System), and the desire to absorb some of this prestige through the fantasy of a glamorous military operation.

68. A thoughtful analysis of the relation between differing diagnostic formulations and differing policy formulations is contained in M. Rein, "Social Science and the Eliminaton of Poverty," *Journal of the American Institute of Planners,* XXXIII (May 1967), 146–163.

Chapter 11

⫴ *An Economic Definition of Poverty*

HAROLD WATTS

INTRODUCTION

The discussions of the poverty seminar, whatever else they did or did not achieve, accomplished one thing most conspicuously. They highlighted two radically different approaches to the definition of "poverty": on the one hand, the "narrow economic" definition, and on the other, the "culture of poverty."

The economic concept is defined in terms of the external circumstances that condition a person's behavior, especially the behavior he displays in economic transactions: buying consumption items, selling productive services, securing professional advice, etc. The cultural concept focuses on the internal attitudes and behavior patterns that a person brings to any particular set of circumstances. The one locates poverty in the person's condition; the other finds it in the person's character.

A program aimed at eliminating economic poverty will measure its success by the increase in command over goods and services that is induced by the program. A program aimed at eliminating the culture of poverty will measure its success by changes in the complex of attitudes and behavior patterns characteristic of that culture. Any program will, in general, influence both economic poverty and the culture of poverty, but not in equal proportions or with equal directness.

Because the external conditions, given a sufficiently long exposure, can affect the patterns of behavior we term "culture," and, in turn, "culture" can and does influence the nature of the external world a person faces, it is not usually possible to attribute exclusive effects on either "economic" poverty or "cultural" poverty to any particular policy or program. It can be argued, however, that much of the current and widespread dissatisfaction with anti-poverty policies is due to a failure to make an explicit choice of a restrictive definition of poverty. In a situation in which each critic can choose from a wide range of poverties—and feels no need to restrict his choice to any single one—it is no hard task to find all policies wide of some target.

A clear notion of what one is trying to do has always been of importance in the formulation of policies. The advantage of choosing the most efficient means of attaining a specific goal is also no new discovery. However, the recent adoption throughout the executive branch of the Federal Government of PPBS (Planning, Programming, Budgeting Systems) does indicate a change in the direction of more explicit and coordinated application of these principles. By requiring agencies to state their objectives and to establish priorities among their program proposals according to the degree that the programs serve those objectives, PPBS enforces a tighter correspondence between objectives and policy decisions.

In the language of the model of economic choice, we may take alternative programs (or increments to them) as the set of objects of choice. PPBS asks an agency such as OEO to consider all possible combinations of programs and to establish a preference ordering among them based on the agency's interpretation of its mission or goal. A determinative choice, of course, requires the addition of constraints—financial, political, or what have you—but these constraints are not finally decided at the agency level. When the choices are made by the Bureau of the Budget and ultimately the Congress, objectives of other agencies must be considered and balanced with the anti-poverty objective.

Hence, it can be seen that the choice of a definition of that poverty that we want to eliminate *must* be made. And that the choice affects not only the setting of priorities among anti-poverty programs, but also the higher level assessment of the relative importance of getting rid of poverty vis-à-vis other objectives of society.

If the problem of poverty is worthy of a distinct name (even of a special agency), then it certainly should be possible to distinguish poverty from the entire collection of social problems. The task of evaluating and ranking programs for their effect on poverty is not responsibly discharged by usurping the Presidential-level problem of balancing the claims of all social objectives. We must distinguish between the Great Society and the Poverty-less Society. The more is subsumed under the definition of "poverty," the more the Poverty-less Society simply *becomes* the Great Society. Every step we take toward an equation of the two goals takes us further toward elimination of the need for, and in fact the possibility of, a separate consideration of poverty as a distinct problem.

It is possible to pay exclusive attention to one or another anti-poverty objective. Moreover, once such a commitment is made, all extraneous consequences must be excluded in order to secure the maximum impact from a given anti-poverty budget. A familiar theorem in economics rules out the possibility of maximizing more than one objective at the same time. If the activities that promote each objective use some of the same scarce resources, and if the objectives are truly different, then one must be prepared to accept a reduced level of success for one objective in exchange for the other; it is impossible to get more of both. Two possible resolutions are: (1) to ignore one of the objectives, or (2) to reformulate the problem by defining a new objective that is an explicit combination of the two objectives, that is, to admit that the original definition of the poverty problem was incorrect.

The concept of poverty developed below is restrictive, both in the sense that any specific concept must be restrictive and in the sense that it excludes from consideration sociological, political, psychological, and physical ills that are weakly or strongly associated with poverty. This does not indicate a presumption that these goals are unimportant. What it does indicate is the presumption that poverty is a specific ill in itself; that poor people, while they share many other problems with the nonpoor, are unique in having a relative shortage of goods and services at their disposal; and that, finally, poverty in the more restricted sense can be eliminated, is worth eliminating, both for its inherent injustice and for its fallout effects on related problems, and will be eliminated more promptly by policies that are aimed at a compact, rather than a diffuse, target.

THE NEOCLASSICAL MODEL OF ECONOMIC CHOICE

The concept developed takes from the basic model of economic choice the idea of separating preferences from constraints. Associating poverty with extremely limiting constraints, the definition incorporates a broader view of the economic constraint derived from Milton Friedman's theory of permanent income.[1] Consideration also is given to the problem of weighting and aggregating varying degrees of poverty and to the notion of a social-welfare function.

A very simple analytic tool, the neoclassical model of economic choice, can provide a framework for analyzing the behavior of decision-making economic units. Its flexibility permits application to consuming units or producing units of varying levels of complexity. The consuming units with which we are immediately concerned are the individual and the family.

Stated most simply, the model postulates that there is a set of objects of choice that the decision-maker ranks according to his particular, and perhaps peculiar, preferences. Confronted with one or more considerations that limit his choice to a sub-set of these objects, the decision-maker will, according to the model, choose the highest ranking alternative available in that sub-set. For example, a family may prefer a suburban bungalow to a high-rise apartment, which in turn is favored over a walk-up flat, and all three are regarded as better than remaining in (or returning to) a rural tar-paper shack. If it is limited by income or discrimination to either the flat or the shack, however, it will choose the former. This is, loosely speaking, the extent of the rationality assumption that is so often used as a club with which to beat economists. It is possible, of course, to make more restrictive assumptions and to get more substantial derivative propositions from the theory. But these are not necessary in general, nor are they needed for the development of the concept that follows.

In more specific terms, consider the set of choice objects to be possible rates of consumption of two categories of consumer goods and services: necessities and luxuries. (We may indulge in the abstraction that there are only two goods, measured in some convenient scale, and each good is perfectly divisible, so that amounts can be varied in a continuous manner.) The decision-making unit, which we may take to be an individual or a family, has a system of preferences among these objects that may be represented by an "indifference map" imposed on a two-dimensional space as in Figure 11–1. Each point in the positive quadrant corresponds to a unique combination of luxury and necessity consumption. The point A in Figure 1 corresponds to consumption of X units of necessities and Y units of luxuries per month. Each curved line consists of points that are considered equally good by the family. (There is such a line through every point—only a few representative ones are drawn.) Points to the northeast of any one curve are all preferred over points on or to the southwest of the same curve. In this manner, a system of indifference curves can describe completely a particular ranking; any pair of consumption levels or two-dimensional points on the diagram can be evaluated as better, worse, or equally good, compared to any other pair.

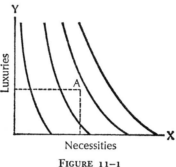

FIGURE 11-1

This system of preferences is regarded as a characteristic of a particular individual and may be quite different for some other individual. The preference ordering represents the tastes, values, and knowledge possessed by the individual; they will reflect his culture. As such, the preferences are not immutable, but, like culture, they are treated as stable enough to make worthwhile the abstraction that they remain constant for analytic purposes.

Given these preferences, now consider which combinations are available to the decision-maker. Assume that he has a fixed income flow to be spent and can purchase any amount of each good at prices that do not depend on the size of his purchase. We may now draw a straight line, PP′, that divides the space into a portion that he can afford and one that he cannot, as shown in Figure 11-2. The point P

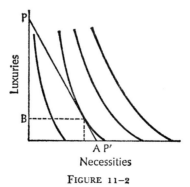

FIGURE 11-2

on the vertical axis is simply the number of luxury units that could be bought if the entire income were spent on luxuries; P' is similarly derived from income and the price per unit of necessities. The model is now complete and indicates that a family with preferences as shown, faced with a budget limit and prices as drawn, would choose to consume necessities at rate A and luxuries at rate B.

The external and relatively objective factors that determine the available alternatives are usually regarded as subject to variation. For example, an increase in income would shift the constraint outward in a parallel manner and, as drawn, would lead to increased purchases of both commodities. A change in relative prices will rotate the constraint and thus alter the level of purchases. Usually an increase in price of one good, other things remaining constant, will result in a reduction of consumption of that good and an increase in the consumption of the other.

POVERTY AND AFFLUENCE AS DEGREES OF CONSTRAINT ON CHOICE

The above excursion into basic economic theory was made to lay a foundation for the concept of poverty. The distinction made between preferences and constraints provides a useful basis for limiting the notion of poverty to the relatively objective constraint side of the problem. Poverty is, in this view, a property of the individual's situation, rather than a characteristic of the individual or of his pattern of behavior. Of course, overt behavior or ex post facto choices will reflect both preferences and constraints (both values or culture and situation), but poverty is associated solely with severe constriction of the choice set. Similarly, affluence corresponds to a much larger area of attainable alternatives. Indeed, poverty and affluence are, in this view, the names we give to the two ends of a scale measuring level of generalized command over real goods and services. Current income is an important part of this command over goods and services, but it is not, as will be argued below, the sole determinant.

There are two features of a definition based on the choice constraint that recommends it. First, it avoids imposing a norm on the tastes and values held by individual decision-makers. Instead of arguing that anyone who consumes less than X units of food or Y units of housing is poor, it would argue that anyone who has sufficient command over goods and services to achieve X and Y simultaneously must be at least as well off if he actually chooses some other combination.

It is, of course, a value judgment on the part of economists that the diversity of tastes and values reflected in different allocations of consumption at the same level of general command ought to be respected. Accordingly, that a particular family allocates a given budget in a way contrary to a typically middle-class outsider's notion of how he would do it or at variance with some statistical average of families at a comparable budget level should not be taken as evidence that the family is worse off or poorer.

The second salutary feature of this definition pertains to the elimination of troublesome questions about the level of satisfaction or happiness achieved by particular families from a given budget. The theory of choice requires only a ranking of alternatives; it does not require any measure of the magnitude or intensity of the distinctions made in rank, nor does it require any absolute measure of the pleasure derived from a particular allocation. Neither economics nor, as far as I know, social science in general can contrive a measure of satisfaction that would make one comfortable about asserting that Mr. A, with very aristocratic tastes and only two Picassos, does not feel more deprivation from want of a third than does Mr. B, who hasn't been able to buy shoes for the last three years. Lacking such a measure and possessing egalitarian tendencies, one is attracted to a definition of poverty that focuses on the means for pursuit of happiness rather than on happiness itself.

GENERALIZED COMMAND OVER GOODS AND SERVICES

The prevailing practice of measuring the extent of poverty according to levels of money income can be construed as a choice of a constraint-oriented poverty concept, as recommended above, combined with a choice of current annual money income as the measure of command over goods and services. Probably everyone remotely connected with developing and working with these statistics has acknowledged the crudity of this measure. But if the argument in favor of a constraint-oriented measure is accepted, then it follows that improvement lies in adopting a more comprehensive measure of the constraint on household choice. The income measure is crude because of its incomplete coverage of sources of command over goods and services and its short time horizon—*not* because it is narrowly economic, lacking in humanity, or oblivious to subjective subtleties. The following paragraphs indicate how the measure can and should be broadened both on conceptual and empirical levels of analysis.

The economic literature contains a concept of income that comes very close to meeting the present need for a comprehensive measure of command over goods and services. Milton Friedman's permanent income concept has proved useful both in clarifying theoretical analysis of household behavior and in improving our ability to predict behavior. The value of the largest sustainable level of consumption is one, slightly circular, way of describing Friedman's more comprehensive concept. More precisely, it is the sum of income flows from property, from sale of labor services, and from transfers (unilateral "gifts"), from other persons, or from governmental units, whether received in money or in "real" form. These flows are evaluated at the normal rate they can be expected to maintain over the long run instead of at the current level. The reason for this is that current income may be higher or lower than normal because of temporary good fortune or misfortune. Friedman terms these deviations "transitory income," which, together with "permanent income," divides current income receipts into two additive components.

Expansion of the time horizon for purposes of measuring income broadens the concept substantially. As developed by Friedman, there are two bases for income via the market: human wealth and non-human wealth. The latter is relatively familiar owing to its similarity to *wealth* in common usage: real and financial property. Money income from this source is usually counted in current measures, although year-to-year variation in profits or dividends may exaggerate the dispersion of the income distribution. However, it is not common to consider the wealth itself, as distinct from the income it generates, as part of a household's command over goods and services. But, considering that households do accumulate wealth with the intent of decumulating it during retirement (or passing it on to succeeding generations), it would seem appropriate to convert net wealth (assets minus liabilities) into equivalent life annuities for purposes of measuring the capacity to sustain a level of consumption. This modification would primarily affect the aged or near-aged family units.

An important example arises from the directly consumed services of owner-occupied housing. The value of such services is, conceptually speaking, a form of income and is no less worthy of inclusion because the income does not accrue in money. The income will be appropriately accounted for if owner-occupied housing is included among the assets used in the net-wealth calculation discussed above. It is specifically singled out here because of the ubiquitousness of home ownership and because it is easily overlooked.

The notion of human wealth is a major improvement over current earnings as a measure of command over goods and services. The effective capacity to earn money income by selling labor services in the market or to produce directly consumed services in the home is the second component of permanent income. As compared with current earnings, it both takes into account a longer period of time and incorporates real income as well as money income. The longer period tends to substitute average rates of unemployment for intermittent full and zero levels of employment. It also offsets the quite low levels of current income usually enjoyed by those who are adding to their stock of capital by education or training.

In terms of this broader concept, an unemployed dishwasher would be counted as poorer than an unemployed plumber, even though both had the same zero level of current earnings. A Negro assembly-line worker who currently earns the same wage as the white worker at his side would be credited with a smaller long-run command over goods and services by being subject to a higher risk of future unemployment.

Another feature of the generalized measure of human wealth is its ability to include the home-produced and home-consumed services of the homemaker and other adult family members. The conventions of income taxation and national-income accounts do not give explicit recognition to this source of income. The anomaly has been pointed out with respect to the national-income accounts, but in the absence of any threat of drastic changes in human nesting patterns, it has not been regarded as an important weakness. When making interfamily comparisons, however, particularly at income levels in which nesting patterns frequently diverge from the ideal nuclear family, it is quite indefensible to ignore the direct contributions of adult family members to the services, or even goods, available to the family.

Finally, there are transfer payments among persons. These may be entirely voluntary, as within a family; or be covered by contract, as in the case of alimony; or arise out of public programs, such as social security. Persons are able to obtain command over goods and services in such ways without a current quid pro quo. Insofar as these claims are secure, either through law or through convention, there is no reason to treat them as different from income that accrues to human or nonhuman wealth.

There are, of course, substantial problems involved in measuring "permanent income." But if it is possible to obtain some general agreement on the suitability of the concept for analysis of poverty, there are many possibilities for improving on the measures now in use. Furthermore, if, as I believe, the generalized concept is relatively free of the many weaknesses criticized in the current money-income concept, then its adoption may make it possible for a wider range of analysts to work within a common conceptual framework.

THE INDEX OF POVERTY

The preceding discussion has argued that a measure of poverty should be related to the individual's or family's "permanent" level of command over goods and services. There remains the problem of specifying standards of comparison that will permit evaluation of commensurate degrees of poverty for families of different size or composition, in different places, and at different times. The "poverty lines" now in use are intended to provide such standards in terms of annual money income. The Orshansky [2] thresholds vary according to family size, they have been adjusted for changes in the consumer price index for intertemporal comparisons, and they allow for differences between farm and nonfarm residence.

In the simplest terms, the poverty lines represent the level of income that divides the families of a particular size, place, and time into the poor and the nonpoor. Hence the set of poverty lines are intended to designate equivalent levels of deprivation. Similar thresholds could be obtained for the more comprehensive constraint measures presented above that could be used to divide the population into poor and nonpoor.

However, it has been argued above that poverty is not really a discrete condition. One does not immediately acquire or shed the afflictions we associate with the notion of poverty by crossing any particular income line. The constriction of choice becomes progressively more damaging in a continuous manner. As a first step, it would seem appropriate to maintain the graduation provided by a continuum, but to seek a scale along which differently situated families can be compared. For this purpose, a ratio of the measure of permanent income to the poverty threshold might be taken as a first approximation. Symbolically, let $\hat{Y}$ (N,L,t) denote the poverty threshold for a family of size N, in place L, at time t. Define a family's "welfare ratio" w as the ratio of its permanent income, Y, to the appropriate poverty threshold, that is,

$$w = Y/\hat{Y} \ (\text{N,L,t}).$$

This scale extends the notion of equivalence *at* the poverty thresholds to equivalence at any proportional distance *from* the poverty thresholds, for example, 15 per cent below.

This welfare ratio will, of course, permit the same bifurcation into poor and nonpoor, the latter having ratios greater than one and the former less than one. But it also preserves the notion that those who are 5 per cent above the threshold are not much better off than those who are 5 per cent below. The welfare ratio also leads into consideration of more sophisticated ways of aggregating the detailed data into one-dimensional measures of the nation's poverty problem.

The "nose count" in poverty is one such measure that has little but its simplicity to recommend it. The "dollar gap," or the total amount by which the incomes of the poor fall short of the poverty lines, is a somewhat better measure because it counts a family that is at half the poverty line as five times as severe a problem as one that is at 90 per cent of the same line. A further improvement would recognize that poverty becomes more severe at an increasing rate as successive decrements of income are considered; in other words, that poverty is reduced more by adding $500 to a family's command over goods and services if the family is at 50 per cent of the poverty line than if it is at 75 per cent.

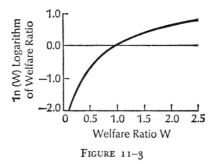

FIGURE 11-3

A simple and mathematically tractable measure that has this property would be the logarithm of the welfare index. It is not, by any means, the only such scale, but it offers a definite improvement over the current practice. The logarithmic function,[3] as shown in Figure 11–3, takes on negative values for fractional welfare ratios (incomes below poverty) and positive values for ratios greater than one. For purposes of more aggregative measures of poverty, it would be appropriate to sum the logarithms of welfare ratios, weighted by family size, over some part or all of the lower half of the distribution of families, that is,

$$P = \sum_{i \epsilon L} N_i \log (W_i)$$

where L is the set of subscripts belonging to families with $W \leq W^* \leq$ median W, N_i is the ith family size, and W_i is the ith family's welfare ratio; log (X) denotes the logarithm of any (positive) number X. W^* is an essentially arbitrary threshold value comparable to the "poverty line."

If $W^* = 1$, then P cannot take on positive values. It would have a limiting value of zero if no one were below the poverty line. The more severe is poverty, according to this scale, the more negative is the value of P. For $W^* > 1$, P could take on positive values and could do so even though some families remained below the poverty line. However, in both cases, an objective of maximizing P would provide a tenable guide to policy formation.

It would be possible to use some old and honorable terminology to add further perspective to the measure proposed here. Without doing excessive violence to the ideas of the utilitarians, one could specify an over-all utility function for society as the sum of *all* welfare ratios:

$$U = \sum_{\text{all } i} N_i \log (W_i) .$$

This magnitude could be broken into two parts:

$$P = \sum_{i \epsilon L} N_i \log (W_i)$$

where L is the set of subscripts for families with $W \leq 1$, and $\overline{L}$ is all the remaining subscripts,

$$A = \sum_{i \epsilon \overline{L}} N_i \log (W_i)$$
$$U = P + A$$

Here P will be a negative number (unless there are no poor) and could be interpreted as the disutility suffered by society because of poverty. The sign of A will be positive and could be termed the affluence level of society, part of which is "wasted" as an offset to P in the calculation of total utility.

It should be explicitly noted that the interpretation discussed above incorporates a fairly radical form of egalitarian value bias. It assumes that, except for the adjustments introduced in defining *W* (family size, location, etc.), all persons have equal needs; and that, other things being equal, including total output of goods and services, society would attain its highest satisfaction from an absolutely equal distribution of incomes. No positive value is attached to dispersion of the income distribution even for the sheer delight of variety. Practically speaking, there is a relation between total output and income dispersion that would almost certainly prevent complete equality from being an optimal or even an attainable solution.

Regarding P as simply an objective function, it is useful to consider how it would tend to allocate effort among the various levels of income. The derivative of P with respect to the welfare ratio of a particular family is an indicator of the relative importance of increasing that family's welfare ratio. That derivative for the logarithmic function is:

$$\frac{dP}{dW} = \frac{N_i}{W_i}$$

for all families with $W_i < W^*$ ($=0$ otherwise). Hence, for a family of four, at half of the poverty line, the derivative is $8 = 4 \div 0.5$. Compared to a family of four only 20 per cent below the poverty line which would have a derivative of $5 = 4 \div 0.8$, it is seen to be 60 per cent more important to raise the welfare ratio of the former. It would be preferable to promote an increase in welfare for the poorer family unless it were 60 per cent more expensive to do so.

CONCLUDING REMARKS

It appears to many that calculations of the sort carried out above are symptomatic of an extreme insensitivity to human values. How can one justify the contention that if it costs too much—when "too much" is given a definite numerical value—it would be better to forsake the poorer family and help the less poor one? The simplest, and least invidious, answer is a pragmatic one. If the 8:5 ratio doesn't seem right, we can specify a function that will make it, say, 100:1. But at some point, with limited budgets for fighting poverty, choices of this sort have to be made. They cannot be made more sensibly by *refusing* to look at the distributional implications than by looking at them. An economist draws very little satisfaction from engaging in interpersonal comparisons that, according to his training, cannot be grounded in objective fact, but must be plainly labeled as value judgments. He cannot profess any expertise in making such judgments, but he can, and must, insist that such judgments be made explicit, both to promote democratic debate and to permit consistent analysis and choice of policy alternatives.

A poverty function of the sort displayed above should be carefully distinguished from an over-all social-welfare function. The former is at best appropriate for guiding the choices of an agency charged with eliminating poverty. For choices that have to be made at the Presidential level, a much larger set of national objectives, inevitably conflicting at the margin, have to be balanced against each other. The poverty level should be one of these, but so should the affluence level, national security, mental health, and at least several others.

Finally, it should not be assumed that because the poverty index depends solely upon the level of command over goods and services, the optimal means of reducing poverty must be to increase that level as directly and as immediately as possible, for example, to hand out money or public jobs. There is nothing in the definition that prevents Head Start or even prenatal nutrition from being the most efficient means of reducing poverty in the sense of amount of poverty reduced *per dollar spent*. Some kinds of direct transfers would almost surely be among the least efficient.

Notes

1. Milton Friedman, *A Theory of the Consumption Function,* National Bureau of Economic Research, General Series 63 (Princeton, N.J.: Princeton University Press, 1957).

2. Mollie Orshansky, "Counting the Poor: Another Look at the Poverty Profile," *Social Security Bulletin* (January 1965), pp. 3–29.

3. Cf. Hugh Dalton, *Principles of Public Finance,* 4th ed. (London: Routledge and Kegan Paul, 1954), p. 68.

Chapter 12

⊂≡ *Identifying the Poor: Economic Measures of Poverty*

GERALD ROSENTHAL

The purpose of this chapter is to discuss the development of *economic* definitions of poverty, most of which are designed to distinguish the poor from the nonpoor. These identification measures are, for the most part, based on income levels, but are in fact attempts to reflect the consumption capability of families. The relationship between income level and consumption will be discussed here in order to indicate the implicit assumptions underlying such measures. In addition, the relationship between poverty-identification measures and the choice among various anti-poverty policies will be examined.

It is possible to distinguish efforts to identify the poor from efforts to describe them. The description exercise requires an initial identification and is usually directed at contrasting the incidence of certain characteristics of the group designated as poor with the incidence within the nonpoor group (or the population at large). Few, if any, characteristics are unique to the poor. However, the relative incidence provides a clearer picture, both of the impact of poverty on the life of the poor and of circumstances that might affect the likelihood of a given family's being poor. Descriptive analyses provide a basis for evaluating certain aspects of the lives of the poor as the objects of specific policies designed to reduce either their impact or their incidence. Identification measures alone are not a sufficient basis for selecting appropiate policies for dealing with poverty. Both descriptive analyses and causality analyses are also essential.

Most of the economic definitions of poverty have been directed at the identification problem. The argument is that being poor implies an inability to participate economically in society with some minimum degree of choice. Intuitively, it is difficult to find a reasonable basis on which to argue with this economic notion of poverty, that is, that poverty is an economically associated circumstance involving low-consumption opportunity. Identifying the poor, therefore, requires an income or consumption-related measure that can be applied to the population at large. Even evaluation of the "culture of poverty," which represents, perhaps, the most advanced development of a descriptive analysis of poverty, proceeds from the identification of families who are poor or areas that are composed primarily of those who are poor and can thus be distinguished from the rest of the population.

A considerable amount of the debate between those who favor economic definitions of poverty and those who prefer social or cultural descriptions relates to the implications for policy. This chapter will discuss the issues involved in developing poverty-identification measures based on economic or consumption-related circumstances and the implications for policy of these poverty-identification measures.

DESIRED ATTRIBUTES OF THE POVERTY-IDENTIFICATION MEASURES

An ideal measure for identifying the poor would be based on the isolation of a single measurable characteristic or group of characteristics that all poor possess and all nonpoor do not possess. Whether the characteristics in question are the cause of poverty or the result is, for this purpose, of no concern.[1] While such an ideal is not achievable, it is difficult to conceive of any measure even approximating this criterion that is not related directly to consumption ability, and it is equally difficult to conceive of any measurement of consumption ability that would not depend primarily on family income. The identification of the poor essentially involves identifying those members of society whose consumption opportunity is low. The reference is to consumption *opportunity,* since it is the inability to consume and not the low consumption itself that generates the disutility of poverty in both the personal and social sense.

There are a number of attributes other than measurability and objectivity that poverty-identification measures should possess. In addition to being related to consumption in a systematic and understandable way, they ought to be sensitive to changes within the group identified as poor. Ideally, such measures would not only distinguish between the poor and the nonpoor, but would also provide a basis for estimating the distribution of degrees of poverty among the poor. Such poverty-identification measures should also permit comparisons, both within a group and among different groups, over time. One would like to be able to ask realistically whether the amount of poverty has decreased, increased, or been fairly constant from one period to another, and whether or not group *A* is or has been poorer than group *B*.

Most of the measures developed to identify the poor have used family income as a basis for identification. However, considerable differences do exist among poverty-identification measures currently in use or being developed.

SOME POVERTY-IDENTIFICATION MEASURES

Among the most elementary poverty-identification measures are those that use a single level of income to represent the cut-off point between the poor and the nonpoor. Although the 1964 report of the Council of Economic Advisers acknowledged the limitations of such a definition, they nevertheless used a figure of $3,000 per year for a family of four, and $1,500 per year for a single individual to designate the poverty income cut-off.[2] There are a number of difficulties with any fixed-income poverty measure. While they do have the advantages of objectivity, reproducibility, and relative unambiguity, they nevertheless tend to be deficient in providing an accurate estimate of the degree to which individuals or groups falling within these limits face the same limitations on consumption opportunity. The relationship between income and consumption will vary considerably with factors such as family size, geographic location, etc.

A more significant difficulty is that the relation of a given income to consumption opportunity does not remain constant over time. The $3,000 per year family-income poverty line would have identified well over 40 per cent of the population in 1929 as poor. It is evident that the degree to which given incomes represent a low level of economic participation in society may be quite different in two time periods.

An alternative approach is to develop separate estimates of poverty cut-off incomes for different subgroups of the population.[3] One type of measure starts from the notion of a minimum level of consumption and attempts to translate that consumption into appropriate income levels. These measures take account of characteristics such as family size, age of head of family, sex of head of family, and geographic location. An attempt is made to determine specific budgets for specific types of families that can support a level of consumption regarded to be minimal. These budgets usually use nutritional requirements adapted to regional food patterns to establish expenditures on food. The total budget is then estimated on the assumption that food will equal one-third of the total budget. These budgets are used as standards for income with which to identify the poor for each subgroup of the population possessing the characteristics for which the given food budget was calculated.

It is evident that such standards fare better than simple income cut-off measures on a number of grounds. While they are considerably more complex because of the variety of circumstances affecting consumption that are considered, they are nevertheless explicitly consumption-related, at least to the degree of adjusting income levels of different groups of poor to their own consumption requirements. In addition, they enable meaningful comparison of various groups at one point in time or evaluation of changes in the number of poor over time. This last task requires constant updating by repricing the budget and, perhaps, revision of what is to be included in the market basket of "minimal" consumption. Nevertheless, these measures do attempt to deal explicitly with some of the problems which straight income cut-off measures do not.

An alternative approach to the development of equivalent poverty incomes for families of different composition and location is based on the varying relationships between share of income spent on food and the size of the income.[4] In the budgets noted above, food was assumed to be one-third of the total budget. However, there is considerable evidence that the fraction of income spent on various forms of consumption tends to change fairly systematically as the level of living of the family changes. This observation leads to a mechanism for deriving different poverty-income levels based on equivalent levels of living for subgroups with different family characteristics. All that is required initially is that some poverty-level income be set for one of the subgroups being considered (the base-line group). Although higher incomes are associated with a reduction in the share of income going to food purchases, larger families will spend on food proportions of their income similar to those of smaller families with smaller incomes. This leads to the obvious point that for a larger family, a higher income is needed to represent the same level of living as for a smaller family. This same approach can be applied to other family circumstances in terms of geographic location, urban-rural distribution, etc. The income level representing the poverty line for each separate group will be the income at which the percentage spent on food is the same as that spent by families in the base-line group at the previously determined poverty-income cut-off point.

It is important to note that by this last set of criteria, each family reflects in its spending patterns its view of its level of living, while in the previous method, budgetary equivalents are based on some explicit, externally established standards for what is a minimally acceptable mix of consumption. While stylistically these are two very different approaches, they nevertheless both represent attempts to incorporate into poverty-identification measures some explicit acknowledgment of factors that cause differences in the consumption opportunity associated with given incomes.

Another approach to the development of measures of poverty is to deal with poverty as a relative phenomenon. The assumption is that the specific disutility (or utility) associated with a given income is a function of the relationship between that income and some societal norm. This has led some to argue that one should assume that the bottom 20 per cent of the income distribution is poor and that policies should be directed at dealing with the social and economic circumstances of this group. Such a poverty-identification criterion is not wholly related to the consumption ability implicit in being at the lower end of the income distribution. One can envision a number of alternative distributions of income with very different implications for consumption for the bottom 20 per cent.

An alternative way of portraying the relative consumption capability of the lower 20 per cent is to examine over time the share of total income going to this group. From 1947 to 1962, the share of total money income going to the lowest 20 per cent ranged from 3.1 per cent to 3.6 per cent.[5] By contrast, the highest 20 per cent of income earners received from 43.1 per cent to 45.6 per cent. As there will always be a lowest 20 per cent, there is no basis in this measure for any policy aimed at reduction in the numbers of poor. Nevertheless, changes in the "size of the pie" and of the distribution of income are likely to lead to different estimates of the economic deprivation suffered by the lowest 20 per cent.

However, there are a number of more sophisticated approaches that also attempt to measure poverty in terms of relative economic levels that do not have this degree of specificity. Perhaps the best example of such an index is based on a suggestion that the poverty-income cut-off line should be approximately 50 per cent of the median income.[6] The cut-off point itself will shift automatically as the economic level of society in the aggregate is improved since such improvement will be reflected in a rising median income. It is evident that there could be a number of income distributions in the lower income levels. Although, by definition, 50 per cent of the population falls below the median, a very small percentage of the population could fall below one-half of the median. On the other hand, if the income distribution were spread out more toward the lowest income brackets, the group within the poverty range would be considerably greater.

There is much to commend this kind of an estimator. It does adapt itself over time to changes in the societal norms as reflected in incomes. Such a poverty-identification measure is easily developed; however, it does not distinguish among different distributions of income below the poverty cut-off line, and in this sense, is not different from the other identification measures noted earlier. This deficiency can be mitigated somewhat by attempts to estimate the "poverty gap," defined as the amount of expenditure that would be required to bring all families under the poverty cut-off income up to that level. Estimates of the poverty gap do reflect the income distribution of the poor; it is quite possible to find radically different poverty gaps for two situations in which the same number of persons fall below a particular poverty-line income.

Recent developments, exemplified by Harold Watts's chapter in this volume (Ch. 11), attempt to incorporate into an economic poverty-identification measure the distribution of incomes within the group designated as poor.[7] In Watts's measure, the degree of economic deprivation associated with being farther below the poverty line is made disproportionately greater than that of being closer to the cut-off line by using a weighting scheme based on the notion of decreasing marginal deprivation as income rises toward the poverty line. Thus, the amount of deprivation associated with a given number of poor would be reduced most by increasing the incomes of those farthest below the poverty line. This result reflects a particular distributional view of relative deprivation that determines the weighting system used; other weights could be chosen. Watts's index permits comparison over time both of the number of poor and of the relative disutility associated with the particular distribution of poverty.

PROBLEM AREAS IN THE ECONOMIC POVERTY-IDENTIFICATION MEASURES

The ideal poverty-identification measure should reflect a single, definable, quantifiable characteristic that all poor families and only poor families possess. It is very difficult to find a measure that identifies only those individuals or families everyone would agree are poor. However, all poverty measures must ultimately relate to ability to consume. Because consumption is a difficult thing to measure, and because there is a considerable degree of ambiguity in determining what the ability to consume means, most poverty-identification measures have centered on adapting information on family income. In all cases the adaptation is directed at one of two problems: either making the measure more consistent with intuitive and theoretical notions of what poverty is or compensating for some explicit breakdown in the "neatness" of the relationship between income and consumption. In this section, a number of the difficulties with the income-consumption relationship will be pointed out in an effort to make clear the potential misinformation incorporated in any poverty-identification measure based solely on income.[8]

The most obvious difficulty is that income-related measures tend to ignore alternative sources of consumption: income-in-kind, which is particularly significant for rural families, alternative sources of income from people who are not part of the household unit, and accumulated wealth. To some extent, wealth as a source of consumption is partly incorporated into indices using a concept of permanent income. The permanent-income concept is based on the assumption that a family's general level of consumption is determined by its long-run stable income, although in any given year income may be higher or lower. Perhaps the most significant association that might be pointed out here is that between ill health and low income. Typically, during periods of illness, families are found to spend considerably more than their incomes by dissaving or absorbing wealth in an effort to maintain a consumption level consistent with their usual practice. The lowness of income in the particular year of illness is considered to be a temporary circumstance. On the other hand, response to windfall income will be quite different from the family response to an increase of income from the regular earning sources which is expected to continue. At any rate, to the extent that there are alternative resources available for consumption, a purely income-based measure will not be wholly indicative of ability to consume.

A second area of difficulty stems from the fact that income measures ignore flows of consumption that are not purchased. Most significant are the public services such as education, fire and police protection, and trash collection. There is evidence of an association between the level of income in a neighborhood and the degree to which expenditures are made on public services. Public expenditures may not affect the distribution between poor and nonpoor, but the degree of relative deprivation associated with a given income may be blurred somewhat by ignoring these forms of consumption. It is likely that the lower level of public services available, for example, in an urban ghetto compared with a high-income community increases the degree of relative deprivation beyond that indicated by estimating only the income differences between the poor and the nonpoor.[9] It may be better to be poor in a rich town than poor in a poor town. One might prefer the latter for the company, but from an economic point of view, it is probably not a good exchange.

It is also possible that the degree of deprivation that a person with a low income feels is less than might be assumed. Certainly, those who do not subscribe to society's norms (a group ranging from hippies on the one hand to rich hermits "living in poverty" on the other) provide exceptions to the argument typically made for the notion of a societal norm as the basis for relative deprivation. It is not likely that such exceptions will make a large numerical difference; however, they illustrate the point that views of "appropriate" consumption or "adequate" incomes are based on collective societal standards and may or may not reflect an individual's view of whether or not he is poor. There is some evidence that many who show up as poor on our indices do not consider themselves poor, while many who would not show up on any poverty identification measure may very well feel themselves economically deprived.

One of the most difficult problems in translating income levels into consumption has to do with the degree to which it is possible to establish a cost for a given amount of consumption. To some extent, the amount of consumption implicit in any income level depends on prices. To the extent that prices change rapidly, any income-based measure of consumption potential used to identify the poor will require constant updating. More significant is the fact that the price levels used in translating specific budgets into an individual's income requirement tend to be based on general price levels in an area. There is considerable evidence that markets and pricing mechanisms are such that the poor tend to pay more, item by item, than those living in the same general area who are not poor.[10] Part of this is a reflection of geographic immobility that limits the markets that are relevant for low-income purchasers and part an inability to buy larger sizes so that the poor are always paying a premium for having little cash or being unable to obtain credit at a reasonable cost.

It is hard to estimate the degree to which the price differences exist, but some indication can be gained from the results of a recent examination of prices in three stores in an urban area, two of which serve primarily a low-income urban population, the third of which is part of a chain serving people throughout a major metropolitan area. In some cases, the prices were the same in the three stores, but in most, the prices in the two stores catering primarily to the poor were between 20 and 50 per cent higher for identical brands and sizes. Even between the two local stores (under the same ownership) price differences were observed, and, more significant, there was a considerable number of items with no prices marked. I am assured by many that the number of goods with no prices marked increases the day that welfare checks are distributed.

It is evident that the relationship between income and consumption is not a perfect one, and that income-based measures of poverty only partly reflect consumption ability. Nevertheless, they remain, and are likely to remain, the least ambiguous and most generally acceptable basis on which to identify the poor. Each of the various poverty-identification measures discussed above attempts to incorporate refinements that would make the income-based measure more reflective of the consumption needs of families.

POLICY CHOICES AND THE IDENTIFICATION MEASURE

It is important to examine some of the ways in which the use of the poverty-identification measure itself will have an impact on the selection of "appropriate" policies for dealing with poverty.

There are three directions for development of poverty policy. The first set of policies is devoted to reducing the number of poor. The second set of policies is directed toward increasing the amount of consumption possible with a given income. The third set relates to decreasing the disutility of poverty. Thus, policies can be directed at raising income, raising consumption, or improving certain environmental, social, and cultural circumstances of the poor that are considered to be inappropriate or undesirable. It is essential to note the implications of the fact that not all policies with regard to poverty are directed at a reduction of the number of poor. Because this is true, changes in the value of identification measures that enumerate the poor and distinguish them from the nonpoor will not serve as a performance measure for all policies directed toward the problems of poverty.

Certain kinds of policies that serve the over-all anti-poverty objectives will not have any impact whatever on any count of the poor. Insistence that income-related economic identification measures serve as the only performance guide favors policies that have some impact on reducing the numbers of the poor. This creates a bias away from policies dealing with cultural difficulties, providing nonincome forms of services, and dealing directly with the consumption-income relationship, a bias that may be inconsistent with the over-all objectives of poverty policy. It stems *not from anything inherent in the use of an economic measure of poverty for identification, but in requiring a poverty count to be a performance reflector for all the policies in operation.*

A difficulty that follows from the above is the shortening of the time horizon for evaluation. To the extent that good policies are considered to be those that reduce the number of the poor and bad policies are those that do not, a high premium will be placed on carrying out activities that take less time to show up in the form of increased income (that is, reduced poor). This means that human capital-investment policies directed at the reduction of the intergenerational transfer of poverty are likely to look worse in terms of performance than those policies that directly transfer resources in sufficient quantity to move individuals above the poverty line. *For example, make-work policies would be preferable to education for children, which has no short-run payoff. It is evident that such a short time-horizon may lead to policies that, over a longer time span, might not prove to be the best means of reducing the number of poor.* Judging activities that represent an investment in future earning capacity by this limited, immediate, economic performance measure tends to make it more likely that policy choices will, in the long run, be less than optimal.

The use of the economic identification measure as the sole performance guide also leads to a tendency to deal with the "easy" poor. By most such measures, some fixed amount of income represents the cut-off point between poor and nonpoor. To the extent that *x* dollars are going to be redistributed to bolster incomes, it would be "better" to concentrate on those individuals whose poverty gap (difference between the poverty cut-off line and their income) is smaller. This means that one would be less likely to devote resources toward improving the income position of an individual the farther his income falls below the poverty cut-off line. This same effect is observable in job-training-program selection criteria. The candidate preferred (and most likely to become a "success") is the one closest to "not needing" the training, just as the success of students from the best schools may be more a function of admission-selection procedures than of educational quality.

Explicit acknowledgment of this potentiality is found in the Watts measure in this volume in that a relatively higher premium is placed on a given unit of increased income for those farthest away from the poverty line than for those closer to it. Under the Watts poverty identification criterion, the optimal policy would be always to act so that resources were distributed to those who were the poorest. Such a decision criterion may be consistent with intuitive preferences, although it could lead to policies that resulted in no reduction in the number of the poor despite large expenditures. In fact, optimal policy might indicate no reduction in the number of poor until everyone was immediately adjacent to the poverty line, that is, the poverty gap for a group would be reduced without regard to the change in the number of poor. Insistence on use of reduction of the number of poor as a performance guide for poverty policies will tend to bias efforts away from longer term policies and policies directed at mitigating the circumstances of the poor, as well as from those that are directed specifically toward changing the amount of consumption attainable with a given income. Certainly, policies directed at improving the markets that serve the poor, increasing competition, making available a more extended purchasing area, and providing consumer counseling, all serve to improve the economic and consumption circumstances of the poor without changing their income levels at all. Such activities may be more fruitful in consumption terms than considerable increases of income although, using reduction of the number of the poor as a criterion, no improvement at all will follow from this type of policy.

FINAL COMMENTS

This chapter has been directed at a discussion of the development of poverty-identification measures based on income and the consumption-income relationship. Some of the implications of excessive reliance on poverty-identification measures as a substitute for more intensive analysis in terms of policy selection have also been described. In this connection, one might ask if raising incomes of the poor above the poverty cut-off for an extended period would leave a subgroup of population still identifiable as being unique and distinct from the rest of the population of the country. A considerable segment of opinion would argue that after an extended period (beyond a single generation or so) of living in poverty, even the elimination of low income would not serve to mitigate significantly many of the constraining circumstances of the poor. On the other hand, there are those who argue that, given a reasonable time period at a higher level of income, an erosion of the circumstances that generate the disutility of poverty would occur, and that, in the long run, it would be difficult to distinguish the previous poor from the previous nonpoor. The answer to this question clearly must come from a more intensive analysis of the characteristics of the poor and the tenacity of such characteristics in the absence of low income or in spite of increases in income.

Notes

1. This is the subject of causality analysis.
2. Council of Economic Advisers, *Annual Report* (January 1964), pp. 57–58.
3. Mollie Orshansky, "Counting the Poor: Another Look at the Poverty Profile," *Social Security Bulletin* (January 1965).
4. Harold Watts, "The Iso-Prop Index: An Approach to the Determination of Differential Poverty Income Thresholds," *The Journal of Human Resources* (Winter 1967), pp. 3–18.
5. Herman Miller, *Income Distribution in the United States*, 1960 Monograph, Bureau of the Census (1966), p. 21.
6. Victor Fuchs, "Toward a Theory of Poverty," in *The Concept of Poverty*, First Report, Task Force on Economic Growth and Opportunity, Chamber of Commerce (1965), pp. 71–91.
7. Harold Watts, "An Economic Definition of Poverty," this volume, Ch. 11.
8. Because the discussion in this chapter is restricted to poverty-identification measures, the important questions of longer run income levels and shifts in the group of poor from year to year are not dealt with. The identification measures typically treat current-year annual income as the appropriate base to reflect

consumption while the permanent-income approach attempts to incorporate a longer run view of income. Obviously, the stability of income may be as relevant as its size in any given year in determining the consumption position of a family. The suggestion, however, that the poor should be identified as those families whose lifetime income is below a lifetime poverty line implies more utility to posthumous designation of the poor than might be desirable. To infer lifetime income while the family head is not dead requires considerable reliance on current or recent previous-period incomes, subject to many of the difficulties noted.

9. See S. M. Miller et al., "Poverty, Inequality, and Conflict," *Annals of the American Academy of Political and Social Science* (September 1967) .

10. David Caplovitz, *The Poor Pay More* (New York: The Free Press of Glencoe, 1963) .

Appendix

☞ *Social Class Research and Images of the Poor: A Bibliographic Review*

Z A H A V A   D.   B L U M   and   P E T E R   H.   R O S S I

INTRODUCTION

Social class and social status may well be the most powerful of all the conceptual tools in the sociologist's kit of ideas about social life. We all share a strong interest in these topics; indeed, part of the power of these concepts is based on the fact that they refer to phenomena of widespread human interest. However, the main reason for the power of the concepts of social class and status is that their use in providing explanations of social behavior has led to increased understanding of the sources of differences among individuals and social groups.

Social class, social status, and their operational counterpart, socio-economic status, really came into their own with the development of large-scale empirical social research in the 1930s. The early community studies by Lynd and Warner drew attention from lay and professional audiences alike. From these investigations we learned in a more definitive way what we knew in our hearts all along: that America was a class society. From the researches that followed (which by now must number in the thousands), we learned things that were not so obvious deep in our hearts. Most important of all, we learned that socio-economic status created pervasive lines of differentiation in our population. We always knew that the poor had higher mortality rates than their more prosperous fellow citizens;

Support for the research underlying this chapter came from a grant from the American Academy of Arts and Sciences, a grant from the Russell Sage Foundation, and was written while the second author was on a Reflective Year Fellowship from Carnegie Corporation of New York. Their help is gratefully acknowledged.

that was an obvious conclusion to draw from the conditions under which the poor lived. However, we did not know many of the other things that empirical research brought to light; for example, socio-economic strata varied in their child-rearing practices, attitudes toward foreign policy, and regard for civil liberties. Even more striking was the fact that they varied in ways that went contrary to conventional commonsense "knowledge."

The tradition of research into the concomitants of socio-economic status is so extensive in time and breadth that it would seem extremely fruitful to examine existing studies in order to bring together what is known about the characteristics of the poor. After all, the poor, by any definition, anchor the bottom end of the socio-economic ladder and should therefore have received more than passing attention in the studies that have been conducted since the beginnings of empirical social research. Indeed, many of the early classics of sociological surveys were concerned with this group, for example, Booth's study of the London poor and the social surveys conducted in city after city in this country during the twenties. Some of this early traditional concern must certainly have been retained by later investigators, or so we thought.

The goal we had in mind in undertaking this survey of empirical findings about the poor was to sort out and display what was definitely known about the characteristics of the poor. Although we did not entirely achieve this goal, for reasons we shall later present, we did manage to uncover enough information to cast *some* light on the nature of socio-economic differences in general and to make *some* assertions about the characteristics of the poor. However, our survey of the literature also brought to light how little is known firmly and definitively about this group.

Like F. Scott Fitzgerald, sociologists have been fascinated by the rich and the powerful. The poor have not been fascinating enough to be studied in detail, although they are usually included in studies that cover the range of socio-economic differentiation.

We encountered other disappointments in our search of the literature. First of all, the writings about empirical findings have been generally stronger than the findings themselves. Americans of different socio-economic status are different in other respects, but there are blurred, rather than clear-cut, lines of distinction. Second, the findings have not been uniform either in direction or strength. Some investigators have found one tendency; others find another. These variations are due partly to method, partly to different time periods under study, and partly to rhetorics of interpretation. Finally, there are few studies that provide data representative of the nation as a whole. Most are community studies of limited generality.

Despite these drawbacks, we believe there is merit in presenting the review and summary of literature that occupies the next pages. We have been able finally to assess the state of our knowledge in this area. In some cases, we have been able to make fairly definite statements; in others, the evidence is so weak and fragile that it is only clear that we do not know very much. We have been able to show that it is not very likely that the poor show characteristics that are distinctively different from those of groups that are close to them in social standing. Socio-economic status is more a continuum than a set of discrete classes. The end result of our endeavors has been to place bounds on our knowledge and to indicate the gaps in our understanding.

A REVIEW OF THE LITERATURE ON SOCIAL CLASS AND POVERTY

Since the literature dealing with social class as a variable is considerable, it was obvious from the start that the entire body of this literature could not be surveyed. Consequently, a number of topics had to be omitted at the outset and some limits established on the inclusion of material. Since our bias is in the direction of empirical sociology, our coverage of a number of related disciplines is undoubtedly incomplete. The most serious omission is the economic treatment of poverty, an area in which we may claim no particular competence. A number of areas within the usual meaning of social stratification (for example, occupational prestige, social mobility, and stratification theory) were excluded from the start. We have also eliminated studies dealing with social-class measurement and methodology.

We began by systematically screening each issue of the major sociological journals, and a number of related publications, from 1950 to 1966.[1] Articles that dealt with the correlates of social-class

1. *American Journal of Sociology, American Sociological Review, Journal of Educational Sociology, Journal of Abnormal and Social Psychology, Journal of Social Issues, Marriage and Family Living, Public Opinion Quarterly, Social Forces, Social Problems, Social Work, Sociometry, Welfare in Review.*

position were read and abstracted. Relevant references to separate monographs or to journal articles not subject to the screening were also read and abstracted. In addition, published collections of articles and conference proceedings dealing with poverty were covered. A preliminary draft of our bibliography was circulated to participants in the seminar on poverty and to other interested persons. As a result of their cooperation, many omissions were called to our attention, and some unpublished material made available to us. An earlier version of this chapter was presented at the August 1967 meeting of the Sociological Research Association, San Francisco, California, and we have incorporated many of the suggestions arising from that presentation in the present revision. In spite of precautions, there are obvious gaps. There is no sure way of estimating the number of relevant articles missed by our screening methods. More serious, since the start of the War on Poverty a great deal of research on the "poor" has been undertaken. Unless, either through chance or sociometric referral, unpublished memoranda from these ongoing researches have passed through our hands, projects that may in a few years contribute the bulk of our knowledge concerning the characteristics of the present-day "poor" are not systematically covered.

Our original screening, plus the referrals, netted approximately 750 articles and books; clearly, some criteria had to be established for putting manageable bounds on the material to allow for integration and analysis. Given our bias toward empirical research, most of the impressionistic articles dealing with the poor have been excluded. Research studies with obvious deficiencies in either research design, sampling methods, or analysis were excluded on the grounds that their findings and interpretations were unknowable or limited of value. In principle, this is a sound approach; in practice, it has its limitations. A number of areas, for example, the place of work in individual self-identification, the possible differential handling of delinquents from various social classes by law-enforcement agencies, the uses of leisure by social class, or the ideology of welfare, are so sparsely researched that we had to rely on every shred of evidence available for interpretation. In a number of other areas, for example, child-rearing practices, educational and occupational aspirations of adolescents, and studies relating socio-economic status and performance on intelligence tests, the literature is so extensive that the citations, perforce, reflect some degree of selection among works we considered to be equivalent in value.

A. THE DATA RECONSIDERED

The published literature dealing with those on the very bottom of the stratification system is on the whole somewhat limited. To begin with, few studies have been concerned with systematically describing the characteristics of the very poor, the outstanding exception being the Survey Research Center's survey of income and labor force participation, based on a probability national sample augmented by oversampling of low-income households (Morgan et al., 1962). We are thus left in the position of creating a collage from numerous findings, collected in different places and at different times. Since few studies have utilized probability samples of the national populace, it is questionable how reliable available results are as estimates of the country's "true" patterns. The available studies lead us to suspect the existence of appreciable regional and ethnic differences in class-related behavior, but these subgroup variations have yet to be systematically documented.

Second, in order to compare findings across studies, it is important that the discrete groupings into which the study populations are divided be consistent. By and large, however, researchers have tended to dichotomize their study populations, the most common being "working/middle-class" or "blue/white-collar" divisions. Even among studies that use the same gross dichotomy, for example, "working/middle-class," the cutting points utilized are often different, so that comparisons are difficult to make. It is obvious that this dichotomization and use of ordinal scales can lead to different interpretations of identical "raw" findings, since a change in the cutting point between groups can lead to a change in the observed percentage differences. A number of researchers have continuously stressed that variations in behavior are present within these groupings that should not be overlooked. Yet, for example, the typology suggested by S. M. Miller (1964) or Walter Miller's (1958) characterization of the lower class in terms of six "focal concerns" has not been rigorously tested.[2] In many instances, data are available from which to

2. The study by Cohen and Hodges (1963) is a notable attempt to characterize the "lower-blue-collar" class and its differences from our groups; but even there, as the authors admit, "the interpretations are post facto attempts to make sense of our data." Another example is the comparison of the child-rearing environment and family functioning of "upper-lower" and "very low-lower" class families by Pavenstedt (1965). The over-all theoretical orientation of this study, however, was psychoanalytic, and the criteria for dividing families into the two groups do not lend themselves to replication.

make finer distinctions, but because the samples are small, the authors collapse their categories and so obliterate finer points.

Third, most of the writers have been so impressed with the finding that socio-economic position (no matter how measured) is associated with a variety of dependent variables that they have generally not taken the further steps of assessing the strength or degrees of relationship or attempting to explain why such relationships are found. Few investigators have employed measures of association that allow the reader to assess how strongly a particular dependent variable is related to socio-economic status. As a consequence, descriptive statements usually lend themselves to somewhat exaggerated views of class differences. For example, the literature on "need achievement" contains findings that, when translated into correlation coefficients, are of the order of .2–.4, but descriptive statements about the findings give the impression that there are strikingly different orientations to achievement by socio-economic status. To some extent, these ambiguities in the literature have carried over into this chapter.

Similarly, the finding that socio-economic status is correlated with some dependent variable is very infrequently followed up with either further empirical specification or speculation concerning the causal nexus between SES and the dependent variable in question. With the notable exceptions of Merton (1957) and Kriesberg (1963), who have attempted to work out rationales for class differences, most social scientists typically regard such findings as ultimate explanations requiring little further exploration. For example, the relationship between SES and tests of intellectual functioning has been documented for decades, yet only recently has one of the prior variables, that is, linguistic development, been studied. The precise effects of some intervening variables, such as quality of education, are still unclear. We could, by drawing elaborate causal models based on numerous studies, reconstruct some of these relationships, but the problem of markedly different sampling designs from study to study would obstruct such an effort. Or, the inverse relationship between socio-economic status and divorce is well documented, but with the exception of William Goode's (1951, 1966) explanation and the Moynihan report, few studies have set out to study this relationship empirically with a sample large enough to allow for the possibility that different mechanisms may be causing the relationship observed at different levels. A study of the structure and functioning of the Negro family in the United States, to the best of our knowledge, has not been published.[3] As a consequence of the research of the past few decades, we know a lot about *what* the differences are among socio-economic groups, but very little about *why* such differences exist.

Two additional problems were encountered, but not solved to our complete satisfaction: comparability of findings and the histori-cal period that the studies cover. The research technology available to social scientists has grown rapidly in sophistication over the period surveyed; researchers in the mid-sixties have access to electronic com-puters that were unavailable to the researcher of the fifties. More funds for research were available in the later period. Consequently, comparisons and juxtapositions of findings from different periods are fraught with danger. Furthermore, we have no way of assessing whether some of the findings reported at the start of our period are still relevant today, or conversely. Consequently the reader is cau-tioned not to regard the empirical information related in our analy-sis as holding for all times and places. For example, the political apathy of the poor is well documented, but under certain circum-stances, such as the 1967 racial riots, politicization of the poor can occur.[4]

WHO ARE THE "POOR"?

In the current literature on the poor and in policy discussions the definition of poverty is an unresolved problem. All agree that those living in poverty are persons and households that have consid-erably less than average access to goods and services and considerably less than average financial and other resources. There is no agree-ment, however, on where to draw the poverty line, that is, on what constitutes minimum adequacy and on how many Americans can be considered "poor." This disagreement can be expected to continue indefinitely for two reasons: First, because no index and no cutting point will do everything that every party to the dispute would desire, and second, because social change will not acquiesce in the preserva-tion of any index.[5]

3. E. Franklin Frazier's (1939) classic study, now more than thirty years old, rests heavily on relatively slight research and is geared to a period in American Negro history that is now long past.

4. In this sense, Marx' characterization of the *lumpenproletariat* as, at best, politically inert, and at worst, counter-revolutionary, was historically conditioned.

5. Examples of these discussions can be found in Gordon (1965), Harrington (1962), Orshansky (1965), W. H. Locke Anderson (1964), and Ferman et al. (1965).

Part of the disagreement over the concepts of the "poor" and of "poverty" stems from the distinction, often implicit, made by many writers, between two types of poverty and of poor people. On the one hand, there are the "respectable" poor, persons who are just like standard middle-class Americans except that they have less income and wealth. On the other hand, there are the "disreputable" poor, those who not only have limited resources, but also behave differently or hold values different from those of standard middle-class Americans. For example, Warner and his students (1949) distinguish a lower-lower class from an upper-lower class primarily on the basis of values and behavior.[6] Marx (1914) used the term *lumpenproletariat* to characterize the most disorganized and bestialized element of the working class. He predicted that the *lumpenproletariat* would be used by counter-revolutionary forces to oppose the righteous revolution of the working class.[7]

Contemporary discussions of the poor distinguish between those who, because of events of their life cycle or the chance happenings of disaster, "happen" to be suffering from a low level of income and wealth (the aged, the sick, the disabled, the victims of economic dislocations) and the "chronic" poor, those who are unable to "make a go of it" because of character deficiencies or lack of skill. It is the latter group upon which the greatest attention is centered. A set of terms has been filtering into the literature to characterize this group: "the new poor," "multiproblem families," the "new working class," "unstable families," "the culture of poverty," and so on. Other terms (for example, the "disreputable poor" and "paupers") have been refurbished, usually encased in quotation marks, presumably to indicate that they are being used without old-fashioned pejorative connotations. Note that all of these terms are used to imply that something more than income is missing in this group. They indicate that these are people who are poor and who cannot cope with their poverty despite their lack of any obvious physical and mental disabilities. These are people who "make noise," "cause trouble," and generally

6. In *Social Class in America*, Warner distinguishes a "common-man" level described by his respondents as "poor but respectable," "poor but honest," and "poor but hardworking," from a "below the common man level" described as "river rats," "peckerwoods," "dirty and immoral," and "those who live like pigs."

7. In the *18th Brumaire*, Marx writes: "Along with ruined *roués* of questionable means of support and questionable antecedents, along with foul and adventure-seeking dregs of the bourgeoisie, there were vagabonds, dismissed soldiers, discharged convicts, runaway galley slaves, . . . —in short, the whole undefined, dissolute, kicked-about mass that the Frenchmen style 'la bohême.'"

create "problems" for the rest of society.[8] The "poor," then, to whom the major amount of attention is addressed in the new literature on poverty, are those whose income is low (excluding the disabled, the retired, and the temporarily poor), who are unable to cope successfully even at a minimal level with their poverty and who present problems to society. Although no single writer employs precisely this definition, we think it covers the essential features of most.[9]

There are two important distinctions of this definition: First, the definition stresses the noneconomic aspects of poverty and hence is more in keeping with social policies that are directed at changing values and behavior than with policies that stress full employment and income maintenance. Second, it is a definition that easily becomes circular: The target population is defined as poor because they manifest certain characteristic problems; the problems are then explained as due to the fact that the target population is poor.

This new literature that describes the specific characteristics of the "lower-lowers" (to use Warner's neutral term) tends to consist of case studies or qualitative field observations rather than extensive, quantitative, systematic analyses of population characteristics. Perhaps because the literature is so meager there is considerable agreement among writers concerning specific characteristics that are manifested by the "lower-lowers." These features include:

1. *Labor-Force Participation*. Long periods of unemployment and/or very intermittent employment. Public assistance is frequently a major source of income for extended periods.

2. *Occupational Participation*. When employed, persons hold jobs at the lowest levels of skills, for example, domestic service, unskilled labor, menial service jobs, and farm labor.

3. *Family and Interpersonal Relations*. High rates of marital instability (desertion, divorce, separation), high incidence of households headed by females, high rates of illegitimacy; unstable and

8. As Matza (1966) points out, this is especially evident in the British term, "problem family," and the American adaptation, "multiproblem family."

9. Jerome Cohen, 1964; Engel, 1966; Harrington, 1962; O. Lewis, 1965; Lockwood, 1960; Matza, 1966; S. M. Miller, 1964a, 1964b; Walter Miller, 1958, 1959; Pavenstedt, 1965; Riessman, 1962, 1964; and Schneiderman, 1964, 1965. Of these writers, S. M. Miller has attempted to elaborate a typology of the lower classes, distinguishing essentially between the "hopeless" poor and those who are attempting to cope with their problems.

superficial interpersonal relationships characterized by considerable suspicion of persons outside the immediate household.

4. *Community Characteristics.* Residential areas with very poorly developed voluntary associations and low levels of participation in such local voluntary associations as exist.

5. *Relationship to Larger Society.* Little interest in, or knowledge of, the larger society and its events; some degree of alienation from the larger society.

6. *Value Orientation.* A sense of helplessness and low sense of personal efficacy; dogmatism and authoritarianism in political ideology; fundamentalist religious views, with some strong inclinations toward beliefs in magical practices. Low "need achievement" and low levels of aspirations for the self.

Although several other characteristics could be added to this inventory, our informal content analysis of the literature indicates that these characteristics are those over which there is considerable consensus and that tend to be stressed as critical features of the "lower-lowers."

Dissent among writers centers around three issues: First, there is the question of whether the "lower-lowers" are "happy" or not. Some writers extol the spontaneity of expression among this group, while others ascribe the same phenomenon to lack of impulse control. Some see the poor as having a fine and warm sense of humor, but others regard their humor as bitter and sad. Some claim that the poor are desperately trying to change their condition, sinking into apathy when it becomes clear to them that the odds are greatly against their being able to do so; others deny that a strong desire for change exists.

The second major point of disagreement arises over whether or not the "lower-lowers" have developed a contra-culture—a rejection of the core values of American society—or whether they are best characterized by what Hyman Rodman (1963) calls "value stretch," a condition in which the main values are accepted as valid, by persons, who, nonetheless, exempt themselves from fulfilling the requirement of norms.[10]

10. As described in Rodman (1963), the concept of "value stretch" is a phenomenon not peculiar to the "lower-lowers." No normative system is adhered to completely by everyone in the society, and depending upon the norms in question,

A third issue over which there is some disagreement concerns the extent to which the characteristics of the poor are "cultural" or "situational." From the point of view of some writers, many features of "lower-lower" life are passed on from generation to generation forming a "culture (or subculture) of poverty," which once started is as difficult to change as any other valid culture (O. Lewis, 1965; Walter Miller, 1958). Other writers stress the situational determinants of these characteristics, indicating that they arise as accommodative responses to the conditions of poverty (Kriesberg, 1963; Rainwater, 1966). Obviously, this issue to some extent overlaps the second area of disagreement described above: A contra-culture is a subculture although a subculture need not necessarily be set up in opposition to the main cultural streams of a society.

Even if we had limited our discussion to those sets of characteristics about which minimal consensus exists, it still would have been a major undertaking to draw a definitive portrait of the poor. The major reason for this difficulty is that the literature describing the "lower-lower" class does not provide us with information on the relative weights to be attributed to these characteristics. Thus, if we take the position that a person (or household) is to be counted as a member of the "lower-lower" group if and only if he manifests each and every one of the characteristics described above, then it is obvious that extremely small numbers of the population would fall into the group so defined. The addition of each characteristic necessarily restricts the eligible population, except when characteristics are very highly correlated with each other. It is doubtful, however, whether such a rigorous definition of the poor is subscribed to by any one of the writers whose orientations we have discussed.

It seems more sensible to apply these defining characteristics according to some sort of scale. However, in this case, the critical question becomes what weight should be given to each of the characteristics, that is, which are the most essential characteristics, the absence or presence of which should more definitely determine whether or not an individual or household is to be a member of the "lower-lower" class. At the simplest level, the presence or absence

---

the latitude given for compliance can be considerable. For example, adultery has undoubtedly been widespread throughout the whole range of American social strata, although there is clear evidence from attitude surveys that legitimate sexual alliances are to be preferred over adulterous ones. If there is any reason for the concept to be applied to the "lower-lowers" with more force than to any other group in American society, it is that their lives (for a variety of reasons) depart from standard American in more areas and more dramatically.

of each characteristic can be weighted in deciding whether or not an individual or household is to be counted among the "lower-lowers." Then the critical question becomes what weight should be given to each of the characteristics, which are the more essential characteristics that should be given greater weight in determining placement among the "lower-lowers." [11]

Although most of the writers have not been particularly clear on this point, we assume that occupation is the sine qua non of the "lower-lowers." Hence, "lower-lower" characterizes persons or households whose main breadwinner is permanently unemployed and/or, when employed, holds down occupations on the lowest-skill and lowest-income levels. However, since, according to the literature, not all such persons should be considered members of the "lower-lower" class, persons in this group have to manifest some, or all, of the other characteristics described in order to be considered members of the "lower-lower" class.

In short, a person—or household—to be considered of the "lower-lower" class displays certain occupational characteristics and also some (as yet unspecified) combination of behavioral or attitudinal characteristics.[12] For the purposes of this chapter it was not necessary to come to grips fully with this question; our main concern was with the general correlates of socio-economic position.

The overview of our knowledge about the poor, presented earlier in this volume, was derived from a synthesis of the empirical literature and a comparison between these findings and the composite picture derived from the qualitative and impressionistic material just presented. If the differences shown in the empirical material between middle class and working class were such that an extrapolation from them resulted in a prediction of "lower-lower" class behavior that is *consistent* with the descriptions provided in our composite portrait, then we would have some basis for inferring that

11. Note that Warner bypasses this question entirely by defining membership in a particular class in terms of some sort of consensus in a community that the individual or household in question belongs in that class (Warner, 1949b). Hence, his definition of the "lower-lowers" is perhaps the least subject to circularity, although the most difficult to apply in a given empirical situation.

12. Obviously, this is not yet a workable definition, since the way in which these secondary characteristics are to be combined in an index or scale has yet to be specified. Exactly how some of the writers on the poor (see especially O. Lewis, 1965) come up with estimates of the proportion of the total population who are "lower-lower" or "living in the culture of poverty" is something of a mystery. We suspect that these estimates are arrived at by considering a combination of income and occupation, eliminating those who are "merely" poor by subtracting the old, disabled, and temporarily unemployed, leaving the residual as those "living in the culture of poverty."

the "lower-lower" class is not qualitatively different from the rest of society but simply more extreme in these behaviors. On the other hand, if extrapolation from known differences had resulted in predictions that were inconsistent with our composite portrait we would have had reason to infer that the poor are indeed qualitatively different from the rest of the population. As argued above, however, our findings indicated that the major differences are *quantitative,* not *qualitative.*

It could be said that our strategy was deficient: On the one hand, we constructed a composite portrait based on nonsystematic and impressionistic evidence and, on the other hand, confronted it with almost two decades of empirical research. Indeed, it may even be argued that this portrait is incorrect and that no conclusive inferences can be made. It is our belief, however, that given the current state of knowledge about the poor, our conclusion was the most reasonable. The question of the accuracy of our inferences and extrapolations cannot be resolved until the large-scale, quantitative studies of representative samples of the poor provide the necessary documentation.

THE CORRELATES OF SOCIO-ECONOMIC STATUS

This part of the chapter is a series of short stories, each covering a substantive area in which some social-class differentials have been found. In condensed form, these sections provide for the reader the "raw data" from which we have drawn many of our inferences about the poor in the United States. The synthesis attempted within each area will also provide a useful entry point for social scientists and laymen to the literature on social class and poverty.

The classification system employed here attempts to be systematic but is clearly not the only way these studies can be grouped. Some readers may find it useful to rearrange findings in what are analytically more useful ways. In the case of small studies or laboratory experiments classification was not difficult, and extracting the major finding was an easy task. When we were confronted with large-scale national surveys, the problem was more difficult. In these cases, we have reported one or two relevant findings and left the fuller richness of the socio-economic status materials to be investigated by the reader.

Both in the text itself and in numerous footnotes we have indicated sources of additional information or corroborative studies. It should be remembered that the main reason for citing a study is not because it is an exemplar of empirical research but because it provides some evidence, no matter how precariously established, concerning socio-economic status and its correlates. We are aware that both our citations and bibliography may leave the reader with an enigma: Namely, was omitted material with which he is personally acquainted merely overlooked or considered inadequate for inclusion? We hope that the discussion of our method and some of the criteria for selection set forth in the preceding section will help resolve such issues.

A. COMMUNITY ORGANIZATION AND PARTICIPATION IN VOLUNTARY ASSOCIATIONS

The literature on poverty and the poor describes the areas inhabited by the "lower-lowers" as severely lacking in community organization; that is, the voluntary associations usually found in many middle-class areas, whose purposes are to look after the collective interests and the commonwealth of the area in question, are not present. Consequently, it is difficult to locate and negotiate with "indigenous" leaders who can legitimately speak for, and make commitments on behalf of, area inhabitants. Even those local voluntary associations that can be found, for example, churches and social clubs, tend to be concerned with their own particular affairs and not with the neighborhood community or public interests in general.

This is not to imply that the areas occupied by the poor are socially disorganized. Whyte (1943) and Gans (1962) both demonstrate that individuals in the slums are connected to each other in complicated networks of peer and kinship groups. However, organizations concerned with community affairs, both internally and in dealing with the larger society, are relatively rare. Gans, for example, notes the relative helplessness of the people he studied to organize sufficiently to halt the redevelopment of their neighborhood.

So rare are those working-class or "lower-lower" neighborhoods that do manage to achieve some degree of community organization that a great deal of attention has been paid to the few examples which exist. Alinsky's (1946) successful organization of the Back-of-the-Yards neighborhood of Chicago during the thirties and his later, even more dramatic, organization of Woodlawn, a "lower-lower"

Negro slum of Chicago (Silberman, 1964) are prime examples of successful organization in types of areas usually characterized as lacking in community organization.[13]

Systematic studies directly touching upon the density of voluntary associations by areas are few. Rossi (1956) studied four areas in Philadelphia and found by canvassing voluntary associations in each area that the two high-status areas had many more voluntary associations than the two low-status areas.[14] Glazer and Moynihan (1963) argue that the main difference that accounted for the rapid rise in social status of some immigrant groups (namely, the Jews) and the relatively retarded rise of others (notably Italians, Negroes, and Irish) was the lack of voluntary mutual-aid associations in areas occupied by the latter.

At the level of individual participation in voluntary associations, research findings are more plentiful. Hausknecht (1962) reanalyzed two national sample surveys and found participation in voluntary associations to be positively related to education, occupation, and income, although also related to stages in the life cycle, with heaviest participation among the middle aged. This study also concurs with our previous statements that not only do participation rates differ, but also the types of organizations to which lower-status individuals belong are different. Wright and Hyman (1958) present evidence from two national probability samples and a number of metropolitan area samples and find similar patterns, along with fairly strong ethnic and religious differences.[15]

Participation in specific voluntary associations also shows the same pattern of higher rates of membership and participation on the part of persons from higher socio-economic levels. Erich Goode (1966) compares the religious behavior of two national samples (the first predominantly white, Protestant, rural, and blue-collar; the second a white, Congregationalist, urban, white-collar, and high-income sample) and finds that church participation (as measured by attend-

13. Other recent examples of concerted attempts to build community organization in unorganized, urban, lower-class areas are Mobilization for Youth, operating on New York's lower East Side, Haryou-Act in Harlem, and the various Community Action Programs sponsored by the Office of Economic Opportunity. Marris and Rein (1967) discuss the evolution of many of the recent programs, giving special attention to the philosophies behind them. Unfortunately, they do not present much information on the success or failure of the attempts to organize these areas.

14. Note that neither low-status area would qualify as being primarily a "lower-lower" neighborhood.

15. Many other researchers working with smaller and less extensive samples report the same findings (for example, Dotson, 1951; Reissman, 1954; Foskett, 1955).

ance, membership, and officeholding in church organizations) is positively associated with social status.[16] Greeley and Rossi (1966) find the same pattern among Roman Catholics, with attendance at mass and the performance of ritual duties more frequent among higher-status Catholics. Demerath (1966) argues that there are differences among socio-economic levels in styles of religious behavior, with the higher levels being more committed to church organization and ritual and lower-status people being more concerned with devotion and "spirit." Erich Goode (1966) suggests that for the middle class, church activity has become secularized, so that it is an extension of over-all associational participation whereas for the lower class it is more intrinsically religious in character.

Participation in political activities is also inversely related to socio-economic levels. Matthews (1954) found that the socio-economic status of legislators on all levels was predominantly upper-middle class, with lawyers constituting a majority of congressmen and senators. Persons with working-class occupations were found very infrequently, and then only on local legislative bodies (for example, city councils in small cities). In a review of a series of studies, Woodward and Roper (1950) found that lower-status individuals are much less likely to vote, belong to organizations that took stands on political issues, discuss political issues with their friends, write or talk to congressmen or other public officials, contribute money to a political party or to a candidate, or attend meetings at which political speeches were made.

Studies of involvement in public decision-making also reveal the same pattern. In a review of studies of participation in decision-making, Wendell Bell et al. (1961) find that working-class individuals are rarely implicated as playing direct or indirect roles in the making of public decisions. Strodtbeck et al. (1965) found that even when lower-status individuals are brought into a decision-making situation as in the case of experimental juries, they tend to participate less in discussion, to be less often elected as jury foremen, and not to be regarded as contributing very much to the discussion by other participants.

The major studies of voting behavior conducted by the Survey Research Center of Michigan (Campbell et al., 1960, 1966) as well as others[17] clearly document the lowered rates of participation in elec-

16. Goode's article contains references to a great many relevant studies dealing with various aspects of social class and church participation.
17. See Lipset et al. (1954) for a review of major voting studies.

tions on the part of lower-status individuals. Particularly important has been the finding that lower-status persons have a lower sense of "political efficacy," that is, they feel that their efforts directed toward influencing the outcome of political decision-making would not have any appreciable effect.

Finally, we turn to studies of participation in informal forms of social interaction. Rossi (1956) found that lower-status individuals have fewer friends and are less likely to visit with relatives and neighbors, a finding also partly reported by Cohen and Hodges (1963).[18] King (1961), reviewing the results of four sociometric studies, showed that although individuals at all status levels tend to choose friends from one's own level, lower socio-economic status (SES) individuals also make unreciprocated upper-status choices. Curtis (1963) reports that lower-class individuals tend to associate more with individuals within their own socio-economic categories than do high-status individuals. In an analysis of social behavior, Muir and Weinstein (1962) find that lower socio-economic status families restrict socializing to their immediate families and neighbors, while higher socio-economic status individuals have a much broader range of friends and acquaintances.

B. MORBIDITY, MORTALITY, AND THE UTILIZATION OF MEDICAL SERVICES

Nineteenth- and early twentieth-century descriptions of the poor heavily stress the higher incidence of physical illnesses among the poor and their relatively short life span. Indeed, the major emphasis of the public-health movement (Simmons, 1958) was on eliminating those conditions that sustained the lowered chances of life of the poor. The success of the public-health movement, coupled with the sharp rise in standards of living, has significantly lowered the incidence of illness and raised the average life expectancy of the total population.

In a review article, Kadushin (1964) argues that socio-economic differentials in the incidence of disease were almost eliminated by the post-World War II period and refers to ten studies that he feels substantiate his position. Recently, Antonovsky (1967) raised some strong objections to this argument, although granting that there is

---

18. Cohen and Hodges report that lower-class respondents say that they interact more with kin both *absolutely* and also relative to their interaction with neighbors, friends from work, and friends they have met elsewhere.

merit in Kadushin's suggestion that there are intervening variables between social class and disease. In re-examining the studies cited by Kadushin, Antonovsky concludes that only a study by Graham (1958) supports Kadushin's hypothesis. The studies that we have found, in addition to those discussed in the debate, present a mixed picture. Thus, Mayer and Hauser (1950) analyzed life tables for Chicago for the period 1920 to 1940 and showed that expectations of life at birth for racial and socio-economic groups converged during this period, although substantial differences still remained between whites and nonwhites. Ellis (1958), in an analysis of mortality records from 1949 to 1951 for the city of Houston, Texas, also finds mortality rates inversely related to socio-economic status, with the major differences between the lowest socio-economic status group and others, and particularly high death rates in this group from chronic diseases. In a unique study of the interaction over time between illness and socio-economic status, Lawrence (1958) examined the prevalence of illness in a sample of 1,310 families in 1923 and 1943 and found an inverse relationship in both periods. However, the data indicate that chronic illness may be more significant as a factor in reducing socio-economic status than as a consequence of status.

In a review article of the social and cultural factors involved in infant mortality, Anderson (1958) concludes that when the gross relationships of infant mortality and various social factors are examined, there is a negative correlation between social status and infant-mortality rates; however, "the nearer the infant-mortality rate approaches a virtually irreducible minimum in terms of our present knowledge, the less operative are the social and environmental factors and the more operative are so-called 'maternal efficiency,' 'copability,' and other personal factors (p. 23)." Two more studies dealing with socio-economic status and infant mortality bear out Anderson's statement: Stockwell (1962), in a study of neonatal mortality in Providence from 1949 to 1951, found that there was not very much difference between class levels, except for deaths, in the post-neonatal period (after one month), at which point the lower socio-economic levels had higher rates due to infectious diseases and accidental deaths. Willie (1959), in a similar study in Syracuse, also finds very little difference in neonatal deaths by socio-economic status.

Graham (1963) in a review of studies of chronic illness finds a confusing and irregular pattern of relationships to socio-economic levels. For example, some studies show that hypertension is positively related to socio-economic status, while others show a negative relationship; or, that cancers at different body sites relate differently to socio-economic status.

Statistics from the U.S. National Health Survey, 1962–1963, showing the number of days of disability according to income class from below $2,000 up to $7,000 were divided into "restricted activity days per person," "bed disability days per person," "days in hospital per hospitalized person," and "days of work-loss due to injury per usually working person." These statistics reveal that, comparing four disability categories, the percentages are higher for those earning below $2,000.[19]

Page 74 of the report states that

1. Rates of disability days are inversely related to the amount of family income, even with adjustment for differences in the age distribution within income intervals.
2. Based on unadjusted data, a person with family income of less than $2,000 has, on the average, 16 days more of restricted activity than a person with an income of $7,000 or more. Comparable differentials were 7 additional days of bed disability and 4 days more lost from work. The rate of days lost from school was fairly constant for all income levels.
3. The number of disability days attributable to chronic illness and impairment was highest among persons with family income of less than $2,000 and decreased consistently with higher amounts of income. Disability days associated with acute illness or injury remained fairly constant regardless of amount of family income. The relatively higher rate of disability days due to chronic illness in the lowest income group is influenced to some extent by the comparatively high proportion of older persons in this group.

It is important to note, however, that the above findings discuss income, and that most of the empirical work discussed earlier considers composite measures of social status.

Studies reporting socio-economic differences in the utilization of medical services are more consistent in their findings: Ross (1962), reanalyzing data from the National Health Surveys for 1957–1959, found a direct relationship between the average number of visits to physicians and social class. When the visits are analyzed in terms of the type of service that was received from the physician, the findings indicate that upper-class persons were more likely to be seeking pre-

19. U.S. National Center for Health Statistics, *Medical Care, Health Status, and Family Income*. Washington, D.C., Department of Health, Education, and Welfare, Public Health Service, 1964, Series 10, No. 9.

ventive services, while lower-class persons mainly go to the doctor due to some acute complaint. Kriesberg and Treiman (1960) found similar tendencies with respect to utilization of dental services in a national sample of 1,862 respondents. Graham (1958) also reports that in the same county in which there are no discernible class differences in illness, 58 per cent of the highest-status respondents had consulted a physician during the study period, while only 40 per cent of the lowest-status group had done so. Laughton et al. (1958), in an analysis of the records of a small sample (N = 105) of families participating in a prepaid medical-care plan in Canada, found that class differences in the utilization of services were not statistically significant. They suggest that under conditions in which financial factors are not important, class differences in the utilization of medical services tend to disappear.[20]

Kadushin (1964), in the review noted earlier, also hypothesizes that lower-class persons are more concerned about illness and experience feeling ill more frequently than upper-class persons. The greater concern over illness expressed by low socio-economic status persons stems from their lesser knowledge of medicine and the greater consequences of disease for their lives. The greater fear of both medicine and the consequences of disease leads to less utilization of medical services. We did find shreds of evidence to support the greater anxiety and lack of knowledge about illness that Kadushin suggests: Deasy (1956) found in a study of the mothers (130) of second-grade children participating in field trials of a polio vaccine that lower socio-economic status mothers were less likely to allow their children to participate and less likely to know the purposes of the field trial. Ossenberg (1962), in a study of 75 patients hospitalized for similar disorders, found that low-status patients were more anxious about their illnesses, less resigned to their illnesses, and more inclined to procrastinate in seeking medical help than high-status patients.[21] Levine (1962), controlling for the adequacy of local medical facilities, shows that lower-class persons are more fearful of serious disease. Jenkins (1966) reports, from a study of 436 respondents in a Florida community, that Negro respondents, perceiving a greater

20. Laughton's sample, however, is not representative of the socio-economic continuum, since membership in a prepaid medical plan is often contingent on regular employment and/or enough funds to maintain monthly payments.

21. In this study, the findings cannot be accounted for by economic factors, since most of the lower-class patients were on welfare relief and payments were not discontinued during hospitalization; moreover, their hospital expenses were covered.

prevalence of tuberculosis than whites, were much more concerned about tuberculosis.

In sum, the data presented above lead us to agree with Antonovsky's (1967) conclusions:

There have doubtless been major changes during the twentieth century in the extent to which there are class differences in the traditional intervening variables—Malthus' "vice and misery"—which linked class to disease. But . . . the data are far from conclusive in demonstrating the disappearance of class differences in disease.

We might add to this that in the utilization of medical services the existence of class differences is very marked.

C. DELINQUENCY

The observation that the lower socio-economic status levels contribute more than their proportionate share to juvenile delinquency and adult criminality is firm enough to require little further documentation. However, it is necessary to keep it in mind that in the statistics usually cited, delinquency and criminality are defined by actions taken by the law-enforcement agencies, processes that offer many points at which selective treatment can enter. In short, no one knows the *true* rates of criminal or delinquent acts, although the *recorded* rates indicate that there is an inverse relationship to socio-economic status.

The possible disparity between *true* and *known* rates of delinquent and criminal acts is well illustrated by the course of research over the past decade on juvenile delinquency. A number of macroscopic studies on officially recorded delinquents show the expected inverse relationship to socio-economic status. Lander's (1954) Baltimore study of over 8,000 cases of recorded delinquency and Bordua's (1958–1959) Detroit study both found that economic factors were important in urban areas having high delinquency rates. More recently, Chilton (1964) reported a reanalysis of the Lander and Bordua data, as well as a comparison of the two earlier studies with data from 1,649 delinquent cases in Indianapolis. He concluded that delinquency in urban areas is related to transiency, poor housing, and economic indices, and is predominantly a lower-class male phenomenon.

Reiss and Rhodes (1961) in a study of 9,238 boys in Nashville, Tennessee, searched juvenile court records to locate delinquent respondents in the sample. They found the usual inverse relationship between socio-economic status and delinquency; furthermore, lower-status boys are more likely to have been charged with more serious delinquent acts and upper-status boys are more likely to have informal records on their activities rather than formal citations.[22]

However, when adolescents themselves are asked whether or not they have committed one or more of a set of delinquent acts, the inverse relationship to socio-economic status lessens or disappears. Nye, Short, and Olson (1958), in a study in three Washington cities and three midwestern towns, using a sample of fourteen- and fifteen-year-olds, found virtually no differences by social class in the amount of self-reported delinquent behavior.[23] A replication by Akers (1964), conducted in a middle-sized Ohio city and using a sample of ninth-grade students, found the same results. A lack of differences by social class is also reported by Clark and Wenninger (1962) in research from four Illinois communities for sixth- to twelfth-grade children and by Dentler and Monroe (1961) for seventh- and eighth-grade students in three Kansas counties. A study conducted by Voss (1966) in Honolulu did find a significant positive association between self-reported delinquency and social class for boys, but the association disappears when delinquency is redefined as the reporting of two or more serious delinquent behaviors. Voss found no relationship between delinquency and social class for girls in the study. In sum, these five studies of self-reported delinquency, conducted in fifteen communities, question whether there is a true inverse relationship between social status and delinquent behavior.

There are two equally plausible ways of explaining these contradictions: First, the findings may indicate that there are severe differences in the way in which law-enforcement agencies handle delinquent acts committed by children from different class levels. A second explanation is that either middle-class children are exaggerating their delinquent acts or that lower-class children are under-reporting theirs. It is obviously hard to choose among these alternatives. Perhaps it is most judicious to simply state that these findings indicate that there are probably socio-economic status differences in the commission of delinquent acts as well as differential treatment of apprehended delinquents by law-enforcement agencies.

22. Similar findings, gleaned from official records, are reported by Bates (1960, 1962), Palmore (1963), Palmore and Hammond (1964), Erickson et al. (1965), and Gold (1966).

23. They report that only 33 of the 756 tests of differences reach a 5 per cent significance level; these few differences can certainly be regarded as spurious.

To date, only fragmentary evidence exists to support the position that both explanations may indeed be plausible; Gold (1966) reports findings from a study of teenagers in Flint, Michigan, that included interviews designed to detect delinquency, the use of informants to validate some of the reported delinquent behavior, and a comparison of the data with police records (N = 522, validation was possible in 125 cases). The findings indicate that an inverse relationship between social status and delinquency does exist for boys but not for girls, that many serious delinquent acts are undetected, and that definite biases do exist in the police records. The police were more likely to record officially offenses committed by lower-status youngsters, and more likely to "handle" the matter unofficially without referring it to court if the offender came from a higher-status family. From the official records, boys from the lowest social strata were apprehended five times as often as boys from the highest. Gold estimates that if records were complete and unselective, the ratio would be closer to 1.5:1. However, the interview data also indicate that, graded on an index of seriousness of offense, boys from the lowest strata were implicated on the highest delinquency level three to four times more than boys from the highest strata. "If we consider these boys to be ones who represent the most pressing social problem and therefore should be apprehended and given attention, then the official bookings rates do not depart so far from truly representing differential delinquency among social status levels (Gold, 1966, p. 44)." [24]

Concerning criminal acts committed by adults,[25] no comparable information is available. Among imprisoned criminals, the lowest economic groups tend to be disproportionately represented; prisoners are generally poorly educated, unemployed, unmarried, and have a prior criminal record. We do not know whether such differentials would be markedly decreased were one to employ the same sort of

24. An observational study of police officers' contacts with juveniles is reported by Piliavin and Briar (1964). The study suggests that wide discretion is exercised by police in dealing with young offenders and that this discretion is affected by criteria such as boys' prior records, race, grooming, and demeanor. When law-enforcement agencies are evaluated by adolescents, one limited study (Chapman, 1956) finds that delinquent and nondelinquent respondents do not differ in their attitudes toward juvenile courts, probation agencies, and reformatories but that the delinquent respondents show significantly greater antagonism toward the police.

25. Characteristics of prisoners are tabulated in U.S. Bureau of the Census. *U.S. Census of Population: 1960. Subject Reports. Inmates of Institutions.* Final Report PC (2) -8A. Washington, D.C. Government Printing Office, 1963.

self-reporting device with adults that Nye and others have used with youths or the interview procedure developed by Gold.

Thus far we have dealt with those who commit crimes. Delinquent and criminal acts, however, can also be viewed in terms of the *victims* of crime. Some findings from a study conducted by the National Opinion Research Center (NORC) for the President's Commission on Law Enforcement and Administration of Justice (Ennis, 1967) are of particular interest in this context: At all levels of income, Negroes have higher rates of victimization for serious crimes against the person compared to whites. For both groups, larcenies and car thefts increase with income. Burglaries, however, decline with a rise of income for whites, but increase for Negroes. When both serious and nonserious crimes against persons and property are tabulated, we find that low-income groups are more likely than high-income groups to be victims of crimes against the person, and that among the low-income group, Negroes are more often victimized than whites. Low-income groups of both races and high-income whites have similar victimization rates in property crimes, with high-income Negroes being twice as likely to be victims of such crimes.

D. SEXUAL BEHAVIOR, FERTILITY, AND
FAMILY STABILITY

Description of the "lower-lower" and cognate groups stresses the "immorality" and instability of family life. O. Lewis's (1965) long and intensive description of a Puerto Rican family living in the "culture of poverty" seemingly devotes more space to these two topics than to almost any other. Similarly, Moynihan (1967) is particularly concerned with the stability of family life and the incidence of illegitimacy among Negroes in the 1960s. Warner's (1949a, 1949b) informants frequently refer to the theme of immorality in their descriptions of the "lower-lower" class. Both Dollard (1937) and Powdermaker (1939), in studies of a Mississippi city, see sexual behavior and family stability as marking off distinct classes within the Negro group.

Empirical studies tend to bear out the qualitative descriptions. Kinsey's (1948, 1953) now-classic studies of human sexual behavior are the best large-scale studies available. Kinsey's samples, methodology, and interpretation have been criticized; certainly, the studies are biased by self-selection of respondent, under-representation of low-income groups, inclusion of prison populations, and reliance on memory and recall.[26] Kinsey reports that for both males and females, the amount of education is more closely related to sexual behavior than any other social characteristic. He reports a sharp and consistent relationship between education and sexual activity among males: Whether we consider age at first premarital intercourse, percentage involved at a given age level, the frequency of premarital intercourse, or extramarital behavior, the less educated are the most sexually active. For females, the incidence and frequency of premarital intercourse is greater among lower-status families, but the relationship becomes less pronounced with age.

More systematic sample survey studies tend to corroborate Kinsey's findings. Reiss (1965) administered a scale of sexual permissiveness to a national sample of adults (N = 1,515) and to several samples of high-school and college students. He found no association between social class and permissiveness among the students, and a weak curvilinear association among adults; the lowest socio-economic groups tended to be more permissive than the high-status group (gamma = .13 in the adult sample). Rainwater and Weinstein (1960), in their study of a small group (N = 96) of upper-lower and lower-lower families in Chicago, found that the lower-lower group tended to have intercourse more frequently, but to have relatively prudish attitudes toward sexual experiences and only crude notions of the physiology of sex.

Several summary reviews of the relationship between socio-economic status and fertility (Westoff, 1954; Jaffe, 1965; and Kingsley Davis, 1965) indicate an inverse relationship, although status differentials have been decreasing over time. Jaffe (1965), reviewing studies of desired family size, finds that there is very little difference between socio-economic levels in the range and averages of *desired* family sizes. The poor, he concludes, get more children because they are not very proficient in avoiding excess fertility. Rainwater and Weinstein (1960) suggest that lower-lower couples have more children than they want because they have little faith in their own abilities to master contraceptive techniques, coupled with an inadequate knowledge of the physiology of conception.[27] The uneven spread of contraceptive knowledge can be documented with many studies showing that the higher the socio-economic status the greater

26. Some of the criticisms and evaluations of the Kinsey reports are contained in Himeloch and Fava (1955).

27. It should be noted that this finding antedates the development of birth control pills and the renewal of interest in the intra-uterine rings.

the use of contraceptives both in terms of sheer usage and effectiveness of use (that is, in the sense of controlling both number and spacing of children) .[28]

The extent to which both sexual practices and lack of contraceptive techniques influence the illegitimacy rates is difficult to evaluate. Official illegitimacy rates, as Moynihan (1967) has shown, are higher for low socio-economic status groups and especially high for Negroes. Vincent (1954), who studied private practitioners and institutions catering to unwed mothers, found that upper-status women were more likely to have illegitimate children delivered by private practitioners; therefore, he questioned whether socio-economic differences in the illegitimacy rates are as large as official statistics indicate.

Studies of marital satisfaction also find inverse relationships with socio-economic status. The major empirical studies of marriage, until as recently as 1957, dealt primarily with middle-class and college-educated segments of the population; there is almost no research before that date that could be considered representative of the entire population (Landis, 1957). However, recent studies (Rainwater et al., 1959; Gurin, Veroff, and Feld, 1960; Blood and Wolfe, 1960; Komarovsky, 1962; Bradburn, 1965; Orden and Bradburn, 1968) have been based on more representative samples. Gurin et al. (1960), analyzing a national sample, and Bradburn (1965) working with samples in metropolitan areas, find that low-socio-economic status couples are more likely to report dissatisfaction with their marriage. Orden and Bradburn (1968) find that the strength of the relationship between self-assessments of happiness in marriage, the scales constructed in the study to measure marital satisfactions and tensions, and socio-economic status are about the same. Both indicators are positively related to socio-economic status and the relationship is stronger for women than for men in both cases. Of special interest to us is the finding by Roth and Peck (1951) [29] that marital adjustment of couples is unrelated to their parents' socio-economic status, and their suggestion that the source of the relationship between adjustment and socio-economic status lies in the present circumstances of the couple studied.[30]

28. See, for example, the studies in Kiser (1962) and the book by Freedman et al. (1959).

29. Roth and Peck re-analyzed Burgess' longitudinal study of 53 couples engaged to be married in the 1930s; "good" adjustment ranges from a high of 52 per cent in the highest socio-economic-status group to 12.5 per cent in the lowest.

30. We have omitted discussion of the quality and form of lower-class marriages in our discussion, as well as the sources of satisfaction and strain. The

In reviewing studies of marital instability, both Hollingshead (1950) and William Goode (1951) find an inverse relationship to socio-economic status. Goode suggests a process in which strain leads to dissatisfaction on the part of the wife who responds with withdrawal from intimacy and an eventual breakup of the marriage. A more recent cross-cultural analysis by William Goode (1966) finds that the inverse relationship between divorce and socio-economic status holds for advanced industrialized societies in which divorce is relatively easy and inexpensive, but not for societies low in economic advancement or in which divorce is difficult or expensive. In a re-analysis of the 1960 Census, Udry (1966) finds that nonwhites are much more likely to report themselves as separated or divorced than whites. When status is measured by educational level, an inverse relationship is found between separation/divorce and status for both men and women and for both whites and nonwhites. When status is measured by occupation, the inverse relationship still holds for men (more clearly for the nonwhites than for whites); for females, the distribution by occupation is not patterned, except that nonwhite rates are higher.

The literature discussed in this section yields results of an uncertain character. It should be kept in mind that we have dealt with tendencies, and not with absolutes. At any one point in time, most of the households in the general population and among the poor are intact, with both husband and wife present. The poor have more dissatisfaction, more divorces, and so on, but the reasons for these tendencies are not completely understood.

E. PARENT-CHILD RELATIONSHIPS AND CHILD-REARING PRACTICES

Our survey indicates that more research has been conducted on social class differentials in the area of parent-child relationships and child-rearing practices than in any other area of sociology. This emphasis arises out of a particular view of the problems of the lower class as being due primarily to deficiencies of character. If character formation is the result of early childhood experiences and orientations, then it is imperative that we specify ways in which the lower class and (more recently) the very poor differ from standard Americans (that is, middle class) in their child-rearing practices. Yet, there is by

reader should consult the intensive studies of Komarovsky (1964), Pavenstedt (1965), Rainwater et al. (1959), and Cohen and Hodges (1963).

no means strong consensus on what precisely *are* standard middle-class, working-class, and lower-class practices.

The early research of Davis and Havighurst (1946), studying a Chicago sample in 1943, found the working class more permissive than the middle class in a number of areas. Later research, conducted in Boston in 1951–1952, by Sears, Maccoby, and Levin (1957), found opposite class differences. Bronfenbrenner's review of numerous studies, covering the period 1930–57, attempts to reconcile the differences among studies by postulating a historical shift in child-rearing toward greater permissiveness, with the middle class showing greater changes than the working class.[31] Reasoning that the middle class is more attentive and responsive to agents of change (for example, popular literature, physicians, and counselors), Bronfenbrenner sees the middle class as changing sufficiently since the thirties to become, in the post-World War II period, more permissive than the working class. Other class differences established in his review include a greater stress on independence training among the middle class, less use of corporal punishment, and less emphasis on authority as the basis for demands of obedience.

Research conducted since Bronfenbrenner's review has tended to emphasize parental values and attitudes toward child-rearing practices, rather than techniques per se.[32] Kohn (1959a, 1959b, 1963) suggests that techniques may have changed, while child-rearing values have remained much the same over time. The main differences in values between middle-class and working-class parents have been the former's concern with developing self-direction in their children and the latter's concern with conformity to external proscription. Thus, the working class stresses obedience, deference to persons of higher status, honesty, cleanliness, and respectability, while the middle class has been concerned with the internalization of rules and norms rather than the rules and norms themselves.[33] Swinehart (1963) reports that middle-class mothers stress the development of morality and character and feel effective in handling children's social and emotional needs, while lower-class mothers are more concerned

31. For a description of the samples utilized in his review, see Bronfenbrenner (1966), Table I, p. 364. The major studies discussed are Davis and Havighurst, 1946; Klatskin, 1952; Sears et al., 1957; Daniel Miller and Swanson, 1958; Martha White, 1957; Boek et al., 1958; Littman et al., 1957; and Kohn, 1959a.

32. A discussion of the methodology used in the child-rearing studies and some criticism of the findings is presented by Johnsen and Leslie (1965).

33. A recent replication of the Kohn study suggests that occupation is related to parental values in much the same ways in both the United States and Italy (Pearlin and Kohn, 1966).

with the physical needs of their children. Similarly, Gurin et al. (1960) report that higher status parents are more concerned with the child-parent relationship, more introspective about their parental role, while lower status parents are more concerned over the provision of adequate physical care and material goods for their children. Kantor et al. (1958) suggest that as one moves from lower to upper socioeconomic levels, mothers express greater clarity and certainty in their views concerning discipline and sex and are less concerned with obedience to parents. In an experimental setting, the results from the work of Hess and Shipman (1966a, 1966b) show that the lower the class level the more likely the mother is to emphasize obedience from her children and the less likely to explain reasons for behavioral rules.

The research reported above ascertained class differences by focusing on parents; a number of investigators, however, have attempted to detect differences through the study of adolescents. For example, in a large study (N = 1,472), Nye (1951) found that socioeconomic level is a significant variable in the differential adjustment of adolescents to parents; with adolescents from high socio-economic status homes, better adjusted to their parents than those in low socioeconomic status homes. Elder (1962) reports that middle-class parents are viewed by adolescents as more likely to be democratic, egalitarian, or permissive; whereas lower-class parents are likely to be considered autocratic or authoritarian. Bowerman (1964) reports that middle-class parents are more often described as supportive and encouraging than are lower-class parents.

A number of studies have focused on the "lower-lower" families: Wortis et al. (1963), in a study of 250 Negro mothers from very poor households, found that they were more concerned with their own convenience than with a "good" theory of child care: They were more punitive than other groups, less demanding of performance and not very rewarding of children's accomplishments. Pavenstedt (1965) presents a distressing portrait of a group of "multiproblem" families whose cooperation was sought in sending their children to pre-nursery school. The mothers were reluctant to cooperate and harbored mistrust and suspicion of the school personnel. The children appeared to be neglected, hardly communicated with by adults, and characterized by a low level of affect and considerable self-devaluation. These findings are supported by Keller (1963) in a study of 46 fifth-grade children from very poor families in New York. These children have derogatory self-images and little communication with adult members of their families. They were best described as living in an intellectually and emotionally impoverished environment.[34]

We note, however, that a much more optimistic picture of poor families is presented in the Child Rearing Study of Low-Income Families in Washington, D.C. On the basis of intensive study of 66 families, the majority of which have a very low income, Hylan Lewis (1961) and Jackson (1966) conclude that the child-rearing values of this group do not differ very much from those of middle-class Americans. However, because of the problems that extreme poverty presents, their attention is mainly devoted to the high-priority items of food, clothing, and shelter, with consequent seeming neglect of their children.[35] The very poor tend to get bogged down in the frustrations of pursuing these high-priority items, and have little energy or desire left to provide a supportive and stimulating environment for their children.

F. NEED FOR ACHIEVEMENT, LEVEL OF ASPIRATION, AND WORK SATISFACTION

Since jobs and occupations play a central role in almost every definition of socio-economic status, the variables grouped together in this section are of prime theoretical importance. Need for achievement is presumably a measure of the strength of individual motivation to achieve some degree of success in the occupational sphere. Levels of aspiration refer to the professed occupational destinations of young people (or held by parents for their children). Finally, work satisfaction can be seen as one of the rewards of occupational position, and hence one of the incentives for remaining in the labor force.

The concept of achievement motivation and a recognized measure thereof using the TAT was developed by McClelland and his associates in experimental laboratory studies, usually with college students as subjects.[36] The importance of achievement motive lies in

34. For a discussion of the lower-class family, see Keller (1966). Extensive documentation of some of the issues discussed in this section is to be found in Berelson and Steiner (1964) and Hoffman and Hoffman (1964).

35. Epstein (1961) presents documentation, based on the Census and information from the National Health Survey and Public Health Service, showing that the milieu of the child of a low-income family comprises improper food, overcrowded living conditions, and lack of preventive dental and medical care.

36. McClelland et al. (1953). Atkinson and Feather (1966) present the theory of achievement motivation and describe the studies conducted since 1957 that provide the main body of evidence for the validity of its behavioral implications.

the central role given to it by McClelland et al. in social change and in individual mobility. Highly motivated individuals are presumed to show persistent striving activity directed toward a high goal in some area involving competition with a standard of excellence. Standards of excellence are first imparted to individuals by their parents, but in time these standards become internalized. A number of studies found a positive relationship between *n* Achievement and socioeconomic status. An early study by Douvan (1956), using a sample of high-school students (N = 313) in a Midwestern community, found that middle-class adolescents manifest higher *n* Achievement than working-class individuals. Rosen (1956), in a study of high-school sophomores in the New Haven area, showed a clear relationship between social position and motivation scores, for example, 83 per cent of the subjects in the highest social class have high scores, as compared with 23 per cent in the lowest. In a later study, Rosen (1959) examined differences in motivation, values, and aspirations of six racial and ethnic groups (427 pairs of mothers and their sons) in four northeastern states. He found that although there were significant differences in religion and ethnicity, social class accounted for more of the variance in motivation scores than either, and (as before) that social class was positively related to high-achievement scores. Finally, Morgan (1962) reported the results from a national probability sample and showed that the *n* Achievement was higher for those respondents whose fathers were better educated, in white-collar occupations, and lived in large cities in the Northeast.[37]

Recently, Kahl (1965) has suggested that distinctions ought to be made between achievement motivation and achievement goals, presenting data to buttress his case. Support for the argument presented by Kahl is reported in a study by Scanzoni (1967) who concludes that basic orientations toward occupational success may not necessarily vary by social class, but that "due to the structural situation of the lower and working classes, occupational achievement and mobility are less often defined as realistic. This gap (anomie) between aspirations and expectations in many cases exists wholly apart from particular methods of child-rearing and resultant personality development. Instead, limited occupational achievement appears to be (in part at least) the product of the limited purview of opportunity inherent within the lower classes (p. 456)."

Closely related to achievement-motive studies is the research fo-

37. The data are drawn from a study of the determinants of income and of intergenerational changes (Morgan et al., 1962).

cused on the "deferred gratification pattern" (DGP), a concept developed by Davis and Dollard (1940) to characterize the differences between middle-class and lower-class Negroes' ability to defer immediate gratification for long-term return. The major empirical study, conducted by Schneider and Lysgaard (1953), involved the completion of self-administered questionnaires by a national sample of 2,500 high-school students. They conclude that middle-class students are more likely than lower-class students to defer gratification by "impulse renunciation." Although the magnitude of the differences is not impressive, lower-class "impulse following" non-DGP behavior includes willingness to engage in physical violence, limited pursuit of education, low-aspiration level, free spending, lack of concern for courtesy and obedience, and limited dependence on parents. A number of other studies have tried to specify the components of the DGP (Beilin, 1956; Straus, 1962; Mischel, 1958), but the results have not provided unequivocal support for the existence of the pattern.

S. M. Miller, Riessman, and Seagull (1965) have reviewed and criticized various aspects of these studies. For example, in the case of spending behavior, they suggest that the general life situation of the middle class makes it easier to defer gratification. The immediate spending of a lower-class youth may simply be an attempt to bring himself up to the same level of consumption as shown by his middle-class counterpart. Or, in the case of limited pursuit of education, the critics do not deny that class differences exist in attitude, dropout rates, and college attendance, but feel "One must be cautious, however, in ascribing a solitary motivation to a particular behavior, since individuals may react in an identical manner for very different reasons (*op. cit.*, p. 294)." S. M. Miller et al. conclude that a final verdict on the DGP cannot be made at present, and that more attention should be paid to the situational rather than the psychodynamic variables involved in these behaviors.

The relatively small number of studies concerning the relationship between socio-economic status and achievement motive and/or DGP is surprising in the light of the considerable attention paid to these two topics in the literature on social stratification and poverty. In contrast, scores of studies are available on educational and occupational aspirations of youths.[38] The research designs and the sam-

38. Our coverage of the literature in this area is, by necessity, incomplete. To wit, a research team at Texas A&M University has published a bibliography of works on educational and occupational aspirations, including unpublished material, which contains over five hundred items (Ohlendorf et al., 1967).

ple sizes of these studies tend to be of a better quality than the material available on achievement motive and DGP.

Educational and occupational aspirations have been typically studied by asking high-school students their ultimate educational goals (for example, whether they intend to attend college or not) and by asking for an occupational choice. In an extensive study of 35,000 seniors, from a national sample of 500 public high schools, Michael (1961) finds that social class, scholastic ability, and "school climate"[39] predicted intended college attendance rates. In the upper half of the ability distribution, social class remains the best predictor of a student's capacity to score in the top quarter of the ability distribution. An earlier study by Sewell et al. (1957) of a random sample of Wisconsin high-school students ($N = 4,167$) found that measured intelligence and social status each make an independent contribution to educational and occupational aspirations. With some modifications, and smaller, less comprehensive samples, the influence of social class on aspirations has been reported by Wilson (1959), Turner (1962), Krauss (1964), and Bennett and Gist (1964).

Antonovsky and Lerner (1959), in a study of youths between the ages of 16 to 20, paid particular attention to the educational and vocational aspirations of Negro and white youths of the same socioeconomic level. They found that Negroes tend to have higher aspirations than whites.[40] Similar results were obtained by Short and Strodtbeck (1965) in a study contrasting gang members with other youths of comparable social status in Chicago.[41] In a comparison of four Chicago samples and two national samples, Rivera and Short (1967) make the distinction between *absolute* and *relative* occupational expectations.[42] When looking at absolute goals, they find that

39. School climates are ordinarily indexed by the proportion of the student body exhibiting various social and personal characteristics, such as the proportion of students from highly educated families, or the proportion of students planning to go on for further education.

40. The higher-educational aspirations of Negro high-school students are also detected in a study conducted in Kansas City by Gist and Bennett (1963).

41. Many researchers comment on the unreasonably high aspirations of Negro youths: One high-school dropout in Short and Strodtbeck's study indicated that he wanted to be a doctor. Oscar Lewis (1965) catches the flavor of these unrealistically high expectations in a quotation from a nine-year-old Puerto Rican girl who states in the context of explaining how much she loves her mother, "That's why when I grow up I want to be a doctor or a chambermaid. So when I work and earn money, I'll put it in the bank and give *mami* the bank book so she can take out what she wants" (p. 246). Note that the second sentence in the quotation shows both the DGP (putting money earned in the bank) and impulse gratification (letting her mother take out money whenever she needs it).

42. These distinctions are made by Empey (1956). *Absolute* goals refer to

nongang lower-class Negroes expect to reach higher occupational levels than nongang whites; with race controlled, the expectations of gang members are lower than those of nongang members. The findings from the national sample indicate no difference in the absolute goals of Negroes and whites. However, when *relative* expectations are compared, they find that within all comparable categories, Negroes anticipate a substantially greater amount of upward mobility than whites, that is, the expectations of Negro gang members are higher than those of white gang members; the expectations of the Negro national sample are higher than those of the white national sample.

As could be anticipated, parental aspirations for children follow much the same pattern suggested above. Hyman (1966), reviewing national sample survey results, found that parents' educational and occupational aspirations for their children are directly related to socio-economic status.[43] Working with a less extensive sample, Robert Bell (1965) found a direct relationship between socio-economic status and Negro mothers' educational aspirations for their children. In Rosen's work (1959), social class is also significantly and directly related to vocational aspirations; however, ethnicity accounts for more of the variance than social class. With the exception of the study by Reissman (1953), the aspirations of adults across social classes have not been investigated. In an Evanston, Illinois, study, Reissman found that upper-status respondents were much more willing to forego immediate gains in order to obtain occupational advancement.[44] Finally, in a cross-cultural comparison of the occupational aspirations of young boys, Lambert and Klineberg (1963) found that the aforementioned socio-economic differentials in aspirations hold, although there were some differences between countries in the kinds of occupations desired.

The difficulty in the interpretation of the findings from aspiration studies has been recognized by many writers. Once goals are elicited, it is often difficult to interpret whether they are aspirations or whether the responses reflect a combination of realizable goals and/or culturally desirable answers (Empey, 1956; Stephenson, 1957;

---

the occupational level an adolescent defines as attainable; *relative* goals specify the amount of mobility beyond status of origin which a respondent expects to achieve.

43. Studies by Gerald Bell (1963) and Simpson (1962) report similar findings; these studies also suggest that parental motivation, as perceived by high-school students, may be more important than social class as a predictor of high ambition.

44. It is also possible to interpret the findings of this study in terms of the deferred gratification pattern discussed above.

Rodman, 1963). Keller and Zavalloni (1964) have argued that ambition, or high aspiration level, has been incorrectly defined solely in terms of desired educational or occupational goals. They contend that a lower-status child aspiring to a college education has higher aspirations than a middle-class child of college-educated parents. Like S. M. Miller et al. (1965), cited earlier, they argue that aspirations ought to be measured by the "distance" between the starting point of the individual and his aspired-for "destination" (for example, the *relative* goals discussed by Empey); furthermore, individual capacities and talents, as well as facilities (for example, income) for achieving a goal, ought to be considered. With measures of this sort, differences among socio-economic levels would be lessened or perhaps reversed, the lower socio-economic displaying relatively higher levels of aspiration than the upper. The key issue in this argument is identifying individuals' points of origin. Sewell et al. (1957) took into account both the abilities of individuals and their socio-economic status and found a positive relationship to aspiration, independent of intelligence.[45] Whatever the merits of the argument advanced by Keller and Zavalloni (1964), it still remains the case that children coming from different socio-economic levels have different educational and occupational intentions.

Turning now to work satisfaction experienced by adults, Blauner (1960), in an excellent review article covering a large number of empirical studies, finds that a majority of adults are satisfied with their jobs,[46] but that those in higher-status jobs are more satisfied than those in lower-status jobs. Blauner states that job satisfaction is directly related to the degree of control over the job's activities exercised by incumbents and is higher in jobs in which men work as teams and perhaps form occupational communities (for example, typographers and printers, or miners). Inkeles (1960) in a cross-national review of job satisfaction found that "The evidence is powerful and unmistakable that satisfaction with one's job is differentially experienced by those in the several standard occupational positions. From country to country, we observe a clear positive correlation be-

45. Sewell's data also show a critical sex difference in educational plans, college attendance, and college graduation. In general, for females, the relative effect of socio-economic status is greater than is the effect of intelligence; for males, the relative effect of intelligence is greater than that of socio-economic status. (The results of the original study are in Little [1958]; some findings from the follow-up study are presented in Sewell and Shah [1967].)

46. According to Robinson et al. (1966), over 400 studies have reported percentages of workers dissatisfied with their jobs in the past thirty years; the median dissatisfaction rate in these studies is 13 per cent.

tween the over-all status of occupations and the experience of satisfaction in them" (p. 12).

Although impressionistic evidence is considerable that high-status persons regard work as important to them and their occupations as more central to their self-definitions, little in the way of systematic study exists on this score. Morse and Weiss (1955) described differences between middle-class men, who gain a sense of accomplishment and purpose from working, and working-class men for whom work was something to keep them busy.[47] Gurin et al. (1960) found that feelings of inadequacy among employed men were linked to job dissatisfaction. There was a higher degree of satisfaction among those who saw their jobs as intrinsically interesting than among those who saw their jobs as mainly providing material rewards and extrinsic status. Their findings showed that higher educational levels and job status led to more ego involvement and greater satisfaction on the one hand, but also to more work problems on the other. Similarly, Lyman (1955) reports that white-collar workers give greater emphasis to the character of the work itself and to freedom from close supervision, while blue-collar workers emphasize rewards and the conditions of work.

At the beginning of this subsection, we suggested that work satisfaction is one of the rewards of occupational position, and available research sustains that position. It may be the case that types of work satisfaction differ for different occupational groups and positions.[48] Clearly, any assessment of these studies should bear in mind that they do not consider work in relation to, or in interaction with, other aspects of life and how these interrelationships may vary by social class.[49]

Leisure-Time Activities. Although studies of uses of leisure are part of the literature on socio-economic status correlates, it is difficult to place these studies properly in a systematic scheme. On the one hand, leisure is looked upon as the use of nonwork time and is closely

47. In this study, respondents were to assume that they were independently wealthy; therefore, they did not have to work for monetary return.

48. Note that we did not discuss the concept of work alienation and its possible sources. For discussion of the concept and reports of studies, see Wilensky (1964b) and Blauner (1964).

49. Some of these interrelationships are discussed in Bradburn and Caplovitz (1965), Ch. 2. In this work, work satisfaction is an independent, rather than a dependent, variable, the focus of the study being on the effects of current environmental forces on psychological well-being. Also see the study by Wilensky and Ladinsky (1967).

related to work satisfaction,[50] occupational aspirations, and the like. On the other hand, leisure-time activities can also be viewed as expressions of value preferences and hence related to the research on differential values of social-class levels. In any event, it is clear that the uses of leisure time constitute an important research topic. Indeed, if, as some commentators suggest, the amount of leisure time available to the American population is increasing,[51] the interest of social scientists in this area of behavior will also increase.

Although a considerable literature exists in this area, much of the empirical work deals with small homogeneous subgroups of the population, or, more usually, with a limited aspect of leisure-time use. Extensive research exists on the utilization of television (Glick and Levy, 1962; Steiner, 1963), outdoor recreation (Outdoor Recreation Resources Review Commission Study Report #20, 1965), and adult educational programs (Johnstone and Rivera, 1965), to mention only a few. Studies of adolescents have typically included mention of leisure-time activities (for example, Coleman, 1961; Havighurst et al., 1962).

A few scattered studies exist that attempt to document the use of leisure by social class without emphasis on a given aspect. In a study of families (N = 673 families containing 1,741 persons over six) in Ohio, White (1955) finds that the use of parks and playgrounds, attendance at church services, and with slight variations, rates for cummunity-chest services, museums, and ethnic-racial organizations are inversely associated with social class (using Warner's ISC classification). The use of libraries, home activities, and lecture-study courses is positively associated with social class. Clarke's (1956) study of 574 white males in Columbus, Ohio, reports similar findings. Clarke, however, divided his respondents into five occupational prestige levels, using the North-Hatt scale. He finds that the lowest prestige group is more likely to watch television, play with children, fish, play card games (excluding bridge), take drives, go to drive-ins, and spend time in taverns and at ball games. The highest prestige group reports cultural activities (theater, concerts, art galleries),

50. See publications and research reports from "Work, Careers, and Leisure Styles: A Study of Sources of Societal Integration," a program of research directed by Wilensky (Wilensky, 1961, 1964); also Anderson (1961), DeGrazia (1962), and the volume edited by Larrabee and Meyersohn (1958). The last-mentioned publication contains an extensive bibliography.

51. Two trends call this assumption into question: First, the apparent slowdown in the tendency toward shorter industrial hours (Zeisel, 1956); second, the increasing entry of women into the labor force and the increase of multiple job-holding.

reading, studying, home entertainment, attendance at conventions, and community-service work.

A study conducted by the Survey Research Center for the Outdoor Recreation Resources Review Commission (ORRRC Study Report #20, 1962) reports leisure-time activities and their relationships to various socio-economic characteristics. It is worth noting that the results clearly show that upper-income people and those with more formal education make more active use of their leisure time than others. According to individuals' own reports, they use leisure for activities and hobbies rather than relaxing and resting, and the number of activities seems to rise with both education and income. Only if we interpret income and education as reflecting, to some extent, social-class differences in life style and interest patterns do these results become meaningful. Thus, some forms of recreation that involve minimal expense, or none at all, rise with income, and those likely to involve more expense and equipment are not always income-related.

Perhaps reflecting a societal view that leisure is a reward for hard work, the leisure and recreational patterns of the underemployed and the unemployed of the past few decades are almost unknown. Clearly, the need for extensive research into both the budgeting of time in general and the forms of leisure of various groups is evident.[52]

G. PERSONALITY AND PERSONAL ADJUSTMENT

Although the literature on the "lower-lowers" does not ordinarily make direct references to personality and personal adjustment, the relevance of this topic seems clear. Sidestepping, for a moment, the difficult problem of the lack of precise meanings of these terms,[53] it is

52. One of the major research projects, currently underway, that will begin to fill in the gaps in our knowledge of time utilization is the Multinational Comparative Time Budget Research Project, directed by Alexander Szalai, Principal Scientific Research Officer of the United Nations Institute for Training and Research (UNITAR) in New York. Szalai (1966) has written a description of the project and presented some preliminary findings. The final results will be published this year. The American contribution to the study was directed by Philip Converse, Survey Research Center, University of Michigan, and is based on a sample of 1,244 individuals. Extensive analyses of the American data will be published by the Survey Research Center.

53. See Jahoda (1958) for a review of the ambiguity of the term "mental health." This ambiguity is shared by other terms involving the assessment of adequacy of functioning. Although the term "mental health" seems almost incapable of being given specific content, the term "physical illness" is not exempt from difficulties either. The problem is similar to that of defining the dividing

pertinent to inquire whether there are class differences in personality. The implications of such differences are important in resolving the disagreement over whether the poor are happy or not, and whether the "lower-lowers" are so badly impaired that the majority cannot escape from their condition for this reason.

Although Brim et al. (1965) estimate that a majority of American adults have taken personality and/or aptitude tests (usually in connection with application for school or for a job), there is remarkably little published literature based on extensive and well-selected samples that contrasts different class levels on attitudinal or personality characteristics.

In 1952 Auld critically reviewed over thirty studies concerned with the relationship of social status to personality. He found very few studies that were based on adequate samples. Most of the studies report social class differences, but in only one-third of the studies are they appreciable. Where such differences were found, upper-status (middle-class) respondents tended to score higher in personal adjustment than lower status (working-class) subjects.

In a later review article, Sewell (1961) evaluated findings concerning social class and childhood personality. He found that there is a relatively low correlation between the position of a child in a social stratification system and some aspects of his personality, including measured personality adjustment. Empirical evidence does not support the view that neurotic personality traits are more prevalent among middle-class children, but suggests that these traits may be more characteristic of the lower-class child. Like Auld (1952), Sewell criticized reviewed research as defective from a theoretical as well as methodological standpoint.

Rosenberg's (1965) study of feelings of self-esteem found that adolescents (5,000 high-school juniors and seniors) from higher social classes are somewhat more likely to accept themselves than those from the lower social strata. The differences are not large (51 per cent of the highest class scored high, as compared to 35 per cent of the lowest group). However, greater differences in self-esteem appear when religious and ethnic groups are considered.

---

line between those who are poor and those who are not. There is consensus over extremes, for example, persons without income and persons in catatonic trances are respectively poor and mentally ill; however, the borders of poverty and mental illness are in dispute. When terms are stated positively, as in the case of mental health and physical health, it is often not merely the absence of negative symptoms that is meant but some positive features as well, over which more disagreement can ordinarily arise.

Numerous other studies report similar and somewhat equivocal findings, although their coverage is less extensive. For example, Mensh et al. (1959) report that rural and small-town children from high socio-economic status families show fewer indications of personality maladjustment than do children from lower status families. A similar finding was provided by Sewell and Haller (1956), who report small correlations of .159 between the child's personality adjustment score and the prestige status of the child's family in the community. In sum, the evidence points to a weak relationship between socio-economic status and measures of personality, while other characteristics play as strong, or stronger, roles.

The best evidence on the relationships between socio-economic status and emotional problems comes from more extensive sample surveys of adult populations. A national sample study conducted by the Survey Research Center (Gurin et al., 1960) asked respondents whether they had ever experienced simple symptoms of mental or emotional upset, sufficient to warrant seeking some sort of help. Nearly one-fourth of the national sample (N = 2,640) indicated having distress serious enough to warrant seeking some help, with the proportions rising inversely with socio-economic status. Gurin et al. (1960) found that better-educated respondents were more introspective, but had a greater sense of well-being and satisfaction with the self. Thus, "high income is associated with greater happiness, fewer worries, more frequent anticipation of future happiness, fewer physical symptoms, and more symptoms of energy immobilization. Low income implies current unhappiness and worries, a lack of confidence in the future, and the expression of anxiety through physical symptoms (page 218)."

In a less extensive study, Bradburn (1967) found that lower-status respondents reported higher levels of negative feelings and lower levels of positive feelings. Indeed, it is the Negro residents of inner-city Detroit who report the lowest amount of positive feelings and the greatest unhappiness. The study also shows that "lower class people tend to repress anger and perhaps feelings in general. Displays of temper, indignation, and anger, the emotional responses to real or supposed wrongs, may well be emotions permitted only to the more well-to-do (Caplovitz and Bradburn, 1964)."

It should be noted that in both the Survey Research Center study (Gurin et al., 1960) and in the Bradburn et al. studies (Bradburn, 1967; Caplovitz and Bradburn, 1964), socio-economic status was not the highest correlate of emotional distress. More important than social-status differences are differences by age and life cycle, the elderly tending to show greater signs of emotional distress than any other group.

Both Gurin et al. (1960) and Bradburn (1967) rely on a sample survey approach using interviewers who are neither professional nor quasi-professionals in the field of mental health. In contrast, the Midtown studies (Srole et al., 1962, and Langner and Michael, 1963) are more intensive and place greater emphasis on interviews and evaluations by mental health professionals. The studies are based on intensive interviews with a representative sample of more than 1,600 persons living in the midtown area of Manhattan. The protocols of the interviews were reviewed by psychiatrists and rated as falling in one of six graded steps of mental health. In addition, private and public mental hospitals in the New York area, outpatient clinics, and private practitioners were contacted for information on any patient who was a midtown resident. The findings indicate an association between impairment (the last three mental-health categories mentioned above) and parental socio-economic status levels. The progression is approximately linear, from 17.5 per cent impaired in the highest group to 32.7 per cent in the lowest. However, in the discussion of individuals in treatment, no such progression is noted.

The same pattern of relationships is also found in studies of hospitalization for psychiatric disorders. The classic study of ecological distribution of mental hospital patients in Chicago by Faris and Dunham (1939) found that schizophrenic patients were more likely to come from the poorer sections of the city; areas characterized by high mobility had especially high rates of prevalence of schizophrenia. However, the ecological distributions of manic-depression and senile psychoses are not related to the socio-economic status of areas.

More recently, Hollingshead and Redlich (1958) reported the class distribution of almost 2,000 psychiatric patients being treated in public and private hospitals, clinics, and by private psychiatrists in New Haven. They find a relatively strong inverse relationship to socio-economic status, with the lowest status group manifesting more than three times the prevalence rates of the highest-status groups.[54]

54. The prevalence rates, adjusted for age and sex, indicate a sharp decrease between the lowest-status group and the other four classes; this suggests that the lowest group in New Haven has qualitatively greater prevalence of mental illness.

When the total rates are decomposed, it is evident that psychoses are inversely related to social class, while neuroses are positively related to social class.

The New Haven and Midtown findings are consistent with a number of earlier studies; for example, Clark (1949) reported a correlation of −0.75 between male first-admission rates of patients to psychiatric hospitals and occupational status.[55] In a study of hospitalized Negro schizophrenics, Kleiner et al. (1960) found inverse relationships, but the data also show a slight decrease of rates for the lowest group. In contrast, Jaco's (1960) study of admissions to Texas public and private psychiatric hospitals reports the highest rates for both unemployed and professional groups.

Attempts to measure the amount of mental illness in nonhospitalized populations lead only to additional confusion. Studies conducted in small communities show either a slight inverse relationship for schizophrenia (Frumkin, 1954) or no relationship at all (Clausen and Kohn, 1959). As a possible explanation for the findings observed in Hagerstown, Maryland, Clausen and Kohn (1959) suggest that selective out-migration of lower-class schizophrenics may account for their failure to confirm other findings. In a comparison of hospitalized and nonhospitalized cases of psychoses in Wellesley, Massachusetts, Kaplan et al. (1956) report that the incidence of nonhospitalized psychoses was higher in the upper as compared to lower-status groups; although when added to hospitalized cases, the total prevalence was greater in the lower class. However, Pasamanick et al. (1959) find a direct relationship between psychoses and social class in nonhospitalized populations; the lowest class in the study shows the lowest incidence. They attribute this finding to the high proportion of Negroes in the lowest group.

To further confound the attempt to establish regularities, there is some evidence that mental health professionals react differently to persons on different levels. Haase (1964) found that when identical Rorschach psychograms, but with varying social-class-background histories, were presented to psychologists for evaluation, the Rorschach tended more frequently to be evaluated as having been produced by a psychotic when low-status identification was attached. Rosengren

55. Clark has computed age-adjusted occupation-specific psychoses rates for each of nineteen occupational groups, ranked these in order of increasing psychoses rates and correlated them with the ranking of occupations in terms of increasing income and prestige. This method leads to higher correlation than if the correlation had been computed over individuals, that is, it is an ecological correlation.

(1962) reports in an analysis of case materials of ex-psychiatric patients (matched by the original diagnosis of illness, age, and sex) that "these materials suggested a perspective [on the part of mental health personnel] toward the lower class child which might be summed as *blame-control,* and a frame of reference for the middle class child which might be summed up as *explain-treat* (p. 18) ." Similarly, Hollingshead and Redlich (1958) found that psychiatrists preferred to deal with upper-status patients and would more often prescribe intensive psychotherapy to such patients.

More recently, a study of 610 children seen in the Children's Psychiatric Hospital of the University of Michigan's Medical Center during 1960–1961 (Harrison et al., 1965) reports a positive correlation between recommendations for psychotherapeutic treatment and the families' higher socio-economic status. The authors note that what is significant about this correlation is not the mental health problems of the children but the greater affinity with higher-status groups on the part of psychotherapists. In another report from the same study (McDermott et al., 1965) , a comparison is made of the historical and psychiatric data on a subgroup of 263 children of "blue-collar" families, dividing them into two groups on the basis of their fathers' occupations, that is, skilled and unskilled. They report that "the 'unskilled' group was seen as having a significantly higher incidence of diagnosed personality and borderline states . . . Although . . . home adjustment ratings were comparable within the two groups, the 'unskilled' group was seen as presenting a significantly greater problem in school. Referrals for professional treatment nonetheless were found to be made relatively later for the 'unskilled.' " [56]

To some degree, lower-status persons show characteristics that tend to complement the treatment they receive from mental-health personnel. Star (1955, 1956) shows that lower-status individuals are less likely to recognize signs of mental disorder when presented with vignettes describing persons manifesting behavior problems.[57] A number of subsequent surveys [58] have also confirmed the findings

56. For specific criticisms of the mental health professions, see Schneiderman (1965) , Riessman and Scribner (1965) , and Riessman et al. (1964) .

57. A recent study in Baltimore by Lemkau and Crocetti (1962) shows considerable changes in the public's ability to correctly identify these vignettes as indicating mental disorder. Whereas in the NORC (Star, 1955) study, only 34 per cent identified simple schizophrenia, in this work, 78 per cent were able to do so. However, the authors do not indicate whether the lower socio-economic group is participating in this general shift toward a more psychogenic interpretation of behavior disorders.

58. Freeman and Kassebaum, 1960; Lemkau and Crocetti, 1962; and Meyer, 1964.

that the higher the educational and occupational level of a respond-ent, "the more optimistic he was about the likelihood of recovery from mental illness, the greater the tendency to recommend profes-sional treatment, the more frequently he qualified his response about the possibility of hereditary factors being involved in mental illness . . . and the less frequently he cited poor living conditions as a cause of mental disease (Halpert, 1965) ." Gurin et al. (1960) also found that education was positively related to whether or not a respondent would seek professional help for an emotional problem, while Hol-lingshead and Redlich (1958) found that low-status patients were puzzled by psychotherapy and unable to grasp the fact that "talking" was the treatment.

The studies cited in this section display heterogeneity in design and coverage; to some unknown degree, this heterogeneity may ac-count for the seeming contradictions manifested in their results. Since the study of both the epidemiology and etiology of personality disorder has been the concern of scholars from varied fields, we are certain that our coverage is limited. We have not, furthermore, dis-cussed the differential care received by low socio-economic status indi-viduals within treatment institutions, social class factors related to length of mental hospital stay,[59] rehospitalization rates for mental ill-ness by social class, nor the acceptance of mental patients by their families and social groups upon discharge.[60]

H. INTELLECTUAL PERFORMANCE AND LINGUISTIC BEHAVIOR

Since the analysis of the relationship between Army Alpha Examina-tion scores and the occupations of World War I draftees,[61] few em-pirical findings have seemed better established than those relating socio-economic status and performance on tests of intellectual func-tioning. Specific studies are too numerous to review, but there is a fair amount of consensus among the studies that the magnitude of the correlation ranges from .40 to .50 (Friedhoff, 1955; Anastasi, 1958; Knief and Stroud, 1959; Wolf, 1965). Similar findings have been doc-umented for the relationship between socio-economic status and aca-demic performance as measured by rank in class, grade-point aver-

59. See, for example, the review by Krause (1967) .

60. A discussion of attitudes toward deviant behavior, by social class, with emphasis on the issue of mental health is presented by Dohrenwend and Chin-Shong (1967) .

61. See the discussion by Miner (1957) , pp. 67–71.

ages, and achievement test scores.[62] Parental socio-economic status tends to correlate between .30 to .60 with measures of performance in school, depending on subject matter (Rossi et al., 1959).

Of special interest to this review are researches on differences between Negroes and whites in both I.Q. tests and school performance. Coleman et al. (1966) find consistent differences in achievement between Negroes and whites, holding a number of background factors constant. Furthermore, they find that the background factors account for more of the variance in achievement at earlier grades than at later ones, the decline, however, being slight. In a report from the Institute for Developmental Studies in New York, Deutsch and Brown (1964) find that at each socio-economic status level Negro children score lower on I.Q. tests than whites and that Negro-white differences increase at each higher socio-economic status level. Recently, Hicks and Pellegrini (1960) evaluated twenty-seven studies of differences in Negro versus white I.Q. and concluded that knowledge of race accounts for only 6 per cent of the variance in I.Q.[63]

In the early 1920s these relationships were first documented on a large scale. They sparked a nature-nurture controversy that diminished only when it became obvious that there was no powerful methodology available to settle the question, nor to partition among heredity or environment their proper shares of the total variance in I.Q. or intellectual performance. Currently, it is generally accepted that some portion of an individual's performance on such tasks is accounted for by genetic [64] differences and some by differences in life experiences and other environmental factors, although the exact proportions may never be fully worked out.[65]

Since linguistic behavior is directly implicated in measures of intellectual performance, studies of the learning and use of language by people of different socio-economic levels lead to further specifications of the relationship between socio-economic status and intellec-

62. A useful summary of the major findings from studies of education and social class is given in Herriott and St. John (1966), Ch. 1.

63. Dreger and Miller (1960) present a review of published psychological studies, 1943–1958, that involve Negro-white comparisons. They note that although Negroes score lower on tests of intellectual functions, they average well within the normal range for whites.

64. Note that "genetic" does *not* imply direct and simple inheritance of traits, but that there are genetic differences in the gene pools of each parent. Thus, the correlation between scores on the National Merit Scholarship Qualifying Test is .9 for identical twins, and .6 for fraternal twins; the latter is not too different from the correlation between parents and their children (Nichols, 1967).

65. For a current discussion of the relationship between genetics and social processes, with special references to the study of intelligence, see Eckland (1967).

tual performance. Consequently, special note should be taken of studies that do investigate the processes that link socio-economic status and linguistic behavior.

Schatzman and Strauss (1955), studying the protocols of interviews with survivors of natural disasters, noted qualitative differences in the way in which persons of different class levels described their experiences. Upper-status respondents tended to be concrete in their descriptions, able to see the disaster from the position of others, and tended to use specific names rather than general pronouns; the language of the lower-status respondents had the opposite characteristics.

Following along the same lines, Bernstein (1958, 1960, 1962, 1964a) provides a more elaborate characterization of class differences in the use of language: He distinguishes between class-differentiated modes of cognition and modes in which the expression of language modifies perception. He postulates (Bernstein, 1958) the existence of "public" and "formal" languages (or, in his later work, "restricted" and "elaborated" codes). "Public" language consists of short, grammatically simple, often unfinished sentences in poor syntax, with an emphasis on emotive rather than logical implications. "Formal" language is rich in personal, individual qualifications (for example, "I believe that . . ."), and its form implies stress on logical relationships among concepts, with tone and volume taking second place to logical meaning. He argues not only that these codes can be distinguished, but that their use is class-correlated and independent of measured intelligence. In particular, the middle-class child is socialized to use both codes, whereas the working-class child is restricted to the "public" language.[66]

Hess and co-workers (Hess and Shipman, 1965, 1966a, 1966b; Bear et al., 1965; Olim et al., 1967) have extended the empirical base of Bernstein's insights and provided knowledge concerning the genesis of class differences in the use of language. Their study was designed to test the existence of a relationship between the child's cognitive development and the mother's verbal ability, maternal teaching style, and characteristic mode of family control. In an early report from this study of 160 Negro mothers and their preschool children drawn from four socio-economic levels, Hess and Shipman (1965) conclude that ". . . the meaning of deprivation is a depriva-

66. Bernstein's own experiments have been restricted to analyzing the verbal behavior of a group of sixteen-year-old boys; however, a later article (Bernstein, 1964b) applies the framework to cover the therapist-patient relationship.

tion of meaning—a cognitive environment in which behavior is controlled by status rules rather than by attention to the individual characteristics of the situation, and one in which behavior is not mediated by verbal cues or by teaching that relates events to one another and the present to the future."

In short, lower-status mothers tell their children what to do without explaining why it should be done.[67]

Not only does class-linked linguistic behavior help us to understand the functioning of different social class levels in the performance of intellectual tasks, but such differences can also serve as indicators of class position (as G. B. Shaw saw so well in *Pygmalion*). In one study, Harms (1961) played to a sample of respondents (N = 180) content-neutral recordings made by speakers from three status groups. He found that respondents were able to identify correctly the social status of the speakers, with a slight tendency to be able to identify members from one's own status group more accurately; listeners also attributed higher ratings of "credibility" to higher-status speakers, regardless of their own social status. Furthermore, there is a positive correlation between the subjective class evaluation of a speaker and the credibility attributed to him (the average correlation over the nine cells is .50). A number of research findings also support the contention that neither racial nor regional dialects of speakers inhibits the ability of listeners to identify the speakers' social class (Putnam and O'Hern, 1955; Harms, 1963; Ellis, 1963). Another implication present in these studies is that education does not completely erase auditory cues that make class distinctions possible. For example, in one series of experiments, Ellis (1967) used college students as speakers. Yet, listeners were able to identify the status of family background.[68]

Labov (1964) has analyzed the linguistic structure of adult subjects in the New York metropolitan area and found that linguistic variables correlate with objective indicators of social-status position. For example, an analysis of the phoneme *th* shows that upper-middle-class respondents depart very little, in all types of linguistic contexts,[69] from the prestige standard of radio and television announcers; however, the lower the class, the more pronounced the

67. A recent review (Cazden, 1966) nicely summarizes the state of knowledge concerning "subcultural" differences in the language of children.

68. The listeners produced mean ratings of the speakers' social status that correlated .80 with Hollingshead's measure.

69. The linguistic interviews obtained samples of careful speech, casual speech, reading style, and pronunciation of specific word lists.

differences between different styles, as well as the distance from the most prestigious style.

It should be borne in mind that although the relationships between socio-economic status and I.Q. are well documented, studies of linguistic processes have yet to move out of the state of small projects accomplished with, at best, haphazard and casual samples. Hess's (1965) study, which can be regarded as the most systematic yet to appear in the literature, is based on observations of Negroes in one neighborhood of Chicago and has not been replicated in other regions of the country with other types of groups. We have also been unable to locate any studies that investigate the consequences of speech behavior as an indicator of social status: If an individual's speech reveals his social status, is this a handicap to lower status individuals, for example, in the job interview situation?

Omitted from this chapter is any discussion of the quality of education available to lower-status groups and possible effects thereof on performance. Linguistic development is one of the prior variables in understanding the relationships between socio-economic status and intellectual performance. The "quality" of educational experiences, however, becomes a possible major intervening variable between individuals and their performance. The most extensive study along these lines (Coleman et al., 1966) indicates that most measures of educational quality are only marginally related to performance on intellectual tasks, once socio-economic status is held constant. Other studies [70] of adults, however, hold forth the possibility that some educational quality effects may yet be found.

I. VALUES AND IDEOLOGY

As a concept in sociology, "values" has a particularly murky position. Indeed, it would have been possible, following at least one definition of "values," to write our preceding subsections entirely in terms of socio-economic differentials in values. Thus, the discussion of child-rearing practices could have been stated in terms of the differences in desired behavioral tendencies sought by middle-class and lower-class

70. Some of these relationships are discussed in the report of the United States Commission on Civil Rights (1967). Unpublished data analyzed by NORC from its study for the Commission indicates that, controlling for parental education, verbal achievement and school quality are positively correlated. For a discussion of facilities available to different groups in one city, see Sexton (1961); the impact of pupil background on teachers has been studied by Herriott and St. John (1966); the possible differential treatments meted out to low-income students and possible solutions are discussed by Riessman (1962).

parents. In order to bypass the difficult question of whether a particular practice or behavioral tendency actually expressed generalized preferences or desired end states, we have preferred to review the literature primarily in terms of behavior and predisposition, leaving to this subsection studies involving highly generalized preferences, views of the world, and the society. For convenience, we have separated values from ideology, the latter being primarily related to evaluations of society and its component parts.

Despite the emphasis on values by writers who subscribe to the view that the "lower-lowers" constitute a subculture, there have been few studies of values seen as generalized world views. Using Kluckhohn's (Kluckhohn, 1950, 1951; Kluckhohn and Strodtbeck, 1961) multidimensional classification of value systems, Schneiderman (1964) administered questionnaires to a small sample of 35 relief clients in St. Paul, Minnesota, a sample of 68 social workers employed by the Department of Public Welfare, and a sample of 52 teachers of the children from the 35 families. Schneiderman found that responses from the teachers and the social workers were in such strong agreement that they could be considered as drawn from the same population. The welfare clients professed value patterns markedly different from the professionals'—a world view that sees man as subjugated to, or in harmony with, nature as opposed to a view that sees man as mastering nature; a present-time orientation as opposed to a future-time orientation; an individualistic orientation as opposed to a lineal or collateral one (showing in this respect little difference from professional social workers or teachers) ; a slight, although not significant, preference for a pessimistic, as opposed to an optimistic, view of human nature; and an orientation to *being* rather than *becoming*.

A more elaborate study was reported in an article by Cohen and Hodges (1963) based on interviews with 2,600 male heads of households in three counties in the San Francisco area. The article presents in a summary form generalizations contrasting the "lower-blue-collar" respondents with others interviewed.[71] This group is characterized as having a simplified experiential contact with the world (that is, a constriction of life experiences) , a sense of deprivation, with accompanying feelings of insecurity, and a consequent inability to cope with the problems of life. Lower-blue-collar respondents are

71. Unfortunately, their presentation does not contain a clear statement of how they distinguish this group from others nor detailed descriptions of the questionnaires used. This appears to be a preliminary report of the research, but we were unable to find a more detailed account of this particular study.

further characterized as anti-intellectual and authoritarian, with corresponding intolerance for violators of conventional morality and for minority groups, a pessimism concerning the future, and a misanthropic view of mankind.

A similar characterization of working-class life has been offered by S. M. Miller and Riessman (1961b) in which they identify the following themes: a concern for stability and security, traditionalism in moral precepts, anti-intellectualism, an appreciation of "excitement" among younger groups, and intensity concerning those things that matter to them. Miller and Riessman make a distinction between the "stable" working class described and a "lower-class" worker, the difference being that "lower class style is considered to be the inability to develop an adequate measure of coping with the environment so that some degree of security and stability ensues (p. 96)."

Walter Miller (1958), in an article summarizing some results of his study of twenty-one street corner groups in Boston, presented a list of "focal concerns" of lower-class culture that foster delinquent behavior. A considerable similarity between these concerns and the previous studies described in this section can be seen from the following list: toughness (masculinity), trouble (contacts with the police or other law-enforcement agencies), smartness (getting by with a minimum of exertion and a maximum of mental agility), excitement (being where the action is), and autonomy (avoidance or rejection of external controls imposed by society).

The sense of powerlessness, inability to control one's fate, and detachment from the larger society is shown in a number of special studies directed at these dimensions. Cited earlier was the finding by Campbell et al. (1960) that members of the working and lower class lack a feeling of political efficacy. A number of studies confirm that anomie [72] is more prevalent on the lower levels of the socio-economic ladder (Bell, 1957; Meier and Bell, 1959; Simpson and Miller, 1963) than on the higher levels.

The extent to which the lower class differs markedly in these respects from other groups in the society is hard to judge from any of these studies. Schneiderman's small-scale study is perhaps the easiest

72. In these studies, anomie is usually measured with a scale constructed by Leo Srole. It attempts to measure the extent to which an individual feels that community leaders are indifferent to his needs; that he can do little to direct his life with any degree of time perspective; feeling of retrogression from goals already reached; loss of meaning of internalized group norms, values, and goals; and lack of confidence in immediate personal relationships.

to evaluate, but its scope is so narrow that confidence in its conclusions cannot be strongly justified. The conclusions of the study by Cohen and Hodges would be considerably strengthened had the authors presented more of their data. Whether descriptions presented by S. M. Miller and Riessman are correct or not is even harder to judge since whatever data may underlay their statements is not documented in their presentations. Finally, the complete analysis of Walter Miller's study of a lower-class area in Boston has not been published; it is therefore difficult to judge the extent to which the "focal concerns" isolated from the study of gangs can be extended to other age and sex groupings.

Somewhat better studies exist of ideology; a fairly large number of studies indicate an inverse relationship between socio-economic status and expressed prejudice or social distance from minority groups. Stember (1966), in an analysis of the relationship of education to anti-Semitism, shows that inverse relationships persist in a large number of national surveys conducted in the post-World War II period. Utilizing data from a representative sample of adults ($N = 1,182$), Hodge and Treiman (1966) show an inverse relationship between socio-economic status and prejudice toward Negroes; this relationship is seen to hold whether socio-economic status is measured by income, education, or occupation (Treiman, 1966). A number of studies have used a Social Distance Scale in the study of prejudice toward ethnic groups and found greater intergroup prejudice among lower socio-economic status levels (Westie, 1952; Westie and Howard, 1954; Westie and Westie, 1957).

In a study of tolerance for political deviants, Stouffer (1955), found that lower socio-economic groups were less tolerant toward socialists, Communists, and atheists, although education played a stronger role in the relationships than occupation or income. Lower socio-economic status groups were more willing to bar Communists and socialists from a variety of positions, including employment in nonsensitive private industries, than middle-class respondents.

Lipset (1959), in a major review article of many studies, argues that the family patterns, educational experiences, characteristic tensions and insecurities, plus the lack of sophistication of low-status individuals, predispose them "to favor extremist, intolerant, and transvaluational forms of political and religious behavior." [73] Lip-

73. The original presentation of the relationship between authoritarianism and prejudice was conceived chiefly in connection with middle-class support for fascist movements (Adorno et al., 1950). Partly due to biased sampling, the find-

sitz (1965) disputes Lipset's findings by showing that for three national sample surveys most of the inverse relationship between authoritarianism and socio-economic status can be eliminated by controlling for the educational attainment of respondents. S. M. Miller and Riessman (1961a) also dispute Lipset's findings, although mainly on the grounds that the measures of authoritarianism employed are biased in favor of the middle class.

The socio-economic differentials in voting behavior and political ideology have been well documented. In a review of the psychology of voting, Lipset et al. (1954) note that in every economically developed country, the lower-income groups vote mainly for parties of the left, while higher-income groups vote for parties of the right. In the United States, a positive association between socio-economic status and voting for the Republican Party is a socological commonplace (Lipset et al., 1954; Campbell et al., 1960, 1966). Studies of political issues indicate that lower socio-economic status groups usually take the more liberal position on a variety of issues affecting support for labor unions, increased welfare activities of the state, and opposition to the power of business (Centers, 1949; Berelson et al., 1954; Campbell et al., 1960, 1966; Stouffer, 1955).[74] Similar findings for other Western countries are reported by Alford (1963).

A further question, and of particular importance in its policy implications, is that of the ideology of relief—whether there exists a discrete set of attitudes about giving and receiving public welfare. The distinction between contributory social insurance and the "dole" has been at the heart of conventional wisdom about the American approach to poverty for the past half century (Brown, 1956). The prevailing image of public opinion has the public reluctant about handing out the dole and the poor uncomfortable about receiving handouts.

Empirical evidence bearing on these assumptions is scant, indeed, and is spread across three decades. As a result, attempts to

---

ing that the lower-middle class is the most prejudiced and authoritarian has not been sustained in subsequent findings. Janowitz and Marvick (1953), for example, find an inverse relationship between authoritarianism (using a short version of the F-scale) and SES. For some of the critiques of the original Adorno et al. work, see Christie and Jahoda (1954); for a summary of the research findings of the many studies in this area, see Christie and Cook (1958).

74. As indicated earlier, working-class liberalism does not extend toward civil liberties for deviant political groups; in those instances, the working class is more likely to take a conservative position. On an individual level, it appears that liberalism on economic issues is often correlated inversely with liberal views on civil rights for deviant groups.

synthesize even what is available are confounded by three historical phenomena: (1) only during the thirties, and not since, was it possible for the public to fix the blame for poverty on a national economic catastrophe; (2) because the poor and the Negro have in recent years become so largely coterminous in the public mind, it is difficult to know when attitudes toward race become confounded with attitudes toward welfare; and (3) the Aid to Dependent Children has overshadowed Old Age Assistance as the dominant public-assistance program in the last decade.

Nevertheless, what evidence is available does not clearly support the stereotypes. In a compendium of national surveys on social security over the past thirty years, Schiltz (1968) notes a marked absence of concern for the allegedly superior aspects of old-age insurance arising from its contributory and non-means-test provisions. Pinner et al. (1959), in a study of OAA recipients in California, found a propensity for the aged to regard their checks as a matter of right. Pinner's indirect evidence supports that of Bond et al. (1954) who found, in another California survey, that the children of the needy aged prefer their parents to go on relief, even if the children are capable of supporting their parents, and that the parents prefer public support to that of their children.[75]

Even more important, the evidence is abundant that the American public, both as taxpayers and as relief consumers, regard the poverty of the aged quite differently from poverty among younger age groups. Schiltz (1968) notes that from 1936 to 1946, old-age programs received nearly unanimous support from all sectors of the population, while unemployment compensation received less support and generated sharp cleavages along urban-rural and educational continua, the college-educated rural resident being the most hostile.

The distinguishing feature seems to be that the aged cannot be expected to work and thus deserve support (Pinner, 1959). Studies of depression unemployment (Bakke, 1940; Angell, 1936) seem to suggest that what demeans is not the acceptance of charity, but the implicit prior assumption that one has failed in not getting and holding a job. Survey evidence is overwhelming that Americans preferred work relief to cash relief during the depression, and there was no difference in this attitude by income class or relief status (Schiltz, 1968). Bakke (1940) notes the restored self-image among those on work relief. Pinner (1959) concludes that the work ethic is stronger

75. Pinner also reports that more OAA recipients are "glad" to be on OAA than are "embarrassed" by it.

among those who have had a marginally successful work history than among those who have not.

In this connection, the findings by Goodchilds and Smith (1963) are relevant. They found, among a small sample of unemployed men, that middle-class respondents tended to lower their self-appraisal as the length of unemployment increased, while working-class respondents' self-appraisal increased. The finding that unemployment apparently had more of a negative effect on middle-class respondents is consistent with Bakke; the finding of increases in positive self-perceptions with the length of unemployment on the part of lower-status respondents needs further clarification.

If there is evidence that the work ethic is salient, there is little evidence that economic self-interest is equally so. In an examination of scores of survey questions related to social-security programs and welfare policy, Schiltz (1968) finds no consistent patterns among income or age lines.

Tangible evidence about the effect of relief on the incentive to work is hard to come by. Lane (1962), in his intensive interviewing of lower-middle-class Westport men, finds a deeply ingrained belief that the lower classes would stop working if their needs were met by a dole. Whether this belief pervades the public generally has *never* been tested.

Clearly widespread is the conviction that relief recipients cheat (Schiltz, 1968; Lane, 1962; Bond, 1954), a conviction that is not strongly influenced by income class; and the implication seems to be that cheating by relief recipients is more reprehensible than analogous white-collar deceptions (Lane, 1962). But this willingness to ascribe "chiseling" to the relief recipient is consistently accompanied by a willingness to sustain or increase present levels of relief. It may be that the American public is caught in a cross-pressure between its philanthropic impulse and its competitive-work ethic. This attitude is caught directly in Lane (1962) and summarized in Schiltz (1968). At the same time, cheating appears to be different from the perspective of the recipient. Bakke (1940) describes the delicate style, developed from experience, necessary to "con" the relief worker into a few extras and suggests that the art of getting the most out of the "system" became, for many depression men, an acceptable status substitute for the art of getting and keeping a job.

Finally, the American public has been rather consistently unwilling to fix responsibility firmly for individual poverty. Schiltz (1968) has shown that during the depression Americans were more willing to attribute poverty to "circumstances" than in the sixties, when they are about equally divided as to whether a person's poverty is his own fault, that of circumstances alone, or due to a combination of the two.

❧ Bibliography

Adorno, T. W.; Frenkel-Brunswik, Else; Levinson, Daniel J.; and Sanford, R. Nevitt. *The authoritarian personality*. New York: Harper & Bros., 1950.

Akers, Ronald. Socio-economic status and delinquent behavior: A re-test. *J. res. crime Delinq.*, 1964, *1*, No. 1 (January), 38–46.

Alexander, C. Norman, Jr., and Campbell, Ernest Q. Peer influence on adolescent educational aspirations and attainment. *ASR*, 1964, *29*, No. 4 (August), 568–575.

Alford, Robert R. *Party and society: The Anglo-American democracies*. Chicago: Rand McNally, 1963.

Alinsky, Saul. *Reveille for radicals*. Chicago: University of Chicago Press, 1946.

Anastasi, A. *Differential psychology*. New York: Macmillan, 1958.

Anderson, Nels. *Work and leisure*. New York: The Free Press of Glencoe, 1961.

Anderson, Odin W. Infant mortality and social and cultural factors. In E. Gartley Jaco (ed.), *Patients, physicians and illness*. New York: The Free Press of Glencoe, 1958. Pp. 10–24.

Anderson, W. H. Locke. Trickling down: The relationship between economic growth and the extent of poverty among American families. *Quart. J. of Econ.*, 1964, *78*. (November), 511–524.

Angell, Robert Cooley. *The family encounters the depression*. New York: Charles Scribner's Sons, 1936.

Antonovsky, Aaron. Social class and illness: A reconsideration. *Sociol. Inq.*, 1967, *37*, No. 2 (Spring), 311–322.

Antonovsky, Aaron, and Lerner, Melvin J. Occupational aspirations of lower class Negro and white youth. *Soc. Prob.*, 1959, *7*, No. 2 (Fall).

Antonovsky, Aaron, and Lorwin, Lewis L. (eds.). *Discrimination and low incomes*. New York: New School for Social Research, 1959.

Atkinson, John W., and Feather, Norman T. (eds.). *A theory of achievement motivation*. New York: John Wiley & Sons, 1966.

Auld, Frank, Jr. Influences of social class on personality test responses. *Psychol. Bull.,* 1952, *49,* No. 4, Part 1 (July), 318–332.

Bakke, E. Wight. *Citizens without work: A study of the effects of unemployment upon the worker's social relations and practices.* New Haven, Conn.: Yale University Press, 1940.

Bates, William. Social stratification and juvenile delinquency. *Amer. Cath. sociol. Rev.,* 1960, *21,* No. 3 (Fall), 221–228.

———. Caste, class and vandalism. *Soc. Prob.,* 1962, *9,* No. 4 (Spring), 348–353.

Bear, Roberta Meyer; Hess, Robert D.; and Shipman, Virginia C. Social class differences in maternal attitudes toward school and the consequences for cognitive development in the young child. Paper presented at the American Educational Research Association, February 19, 1965, Chicago, Illinois.

Beilin, Harry. The pattern of postponability and its relation to social class and mobility. *J. soc. Psychol.,* 1956, *44,* 33–48.

Bell, Gerald D. Processes in the formation of adolescents' aspirations. *SF,* 1963, *42,* No. 2 (December), 179–186.

Bell, Robert R. Lower class Negro mothers' aspirations for their children. *SF,* 1965, *43* (May), 493–500.

Bell, Wendell. Anomie, social isolation, and the class structure. *Sociometry,* 1957, *20,* No. 2 (June), 105–116.

Bell, Wendell; Hill, Richard J.; and Wright, Charles R. *Public leadership.* San Francisco: Chandler, 1961.

Bendix, Reinhard, and Lipset, Seymour M. (eds.). *Class, status and power: Social stratification in comparative perspective.* (2nd ed.) New York: The Free Press of Glencoe, 1966.

Bennett, William S., Jr., and Gist, Noel P. Class and family influences on student aspirations, *SF,* 1964, *43,* No. 2 (December), 167–173.

Berelson, Bernard R., and Janowitz, Morris (eds.). *Reader in public opinion and communication.* (2nd ed.) New York: The Free Press of Glencoe, 1966.

Berelson, Bernard R.; Lazarsfeld, Paul F.; and McPhee, William N. *Voting: A study of opinion formation in a presidential campaign.* Chicago: The University of Chicago Press, 1954.

Berelson, Bernard R., and Steiner, Gary. *Human behavior: An inventory of scientific findings.* New York: Harcourt, Brace & World, 1964.

Bernard, Sydney E. *Fatherless families: Their economic and social adjustment.* Waltham, Mass.: The Florence Heller Graduate School for Advanced Studies in Social Welfare, Brandeis University, 1964.

Bernstein, Basil. Some sociological determinants of perception. *Brit. J. Sociol.,* 1958, *9,* No. 2 (June), 159–174.

———. Language and social class. *Brit. J. Sociol.,* 1960, *11,* No. 3 (September), 271–276.

———. Social class, linguistic codes, and grammatical elements. *Lang. Speech,* 1962, *5,* 221–240.

——— (a). Social class and linguistic development: A theory of social learning. In A. H. Halsey et al. (eds.), Education, economy and society. New York: The Free Press of Glencoe, 1964. Pp. 288–314.

——— (b). Social class, speech systems and psychotherapy. *Brit. J. Sociol.,* 1964, *15,* No. 1 (March), 54–64.

Blauner, Robert. Work satisfaction and industrial trends in modern society. Reprint No. 151, Institute of Industrial Relations, University of California, Berkeley, 1960. Also in Walter Galenson and Seymour M. Lipset (eds.), Labor and trade unionism. New York: John Wiley & Sons, 1960. Pp. 339–360.

———. *Alienation and freedom.* Chicago: University of Chicago Press, 1964.

Blood, Robert O., Jr., and Wolfe, Donald M. *The dynamics of married living.* New York: The Free Press of Glencoe, 1960.

Bloom, Richard, Whiteman, Martin, and Deutsch, Martin. Race and social class as separate factors related to social environment. *AJS,* 1965, *70,* No. 4 (January), 471–476.

Blum, Zahava D., and Rossi, Peter H. *Social class and poverty: A selected and annotated bibliography.* Boston: American Academy of Arts and Sciences, 1966. (Mimeographed.)

Boek, Walter E.; Sussman, Marvin B.; and Yankauer, Alfred. Social class and child care practices. *Marr. fam. Living,* 1958, *20,* No. 4 (November), 326–333.

Bond, Floyd A.; Barber, Ray E.; Vieg, John A.; Perry, Louis B.; Scaff, Alvin H.; and Lee, Luther J., Jr. *Our needy aged: A California study of a national problem.* New York: Henry Holt, 1954.

Bordua, David J. Juvenile delinquency and "anomie": An attempt at replication. *Soc. Prob.,* 1958–1959, *6,* 230–238.

Bowerman, Charles E., and Elder, Glen H., Jr. Variations in adolescent perception of family power structure. *ASR,* 1964, *29,* No. 4 (August), 551–567.

Bradburn, Norman M. *The structure of psychological well-being.* Chicago: Aldine, 1968.

Bradburn, Norman, and Caplovitz, David. *Reports on happiness.* Chicago: Aldine, 1965.

Brim, Orville G.; Neulinger, John; and Glass, David. *Experiences and attitudes of American adults concerning standardized I.Q. tests.* Technical Report No. 1 on the Social Consequences of Testing. New York: The Russell Sage Foundation, 1965.

Bronfenbrenner, Urie. Socialization and social class through time and space. In Reinhard Bendix and Seymour M. Lipset (eds.), *Class, status and power.* New York: The Free Press of Glencoe, 1966, pp. 362–377.

Brown, J. Douglas. The American philosophy of social insurance. *Soc. serv. Rev.,* 1956, *30,* No. 1 (March), 1–8.

Burchinal, Lee; Gardner, Bruce; and Hawkes, Glenn R. Children's personality adjustment and the socio-economic status of their families. *J. genet. Psychol.,* 1958, *92* (June), 149–159.

Burgess, M. Elaine, and Price, Daniel O. *American dependency challenge.* Chicago: American Public Welfare Association, 1963.

Campbell, Angus; Converse, Philip E.; Miller, Warren E.; and Stokes, Donald E. *The American voter.* New York: John Wiley & Sons, 1960.

———. *Elections and the political order.* New York: John Wiley & Sons, 1966.

Caplovitz, David. *The poor pay more.* New York: The Free Press of Glencoe, 1963.

Caplovitz, David, and Bradburn, Norman M. *Social class and psychological adjustment: A portrait of the communities in the "happiness" study.* A preliminary report. Chicago: National Opinion Research Center, January, 1964.

Cazden, Courtney B. Subcultural differences in child language: An interdisciplinary view. *Merrill-Palmer Q.,* 1966, *12,* No. 3 (July), 185–219.

Centers, Richard. *The psychology of social classes.* Princeton, N.J.: Princeton University Press, 1949.

Chapman, Ames W. Attitudes toward legal authorities by juveniles. *Sociol. soc. Res.,* 1956, *40,* No. 3 (January–February), 170–175.

Chilman, Catherine S. Child-rearing and family relationship patterns of the very poor. *Welf. in Rev.,* 1965, *3,* No. 1 (January), 9–19.

———. Growing up poor. Washington, D.C.: United States Department of Health, Education, and Welfare, Welfare Administration Publication No. 13 (May), 1966.

Chilton, Roland J. Continuity in delinquency area research: A comparison of studies for Baltimore, Detroit, and Indianapolis. *ASR,* 1964, *29,* No. 1 (February), 71–83.

Christie, Richard, and Cook, Peggy. A guide to published literature relating to the authoritarian personality. *J. of Psychol.,* 1958, *45* (April), 171–199.

Christie, Richard, and Jahoda, Marie (eds.). *Studies in the scope and method of the authoritarian personality: Continuities in social research.* Glencoe, Ill.: The Free Press, 1954.

Clark, John P., and Wenninger, Eugene P. Social-economic class and area as correlates of illegal behavior among juveniles. *ASR,* 1962, *27,* No. 6 (December), 826–834.

Clark, Robert E. Psychoses, income and occupational prestige. *AJS,* 1949, *54,* No. 5 (March), 433–440.

Clarke, Alfred C. The use of leisure and its relation to levels of occupational prestige. *ASR,* 1956, *21,* No. 3 (June), 301–307.

Clausen, John A., and Kohn, Melvin L. Relations of schizophrenia to the social structure of a small city. In Pasamanick, Benjamin (ed.), *Epidemiology of mental disorder.* Washington, D.C.: American Association for the Advancement of Science, 1959.

Cloward, Richard A., and Ohlin, Lloyd E. *Delinquency and opportunity.* New York: The Free Press of Glencoe, 1960.

Cohen, Albert K. *Delinquent boys.* New York: The Free Press of Glencoe, 1955.

Cohen, Albert N., and Hodges, Harold M., Jr. Characteristics of the lower-blue-collar class. *Soc. Prob.,* 1963, *10,* No. 4 (Spring), 303–333.

Cohen, Jerome. Social work and the culture of poverty. *Soc. Wk.,* 1964, *9,* No. 1 (January), 3–11.

Coleman, James S. *The adolescent society.* New York: The Free Press of Glencoe, 1961.

Coleman, James, et al. *Equality of educational opportunity.* Washington, D.C.: Office of Education (OE-38001), 1966.

————. *Equality of educational opportunity: Supplemental appendix.* Washington, D.C.: Office of Education (OE-38oo01—Supplement), 1966.

Cooper, Homer Chassell. Social class identification and political party affiliation. *Psychol. Rept.,* 1959, *5,* 337–340.

Coser, Lewis A. Sociology of poverty. *Soc. Prob.,* 1965, *13,* No. 2 (Fall), 140–148.

Curtis, Richard F. Differential association and the stratification of the urban community. *SF,* 1963, *42,* No. 1 (October), 68–76.

Davis, Allison, and Dollard, John, Jr. *Children of bondage: The personality development of Negro children in the urban south.* Washington, D.C.: American Council on Education, 1940.

Davis, Allison, and Havighurst, Robert J. Social class and color differences in child rearing. *ASR,* 1946, *11,* 698–710.

Davis, Kingsley. Some demographic aspects of poverty in the United States. In Margaret S. Gordon (ed.), *Poverty in America.* San Francisco: Chandler, 1965, 299–319.

Deasy, Leila Calhoun. Socio-economic status and participation in the poliomyelitis vaccine trial. *ASR,* 1956, *21,* No. 2 (April), 185–191.

DeGrazia, Sebastian. *Of time, work and leisure.* New York: Twentieth Century Fund, 1962.

Demerath, Nicholas J., III. Social class, religious affiliation, and styles of religious involvement. In Reinhard Bendix and Seymour M. Lipset (eds.), *Class, status and power.* New York: The Free Press of Glencoe, 1966, 388–394.

Dentler, Robert A., and Monroe, Lawrence J. Social correlates of early adolescent theft. *ASR,* 1961, *26,* No. 5 (October), 733–743.

Deutsch, Martin. The role of social class in language development and cognition. *Amer. J. Orthopsychiat.,* 1965, *35,* No. 1 (January), 78–88.

Deutsch, Martin, and Brown, Bert. Social influences in negro-white intelligence differences. *J. soc. Issues,* 1964, *20,* No. 2 (April), 24–35.

Dohrenwend, Bruce P., and Chin-Shong, Edwin. Social status and attitudes toward psychological disorder: The problem of tolerance of deviance. *ASR,* 1967, *32,* No. 3 (June), 417–433.

Dollard, John. *Caste and class in a southern town.* New Haven, Conn.: Yale University Press, 1937.

Dotson, Floyd. Patterns of voluntary association among urban working class families. *ASR,* 1951, *16,* No. 5 (October), 687–693.

Douvan, Elizabeth. Social success and success striving. *J. abnorm. soc. Psychol.,* 1956, *52,* 219–233.

Dreger, Ralph Mason, and Miller, Kent S. Comparative psychological studies of Negroes and whites in the United States. *Psychol. Bull.,* 1960, *57,* No. 5 (September), 361–402.

Duncan, Otis Dudley, and Hodge, Robert W. Education and occupational mobility: A regression analysis. *AJS,* 1963, *68,* No. 6 (May), 629–644.

Eckland, Bruce K. Genetics and sociology: A reconsideration. *ASR,* 1967, *32,* No. 3 (April), 173–194.

Elder, Glen H., Jr. Structural variations in the child rearing relationship. *Sociometry,* 1962, *25,* No. 4, 241–262.

Ellis, Dean S. Speech and social status in America. *SF,* 1967, *45,* No. 3 (March), 431–437.

———. The identification of social status from limited vocal cues. Unpublished paper, Purdue University, Communications Research Center, 1963.

Ellis, John M. Socio-economic differentials in mortality from chronic diseases. In E. Gartly Jaco (ed.), *Patients, physicians and illness.* Glencoe, Ill.: The Free Press, 1958, 30–37.

Empey, LaMar T. Social class and occupational aspiration: A comparison of absolute and relative measurement. *ASR,* 1956, *21,* No. 6 (December), 703–709.

Engel, Madaline H. A reconsideration of the concept of "American lower class": A study of urban subculture. Unpublished doctoral dissertation, Fordham University, 1966.

Ennis, Philip H. *Adult book reading in the United States: A preliminary report.* Chicago: National Opinion Research Center, September, 1965.

———. *Criminal victimization in the United States: A report of a national survey.* Washington, D.C.: Government Printing Office, 1967. Field Studies II, U.S. President's Commission on Law Enforcement and the Administration of Justice.

Epstein, Lenore A. Some effects of low income on children and their families. *Soc. sec. Bull.,* 1961, *24,* No. 2 (February), 12–17.

Erickson, Maynard L., and Empey, LaMar T. Class, position, peers and delinquency. *Sociol. soc. Res.,* 1965, *49,* No. 3 (April), 268–282.

Eron, Leonard D.; Walder, Leonard O.; Toigo, Romolo; and Lefkowitz, Monroe M. Social class, parental punishment for aggression, and child aggression. *Child dev.,* 1963, *34* (December), 849–867.

Faris, Robert, and Dunham, Warren. *Mental disorders in urban areas.* Chicago: University of Chicago Press, 1939.

Ferman, Louis A.; Kornbluh, Joyce L.; and Haber, Alan (eds.). *Poverty in America.* Ann Arbor: University of Michigan Press, 1965.

Findlay, Donald C., and McGuire, Carson. Social status and abstract behavior. *J. abnorm. soc. Psychol.,* 1957, *54* (January), 135–137.

Foskett, John M. Social structure and social participation. *ASR,* 1955, *20,* No. 4 (August), 431–438.

Frazier, E. Franklin. *The Negro family in America.* Chicago, Ill.: University of Chicago Press, 1939.

Freeman, Howard E., and Kassebaum, Gene G. Relationship of education and knowledge to opinions about mental illness. *Ment. Hyg.,* 1960, *44* (January), 43–47.

Freeman, Howard E., and Simmons, Ozzie G. Social class and posthospital performance. *ASR,* 1959, *24,* No. 3 (June), 345–351.

Freedman, Ronald; Whelpton, Pascal K.; and Campbell, Arthur A. *Family planning, sterility, and population growth.* New York: McGraw-Hill Book Company, Inc., 1959.

Freedman, Ronald; Whelpton, Pascal K.; and Smit, John W. Socio-economic factors in religious differentials in fertility. *ASR,* 1961, *26,* No. 4 (August), 608–614.

Friedhoff, W. H. Relationship among various measures of socio-economic status, social class identification, intelligence, and school achievement. Dissertation Abstracts, 1955, Vol. 15.

Frumkin, Robert M. Social factors in schizophrenia. *Sociol. soc. Res.*, 1954, *38*, No. 6 (July–August), 383–386.

Gans, Herbert J. *The urban villagers.* Glencoe, Ill.: The Free Press, 1962.

Gist, Noel P., and Bennett, William S., Jr. Aspirations of Negro and white students. *SF*, 1963, *42*, No. 1 (October), 40–48.

Glazer, Nathan, and Moynihan, Daniel Patrick. *Beyond the melting pot.* Cambridge, Mass.: M.I.T. and Harvard University Presses, 1963.

Glick, Ira O., and Levy, Sidney J. *Living with television.* Chicago: Aldine, 1962.

Glick, Paul C., and Carter, Hugh. Marriage patterns and educational level. *ASR*, 1958, *23*, No. 3 (June), 294–300.

Gold, Martin. Undetected delinquent behavior. *J. res. Crime and Delinq.*, 1966, *3*, No. 1 (January), 27–46.

Goodchilds, Jacqueline D., and Smith, Ewart E. The effects of unemployment as mediated by social status. *Sociometry*, 1963, *26*, No. 3 (September), 287–293.

Goode, Erich. Social class and church participation. *AJS*, 1966, *72*, No. 1 (July), 102–111.

Goode, William J. Economic factors and marital stability. *ASR*, 1951, *16*, No. 6 (December), 802–812.

―――. Marital satisfaction and instability: A cross-cultural analysis of divorce rates. In Reinhard Bendix and Seymour M. Lipset (eds.), *Class, status, and power.* New York: The Free Press of Glencoe, 1966, 377–387.

Gordon, Margaret S. (ed.). *Poverty in America.* San Francisco: Chandler, 1965.

Gosnell, Harold F. *Machine politics: Chicago style.* Chicago: University of Chicago Press, 1937.

Graham, Saxon. Socio-economic status, illness, and the use of medical services. In E. Gartly Jaco (ed.), *Patients, physicians and illness.* Glencoe, Ill.: The Free Press, 1958, 129–134.

―――. Social factors in relation to chronic illnesses. In Howard E. Freeman et al. (eds.), *Handbook of medical sociology.* Englewood Cliffs, N.J.: Prentice-Hall, 1963, 65–98.

Graham, Saxon; Levin, Morton; and Lilienfeld, Abraham M. The socioeconomic distribution of cancer of various sites in Buffalo, N.Y. *Cancer*, 1960, *13*, No. 1 (January–February), 180–191.

Gray, Susan W., and Klaus, Rupert A. An experimental preschool program for culturally deprived children. *Child Dev.*, 1965, *36*, No. 4 (December), 887–898.

Greeley, Andrew M. *Religion and career.* New York: Sheed and Ward, 1963.

Greeley, Andrew M., and Rossi, Peter H. *The education of Catholic Americans.* Chicago: Aldine, 1966.

Gurin, Gerald; Veroff, Joseph; and Feld, Sheila. *Americans view their mental health: A nation-wide interview survey.* New York: Basic Books, 1960.

Haase, William. The role of socioeconomic class in examiner bias. In Frank

Riessman et al. (eds.), *Mental health in the poor.* New York: The Free Press of Glencoe, 1964, 241–247.

Haggstrom, Warren C. The power of the poor. In Louis Ferman et al. (eds.), *Poverty in America.* Ann Arbor: University of Michigan Press, 1965, 315–335.

Haller, Archibald O., and Shailer, Thomas. Personality correlates of the socio-economic status of adolescent males. *Sociometry,* 1962, *25,* No. 4 (December), 398–404.

Halpert, Harold P. Surveys of public opinions and attitudes about mental illness: Implications for communications activities. *Publ. Hlth. Rep.,* 1965, *80,* No. 7 (July), 589–597.

Handel, Gerald, and Rainwater, Lee. Persistence and change in working-class life style. *Sociol. soc. Res.,* 1964, *48,* No. 3 (April), 281–288.

Harms, L. S. Listener judgments of status cues in speech. *Quart. J. Speech,* 1961, *47,* No. 2 (April), 164–188.

———. Speaking ability and social class. Paper presented at the 1963 convention of the National Society for the Study of Communication, Denver, Colorado.

Harrington, Michael. *The other America.* New York: Macmillan, 1962.

Harrison, Saul I.; McDermott, John F.; Wilson, Paul T.; and Schrager, Jules. Social class and mental illness in children. *Arch. of gen. Psychiat.,* 1965, *13,* No. 5 (November), 411–417.

Hausknecht, Murray. *The joiners: A sociological description of voluntary association membership in the United States.* New York: Bedminster Press, 1962.

Havighurst, Robert J.; Bowman, Paul H.; Liddle, Gordon P.; Matthews, Charles V.; and Pierce, James V. *Growing up in River City.* New York: John Wiley & Sons, 1962.

Herriott, Robert E., and St. John, Nancy Hoyt. *Social class and the urban school.* New York: John Wiley & Sons, 1966.

———. Early experiences and the socialization of cognitive modes in children. *Child Dev.,* 1965, *36,* No. 4 (December), 869–885.

Hess, Robert D., and Shipman, Virginia C. (a). Cognitive elements in maternal behavior. Unpublished paper, University of Chicago, 1966.

——— (b). Maternal attitudes toward the school and the role of the pupil: Some social class comparisons. In A. Henry Passow (ed.), *Fifth work conference on curriculum and teaching in depressed areas.* New York: Bureau of Publications, Teachers College, Columbia University, 1966.

Hicks, Robert A., and Pellegrini, Robert J. The meaningfulness of negro-white differences in intelligence test performance. *Psychol. Rec.,* 1966, *16,* No. 1 (January), 43–46.

Himeloch, Jerome, and Fava, Sylvia F. (eds.). *Sexual behavior in American society: An appraisal of the first two Kinsey reports.* New York: W. W. Norton & Company, Inc., 1955.

Hodge, Robert W., and Treiman, Donald J. Occupational mobility and attitudes toward Negroes. *ASR,* 1966, *31,* No. 1 (February), 93–102.

———. Class identification in the United States. *AJS,* forthcoming.

Hodge, Robert W.; Treiman, Donald J.; and Rossi, Peter H. A comparative study of occupational prestige. In Reinhard Bendix and Seymour M.

Lipset (eds.), *Class, status, and power.* New York: The Free Press of Glencoe, 1966, 309–321.

Hodge, Robert W.; Siegel, Paul M.; and Rossi, Peter H. Occupational prestige in the United States: 1925–1963. In Reinhard Bendix and Seymour M. Lipset (eds.), *Class, status, and power.* New York: The Free Press of Glencoe, 1966.

Hoffman, Martin L., and Hoffman, Lois W. (eds.). *Review of child development research.* New York: Russell Sage Foundation, 1964.

Hoffman, Martin L.; Mitsos, Spiro B.; and Protz, Roland E. Achievement striving, social class and test anxiety. *J. abnorm. soc. Psychol.* 1958, *56,* No. 3 (May), 401–403.

Hollingshead, August B. Class differences in family stability. *Annals,* 1950, 272 (November), 39–46.

Hollingshead, August B., and Redlich, Fredrick C. *Social class and mental illness: A community study.* New York: John Wiley & Sons, 1958.

Hylan, Lewis. Child rearing among low-income families. In Louis Ferman et al. (eds.), *Poverty in America.* Ann Arbor: University of Michigan Press, 1965, 342–353.

Hyman, Herbert H. The value systems of different classes: A social psychological contribution to the analysis of stratification. In Reinhard Bendix and Seymour M. Lipset (eds.), *Class, status, and power.* New York: The Free Press of Glencoe, 1966, 488–499.

Inkeles, Alex. Industrial man: The relation of status to experience, perception and value. *AJS,* 1960, *66,* No. 1 (July), 1–31.

Jackson, Luther P. *Poverty's children.* Washington, D.C.: The Health and Welfare Council of the National Capital Area, March, 1966. (Mimeographed.)

Jaco, E. Gartley. *The social epidemiology of mental disorders.* New York: Russell Sage Foundation, 1960.

Jaffe, Frederick S. Family planning and poverty. In Louis A. Ferman et al. (eds.), *Poverty in America.* Ann Arbor: University of Michigan Press, 1965, 335–341.

Jahoda, Marie. *Current concepts of positive mental health.* New York: Basic Books, 1958.

James, Rita M. Status and competence of jurors. *AJS,* 1964, *59,* No. 6 (May), 563–570.

Janowitz, Morris, and Marvick, Dwaine. Authoritarianism and political behavior. *Pub. Opin. Q.,* 1953, *17,* No. 2 (Summer), 185–202.

Jenkins, C. David. Group differences in perception: A study of community beliefs and feelings about TB. *AJS,* 1966, *71,* No. 4 (January), 417–429.

Johnsen, Kathryn P., and Leslie, Gerald R. Methodological notes on research in child rearing and social class. *Merrill-Palmer Q.,* 1965, *11,* No. 4 (October), 345–358.

Johnson, Cyrus M., and Kerckhoff, Alan C. Family norms, social position, and the value of change. *SF,* 1964, *43,* No. 2 (December), 149–156.

Johnstone, John W. C., and Rivera, Ramon J. *Volunteers for learning.* Chicago: Aldine, 1965.

Kadushin, Charles. Social distance between client and professionals. *AJS,* 1962, *67,* No. 5 (March), 517–531.

————. Social class and the experience of ill health. *Sociol. Inq.*, 1964, *34*, No. 1 (Winter), 67–80. Also in Reinhard Bendix and Seymour M. Lipset (eds.), *Class, status, and power.* New York: The Free Press of Glencoe, 1966, 406–412.

————. Social class and ill health: The need for further research. A reply to Antonovsky. *Sociol. Inq.*, 1967, *37*, No. 2 (Spring), 323–332.

Kahl, Joseph A. Some measurements of achievement orientation. *AJS*, 1965, *70*, No. 6 (May), 669–681.

Kantor, Mildred B.; Glidewell, John C.; Mensh, Ivan H.; Domke, Herbert R.; and Glides, Margaret C. L. Socio-economic level and maternal attitudes toward parent-child relationship. *Hum. Org.*, 1958, *16*, No. 4 (Winter), 44–48.

Kaplan, Bert; Reed, Robert; and Richardson, Wyman. A comparison of the incidence of hospitalized and non-hospitalized cases of psychosis in two communities. *ASR*, 1956, *21*, No. 4, 474–479.

Keller, Suzanne. The social world of the urban slum child: Some early findings. *Amer. J. Orthopsychiat.*, 1963, *33*, No. 5, 823–831.

————. *The American lower class family.* Albany: New York State Division for Youth. Research Document, 1966.

Keller, Suzanne, and Zavalloni, Marisa. Ambition and social class: A respecification. *SF*, 1964, *43*, No. 1 (October), 58–70.

King, Morton B., Jr. Socioeconomic status and sociometric choice. *SF*, 1961, *39*, 199–206.

Kinsey, Alfred, et al. *Sexual behavior in the human male.* Philadelphia: Saunders, 1948.

————. *Sexual behavior in the human female.* Philadelphia: Saunders, 1953.

Kiser, Clyde V. (ed.). *Research in family planning.* Princeton, N.J.: Princeton University Press, 1962.

Klatskin, Ethelyn H. Shifts in child care practices in three social classes under an infant care program of flexible methodology. *Amer. J. Orthopsychiat.*, 1952, *22*, 52–61.

Kleiner, Robert J., and Parker, Seymour. Goal-striving, social status, and mental disorder: A research review. *ASR*, 1963, *28*, No. 2 (April), 189–203.

Kleiner, Robert J.; Tuckman, Jacob; and Lavell, Martha. Mental disorder and status based on race. *Psychiatry*, 1960, *23*, No. 3 (August), 271–274.

Kluckhohn, Florence R. Dominant and substitute profiles of cultural orientations: Their significance for the analysis of social structure. *SF*, 1950, *28*, No. 4 (May), 376–393.

————. Dominant and variant cultural value orientations. *Soc. Welf. For.*, 1951, 97–113.

Kluckhohn, Florence R., and Strodtbeck, Fred L. *Variations in value orientation.* New York: Row, Peterson, 1961.

Knief, Lotus M., and Stroud, James B. Intercorrelations among various intelligence, achievement, and social class scores. *J. of educa. Psychol.* 1959, *50*, No. 3 (June), 117–120.

Knupfer, Genevieve. Portrait of the underdog. *Pub. Opin. Q.*, 1947, *11*, No. 1 (Spring), 103–114.

Kohn, Melvin L. (a). Social class and parental values. *AJS*, 1959, *64*, No. 4 (January), 337–351.

―――― (b). Social class and the exercise of parental authority. *ASR*, 1959, *24*, No. 3 (June), 352–366.

――――. Social class and parent-child relationships: An interpretation. *AJS*, 1963, *68* (January), 471–480.

Kohn, Melvin L., and Carroll, Eleanor E. Social class and the allocation of parental responsibilities. *Sociometry*, 1960, *23*, No. 4 (December), 372–392.

Komarovsky, Mira. *Blue-collar marriage.* New York: Random House, 1964.

Krause, Elliott A. *Factors related to length of mental hospital stay: A review of the literature.* Boston: Massachusetts Department of Mental Health, 1967, publication No. 3M-6-66-943307.

Krauss, Irving. Sources of educational aspirations among working-class youth. *ASR*, 1964, *29*, No. 6 (December), 867–879.

Kriesberg, Louis. Socioeconomic rank and behavior. *Soc. Prob.*, 1963, *10*, No. 4 (Spring), 334–352.

Kriesberg, Louis, and Treiman, Beatrice R. Socioeconomic status and the utilization of dentists' services. *J. Amer. Coll. Dentists*, 1960, *27*, No. 3 (September), 145–167.

Labov, William. Phonological correlates of social stratification. *Amer. Anthro.*, 1964, *66*, No. 6, Part 2 (December), 164–176.

Lambert, Wallace E., and Klineberg, Otto. Cultural comparisons of boys' occupational aspirations. *Brit. J. soc. clin. Psychol.*, 1963, *3*, No. 1 (February), 56–65.

Lander, Bernard. *Towards an understanding of juvenile delinquency: A study of 8,464 cases of juvenile delinquency in Baltimore.* New York: Columbia University Press, 1954.

Landis, Judson. Values and limitations of family research using student subjects. *Marr. fam. Living*, 1957, *19*, No. 1 (February).

Lane, Robert E. *Political ideology: Why the common man believes what he does.* New York: The Free Press of Glencoe, 1962.

Langner, Thomas S., and Michael, Stanley T. *Life stress and mental illness.* New York: The Free Press of Glencoe, 1963.

Larrabee, Eric, and Meyersohn, Rolf (eds.). *Mass leisure.* Glencoe, Ill.: The Free Press, 1958.

Laughton, Katherine B.; Buck, Carol W.; and Hobbs, G. E. Socio-economic status and illness. *Mil. Mem. Fund Q.*, 1958, *36*, No. 1 (January), 46–57.

Lawrence, P. S. Chronic illness and socio-economic status. In E. Gartly Jaco (ed.), *Patients, physicians, and illness.* Glencoe, Ill.: The Free Press, 1958, 37–49.

Lazarsfeld, Paul F.; Berelson, Bernard R.; and Gaudet, Hazel. *The people's choice.* New York: Columbia University Press, 1948.

Lefton, Mark; Angrist, Shirley; Dinitz, Simon; and Pasamanick, Benjamin. Social class, expectations, and performance of mental patients. *AJS*, 1962, *68*, No. 1 (July), 79–88.

Lemkau, Paul V., and Crocetti, Guido M. An urban population's opinion and knowledge about mental illness. *Amer. J. Psychiat.*, 1962, *118*, No. 8 (February), 692–700.

Leslie, Gerald R., and Johnsen, Kathryn P. Changed perceptions of the maternal role. *ASR*, 1963, *28* (December), 919–928.

Levine, G. N. Anxiety about illness: Psychological and social bases. *J. Hlth. hum. Behav.*, 1962, *3*, No. 2 (Spring), 30–34.

Lewis, Hylan. Child rearing among low-income families. Address to the Washington Center for Metropolitan Studies, Washington, D.C., June 8, 1961. (Mimeographed.)

Lewis, Oscar. *Five families*. New York: Basic Books, 1959.

———. *The children of Sanchez*. New York: Random House, 1961.

———. *La vida: A Puerto Rican family in the culture of poverty—San Juan and New York*. New York: Random House, 1965.

Liebow, Elliott. *Tally's Corner: A study of negro street corner men*. Boston: Little Brown, 1967.

Linn, Erwin L. Patients' socioeconomic characteristics and release from a mental hospital. *AJS*, 1959, *65*, No. 3 (November), 280–286.

Lipset, Seymour M. Democracy and working class authoritarianism. *ASR*, 1959, *24*, No. 4 (August), 482–501.

———. The value patterns of democracy: A case study in comparative analysis. *ASR*, 1963, *28* (August), 515–531.

Lipset, Seymour M.; Lazarsfeld, Paul F.; Barton, Allen H.; and Linz, Juan. The psychology of voting: An analysis of political behavior. In Gardner Lindzey (ed.), *Handbook of Social Psychology*. Reading, Mass.: Addison-Wesley, 1954, 1124–1175.

Lipsitz, Lewis. Working class authoritarianism—A re-evaluation. *ASR*, 1965, *30*, No. 1 (February), 103–110.

Little, J. Kenneth. *A statewide inquiry into decisions of youth about education beyond high school*. Madison: School of Education, University of Wisconsin, 1958.

Littman, Richard A.; Moore, Robert C. A.; and Pierce-Jones, John. Social class differences in child rearing: A third community for comparison with Chicago and Newton. *ASR*, 1957, *22*, No. 6 (December), 694–704.

Lockwood, David. The "new working class." *Eur. J. Sociol.*, 1960, *1*, No. 2, 248–259.

Lyman, Elizabeth L. Occupational differences in the value attached to work. *AJS*, 1955, *61*, No. 2 (September), 138–145.

Marris, Peter, and Rein, Martin. *Dilemmas of social reform: Poverty and community action in the United States*. New York: Atherton Press, 1967.

Marx, Karl. *The eighteenth brumaire of Louis Bonaparte*. Translated by Daniel De Leon. Chicago: Charles H. Kerr, 1914.

Matthews, Donald R. *Social background of political decision makers*. New York: Random House, 1954.

Matza, David. The disreputable poor. In Reinhard Bendix and Seymour M. Lipset (eds.), *Class, status, and power*. New York: The Free Press of Glencoe, 1966, 289–302.

Mayer, Albert J., and Hauser, Philip M. Class differentials in expectations of life at birth. *Rev. inst. intern. statistique* (Review of the International Statistical Institute), 1950, *18*, 197–200.

McClelland, D. C.; Atkinson, J. W.; Clark, R. A.; and Lowell, E. L. *The achievement motive.* New York: Appleton-Century-Crofts, 1953.

McDermott, John F.; Harrison, Saul I.; Schrager, Jules; and Wilson, Paul. Social class and mental illness in children: Observations of blue-collar families. *Amer. J. Orthopsychiat.,* 1965, *35,* No. 3 (April), 500–508.

Meier, Dorothy L., and Bell, Wendell. Anomia and differential access to the achievement of life goals. *ASR,* 1959, *24,* 189–202.

Mensh, Ivan N.; Kantor, Mildred B.; Domke, Herbert R.; Gildea, Margaret C. L.; and Glidewell, John C. Children's behavior symptoms and their relationship to social adjustment, sex, and social class. *J. soc. Issues,* 1959, *15,* No. 1, 8–15.

Merton, Robert K. Continuities in the theory of social structure and anomie. *Social theory and social structure.* Glencoe, Ill.: The Free Press, 1957, 161–194.

Meyer, J. K. Attitudes toward mental illness in a Maryland community. *Pub. Hlth. Rep.,* 1964, *79,* No. 9 (September), 769–772.

Michael, John A. High school climates and plans for entering college. *Pub. Opin. Q.,* 1961, *25,* No. 4 (Winter), 585–595.

Miller, Daniel R., and Swanson, Guy E. *The changing American parent.* New York: John Wiley & Sons, 1958.

Miller, Henry. Characteristics of AFDC families. *Soc serv. Rev.,* 1965, *39,* No. 4 (December), 349–409.

Miller, S. M. (a). The American lower classes: A typological approach. *Soc. Res.,* 1964, *31,* No. 1 (Spring), 1–22.

———(b). The "new" working class. In Arthur B. Shostak and William Gomberg (eds.), *Blue-collar world: Studies of the American worker.* Englewood Cliffs, N.J.: Prentice-Hall, 1964, pp. 2–9.

Miller, S. M., and Riessman, Frank (a). Working class authoritarianism: A critique of Lipset. *Brit. J. Soc.,* 1961, *12,* 263–273.

———(b). The working class sub-culture: A new view. *Soc. Prob.,* 1961, *9,* No. 1 (Summer), 86–97.

Miller, S. M.; Riessman, Frank; and Seagull, Arthur A. Poverty and self-indulgence: A critique of the non-deferred gratification pattern. In Louis Ferman et al. (eds.), *Poverty in America.* Ann Arbor: University of Michigan Press, 1965.

Miller, Walter B. Lower class culture as a generating milieu of gang delinquency. *J. soc. Issues,* 1958, *14,* No. 3, 5–19.

———. Implications of urban lower-class culture for social work. *Soc. serv. Rev.,* 1959, *33,* No. 3 (September), 219–236.

———. *City gangs.* New York: John Wiley & Sons, forthcoming.

Miner, John B. *Intelligence in the United States.* New York: Springer, 1957.

Mischel, Walter. Preference for delayed reinforcement: An experimental study of cultural observation. *J. abnorm. Psychol.,* 1958, *56,* 57–61.

Moles, Oliver C., Jr. Training children in low-income families for school. *Welf. in Rev.,* 1965, *3,* No. 6 (June), 1–11.

———. Child training practices among low-income families. *Welf. in Rev.,* 1965, *3,* No. 12 (December), 1–19.

Morgan, James N. The achievement motive and economic behavior. In

John W. Atkinson and Norman T. Feather (eds.), *A theory of achievement motivation*. New York: John Wiley & Sons, 1966, pp. 205–230.

Morgan, James N.; David, Martin H.; Cohen, Wilbur J.; and Brazer, Harvey E. *Income and welfare in the United States*. New York: McGraw-Hill, 1962.

Morse, Nancy C., and Weiss, Robert S. The function and meaning of work and the job. *ASR*, 1955, *20*, No. 2 (April), 191–198.

Moynihan, Daniel P. The Negro family: The case for national action. In Lee Rainwater and William L. Yancey (eds.), *The Moynihan report and the politics of controversy*. Cambridge, Mass.: M.I.T. Press, 1967.

Muir, Donald E., and Weinstein, Eugene A. The social debt: An investigation of lower class and middle class norms of social obligation. *ASR*, 1962, *27*, No. 4 (August), 532–539.

Mulligan, Raymond A. Socioeconomic background and minority attitudes. *Sociol. soc. Res.*, 1961, *45*, No. 3 (April), 289–294.

Nichols, Robert C. Nature and nurture in adolescence. In J. S. Adams (ed.), *Contributions to the understanding of adolescence*. Boston: Allyn & Bacon, 1967.

Nye, F. Ivan. Adolescent-parent adjustment—Socio-economic level as a variable. *ASR*, 1951, *16*, No. 3 (June), 341–349.

Nye, F. Ivan, and Hoffman, Lois W. *The employed mother in America*. Chicago: Rand McNally, 1963.

Nye, F. Ivan; Short, James F.; and Olson, Virgil J. Socio-economic status and delinquent behavior. *AJS*, 1958, *63*, No. 4 (January), 381–389.

Ohlendorf, George; Wages, Sherry; and Kuvlesky, William P. *A bibliography of literature on status projections of youth*. College Station, Texas: Texas A&M University, Texas Agricultural Experiment Station, 1967.

Olim, Ellis G.; Hess, Robert D.; and Shipman, Virginia C. Role of mothers' language styles in mediating their pre-school children's cognitive development. *Sch. Rev.*, 1967, *75*, No. 4 (Winter), 414–424.

Olsen, Marvin E. Distribution of family responsibilities and social stratification. *Marr. fam. Living*, 1960, *22*, No. 1 (February), 60–65.

Orden, Susan R., and Bradburn, Norman M. Dimensions of marriage happiness. *AJS*, 1968, *73*, No. 6 (May), 715–731.

Orshansky, Mollie. Counting the poor: Another look at the poverty profile. *Soc. sec. Bull.*, 1965, *28* (January), 3–29.

Ossenberg, Richard J. The experience of deviance in the patient-role: A study of class differences. *J. Hlth. hum. Behav.*, 1962, *3*, No. 4 (Winter), 277–282.

Outdoor Recreation Resources Review Commission. *Participation in outdoor recreation: Factors affecting demand among American adults*. Report No. 20. Washington, D.C.: Government Printing Office, 1962. (Report by Eva Mueller and Gerald Gurin.)

Palmore, Erdman. Factors associated with school dropouts and juvenile delinquency among lower-class children. *Soc. sec. Bull.*, 1963, *26*, No. 10 (October), 4–9.

Palmore, Erdman, and Hammond, Phillip E. Interacting factors in juvenile delinquency. *ASR*, 1964, *29*, No. 6 (December), 848–854.

Parsons, Talcott. A revised analytical approach to the theory of social stratification. *Essays in sociological theory* (rev. ed.). Glencoe, Ill.: The Free
Press, 1954, pp. 386–439.

Pasamanick, Benjamin; Dinitz, Simon; and Lefton, Mark. Psychiatric orientation and its relation to diagnosis and treatment in a mental hospital.
Amer. J. Psychiat., 1959, *116*, No. 1 (July), 127–132.

Pavenstedt, Eleanor. A comparison of the child-rearing environment of
upper-lower and very low-lower class families. *Amer. J. Orthopsychiat.*,
1965, *35*, No. 1 (January), 89–98.

Pearl, Arthur, and Riessman, Frank. *New careers for the poor.* New York:
The Free Press of Glencoe, 1965.

Pearlin, Leonard I., and Kohn, Melvin L. Social class, occupation and
parental values: A cross-national study. *ASR*, 1966, *31*, No. 4 (August),
466–479.

Piliavin, Irving, and Briar, Scott. Police encounters with juveniles. *AJS*,
1964, *70*, No. 2 (September), 206–214.

Pinner, Frank A.; Jacobs, Paul; and Selznick, Philip. *Old age and political
behavior.* Berkeley and Los Angeles: University of California Press,
1959.

Powdermaker, Hortense. *After freedom: A cultural study in the deep south.*
New York: Viking Press, 1939.

Putnam, G. N., and O'Hern, E. M. The status significance of an isolated
urban dialect. *Language*, 1955, *31*, No. 4 Part 2 (October–December),
1–32.

Rainwater, Lee. *The problem of lower class culture.* Pruitt-Igoe Occasional
Paper 8, September 23, 1966. (Mimeographed.)

Rainwater, Lee; Coleman, Richard P.; and Handel, Gerald. *Workingman's
wife.* New York: Oceana Publications, 1959.

Rainwater, Lee, and Weinstein, Karol Kane. *And the poor get children.*
Chicago: Quadrangle Books, 1960.

Reiss, Albert J., Jr., and Rhodes, Albert Lewis. The distribution of juvenile
delinquency in the social class structure. *ASR*, 1961, *26*, No. 5 (October), 720–732.

———. Status deprivation and delinquent behavior. *Sociol. Q.*, 1963, *4*, No.
2 (Spring), 135–149.

Reiss, Ira L. Social class and premarital sexual permissiveness: A re-examina-
tion. *ASR*, 1965, *30*, No. 5 (October), 747–756.

Reissman, Leonard. Levels of aspirations and social class. *ASR*, 1953, *18*,
No. 3 (June), 233–242.

———. Class, leisure and social participation. *ASR*, 1954, *19*, No. 1 (February), 76–84.

Riesman, David. *Individualism reconsidered.* Glencoe, Ill.: The Free Press,
1954.

Riessman, Frank. *The culturally deprived child.* New York: Harper Row,
1962.

———. Lower income culture: The strengths of the poor. *J. Marr. fam.
Living*, 1964, *26*, No. 4 (November), 417–421.

Riessman, Frank; Cohen, Jerome; and Pearl, Arthur (eds.). *Mental health
of the poor.* New York: The Free Press of Glencoe, 1964.

Riessman, Frank, and Miller, S. M. Social class and projective tests. *J. prof. Techn.,* 1958, *22,* No. 4 (November), 432–439. Also in Frank Riessman et al. (eds.), *Mental health of the poor.* New York: The Free Press of Glencoe, 1964.

Riessman, Frank, and Scribner, Sylvia. The under-utilization of mental health services by workers and low-income groups: Causes and cures. *Amer. J. Psychiat.,* 1965, *121,* No. 8 (February), 798–801.

Rivera, Ramon J., and Short, James F. Occupational goals: A comparative analysis. In Malcolm W. Klein (ed.), *Juvenile gangs in context.* Englewood Cliffs, N.J.: Prentice-Hall, 1967.

Robins, Lee N.; Gymon, Harry; and O'Neal, Patricia. Interaction of social class and deviant behavior. *ASR,* 1962, *27,* No. 4 (August), 480–492.

Robinson, H. Alan; Connors, Ralph P.; and Whitacre, G. Holly. Job satisfaction researches of 1964–65. *Personnel and guidance J.,* 1966, *45,* No. 4 (December), 371–379.

Rodman, Hyman. On understanding lower class behavior. *Soc. econ. Stud.,* 1959, *8* (December), 441–450.

———. The lower class value stretch. *SF,* 1963, *42,* No. 2 (December), 205–215.

Rodman, Hyman, and Grams, Paul. Juvenile delinquency and the family: A review and discussion. In the President's Commission on Law Enforcement and Administration of Justice, *Task force report: Juvenile delinquency and youth crime.* Washington, D.C.: Government Printing Office, 1967, pp. 188–221.

Rosen, Bernard C. The achievement syndrome: A psychocultural dimension of social stratification. *ASR,* 1956, *21,* No. 2 (April), 203–211.

———. Race, ethnicity, and the achievement syndrome. *ASR,* 1959, *24,* No. 1 (February), 47–60.

Rosen, Bernard C., and D'Andrade, Roy. The psychosocial origins of achievement motivation. *Sociometry,* 1959, *22,* 185–218.

Rosenberg, Morris. Society and the adolescent self-image. Princeton, N.J.: Princeton University Press, 1965.

Rosengren, William R. (a). Social status, attitudes toward pregnancy and childrearing attitudes. *SF,* 1962, *41,* No. 2 (December), 127–134.

——— (b). The hospital careers of lower and middle-class child psychiatric patients. *Psychiatry,* 1962, *25,* No. 1 (February), 16–22.

Ross, John A. Social class and medical care. *J. Hlth. hum. Behav.,* 1962, *3,* No. 1 (Spring), 35–40.

Rossi, Peter H. *Why families move.* Glencoe, Ill.: The Free Press, 1956.

Rossi, Peter H.; Raphael, Edna; and Davis, James A. *Social factors in academic achievement.* National Opinion Research Center, July, 1959. (Multilithed.)

Roth, J., and Peck, R. F. Social class and social mobility factors related to marital adjustment. *ASR,* 1951, *16,* No. 4 (August), 478–487.

Scanzoni, John. Socialization, *n* Achievement, and achievement values. *ASR,* 1967, *32,* No. 3 (June), 449–456.

Schatzman, Leonard, and Strauss, Anselm. Social class and modes of communication. *AJS,* 1955, *60,* No. 4 (January), 329–339.

Schiltz, Michael E. *Public attitudes toward social security, 1935–1965.* Chicago: National Opinion Research Center, 1968.

Schneider, Louis, and Lysgaard, Sverre. The deferred gratification pattern: A preliminary study. *ASR,* 1953, *18,* No. 2 (April), 142–149.

Schneiderman, Leonard. Value orientation preferences of chronic relief recipients. *Soc. Wk.,* 1964, *9,* No. 3 (July), 13–18.

———. Social class, diagnosis and treatment. *Amer. J. Orthopsychiat.,* 1965, *35,* No. 1 (January), 99–105.

Sears, R. R.; Maccoby, E. E.; and Levin, H. *Patterns of child rearing.* Evanston, Ill.: Row, Peterson, 1957.

Sewell, William H. Social class and childhood personality. *Sociometry,* 1961, *24,* No. 4 (December), 340–356.

Sewell, William H., and Haller, Archibald O. Social status and personality adjustment of the child. *Sociometry,* 1956, *19,* No. 2 (June), 114–125.

Sewell, William H.; Haller, Archibald O.; and Strauss, Murray A. Social status and educational and occupational aspiration. *ASR,* 1957, 22, No. 1 (February), 67–73.

Sewell, William H., and Shah, Vimal P. Socioeconomic status, intelligence and the attainment of higher education. *Sociol. Educ.,* 1967, *40,* No. 1 (Winter), 1–23.

Sexton, Patricia C. *Education and income: Inequalities of opportunity in our public schools.* New York: Viking Press, 1961.

Short, James F., and Strodtbeck, Fred L. *Group process and gang delinquency.* Chicago: University of Chicago Press, 1965.

Short, James F., et al. Perceived opportunities, gang membership and delinquency. *ASR,* 1965, *60,* 56–67.

Shostak, Arthur B., and Gomberg, William. *Blue-collar world: Studies of the American worker.* Englewood Cliffs, N.J.: Prentice-Hall, 1964.

Silberman, Charles E. *Crisis in black and white.* New York: Random House, 1964.

Siller, Jerome. Socioeconomic status and conceptual thinking. *J. abnorm. soc. Psychol.,* 1957, *55,* No. 3 (January), 365–371.

Simmons, Ozzie G. *Social status and public health.* Social Science Research Council, Pamphlet No. 13, May, 1958.

Simpson, Richard L. A note on status, mobility and anomie. *Brit. J. Sociol.,* 1960, *11,* No. 4 (December), 370–372.

———. Parental influence, anticipatory socialization and social mobility. *ASR,* 1962, 27, No. 4 (August), 517–522.

Simpson, Richard L., and Miller, H. Max. Social status and anomia. *Soc. Prob.,* 1963, *10,* No. 3 (Winter), 256–264.

Simpson, Richard L., and Simpson, Ida Harper. Social origins, occupational advice, occupational values, and work careers. *SF,* 1962, *40,* No. 3 (March), 264–271.

Srole, Leo; Langner, Thomas S.; Michael, Stanley T.; Opler, Marvin K.; and Rennie, Thomas A. C. *Mental health in the metropolis: The midtown Manhattan study.* New York: McGraw-Hill, 1962.

Star, Shirley A. The National Opinion Research Center study. In *Psychiatry, the press, and the public.* Washington, D.C.: American Psychiatric Association, 1956, pp. 1–5.

————. The public's ideas about mental illness. Presented at annual meeting of the National Association for Mental Health, Indianapolis, Indiana, November, 1955. (Mimeographed.)

Steiner, Gary A. *The people look at television.* New York: Alfred A. Knopf, 1963.

Stember, Charles H., et al. *Jews in the mind of America.* New York: Basic Books, 1966.

Stephenson, Richard M. Mobility orientations and stratification of 1,000 ninth graders. *ASR,* 1957, *22* (April), 204–212.

Stockwell, Edward G. Infant mortality and socio-economic status: A changing relationship. *Mil. Mem. Fund Q.,* 1962, *40,* No. 1 (January), 101–111.

Stouffer, Samuel A. *Communism, conformity and civil liberties.* Garden City, N.Y.: Doubleday, 1955.

Straus, Murray A. Deferred gratification, social class, and the achievement syndrome. *ASR,* 1962, *27,* No. 3 (June), 326–335.

Strodtbeck, Fred L. Family interaction, values, and achievement. In McClelland, David C., et al. (ed.), *Talent and society.* Princeton, N.J.: Van Nostrand, 1958, pp. 135–194.

Strodtbeck, Fred L.; Simon, Rita James; and Hawkins, Charles. Social status in jury deliberations. In Ivan D. Steiner and Martin Fishbein (eds.), *Current studies in social psychology.* New York: Holt, Rinehart & Winston, 1965, pp. 333–341.

Swinehart, James W. Socioeconomic level, status aspiration and maternal roles. *ASR,* 1963, *28,* No. 3 (June), 391–398.

Szalai, Alexander. The multinational comparative time budget research project. *Amer. behav. Sci.,* 1966, *10,* No. 4 (December), 1–13.

Thernstrom, Stephan. *Progress and poverty: Social mobility in a nineteenth century city.* Cambridge, Mass.: Harvard University Press, 1964.

Treiman, Donald J. Status discrepancy and prejudice. *AJS,* 1966, *71,* No. 6 (May), 651–664.

Triandis, H. C., and Triandis, L. M. Race, social class, religion and nationality as determinants of social distance. *J. abnorm. soc. Psychol.,* 1960, *61,* 110–118.

Turner, Ralph H. Some family determinants of ambition. *Sociol. soc. Res.,* 1962, *46,* No. 4 (July), 397–411.

Udry, J. Richard. Marital instability by race, sex, education, and occupation using 1960 census data. *AJS,* 1966, *72,* No. 2 (September), 203–209.

U.S. Bureau of the Census. *Current population reports, technical studies,* "Lifetime occupational mobility of adult males: March, 1962." Washington, D.C.: Government Printing Office, 1964, Series P–23, No. 11.

U.S. Bureau of the Census. U.S. Census of Population: 1960. Subject Reports. *Inmates of Institutions.* Final Report PC (2) –8A. Washington, D.C.: Government Printing Office, 1963.

U.S. Commission on Civil Rights. *Racial isolation in the public schools.* 2 vols. Washington, D.C.: Government Printing Office, 1967.

U.S. Department of Labor, Office of Policy Planning and Research. *The Negro family: The case for national action.* Washington, D.C.: Government Printing Office, 1965. (Study authored by Daniel Patrick Moynihan.)

U.S. National Center for Health Statistics, *Medical care, health status, and family income.* Washington, D.C.: Department of Health, Education and Welfare, Public Health Service, 1964 (Series 10, No. 9).

Vincent, Clark E. The unwed mother and the sampling bias. *ASR,* 1954, *19,* No. 5 (October), 562–567.

Voss, Harwin L. Differential association and reported delinquent behavior: A replication. *Soc. Prob.,* 1964, *12* (Summer), 78–85.

———. Socio-economic status and reported delinquent behavior. *Soc. Prob.,* 1966, *13,* No. 3 (Winter), 314–324.

Warner, W. Lloyd, et al. (a). *Democracy in Jonesville.* New York: Harper & Row, 1949.

——— (b). *Social class in America.* Chicago: Science Research Associates, 1949.

Westie, Frank R. Negro-white status differentials and social distance. *ASR,* 1952, *17,* No. 5 (October), 550–558.

Westie, Frank R., and Howard, David H. Social status differentials and the race attitudes of Negroes. *ASR,* 1954, *19,* No. 5 (October), 584–591.

Westie, Frank R., and Westie, Margaret. The social distance pyramid: Relationship between caste and class. *AJS,* 1957, *63,* No. 2 (September), 190–196.

Westoff, Charles F. Differential fertility in the United States. *ASR,* 1954, *19,* No. 5 (October), 549–561.

White, Martha Sturm. Social class, child-rearing practices and child behavior. *ASR,* 1957, *22* (December), 704–712.

White, R. Clyde. Social class differences in the uses of leisure. *AJS,* 1955, *61,* No. 2 (September), 145–510.

Whyte, William F. *Street corner society.* Chicago: University of Chicago Press, 1943.

Wilensky, Harold L. (a). Mass society and mass culture: Interdependence or independence? *ASR,* 1964, *29,* No. 2 (April), 173–197.

——— (b). Varieties of work experience. In Henry Borow (ed.), *Man in a world at work.* Boston: Houghton Mifflin, 1964. Pp. 125–154.

Wilensky, Harold L., and Ladinsky, Jack. From religious community to occupational group: Structural assimilation among professors, lawyers, and engineers. *ASR,* 1967, *32,* No. 4 (August), 541–561.

Willie, Charles V. A research note on the changing association between infant mortality and socioeconomic status. *SF,* 1959, *37,* No. 3 (March), 221–227.

Wilson, Alan B. Residential segregation of social classes and aspirations of youth. *ASR,* 1959, *24,* No. 6 (December), 836–845.

Wolf, R. The measurement of environments. Proceedings of the 1964 Invitational Conference on Testing Problems, Princeton, N.J.: Educational Testing Service, 1965.

Woodward, Julian, and Roper, Elmo. The political activity of American citizens. *Amer. pol. sci. Rev.,* 1950, *44,* No. 4 (December), 872–885.

Wortis, Helen; Bardach, J. L.; Cutler, R.; Rue, R.; and Freedman, A. Child rearing practices in a low socio-economic group. *Pediatrics,* 1963, *32,* No. 2 (August) , 298–307.

Wright, Charles R., and Hyman, Herbert H. Voluntary association memberships of American adults: Evidence from national sample surveys. *ASR,* 1958, *23* (June) , 284–294.

Yinger, J. Milton. Contraculture and subculture. *ASR,* 1960, *25,* No. 5 (October) , 625–635.

Zeisel, Joseph S. The workweek in American industry, 1850–1956. U.S. Department of Labor, *Monthly Labor Rev.,* 1958, *81,* No. 1 (January) , 23–29.

⊂⊋ *Index*